The History of Civilization

Edited by C. K. OGDEN, M.A.

Ancient India and Indian Civilization

The History of Civilization

Edited by C. K. Ogden, M.A.

Introduction and Pre-History

*Social Organization . . . . . . W. H. R. Rivers, F.R.S.
The Earth before History . . . Edmond Perrier
Prehistoric Man . . . . Jacques de Morgan
Language: A Linguistic Introduction . Professor J. Vendryès
A Geographical Introduction to History Professor Lucien Febvre
Race and History . . . . Professor E. Pittard
From Tribe to Empire . . . . . . Professor A. Moret
*Life and Work in Prehistoric Times . . Professor G. Renard
*Money and Monetary Policy in Early Times . . A. R. Burns
*The Migration of Symbols . . . . . . Donald A. Mackenzie
*The Dawn of European Civilization Professor V. Gordon Childe
*The Aryans . . . . Professor V. Gordon Childe

The Early Empires and Greece

The Nile and Egyptian Civilization . . Professor A. Moret
Israel, from its Beginnings to the Eighth Century Professor A. Lods
Mesopotamia . . . . Professor L. Delaporte
The Ægean Civilization . . . . . . Professor G. Glotz
*Minoans, Philistines, and Greeks . . . . A. R. Burn
The Formation of the Greek People . . Professor A. Jardé
*Ancient Greece at Work . . . . . . Professor G. Glotz
Art in Greece . . . . . . W. Deonna and A. de Ridder
Greek Thought and the Scientific Spirit . . Professor L. Robin
The Greek City and its Institutions . . Professor G. Glotz
Macedonian Imperialism . . . . . Professor P. Jouguet

Rome and Beyond the Roman Empire

Primitive Italy and Roman Imperialism . Professor Léon Homo
The Roman Spirit in Religion, Thought, and Art Professor A. Grenier
Roman Political Institutions . . . . Professor Léon Homo
Rome the Law-Giver . . . . . Professor J. Declareuil
Economic Life of the Ancient World . . . J. Toutain
The Roman World . . . . . . Professor Victor Chapot
*Ancient Rome at Work . . . . Paul Louis
Ancient Persia and Iranian Civilization . Professor Clement Huart
*A Thousand Years of the Tartars . . Professor E. H. Parker
*The Heroic Age of India . . . . Professor N. K. Sidhanta
*Caste and Race in India . . . . . . Dr. G. S. Ghurye
*The Life of Buddha . . . . . . E. J. Thomas, D. Litt.
*The History of Buddhist Thought . . E. J. Thomas, D. Litt.
Chinese Civilization . . . . Professor M. Granet
The Rise of the Celts . . . . . . The late H. Hubert
The Greatness and Decline of the Celts . The late H. Hubert
*Nomads of the European Steppe . . . . G. F. Hudson
Ancient India and Indian Civilization Paul Masson-Oursel; Helena De Willman-Grabowska; Philippe Stern

Middle Ages to Modern Times

The End of the Ancient World . . . . Professor F. Lot
*Travel and Travellers of the Middle Ages (Ed.) Prof. A. P. Newton
*Chivalry . . . . (Ed.) Professor E. Prestage
*The Court of Burgundy . . . . . . Otto Castellien
*Life and Work in Medieval Europe . . . P. Boissonnade
*Life and Work in Modern Europe . G. Renard and G. Weulersse
*London Life in the Eighteenth Century . M. Dorothy George
*China and Europe in the Eighteenth Century . A. Reichwein

Historical Ethnology

*The Peoples of Asia . . . . . . L. H. Dudley Buxton
*The Threshold of the Pacific . . . . . Dr. C. E. Fox
*The South American Indians . . . Professor Rafael Karsten
*The American Indian Frontier . . . Professor W. C. Macleod
*Death Customs . . . . E. Bendann

Subject Histories

*The History of Medicine . . . . . . C. G. Cumston, M.D.
*The History of Witchcraft . . . . . Montague Summers
*The Geography of Witchcraft . . . . . Montague Summers
*The History of Music . . . . Cecil Gray
*History of Latin Christianity . . . Professor P. de Labriolle

* An asterisk indicates that the volume does not form part of the French collection "L'Évolution de l'Humanité".

A full list of the Series *will be found at the end of this volume.*

B

C

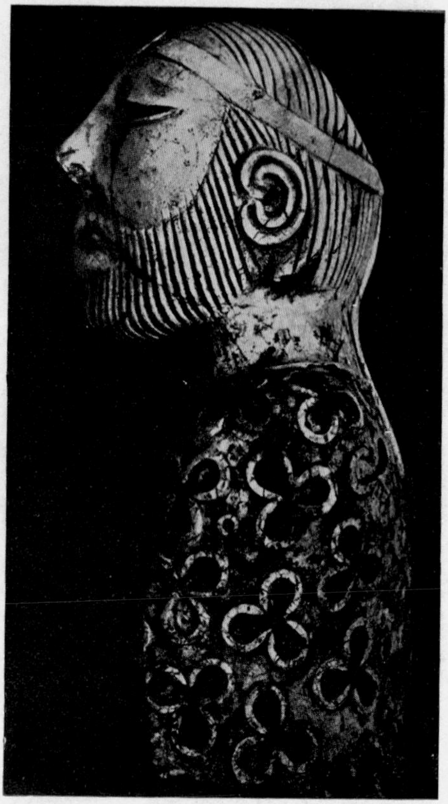

A

OBJECTS FROM MOHENJO-DARO

A. Bust. B. Seal with bull. C. Seal with zebu.

(*From* Coomaraswamy, *History of Indian and Indonesian Art*)

Ancient India and Indian Civilization

By

PAUL MASSON-OURSEL

Directeur d'Études at the École des Hautes-Études

HELENA DE WILLMAN-GRABOWSKA

Professor at the University of Cracow

PHILIPPE STERN

Assistant Keeper at the Musée Guimet

With 5 maps, 16 plates, and 24 black-and-white illustrations

LONDON:

KEGAN PAUL, TRENCH, TRUBNER & CO., LTD.

BROADWAY HOUSE: 68–74 CARTER LANE, E.C.

1934

Translated from the French by

M. R. DOBIE

Keeper of Manuscripts in the National Library of Scotland

PRINTED IN GREAT BRITAIN BY
STEPHEN AUSTIN AND SONS, LTD., HERTFORD

CONTENTS

PART THREE

SPIRITUAL LIFE. RELIGIONS AND PHILOSOPHIES

PART FOUR

ÆSTHETIC LIFE

BOOK ONE

THE LITERATURE OF INDIA

BOOK II

THE ART OF INDIA

PLATES

ILLUSTRATIONS

PLATES

MAPS

TABLE

FOREWORD

THE INDIAN GENIUS

IN the Forewords to the two volumes on China in this series, I have at once pointed out the unity of human history and justified the separate position which we have given to two ancient civilizations of the East and the Far East—civilizations which are great, both in the numbers of the people whose native genius they express and in the brilliance or originality of certain manifestations of thought or art. The peoples of China and India were not, indeed, cut off from communication, material or intellectual, with the other sections of mankind—here Persia acted as intermediary—but they were nevertheless confined to very distinct regions, and did not give or receive to a great extent until a late period. Moreover, their fundamental conceptions present such marked differences from Western thought that recent writers have been inclined to describe East and West as two distinct worlds, whether they wished to show the irreconcilable antinomy between them or to resolve a contradiction which they regarded as merely provisional.

By very reason of its strong individuality—not political, but psychological—India, like China, is of the greatest interest in the history of mankind, which, as our colleague, Masson-Oursel, observes in a striking phrase, is the only real history.

History properly so-called, it is usually said, India has none.[1] *Let us be clear what the word " history " means. It has two meanings, one objective and the other subjective. History can be events, or the memory of events.*

The Indians have lacked the memory of events, or rather they have lacked not writing, but the use of writing, to record them. " Very little writing was done, and that very late." Knowledge was " a personal gift and a caste privilege ", and

[1] " *India has no history* " (*Sylvain Lévi, in* " *L'Inde et le monde* ", *in* Revue de Paris, 1*st February*, 1925, *p.* 332). " *It has often been said : this people has no history, or at least it has had no historians* " (*C. Bouglé, in* Essais sur le régime des castes, *p. xi*).

"*every opposition was made to the spread of knowledge. Therefore it was not entrusted to writing, which was accessible to all*" (*p.* 221). *Moreover, the very mind of the Indians* "*seems to have a distaste for history*" (*p.* 22). *The details of past events do not interest them, or it would be better to say that their interest in the past is* "*not that of dispassionate curiosity but that of loyalty*" (*p.* 209); *they turn to it for lessons and for claims to glory. The truth does not concern them.*

The earliest works have no connection with history except that of the Bible or the chansons de geste.[1] *Even in times nearer our own, in the twelfth century, in Kalhana or Bilhana poetic imagination and moral purpose militate against the author's intention of presenting the facts.*[2] *It is true that one can, if one is cautious, extract some historical data from Indian literature. But it is mainly from the peoples which have a history, in so far as they have had dealings with India, that we learn something of that country's past.*[3] *For early times, it is ethnology, philology, and archæology that give and will give us some notion of the truth. From archæology much is to be expected. Masson-Oursel more than once emphasizes its possibilities as a source; and once again I may call attention to all the complementary and new knowledge which must be brought to the evocation of the past by the* "*militant history*" *of explorers and excavators.*[4]

So India has had no historians. But that is not all. There is also some objective truth in the tradition of "*India without a history*". *It has no history, first, in the sense that its past does not offer clearly distinct phases, such as our own antiquity and Middle Ages or the periods before and after Christ. From the Aryan invasion to the coming of Islam, India is extraordinarily continuous in time. In space, on the other hand, it is extraordinarily discontinuous.*

This immense region was peopled by a great number of immigrations. Although it is a peninsula with partly inhospitable coasts, defended on the north by the highest mountains on the earth, it is accessible by a few passes, chiefly in the west, and by sea, chiefly in the east.

[1] *Purāṇas*, avadānas. *See pp.* 260, 272.

[2] *See pp.* 280, 287.

[3] *See pp.* 23, 34.

[4] "*An immense supply of notes on folklore, a searching examination of manners, a thorough clearing of overgrown jungles of literature, and an abundant booty of archæological finds would be necessary everywhere before a few inferences could be drawn*" (*p.* 117); *cf. pp.* 158, 160, 343–4.

"*India*," *Pittard says*, "*was never an uninhabited land, over which a flood of comparatively late civilizations was to flow with the first races to occupy it . . . From the Quaternary onwards the soil of India has been trodden by the foot of man.*" [1] *In the mass of Indian peoples with all their various types, ethnologists distinguish two chief groups—the Aryans or Indo-Afghans and the Melano-Indians or Dravidians, both long-headed but the latter smaller and darker.*[2] *A round-headed Mongolian element was added by continuous infiltration and occasional irruption. The philologists distinguish archaic languages (Munda), which are earlier even than Dravidian, and various Dravidian tongues, superimposed on and mingled with which is the contribution of the Indo-European immigrants. Aryan or Indo-Iranian is the original speech of the Indo-European group which settled on the plateau of Iran and the plains of the Indus. The Aryan spoken in India came to differ from that of Iran and to take various forms in India itself.*

It was between the fifteenth and twelfth centuries B.C., *according to J. de Morgan,*[3] *that the Aryans entered India. They became the preponderant element in the country. But the other elements—the early inhabitants, who are called Austro-Asiatic, and the Dravidians, whom some connect with the Sumerians—not only survived but continued to be of importance in some parts of the peninsula. To make India something infinitely complex and heterogeneous, the* "*inextricable mixture*" *of the population (p.* 81) *has been further complicated in that enormous area by local environments of the most different kinds. Natural obstacles divide the country into regions which are unlike in climate, fauna, and flora, some being desert or mountainous and others luxuriantly fertile.*[4]

"*The world of ancient India is a chaos, because of differences of race and language and multiplicity of traditions and beliefs*" (*p.* 59 ; *cf. pp.* 85, 210). *Politically the country was broken up to an extraordinary extent, with a quantity of small republics*

[1] Race and History, *in this series, p.* 388.
[2] *Ibid., p.* 390.
[3] *See* Ancient Persia, *in this series, p. xi.*
[4] *On the modes and limits of the influence of geographical environment, see L. Febvre,* A Geographical Introduction to History, *in this series. Cf. H. Bidou,* "*Au-dessus de l'Asie,*" *in* Rev. de Paris, 15*th March,* 1933—*impressions of a flight over India, with sandy desert dotted with rocks and the* "*soaked, rank*" *landscape of Bengal (pp.* 299–306).

(p. 88) alongside of monarchies which were always on the point of collapsing.

That, no doubt, is, from the objective point of view, the fundamental reason for saying that India has no history. Its past is too broken up—so much so that even a social principle as strict and as characteristic of the country as that of caste-distinctions is an ideal rather than the universal rule (p. 85). Apart from irruptions and invasions—of Indo-Europeans, Huns, Turco-Mongols—among the infinite multitude of facts of which the past of India is made up few have been sufficiently large and outstanding to be events. *That happened when a " King of Kings ", as in Persia, succeeded in founding an empire—a " short-lived combination " (p. 93) ; thus " the ancient, permanent solidarity which united India to Iran " asserted itself (p. 59). Such figures as Asoka, one of the noblest in the history of the world,*[1] *Kanishka, Samudragupta, Siladitya, stand out brilliantly against the neutral background of India's past.*

" Only unified peoples can have a history." India has had some episodes, but no history, for it has never been an empire, nor a patria, *nor a nation.*[2]

There is no Indian " nation ", but there is an Indian civilization, an Indian life, wherein religion plays a part which must be examined.

" While it is true in general," says Masson-Oursel, " that among the various peoples the manifold functions of spiritual life, social or individual, only gradually break away from religion, it is particularly true of the civilization of India " (p. 61). Let us be quite clear about this. The functions of social life and the thought of the individual have had difficulty in " breaking away " from religion after the phase in which they were deeply involved in it. But I do not believe—it is fairly generally known[3]*—that religion is* in essence *social, or that social organization is* originally *religious. In India, as everywhere else, there was development, and that is what appears in the cautious pages of Masson-Oursel.*

[1] See *Söderblom,* Manuel d'histoire des religions *p.* 259.

[2] *See p.* 100. *Cf. J. Sion, " L'Asie des moussons," in* Géographie universelle, *vol. ix, p.* 369.

[3] *See especially Sourdille,* The Religious Thought of Greece, *in this series, Foreword.*

India has no more idea of evolution than historic sense. The West worships it, perhaps superstitiously. As our collaborator says, " in assuming a priori *a development in the world of Indian thought, we run against native sentiment. Let us admit that the impulse to look for development in every domain, even when the facts do not compel us to do so, may be a European prejudice " (pp. 117–18). But, this reservation having been made, by a thinker whose sympathy with the East inclines him to defend its attitude of mind, he says that " we can and must attempt to look for changes in the course of the ages ".*

Now, we see here clearly that the social order among the peoples of India sprang, as in all countries, from the need inherent in every human group to maintain itself. At the beginning the Dravidians are in small agricultural communities, and the Indo-Europeans in clans. Religion does no more than reinforce the structure of the groups. The very special and remarkable institution of caste did not exist from the beginning, and it had many causes (p. 81). It was created by a " development " (p. 82), in which the Brahmans doubtless took a large part. They seem, not without struggles, to have superimposed a theory of their own on Aryan manners (endogamy within the phratry).[1] *Where other civilizations unify, mobilize, and level, India tends to divide, to specialize, to arrange in order of rank.*[2] *The* Āryas *are a class apart ; for the race of the " free element ", which alone " can lawfully own property ", must be preserved (pp. 85, 113). Among the* Āryas *themselves, there are three classes, kept strictly separate—the Brahmans, depositories of holiness and living gods, who aspire to theocracy ; the warriors, who, under the lead of the Brahmans, exercise temporal power ; and the husbandmen and traders. The immobility, the petrification found in India, is explained by the religious character and theoretic rigidity assumed by the social order.*[3] *But it must not be supposed that the ideal of the system quite represents the reality of things.*[4] *Various circumstances mixed the castes somewhat and also increased their number, restricted the power of the Brahmans, and gave the*

[1] *p.* 84 ; *cf. pp.* 235, 240, 251, 253, 258.

[2] *See Bouglé, op. cit., p.* 84. " *Repulsion, hierarchy, hereditary specialization* "*—so he defines the caste system (p.* 4).

[3] *Caste partly explains why India is not a nation. See Sion, op. cit., p.* 369.

[4] *pp.* 86, 88, 95, 109, 113.

So it is that one finds in the poetry of India gentle scenes of family life and human compassion.[1] *One finds sympathy for all that lives, beast or plant,*[2] *and a deep sense of nature—hours and seasons, colours and scents. One finds, lastly—in the place of activity—a very lively imagination, addicted to the marvellous, to fairy-tales, to magic, to beautiful dreams in which real and impossible are allied.*[3] *All these elements appear combined into endless stories, which are often, like the Arabian Nights, set one inside another.*

The actual form of these works suits their matter—sometimes sweetness and harmony, almost always profusion of ornaments and images and dazzling colour, in addition to " tricks of the trade " (p. 279), stylistic acrobatics, and metrical complexities. Everything aims at lively sensation or at some mental trick of a subtle and futile kind.

In the plastic arts, Philippe Stern, distinguishing the truly Indian element from Iranian and Greek influences, reveals characteristics similar to those presented by literature. It is a " sensual " (p. 342) art, in which he first emphasizes the grace and harmony, " a keen sense of life " in sculpture, " a love of story-telling, immediate contact with reality, a movement which is never violent, and straightforward, simple love of all creatures " (p. 374), and then shows how the voluptuous and the influence of an overflowing imagination become more marked. Then decoration swarms over the stone masses of a sumptuous architecture, and art seems to adapt itself to the general immoderateness of everything.[4]

It was a mighty æsthetic effort, revealing an intense desire to live and to enjoy life—often ending in disillusionment and disgust. " Vain has been the life of a man who has not sought wisdom and knowledge," is the answer made in a dialogue to one who has said, " Vain has been the life of a man who has not tasted the joys of love " (p. 288). By renunciation, those who seemed to have everything tend to join those who have nothing. Literature shows this " oscillation between two poles, frantic desire to live and complete abnegation " (p. 285). They are " very Indian " things. Perhaps here one should call attention

[1] *pp.* 268, 271, 277.
[2] *pp.* 264, 314, 324.
[3] *pp.* 308–9, 324, 339.
[4] *pp.* 342, 350, 360 ; *Cf. P. Lorquet,* L'Art et l'histoire, *pp.* 227–238. "*India, which loves the colossal, excels no less in the dainty*" (*ibid., pp.* 236–7).

to the effects of an overwhelming nature, a variable and deceptive climate. In a monsoon country human prosperity is particularly unstable. A dry and fairly cold winter is followed by a torrid spring, which already puts a check on life, and the torrential rains of summer. But in the less well-watered parts of India there is not always sufficient rainfall to feed the swarming masses of humanity, and the population is decimated and exhausted by famines. In districts where the waters of heaven and earth cause vegetation to run riot, the heavy, sodden atmosphere softens and weakens man and destroys his courage.[1]

" *The wretched existence of the immense majority of Hindus* " *partly explains the character of personal religion and philosophic thought. In these masses* " *it has created a melancholy pessimism, a hatred of life* ", *and* " *inspired, by the transposition of facts into ideals, the conviction that under-nourishment and diminished activity were means to salvation* ". *Sects of the non-possessors,* which do not aim at changing the social order, " *take to themselves mighty compensations and incomparable reparations in the spiritual order* " (*p.* 116). *As for the privileged classes, satiety of goods, combined with physical exhaustion, drives them likewise in great numbers to spiritual escape.*

Indian thought—certain elements of which are incorporated in art and literature—is described by Masson-Oursel in a remarkable study, at once very rich and very sober, of religions and philosophies. Here it is that one must look for the essence of India. It is true that many and varied influences have been active in this domain ; but here we really find all that is most characteristic and original in India. Through the diversity and multitude of doctrines, which are such that their history, " *far from being written, is hardly possible to write* " (*p.* 117), *and in their evolution, Masson-Oursel discerns the principle of unity which makes the special genius of India.*

We know that religion and magic are at first indistinguishable.[2] *The magical character of the early religion of the Aryans,*

[1] *See J. Sion,* L'Asie des moussons, *pp.* 12, 14–15, 21, 54. *Cf. the still interesting pages of Buckle,* History of Civilization in England, *vol. i, chap. ii.* " *In the great centre of Asiatic civilization, the energies of the human race are confined, and as it were intimidated, by the surrounding phenomena* " (*p.* 138, 1882 *ed.*). *He contrasts India with Greece.*

[2] *See* The Religious Thought of Greece, *in this series, Foreword.*

especially the Aryans of India, is very marked. What they sought to obtain "was the goods of this world—subsistence, a minimum of well-being, even wealth, a full life, not cut off by premature death, and male descendants" (*p.* 123). Means *had to be found to affect things, the appropriate* formula (*this was not, Masson-Oursel remarks,* truth*; for a formula enables you to obtain something contrary to natural laws*). "*Being is thought of only in relation to action*" (*p.* 126). *The mythology of the Vedas, in part inherited from Indo-Iranian times, a mixture of different elements gradually accumulated in fairly arbitrary fashion, has far less significance and importance than the sort of "religious physical science"* (*p.* 131) *which catalogues and manipulates cosmic forces.*[1] *At the beginning is action*—esse sequitur operari (*p.* 132). *The sacrificial operation creates, preserves, transforms the world.*[2] *Words, accents, intonations, gestures, and chants have a mystical value, an efficience. The notion of activity,* karman, *and the ritual formula,* brahman [3]—*these, in religion, are what will provide the basis for a philosophy, which, indeed, will not be clearly distinguished from religion, for in India religion itself is abstract and philosophical rather than mythical,*[4] *as it tends to be more individual than social.*

Brahmanism is later than the Vedic tradition, and it inherits and exploits it. This exploitation of brahman *by the caste which holds it constitutes orthodoxy. But Brahmanism inevitably developed. A "decisive turning-point" makes meditation "an act more efficacious than the rite itself", and tends to substitute knowledge for sacrifice, knowing being only one case, particularly operative, of acting* (*p.* 134). Brahman, *ritual potency, was the expression of the virtue of the priesthood and the justification of its supremacy;* ātman, *the essence of every being and an element of universal life, reveals the absolute to the individual consciousness and gives it eternity in a kind of levelling pantheism.*

[1] *On the gods of India, see Chantepie de la Saussaye, op. cit., pp.* 324–336; *they are "the product of several races and several peoples"; "3,339 gods did honour to Agni," a Vedic hymn says. In the popular religion there is "a horde of spirits and demons", ibid., p.* 406.

[2] *The difference between sacrifice and magic "is simply that magic is addressed to demons and occult powers, while sacrifice is as it were official magic, practised on recognized gods"* (*ibid., p.* 341).

[3] *Before* brahman *became the potent formula it was perhaps force,* mana. *Cf. Söderblom,* Manuel d'hist. des religions, p. 242.

[4] *pp.* 129 *ff.; cf. pp.* 192–3, 244, 246.

In the sixth century B.C. *heterodoxy all at once adapted itself to the evolution of Brahmanism, corrected it by its concern with moral matters, and reacted on it. One follows with the keenest interest in Masson-Oursel's survey the opposition and mutual penetration of Brahmanism and Buddhism. The latter, greatly influenced by Iran,*[1] *and favoured by continual invasions from the north-west, developed, like Jainism, " in an environment only slightly Aryanized and still less Brahmanized," in the north of the lower Ganges basin.*[2]

In contrast to Brahmanic optimism, the heir of the Vedic tradition, which holds that man's needs can be satisfied, heterodoxy is fundamentally pessimistic ; it proclaims the instability of the human condition, the misery of existence (*p.* 139). *It expresses a kind of " collective despair ". Transmigration*—saṃsāra, *a conception peculiar to India and not the same as metempsychosis—condemns all to an eternal becoming, a universal disintegration. Here* karman *is the activity which " steeps us in relativity and misery "* (*p.* 140). *Salvation will consist solely in escaping from the life of desire and passion, in seeking deliverance " beyond good and evil ", which enslave man equally. One must turn away from the world and by knowledge, examining the conditions of existence, one must liberate oneself. For Buddhism, like Brahmanism in its later development, but from another point of view, stimulates thought.*[3] *" There are two terms from which he who would live a spiritual life must remain remote. What are these two terms ? One is the life of pleasure, given up to delights and enjoyment ; it is low, without nobility, contrary to the spirit, unworthy, vain. The other is the life of mortification ; it is melancholy, unworthy, vain. From these two terms the perfect man keeps aloof ; he has seen the Middle Way . . . which leads to rest, to knowledge, to illumination, to Nirvana." Thus speaks Buddha, after his illumination, in the famous Sermon of Benares.*[4]

Two Saviours, Jina and Buddha, both " of princely, not priestly family " (*p.* 138), *stand at the origin of communities of monks and laymen, which were to increase and become diversified steadily. Buddhism, in particular, spread from Nepal,*

[1] *On this point, see S. Lévi, articles quoted,* Rev. de Paris, *February,* 1925, *pp.* 542, 800.

[2] *See pp.* 45, 59–60, 137, 159.

[3] *On the influence of the dialectic of the sophists, see p.* 143.

[4] *Chantepie de la Saussaye, op. cit., p.* 380. *Although Buddhism was influenced by Yoga, an ascetic sect, it condemns excessive asceticism.*

where it had its birth, in every direction, and produced an immense literature. Brahmanism was a national religion; Jainism is a sect; Buddhism is sufficiently human to profit by every movement of the peoples of Asia (*pp.* 205–6). *It is one of those religions of universal appeal, "proselytizing faiths," of which Cournot, in his profound observations on "the concatenation of fundamental ideas", says that their advent, in periods which are close together in the scale of world-history, is a "general revolution" or a "crisis" of that history.*[1]

The problem of deliverance, which is at the centre of the heterodox doctrines, enters Brahmanism. This religion does not give up its absolute—here is its fundamental difference from Buddhism, which denies all substantiality—but it comes to accept an evolutionary, pantheistic, and subsequently even theistic conception,[2] *a metaphysical first principle becoming incarnate in successive saviours of mankind. Masson-Oursel well shows that philosophies and religions, "collective traditions regarding salvation and the pursuit of it"* (*pp.* 176–7), *are hardly to be distinguished; and that, while there is always a Brahman orthodoxy—gnosis, form, etiquette—bound up with the dogma of caste, in reality spiritual life is infinitely and freely varied and is syncretic. For Buddhism, on its side, in the course of its expansion over the East, on the one hand takes in masses of popular "fables and superstitions"* (*p.* 181), *and on the other develops philosophic theories in which* dharma, *Buddha, and Nirvana are conceived variously; a dogmatic complexity with infinite shades of difference corresponds to the proliferation of sects* (*p.* 192). *Orthodoxy, reacting, codifies itself and, the better to defend itself against Buddhism, which it drives out of India, it takes over part of its principles—"transmigration, universal emptiness, compassion for all creatures"* (*p.* 206).

Masson-Oursel moves with ease among innumerable books and brings into the chaos as much order as is at present possible. In the end he succeeds in describing a mental type which is as different from the Western type as from the Chinese.

We have seen the Aryans of India creating a brilliant civilization, without becoming strongly attached to it, and, unlike

[1] Traité, *ed. Lévy-Bruhl, p.* 650.

[2] *Corresponding to this theism is* bhakti, "*confident worship*" (*p.* 171); *and this vein of religious love shows similarities between Hinduism and Christianity, without necessarily implying a connexion.*

the Aryans of Iran, who directed their energies to outward action, gradually turning their activity inwards.

As the realities of life do not fully satisfy those whom they favour, so they do not revolt those on whom they bear hard. Each man has his dharma. *One must accomplish one's destiny —or, better, surmount it. Life is of consequence only in the mind, by the liberating power of the mind. Asceticism prepares the way for enfranchisement; knowledge procures it. But what is this knowledge?*

India has never been interested in facts. Masson-Oursel observes that even when it formulates technical methods, it is not so much by experience as by "comparatively a priori *canons".*[1] *India has not been interested in facts; it has pursued transcendental ends, "quite outside the natural order and often running contrary to nature."*

Yet it is not to the "heart", like Pascal, that it has turned for revelation. As Masson-Oursel says, it would not admit a Credo quia absurdum. *Knowledge for India is action. Sensation and imagination are something dynamic; understanding and will are not distinct. The norms are merely successful creation, right conduct. Reason is a Greek fiction.*

In this attitude of mind, how much is due to theory and how much to mental structure? It seems that each has fortified the other.

When all is said and done, the essential contribution of the Indian genius to mankind is a psychical element, the value of which must be neither underestimated nor exaggerated— the sense of creative activity. Masson-Oursel indicates, for example, the interest and fruitfulness of the dynamistic biology of the East. No doubt, reason is the most solid possession of mankind. Its origins are merged in those of thought itself. It is one of the merits of the Greek genius, one of the aspects of the Greek miracle, to have isolated and strengthened reason, to have created our science. But reason is not bound to an absolute mechanism, and positivity does not exclude anything entailed by reality.

I think that the attractive personality of India will emerge

[1] *Hence the many scholastic treatises on the most varied subjects; see, for example, pp.* 95, 100, 104, 235, 244, 260, 293, 300–1, 325. *On the contribution of India to science, see pp.* 207 *ff., and Rey,* La Science orientale, *bk. v, pp.* 407–429.

from this book, which is both three and one. While the three collaborators whom I have had the fortune to bring together stand at different points of view to study India, they have one same object, which is to understand India.[1]

I must add that someone else, invisibly present, has collaborated in the work. He is the master who, in France, after our Burnoufs and Bergaignes and Senarts, has caused Indian studies to make such great strides—Sylvain Lévi. He has collaborated, first, through what all who work in this field owe to his knowledge and his inspiration. He has also collaborated by helping me, at the outset of my enterprise, to organize this volume. The tribute which I pay him is a duty, and it is a pleasure ; for between us, besides scientific ties, there are those of a friendship born in the distant years of " apprenticeship ".

HENRI BERR.

TRANSLATOR'S NOTE.—In the body of the text, diacritical marks and long and short signs have been omitted in names of persons, peoples, and places and some common words and names such as Nirvana. They are given in the Index.

[1] *The first three parts and Conclusion are the work of P. Masson-Oursel ; the section on literature has been written by Mme de Willman-Grabowska and that on art by Philippe Stern.*

INTRODUCTION

Country and Population

CHAPTER I

The Country

INDIA was predestined by its geographical structure to be one of the great breeding-grounds of humanity. In the diversity of its natural conditions it forms a whole world in itself, but it is kept to itself by comparative isolation. It is the great land of asceticism, which seeks to enrich spiritual life by detaching the individual from his surroundings, and it owes its complex originality to its separation from the rest of our planet.

Yet a man who would try to explain India by itself alone would condemn himself to understanding nothing of it. The peculiar nature of Indian things and Indian ideas can be appreciated objectively only if they are placed side by side with the material and moral possessions of other sections of mankind.[1] Besides, this country was all the more sensitive to outside influence because it lived in such a secluded fashion. There is nothing more decisive in its history than the successive influences which it has undergone.

The name *India* has been used in different periods for very different regions. In its original Persian sense it meant the Sindhu River, the *Indos* of the Greeks, and so, by derivation, all the land lying beyond the Indus for a man entering the country from the west, both the northern plains of Hindustan and the Deccan, otherwise called the " South ", that triangular plateau which separates the Arabian Sea from the Bay of Bengal. That is the orthodox meaning of the name. Accidents, and indeed geographical mistakes,

[1] In my *Philosophie comparée* (Alcan, Paris, 1923) I have tried to justify this use of the comparative method for an impartial knowledge of the various types of human mind and in particular for the interpretation of the Indian mentality.

are to blame for the fact that the Indo-Chinese Peninsula has been called Transgangetic India and that the American continent was called the West Indies, in opposition to those of Asia. In this work, India will mean the portion of Asia comprised between the 37th and 8th degrees of latitude north (Ceylon reaches south to the 6th) and the 67th and 98th degrees of longitude east, having an area of about 1,900,000 square miles.

The most ancient part of this vast country is the Deccan, which was an island when Hindustan was still under the sea. That "Land of Gondwana", as prehistorians call it, was itself the result of the dislocation of an Austral continent, which may have extended from Australia to South Africa and has left remnants in Ceylon, the Andaman and Nicobar Islands, and the Malay Peninsula. A volcanic upheaval, which submerged very ancient lands, gave the Deccan its peninsular shape, while in the north cretaceous sea-bottoms not only appeared above the water but rose to heights nearly double those of the highest peaks of Europe. By that tipping of the scales India, hitherto joined to an Austral continent, became an integral part of the Northern Hemisphere. A wide, deep gulf extended on each side of the plain, only just raised above sea-level, which connected the Deccan with the Himalaya, and the waters which streamed tumultuously off the huge, newly arisen massif, the Five Rivers of the upper Indus basin on one side and the multitude of torrents which feed the Ganges on the other, brought with them great masses of silt which transformed a great part of the two gulfs into river basins.

The Himalaya, the "Dwelling of the Snows", bounds India on the north, in a crescent tilted from north-west to south-east, its northern, concave side enclosing the plateau of Tibet, which is higher than Mont Blanc. The highest summits, Everest and Kinchinjunga (nearly 29,000 feet), dominate the steep glaciers of eastern Nepal and Sikkim. In the extreme north-west the range, continuing in the Karakoram, splits into the Pamir, the "roof of the world", and is carried on by the Hindu Kush into the crest of the Iranian plateau (between 6,000 and 13,000 feet). Eastwards it merges in the Burmese chaos of mountain-chains running north and south. Thus India is hermetically closed on the north of its great river-basins and on the east of Bengal. In the west, the right bank of the Indus is dominated by the highlands of Afghanistan and Baluchistan ; but here access is given to the Indian plain by passes famous in history.

The rest of the country is surrounded by the sea. Southwards it grows very much narrower. The Deccan, properly so called, stops at the Nilgiri Hills, east of Calicut, but is continued in a subsidiary massif which forms Cape Comorin. On the north it begins on the southern slope of the contrary valleys of the Son and the Narbada, its last spur to the north-east being the Rajmahal Hills, round which the Ganges flows before spreading out into a delta. Along the sides of the plateau run two ranges of Ghats. The Western Ghats form an unbroken line along the coast from the Narbada to the extreme south, varying in height between 1,900 and 4,000 feet but rising in the south above 6,500 (Dodabetta, 8,660 feet). This mountain wall makes the west coast extremely difficult of access. At various points in it, often quite close to the west coast as the crow flies, watercourses arise which flow into the sea on the east coast. They only reach it after passing through the more broken barrier of the Eastern Ghats, which are not so high (from 1,900 to 4,000 feet). The alluvium of these rivers has created, all along the eastern edge of the plateau, a belt of plains of an average breadth of 50 miles. Along the northern edge of the Deccan are the Vindhya Mountains, which extend from the northern slope of the valley of the Narbada to the plain of the Ganges. The Aravallis, in the west, are the highest part of this terrace, which falls gently eastwards. Thus the whole plateau, from north to south, slopes from west to east, and this must be noted as one of the most important facts in the geography of India. Lastly, the massif of the Cardamoms, the skeleton of Cape Comorin, is continued by a causeway of reefs which stand like the piers of a bridge between the mainland and Ceylon, crowned by Adam's Peak.

The river-system depends on the orographic structure of the country, but it has modified it in its turn. Not only have the rivers of the Deccan broken the line of the Eastern Ghats into sections, but the Himalaya itself is pierced by the Indus and its tributary the Sutlej and by the Gogra and Brahmaputra, which flow into the Ganges.

The two great rivers of Hindustan are marked by a kind of inverse symmetry. The Five Rivers of the upper basin of the Indus, the Punjab, form what is like a delta upside-down, traversed by rich valleys, while the lower course of the river is between two torrid deserts, where it seems to flow out of the world of man. The Ganges, on the other hand, runs through fertile land all the way, collecting the streams of the whole southern slope of the Himalaya, but divides its waters in a delta in which the luxuriance of life baffles the European imagination. And if we look, not at the Ganges, but at the Brahmaputra, the parallelism with the Indus is even more striking. The Indus and Tsan-po (the Tibetan name of the Brahmaputra) rise fairly close together on the northern slope of the Himalaya, flow in opposite directions, turn the mighty barrier in parallel gorges, and then burst suddenly out on the lowlands.

The Jumna, the twin sister, as it were, of the upper Ganges, receives the water of the Vindhyas by the Chambal and contributes them to the main stream. Lower down, still on the right bank, the Son brings into the Ganges the rainfall of the north-eastern fringe of the Deccan. The irrigation of the plateau is the work of the rivers which I have mentioned, flowing from west to east—the Mahanadi, Godavari, Kistna, and Cauvery. Only two really big streams make their way from the north-western part of the plateau to the Arabian Sea, the Narbada and Tapti, which flow parallel at no great distance.

Two chief factors govern the hydrography of India—the inexhaustible reserve of ice and snow stored in the Himalayan heights and the névés of Tibet, and the wind which in summer and again in autumn blows from south to north across the Bay of Bengal. This latter is the monsoon, which bears torrential rain against the Himalaya. In Bengal the rains attain an intensity unequalled anywhere else in the world, and they are heavy all over the northern side of the Ganges basin, though they become less as one goes up the river. Between the Ganges and the Indus irrigation becomes scantier, and a vast desert extends to the Arabian Sea. Beyond that, westwards, is Baluchistan, the driest part of Iran and one of the regions of the earth which have the least rainfall. In other words, whereas the Indus is fed chiefly by the snows of the Karakoram and Hindu Kush, the Ganges receives an immense amount of rain-water in addition to the constant flow from the glaciers, and its valley grows more and more fertile as it descends.

The rains brought by the west wind have little effect on Hindustan, the irrigation of which increases in intensity as one moves eastwards, for Iran and Afghanistan are traversed chiefly by very dry land-winds. On the other hand, the clouds which form over the Indian Ocean water the west coast of the Deccan very plentifully; but they are in great part caught by the Western Ghats, so that the eastern regions of the peninsula receive little rain.

So the year falls into two very clearly marked seasons (that is the meaning of the Arabic *mausim*, which the Portuguese turned into *monção*, whence our "monsoon") —one from November to May, with prevalent north-easterly wind, cool in January (54·9° F. at Lahore, 77° F. at Trichinopoly) and hot in May (89·2° and 90·3° F.); and one from June to October, with south-west wind, intense rain and great heat in summer (up to 125° F. at Jacobabad). The alternation of periods of high pressure with dry land-wind and periods of low pressure with sea-wind bearing clouds is due to the fact that the Indian mainland is for part of the year hotter and for part of the year colder than the surrounding seas. The mean temperature is 80° F.

The result of these many and various physical conditions is that fertile land is very unequally distributed. The valleys of the Punjab are productive, but the basin of the lower Indus is only saved from sterility by artificial irrigation. Beyond the Thar, or Great Desert of Rajputana, the alluvium of the Baroda district, between Ahmadabad and Surat, is remarkably fertile. The volcanic subsoil of the valley of the Narbada and the plateau of Kathiawar is favourable to cultivation. But the grey dust of the western half of the Gangetic basin is in marked contrast to the exuberant richness of the eastern half. The Carnatic plain, from Madras to Tuticorin, contains some of the best land.

In fertile districts which have not been cleared jungle reigns, for example the Tarai in Bengal, a very damp plain along the edge of the mountains. There wild flora and fauna abound—bamboos, reeds, india-rubber plants, teak, sandal, quinquina, and above all banyans, whose branches, drooping to the ground, take root and form new trees; tiger, panther, leopard, buffalo, and many varieties of reptile. The arable land yields rice, wheat, barley, millet, cotton, jute, and oleaginous plants. One gets an idea of the agricultural value of the Gangetic plain if one thinks of its size—300,000 square miles, on an average breadth varying between 90 and 300 miles.

It would be very rash to suppose that ancient India was exactly like the India of to-day. The country is far from being completely cleared now, and how much less it was so a thousand or two thousand years ago? Antiquity was not acquainted with all the crops which are grown at present. The water system has certainly changed. More than one river has shifted its course. The middle basin of the Indus and even its lower basin do not seem to have been always as dry and torrid as they are now.

Natural Roads

The various regions of this vast country are isolated by many obstacles.

The only easy entrance by land being in the north-west, the Punjab is the forehall of India. To proceed from it to the basin of the Ganges, one must go up the easternmost tributary of the Indus, the Sutlej, and come on to the upper Jumna above Delhi. There is not the least hillock to mark the watershed, but there is not a wide interval between the spurs of the Himalaya and the northern point of the desert which extends to the Arabian Sea. This passage is a strategic point of the greatest importance; the destinies of India have been many times decided there.

From the mouths of the Indus to the region of Baroda communication is hampered by immense swamps along the edge of the desert. At all times, therefore, Surat has been approached chiefly by the sea, as we now land at Bombay. But one then comes on the shut-in valleys of the Narbada and Tapti, and behind them the mountains from which they flow. The rest of the coast is unfriendly to the mariner and offers no breach through the Ghats; or rather, there is none save the Coimbatore Gap, south of Calicut, between the Nilgiris and the Cardamoms. This natural route played a part in the history of the Deccan, but only affected the extreme south. On the other hand there is very easy communication all along the Coast of Coromandel from Cape Comorin to the Ganges delta. So the best way of reaching the south is in the very east, right at the end of the Ganges valley. This is a most important fact.

Now we must consider the chief ways by which the traveller by land can enter that almost closed world of Hindustan. Let us work from west to east.

On the western frontier India is overlooked by the outliers of the Iranian plateau. A first route runs by the edge of that plateau along the coast of Baluchistan. Part of Alexander's armies took this road on their return, with disastrous results. A second, from Seistan (Drangiana), follows the Helmand, leaves it for Kandahar, the ancient Arachosian Alexandria, and there turns south-east to cross the Bolan Pass, now blocked by the fort of Quetta. This was the route by which Crateros led back the part of Alexander's army which had elephants. The ancients often followed the course of the Mula, further south, and the valleys of three torrents, the Gumal, Tochi, and Kurram, further north. A third route, which can be used by a man coming from Seistan, by one coming from Herat by the Hari Rud, and by one who has travelled from the low plains of the Oxus, north of the Iranian plateau, by Balkh and Bamiyan, runs down the Kabul River, a tributary of the Indus, and over the Khyber Pass. The citadel of Peshawar, the ancient Purushapura, commands this defile, which is the chief entrance to India.

On the northern frontier the Himalaya presents a line of obstacles which are almost everywhere unsurmountable. The approaches to Kashmir, except the course of the Indus, are full of difficulties, but the pass of the Dras is practicable most of the year (11,296 feet). A breach is next made in the range by the upper Sutlej, leading to the Punjab. Entrance into Tibet may be attempted in certain months by the gorges north of Almora, near the western end of Nepal, and at the other end through Sikkim, on the eastern slope of Kinchinjunga.

On the east there is no easy communication with Burma

except by sea. The parallel chains, running north and south, which separate the valleys of the Irrawaddy, the Salween, and the Mekong, the last of which is quite near the upper Yangtze Kiang, make the journey into China very difficult, although between the 25th and 30th degrees of latitude the rivers which flow into the Bay of Bengal are remarkably close to those which flow into the Pacific.

CHAPTER II

THE POPULATION

I

RACIAL AND LINGUISTIC CRITERIA

OUR information about the demography of India through the ages is very uncertain. Since it was occupied by settled peoples it has been in great part an agricultural country. At the time of the census of 1911 there was still only 9·5 per cent of the population living in towns. The density varies greatly, according to the suitability of the soil for cultivation ; for instance, at the same date, there were only 6 inhabitants to the square mile in Baluchistan and 37 in Kashmir, whereas there were 551 in Bengal and 675 in Cochin. In the Punjab there were only 177, in Madras 302, in Bihar and Orissa 344, in the United Provinces 427, and in Travancore 452.[1] The contrast between the comparative sterility of the west and the fertility of the east is as marked in the matter of human fruitfulness as in that of the return of the soil. The law which governs both lies in the irrigation of the country. This is proved by the development of certain districts of the Punjab since they have been better irrigated.

The distribution of the population varies not only in quantity but in nature. No country contains such differences of human types. In the west, from Kashmir to Rajputana, one finds the purest white race. The black element predominates in the Deccan, but does not present the hair and lips of the negroids. Yellow-skins with high cheek-bones live in the neighbourhood of Tibet and Upper Burma. Although these various types have been infinitely mixed by crossing, districts keep a population which is all the more characteristic if the country is less easily cultivated, whether it be desert or mountainous. There are still, for example, very primitive elements in the Deccan.

[1] [Figures for 1921 : Baluchistan 6, Kashmir 39, Bengal 578, Cochin 662, Punjab 183, Madras 312, Bihar and Orissa 340, United Provinces 414, Travancore 525.]

The presence of large bodies of men in the better-watered plains, chiefly in Bengal, shows that these lands attracted great immigrations. The dissimilar strata of population which are superimposed one on another or merged in the mass of the Indian people represent successive influxes. What we might well call "the law of the water" did not work within the Indian world as in a closed vessel; the peoples which broke into the basins of the Indus and Ganges came from the surrounding regions. It may perhaps seem strange that a land surrounded by such sparsely populated countries should have been able to receive immigrants in sufficient numbers to implant types which survived or reappeared in spite of crossings. The difficulty can be solved only if we grant that physical conditions in the past were not as they are now. What we know of the evolution of the climates of Central Asia and the parts west of it suggest a gradual desiccation, which made countries once very populous into almost desert regions, such as Turkistan and Baluchistan. Driven by famine, many peoples gradually filtered into India. Then we have to explain how large bodies of immigrants made their way into a land so shut off by nature. The very ancient invasions may perhaps have occurred in ages when the Himalayan range was not so high as it is to-day. The rising of huge mountain masses would deprive certain regions of rain, and communication with Iran or China did not always entail such rough travelling as it now does. Lastly, the increasing barrenness of the countries bordering on India may also be explained by unwise deforestation.

The rough-and-ready distinction between whites in the west, yellows in the east, and blacks in the south is evidence of the presence of several races. But the criterion of race is so fluid that it seems wise to resort to it as little as possible. The data of language, on the other hand, are strictly objective. The distinction between families of languages and the connection of idioms of the same family offer facts which are certain as the facts of ethnology cannot be. We must allow, then, under the influence of an admirable school of language-study, that it is chiefly languages that we must consider in order to inquire what elements make up the peoples of India. Yet we cannot shirk the problems of race. The best way to reduce the risk of mistakes is to bear in mind the principle that one should never postulate a constant correspondence between the distribution of peoples and that of languages. It is, for example, established that the term "Indo-European" designates a community of idiom, not a homogeneous racial type.[1]

The oldest foundation of the population must have spoken the Munda or Kolarian languages (Kol), which are related to the Mon-Khmer group of Indo-China.[2] They are still spoken in some parts of the Central Provinces (among the Kurku tribe in the Mahadeo Hills) and in the Himalaya (100,000 persons), but most of all in Chota Nagpur (Mundari, Kharia, Korwa, Santali, 3,000,000). The way in which the human islands speaking languages of this type are scattered far and wide shows what an extent of territory they must originally have covered, and it is confirmed by place-names.[3] Father Schmidt, who classes these idioms together under the name of "Austro-Asiatic", regards them as a section of the family of "Austric" languages and a "connecting link between the peoples of Central Asia and those of Austronesia". A connecting link they certainly are; but have they any connection with a wider family? J. Przyluski, an excellent judge, is of opinion that the theory is still only conjectural, for it is rash to place agglutinative Munda and monosyllabic Annamite in the same group. This linguistic stratum must lie on the top of other still older languages, of which vestiges survive in Malaysia.[4]

The peoples which speak Munda languages—the comparatively fair-skinned Kols, and men with wavy, not frizzy, hair, like the aborigines of Burma, Assam, Indo-China, and Australia, related to the Veddas of Ceylon, the Toalas of Celebes, and the Batin of Sumatra—have recently been connected, by Uxbond's hypothesis (1928), with the Magyar race. They were submerged by the inflowing tide of Dravidians, who were very dark. In their ignorance

[1] The question of language will be discussed more fully later in this work. Here we touch on it only in connection with the racial problem.

[2] Pegu, Cambodia, Annam, Assam, Burma, Nicobar Islands. The idioms are Mon or Talaing, Khmer or Cambodian, the Moi of the Annamite range; various speeches of the valleys of the Salween and Mekong and the Malay Peninsula; Nicobarese; the Khasi spoken in Assam (Przyluski, in **XXXVIII**, p. 390).

[3] S. Levi, **XV**, 1923.

[4] In **XXXVIII**, p. 390.

of the origin of these Dravidians, scholars have connected them with the Australians, with the Etruscans, with the Finno-Ugrians.[1] *Drāviḍa* is only a transcription of *Damila*, "Tamil", and tells us nothing about racial origin. The prevailing race in the Deccan may be taken as characteristic of this people—small stature, black skin, long face, broad nose. The Dravidian languages, spoken by 63,000,000 Indians (about a fifth of the whole population), prevail in the peninsula, except in the north-west of the Deccan to Goa, where Marathi is spoken. Kanarese and Malayalam in the western half of the Deccan and Tamil and Telugu in the eastern form one compact block. Gondi and Kolami in the Central Provinces and Kui and Kurukh in Orissa and Bihar are reduced to islands, which are becoming more and more broken up. But the survival of Malto between Bihar and Bengal, north-west of the Ganges delta, and, still more, that of Brahui, a Dravidian dialect, in Baluchistan, in the midst of Iranian languages, show that the languages of the Dravidian type must have been widely spread over the whole of India. The northern groups speaking these tongues are peoples of very low culture, the Gonds and the Bhils; they live next to Munda-speaking aborigines. The Dravidians of the south, on the other hand, are highly civilized, and their languages gave rise to refined literatures—under the influence, it is true, of Sanskrit literature. "Telugu literature," says J. Bloch, "is not earlier than the year 1000; the oldest Kanara text dates from about 500; Tamil literature is doubtless older; but all the Dravidian alphabets are derived from alphabets of Northern India of the fourth or fifth century."[2] Although their literatures are late, the Dravidians had a civilization of their own in early times, and Dravidian dynasties, the names of which survived, played an important part in the third century B.C.

Dravidian India was conquered by Indo-European immigrants about 1500 B.C. The invaders encountered the natural obstacles which divide the country into dissimilar regions, and also the hostility of the relatively indigenous peoples. Assimilation was therefore very unequal, according to the region and according to the period. Thus, the invaders

[1] F. O. Schrader, in *Zeitschr. f. Indologie*, iii, 1, 112.
[2] In **XXXVIII**, p. 350.

having come in by the north-west, the Punjab has been Indo-European for about 3,000 years, but the Ganges valley was only gradually subdued in the course of the last millennium before Christ, and the attack on the Deccan succeeded only in the west and north of the plateau, and to this day it meets a resistance which has not been overcome. Moreover, across the Himalaya and the Burmese valleys, a continuous infiltration of Mongols has taken place; this factor is considerable all along the Ganges valley and predominant in Bengal. These two elements, Indo-European and Mongolian, one Western and the other Eastern, complete the demographic structure of Northern India.

The Mongols of India present, in varying degrees, the characteristics of their race—broad face, brownish-yellow complexion, small stature, high cheekbones, Chinese eyes. This type is plentiful in Tibet and the high valleys of Bhutan, Kashmir, and Nepal. In Bengal it has blended with the Dravidian element and produced a hybrid race in which there is a smaller infusion of Indo-European blood. But it also appears on the north-western borders, among the Hezara and Aimak of Afghanistan, settled between Herat and Kabul and numbering half a million, who are at present abandoning their own language in favour of Persian. Only on exceptional occasions did the immigration of these Mongoloids take the form of a violent invasion—when the Hiung-nu changed their abode and at the time of Genghis-Khan. The empire of Tamerlane and the Indian dynasty of the Grand Moguls were connected only distantly with their original stock; they were derived from Turkish and Moslem factors.

The Indo-European invasion, on the other hand, led to a progressive conquest which fills history. It established the rule of a higher civilization over a collection of unequally mixed races, and it imposed on Indian culture its most characteristic features.

II

THE INDO-EUROPEAN STOCK AND THE ARYAN BRANCH

That most of the languages of Europe and those of the western half of Asia, except the Turkish and Semitic tongues, have a common foundation was a discovery of immense importance. The path was opened by a paper addressed by Sir William Jones to the mother of Asiatic Societies, the Asiatic Society of Bengal; in this he proved a connexion between Sanskrit and the languages of ancient Persia, Greece, and Rome, and of the Celts, Germans, and Slavs. This brilliant intuition was systematically developed by F. Bopp (1791–1861) in his comparative grammar.

The place occupied by the Indo-European languages of India among the various tongues of the same family will be considered in detail further on. Here let us confine ourselves to the problem of the geographical distribution of the peoples speaking those languages. Since philology has not given a satisfactory answer to the question, the word lies with archæology, but archæology has not yet declared itself.

Linguistic indications are obtained by looking for words common to the many Indo-European languages. The original people, speaking the parent tongue, must have lived in a country where there were birches and beeches, where barley was grown and horses were bred. Bactriana and Chinese Turkistan have been suggested. But the beech does not grow east of a line drawn from Königsberg to Sebastopol, and thence due south across Asia Minor. Can we determine, west of that line, a country where there were both agriculture and pasture? German scholars have proposed Germany, but their preference does not seem to be justified, for in prehistoric times and long afterwards that country was covered with forests; besides, Sigmund Feist has proved that the Germans, though they learned an Indo-European dialect, were not of Indo-European stock. Let us, therefore, beware of using the very frequent term "Indo-Germanic" for "Indo-European". Giles places the habitat of the oldest nation speaking an Indo-European language in the region bounded on the east by the Carpathians and on the south by the Balkans, that is in the plains of the middle Danube. The steppes of Southern Russia may also be taken into consideration. So the migrations to Asia went either by the north of the Black Sea and by the Caucasus (H. Hirt) or by the other side of the Caspian, or else over the Bosphorus and through Asia Minor (Giles). J. de Morgan places the ancient cradle of the Indo-Europeans in Western Siberia; according to his view, the population of Siberia poured out both towards the Danube and towards Iran or the Far East. Of his theory let us at least bear in mind one big fact—that Siberia grew colder, and so the inhabitants of the steppes were forced to emigrate.[1]

To trace the line of the Indo-European invasions is still far beyond what we can hope to do. Certain data are interpreted variously, according to the hypotheses which I have just mentioned. The presence of the Tokharians between Kucha and Turfan, north of Lop Nor, speaking an Indo-European language, during the first six centuries of our era, bears witness to an Indo-European migration established on the borders of Eastern Asia; and their language was of the Western, *centum* type, not of the Indo-Iranian *śatam* type. On the other hand, the ancestors of the Indo-Iranians passed through Cilicia or settled there, as is shown by the excavations of Boghaz-Keui (1909), the site of the ancient capital of the Hittites. Already the Hittite language is akin to Indo-European, whether it is like it in all respects (Hrozny, 1916; Marstrander, 1919) or the Indo-European flexion comes from Hittite (Sayce, 1920). More interesting still, the kingdom of Mitanni on the Upper Euphrates, in making a treaty with the Hittite Empire about 1400 B.C., invokes as witnesses deities who are identical with those of India—Mitra and Varuna, Indra and the Nasatyas.[2] No one, it is true, has refuted the contention of Sten Konow, that these cults spread from India to the borders of Cappadocia, but it seems more likely that we have here proof that the proto-Aryans made their way into Asia Minor and Syria, just as they migrated to Iran. There are affinities between Indo-European place-names and those of the Kassites, a people of which we hear about 1600 B.C. between Iran and Chaldaea, which it occupied.

Since there is no record of any trace of early Aryan influence in Armenia, it hardly seems likely that the Aryans came from Europe by way of the Caucasus. It seems preferable to suppose that from an early habitat in Central Asia they spread westwards towards the Gulf of Alexandretta and also to Iran and after that to India in the east.

[1] *Revue de Synthèse historique*, xxxiv.
[2] Note, however, the reservation made by R. Grousset, **LXIX**, p. 9, n. 1.

The very name of Iran means "abode of the Aryans" (*āryāṇām*). The Indo-European-speaking immigrants distributed themselves in the country in several sections—Medes, Persians, Bactrians, Sogdians. A branch of the same stock made its way by the valley of the Kabul to India. The original linguistic identity of all these branches is proved by the very close similarity between the language of the early parts of the Avesta, the *Gathas*, and Vedic or pre-Sanskrit. Thus the oldest religious texts of Persia and India bear witness to a common language and thought, which prove identity of origin. Formerly the name Aryan was applied to the whole of the Indo-Europeans, but it is better to use the word only for the proto-Iranian and proto-Indian stock.

Our inferences about the life of the Indo-Europeans are very uncertain. They used bronze and gold, wove garments, and, though capable of agriculture, went in chiefly for stock-breeding. They must have had some organization which made them capable of conquering and ruling less advanced peoples. Their families were of agnatic type. They practised a worship of fire, and their gods were natural forces; the word *deiwos*, from which *deva*, *θεός*, *deus* may be derived, means a being of light, of the sky. Although there are quantities of books on a subject like this, it would be very rash to particularize further, or even to state too positively what I have ventured to suggest. On the other hand, the Aryan branch, thanks to the similarities between the Avesta and the *Ṛigveda*, is comparatively well known to us. Without speaking more of this subject in this chapter, we should mention that J. Vendryès has noted important analogies between two branches of the Indo-European stock which are furthest removed from each other—Italo-Celtic and Indo-Iranian. *Brahman* is the same as *flamen*; *sepelire* "to pay funeral respects" is equivalent to *saparyati* "to pay respect"; the verb *credo* corresponds to the substantive *śraddhā*. In both cases there were colleges of priests, a sort of priestly aristocracy. They were of great importance in the world of India.[1]

[1] *Mem. Soc. Ling.*, xx, p. 165; xxi, p. 40.

PART ONE

HISTORY

CHAPTER I

The Prehistoric Period

INDIA hardly has a history, and such written documents as we have for retracing the chief factors in that history do not even go back to the time of Alexander. That means that the uncertainties of prehistory continue in this land to a late period.

The most backward peoples of modern India, such as the Gonds, who are still in the Stone Age, may tell us something of the way in which the early inhabitants of the Deccan lived, when that most ancient part of Indian soil belonged not so much to Asia as to Austronesia. They provide for their needs by hunting, using bows and arrows. R. B. Foote has discovered in the district of Bellary (Madras Presidency) a potter's workshop dating from Neolithic times, which already shows an advance upon the men of the Quartzite period, who used only stone vessels. The tombs discovered by Cockburn in the district of Mirzapur are evidence of the Neolithic Age. The megalithic tombs erected later contain the first metal objects ; they belong to a civilization which practised the mining industry, and also fishing for pearls, of which there are many traces in the cemeteries in the district of Tinnevelly. Nowhere in India does bronze appear before the Iron Age ; E. J. Rapson holds that the *Rigveda* means copper by the word *ayas* (Latin *aes*), and that " black copper ", *śyāma ayas*, or iron, first appears in the *Yajurveda* and *Atharvaveda*.[1] It was the Aryans who introduced iron into the Deccan. The shapes of metal objects were at first copied from those of objects of stone and earthenware ; thus progress must have been continuous in the use of one material after another and in the nature of the articles

[1] **LXXIII**, p. 56.

manufactured. No doubt the metal weapons and tools of the Aryans gave them an advantage over foemen who were still in the Stone Age. The fact is that in Southern India iron appears immediately after stone, whereas in the north a Copper Age comes between the two periods. The discoveries made at Chota Nagpur and at Cawnpore are evidence of this. The absence of a Bronze Age between those of stone and iron is a special feature of Indian prehistory; and we should add that the bronze objects found in the tombs of Tinnevelly are never weapons.

What I have said about human geography entails a hypothetical reconstruction of prehistory. We shall not return here to the subjection of the Munda-speaking peoples by the Dravidians, nor to the later conquest of the Dravidian nations by the Aryans, although these were the decisive events of Indian prehistory. Whether the aborigines are or are not of the Malayo-Polynesian family; whether the Dravidians are related to the Australians or to the Samoyeds; whether the Aryans came from the plains of the Danube or from the steppes of Siberia; in any case, the population resulting from their crossing is a chaos of races, and one can understand that India is to-day still looking for her unity.

Since 1924 a new factor has had to be considered by historians—the discovery of a pre-Aryan civilization, apparently akin to that of Mesopotamia, in the basin of the Indus. The excavations were conducted at Mohenjo-Daro, in the district of Larkana, Province of Sind, by Rakhal Das Banerji, and at Harappa, in the district of Montgomery, Punjab, by Daya Ram Sahni. Buildings were unearthed, in which were found jewels, knives, seals covered with a script not yet deciphered, and figures of bulls remarkably like Sumerian objects of the beginning of the third millennium before Christ (C. J. Gadd and Sidney Smith). When Sir John Marshall published these results obtained by the Archæological Survey,[1] he met with an immediate and

[1] *Illustrated London News*, 20th and 27th September, 4th October, 1924, and 6th March, 1926; Sayce, ibid., 27th September, 1924. Arrian (*Indica*, i, 1–3, quoted in **LXXIII**, 332) had already said that before the peoples living on the Indus were ruled by the Medes they had been subject to the Assyrians. Cf. Marshall, in **IX**, 1923–4, p. 49, and *Times*, 26th February, 1926; C. Autran, *L'Illustration*, 28th March, 1925; E. Mackay, *Sumerian Connexions with*

sympathetic response from A. J. Sayce, who was struck by the similarity of the bulls to those of Susiana. It would be unwise to conclude too much from these affinities ; we seem, however, to have here a Sumero-Dravidian culture, which built in brick with remarkable skill and adorned its dwellings with real works of art. In any case, we can safely say that even before the Aryan conquest north-western India was in contact with the Mesopotamian powers.[1] It is not impossible that copper, which was introduced late into the Punjab civilization revealed by the finds at Mohenjo-Daro, was imported from Babylonia. On the other hand, Sir John Marshall is alone in connecting this civilization with that of the Ægean, on the strength of similarities in the pottery, which, moreover, have likewise caused a parallel to be drawn between pre-Aryan India and Memphite Egypt.

The Dravidians of Baluchistan (a vestige of whom survives in the Brahui linguistic island) and those of the Indus were the first to be submerged by the Aryan wave. Vedic literature mentions black men, the Dasyus or "brigands", frequently transformed into devils by legend, whom the Indo-Europeans conquered. The latter brought various instruments of domination—a metal, which was iron, an animal, the helper of man in work and war, which was the horse, and, above all, aristocratic institutions favourable to hegemony, to which I have already alluded and about which I shall speak more fully. The destruction of the Dravidian civilization in the East seems to have formed a pendant to the destruction of the Ægean civilization, also by Indo-Europeans, in the West. It was not complete destruction, and doubtless it allowed much of importance to survive.

Although the Aryan conquest of the valley of the Indus and of the tract connecting it with the basin of the Ganges belongs to prehistory, we have evidence regarding it which is of quite capital importance, since it is the very foundation of Indian culture. First, the Vedas, which are revealed

Ancient India, in **XXI**, October, 1925. In 1931, the principal work of Sir J. Marshall and his collaborators on the subject appeared : *Mohenjo-Daro and the Indus Civilization*, London, 3 vols.

[1] A disturbing suggestion, which may have much in it, is coming to the fore in the comparisons which Guillaume de Hervey draws between the civilization of Mohenjo-Daro and that of Easter Island (1932).

scriptures, tell us of the institutions of the Aryans of India. Secondly, the Epics, which are traditional works, followed by the Purāṇas, which are collections of legends about the "old time", contain many allusions to the wars in which the Aryans gradually invaded Hindustan from west to east, and then the Deccan from north to south. But the most ancient of these documents, the *Ṛigveda*, is composed of hymns in honour of various deities, and its priestly origin and its entirely religious object make it anything but a historical narrative. It must have been, not indeed written, but composed, at a time when the Aryans, whether they were still in Iran or had just come down into the Indus valley, were approaching the Punjab and establishing themselves there; it reflects a proto-Indian age and a culture which was not so much Hindu as Aryan. The Epics, on the other hand, which seem to have been composed about a thousand years after that ancient Veda, contain the story of the wars by which the conquest was accomplished only in the form of heroic memories and, one might say, *chansons de geste*. They are full of non-Aryan elements, and even furnish a corpus of Hinduism. The historical value of the Purāṇas is necessarily still more dubious, since they are poetic and philosophical compilations of a yet later date. The history which lies in these various sources cannot be separated from the legend and theory until archæology has confirmed or corrected traditional information.

Without agreeing with native tradition that the *Mahābhārata* describes the very origins of Indian society, Western criticism does not deny that the story told in that epic may be a magnified echo of some historical event. The scene of the conflict lies further east than the country in which the *Ṛigveda* came into being; this proves that the Aryans had advanced eastwards in the interval. Kurukshetra, the "Field of the Kurus", lies on the edge of the Ganges basin, near the west bank of the Jumna, in that district north of Delhi, the ancient Indraprastha, where many decisive battles have been fought. The Kauravas, the champions of the Kuru cause, the hundred sons of Dhritarashtra, led by Duryodhana, fight the five Pandavas, the sons of Dhritarashtra's brother Pandu, led by Yudhishthira, for eighteen days near Thanesar. The former army comprises troops from eastern Bihar, Bengal, the Himalaya, and the Punjab; in the second are warriors from regions which are now western Bihar, Agra, Oudh, Rajputana, Gujarat, and the Dravidian states of the south. Although the whole of ancient India is thus represented as embroiled in this war, it is plain that the conflict centres on the rivalry of two closely related Aryan clans, fighting for the possession of the Doab.[1] The *Rāmāyaṇa*, a work in which still greater freedom is given to poetic fancy, shows the Deccan and Ceylon as integral parts of Aryan India.

[1] A kind of "Mesopotamia" lying between the Ganges and Jumna.

CHAPTER II

The Beginnings of History. The Sixth and Fifth Centuries Before Christ

THE darkness enveloping the past of India is partly due to our ignorance, and archæology will gradually dispel it to some extent. But it is also due to the nature of the Indian world. In that amalgam of diverse races and tongues, the most heterogeneous traditions arose and endured, and were never brought into unity. History is impossible except for united peoples. In India history is reduced to unconnected genealogies. Each caste, each sect or racial stock, each literature has or may have its independent tradition, the lucidity of which depends on the degree of culture to which it has risen. The highest culture belongs to the priestly caste, but that caste, which has for its heritage the understanding and religious exploitation of the Vedas, devotes itself to speculation on abstract technicalities, and only very reluctantly reflects all the confusion of the life around it. Political power lies with another caste, the nobles; but history is usually subservient to the political power, preserving the memory of its great achievements in order to glorify it. It is only by chance that the other elements of the population have their history, and it is the history which one would expect from a minority cast back on itself and making itself the centre of the world.

So we find in India a multitude of annals but not the materials of a history, for it was only at intervals that unity, religious, political, or social, was imposed on some vast portion of the Indian world. But there is a further difficulty: thought in this country seems to have a distaste for history. The exact details of human happenings interest it no more than the laws of nature; later we shall have to determine some of the causes which have produced this bent of mind. Lacking any notion of historical objectivity comparable to our own, the Hindus blend imagination with facts, and their historians are usually poets. The result is a bewildering uncertainty about the period in which one should place the really important milestones of the last three thousand years. The dates of Asoka and Kanishka, though no longer as uncertain as they were twenty-five years ago, are still suspect or approximative, and we should never be able to determine them exactly if we had to rely on evidence of Indian origin. Religious books, great deeds, and the origin of traditions are placed by the natives of India in a far distant and accordingly impressive past. European criticism places most of the dates late, for, in virtue of a wise principle, which, however, is likewise apt to beget errors, it refuses to admit the truth of any fact until the oldest dated document vouching for it has come to light. The truth must often lie somewhere between these extreme interpretations, one of which is very arbitrary while the other errs from excess of caution. But the most baffling thing is that in this Indian world, apart from events properly so called—a reign or a battle—most factors, such as institutions, doctrines, or the development of literary works, hardly allow of strict dating. Everything is older than the first instance in which its existence is observed, and everything lasts long after the time when it appears to come to an end. We must accept the fact that among peoples which had not the same rhythm of life as ourselves, which had infinitely less desire to innovate unceasingly and had not our pre-established sense of a constant and universal evolution, distinctions of time are of less importance than they are in our own civilization.

At all events, it is to the West that India will owe the reconstruction of her history. It could never have been done without the impartiality which European scholarship brings to such a subject and the objective knowledge, so important to us, supplied by the non-Indian sources for Indian history. These foreign sources are chiefly Greek and Chinese, but the archæological and linguistic exploration of Central Asia has brought to light unexpected information, thanks to which the historical as well as the geographical unity of Eurasia is revealed.

The first definite date in Indian history is that of the Macedonian descent on the Indus in 326 B.C. We know, however, that the Persian Empire founded by Cyrus

(558–529) on the ruins of the Semitic empire of Assyria had extended to the Punjab in the reign of Darius (521–485). This was hardly a foreign conquest, so much did the two branches of the Aryans still have fundamentally in common. Yet the event had very great consequences, some religious, if it is true, as one feels, that there was some connection between the development of Buddhism and Jainism and the Iranian reformation of Zoroaster, and others cultural, since it gave the country a writing, namely Kharoshthi, the Aramaic script used by the scribes of the Great King.

Two early events of a purely Indian character to which we should try to give dates are the beginnings of Buddhism and of Jainism. Let us see why their dates cannot be fixed exactly, but how they can be established approximately. If we take the two traditions separately, we find that Mahavira, the founder of Jainism, died in 528 B.C.; but in that case he could not have preached at the same time as Buddha, who, according to the writings of his sect, died about 480. The date of the Nirvana of Buddha is placed by the Ceylon Chronicles in the year 218 before Asoka, but the exact date of the Asoka's accession (in the third century) is not known. European scholars have proposed 487 or 477 for the Nirvana and 477 or 467 for the death of Mahavira. An inscription of Kharavela, King of Kalinga (middle of the second century B.C.), discovered in the cave of Hathigumpha, was held by Vincent Smith [1] to imply earlier dates, and so to justify the Jain tradition mentioned above, on the ground that it makes Mahavira and Buddha contemporaries of Kings Bimbisara and Ajatasatru, the latter of whom reigned from 554 to 527. But the inscription is badly damaged and its interpretation is very doubtful. We have no strong grounds for denying that Buddha, who lived eighty years, was born about 560 and died about 480.

The sixth century before our era, in the course of which the two anti-Brahmanical "heresies" arose almost simultaneously, at the time when the Persian Empire was stretching out towards India,[2] was without any doubt a decisive epoch. Without going so far as to say, with Sir George Grierson,

[1] **LXXIVa**, 48, 52.

[2] The Persian conquest of the Indus took place about 518, but Cyrus had previously reached and occupied Gandhara.

that the Kauravas of the epic represent orthodoxy while the Pañchalas stand for tendencies outside the priesthood, we can take it for certain that Brahmanism was at the time passing through a crisis, and that in particular the Pandavas with their roughness and the Kauravas with their diplomacy bear witness to cultures of unequal refinement or to different mentalities.[1] The crisis seems to have been due both to foreign influence and to the spread of the Aryans further and further eastwards down the Ganges. The centre of the Indian world, passing from the Punjab to Kurukshetra, the region contained between the Sarasvati and the Drishadvati, grew until it embraced the whole of Madhyadesa, the "Middle Country" of the immense river-basin, corresponding to the modern United Provinces, from Delhi to Benares. Kosala (Oudh), Videha, Magadha, and the country of the Angas (northern, southern, and eastern Bihar respectively) assume an increasing importance, and it is there that the torch of Buddhism will be lit, as against the Kuru and Pañchala country, the home of Brahmanism.

This period is filled by the rivalry of two kingdoms, Kosala and Magadha. The power of Kosala was acquired in wars against Kasi (Benares), which was conquered by King Kamsa. From the seventh century Magadha was ruled by the house of Sisunaga. The fifth king of that line, Bimbisara or Srenika (582–554, according to Vincent Smith), is claimed by both Jains and Buddhists as one of their sect. He conquered the Angas and built his capital at Rajagriha (Rajgir). He was probably murdered by his son Ajatasatru, the Kunika of the Jains (554–527), although there is reason to doubt the truth of the Buddhist story that the parricide was committed at the instigation of Devadatta, Buddha's wicked cousin.[2] This Ajatasatru, after a first victory in his war on Prasenajit (Pasenadi) of Kosala, was captured by him, and then was set at liberty and received his daughter in marriage. This did not prevent him from afterwards defeating Kosala and taking possession of it. He built a fort which was one day to become an imperial city, Pataliputra (Patna).

[1] **LXXIII**, 266, 275.

[2] Perhaps the Buddhists presented events in this manner simply for the sake of the moral story of a remorse-stricken monarch taking refuge with the Master and being admitted to communion with him (*Vinaya*, ii, 190; *Digha*, i, 861).

The absorption by Magadha of Kosala, which occupied a central position on the Ganges, and its subsequent conquest of the Anga country near the delta show a steady eastward shift of the political axis in early Buddhist times. These states had been created shortly after a great colonizing movement on the part of the Aryan invaders, who had won ground from the jungle no less than from the coloured inhabitants. In such regions Brahmanism had only recently been introduced and was not deeply rooted, and that is doubtless why they took so readily to Buddhism. We should note, too, that a drive on a smaller scale towards the Deccan had carried Aryan culture to the southern confines of the Ganges basin—among the Vamsas or Vatsas, whose capital, Kausambi, must have been on the lower Yamuna, and in the upper valleys of the southern tributaries of that river, about the sources of the Charmanvati, where the kingdom of Avanti had been founded. The capital of that state, Ujjayini (Ujjain) seems to have been the birthplace of Pali, that *κοινή* of the tongues then spoken in Hindustan, the language in which the Buddhist Canon was composed before it was found necessary to translate it into the sacred language of the Brahmans, Sanskrit.[1]

The Buddhism which developed in this south-western corner of the Indian world had had its birth on the northern border. The region lying east of Kosala between the Himalayan heights and the Ganges contained, in contrast to the huge monarchical states mentioned above, a quantity of small republics, born of independent clans. The confederation of the Vrijis (Vajjians) consisted of eight states, the chief of which, that of the Lichchhavis, had its capital at Vaisali. There were two groups of Mallas, with towns at Kusinagara and Pava. The city of the Sakyas, on the border of modern Nepal, was Kapilavastu; they were nominally rather than effectively subject to Kosala. In this state of at most a million inhabitants Buddha was born, the "Sage of the Sakyas" (Sakyamuni). The name of this people is like *Śaka*, the Indian name of a Scythian people which was settled between the upper Indus and the Oxus and was at that time part of the Persian Empire,[2]

[1] Przyluski, **CCVII**, 330.
[2] For the Sacae (*Sakai*) of Herodotus, the inhabitants of Sacastene (Seistan),

and would invade India in the first century of our era. Various indications suggest an affinity, which is geographically plausible, between these clans and the population of Tibet—the exposure of the dead on trees, the fact that the first King of Tibet came of the family of a Lichchhavi named Sakya, and the racial types portrayed in the sculptures of Bharhut and Sañchi (about 200 B.C.). This was enough to convince Vincent Smith that the environment in which Buddha was born was Mongolian, just as the Gurkha hillmen and Tibetans are connected with the Mongols.[1] Certainly there was little that was Aryan in that environment.

What we know of the Gangetic states of the sixth and fifth centuries comes from the literatures of the country—Brahman works in Sanskrit, Buddhist in Pali (in Ceylon) or Sanskrit (in Nepal), and Jain in Magadhi, Sauraseni (at Muttra), or Maharashtri (in the Maratha country). Their indifference to history may be judged from the fact that if we were confined to these sources we should not even know that Darius reduced Sind to a satrapy.

Here we turn to Persian sources. The Behistun Inscription, apart from the fifth column, was written between 520 and 518, and it does not mention Sind among the possessions of Darius. On the other hand, that country appears in the lists of provinces given on two tablets from Persepolis (518–515) and the inscriptions of Naksh-i-Rustam (shortly after 515). Here is definite information of great value. For later ages Persian coins, followed by Greek, and Greek science bring their light.

At first Greek science worked for the Great King. The cruise of Scylax, who studied the Indus from the point where it becomes navigable to its mouth and afterwards sailed to Egypt by the Indian Ocean, must have been meant to serve the ambition of Darius. The explorer brought back yarns like that about the Skiapodes, who shaded themselves from the sun with their feet, but he also provided Persian policy with much useful geographical information. Hecatæos of Miletus, another Greek of Asia Minor, distinguished various

who were reduced to subjection by Darius I and were allies of Darius III against Alexander, see **LXXIII**, 338, 341. They must have been very slightly Iranianized. See below, Chap. IV.

[1] **LXXIVa**, 47.

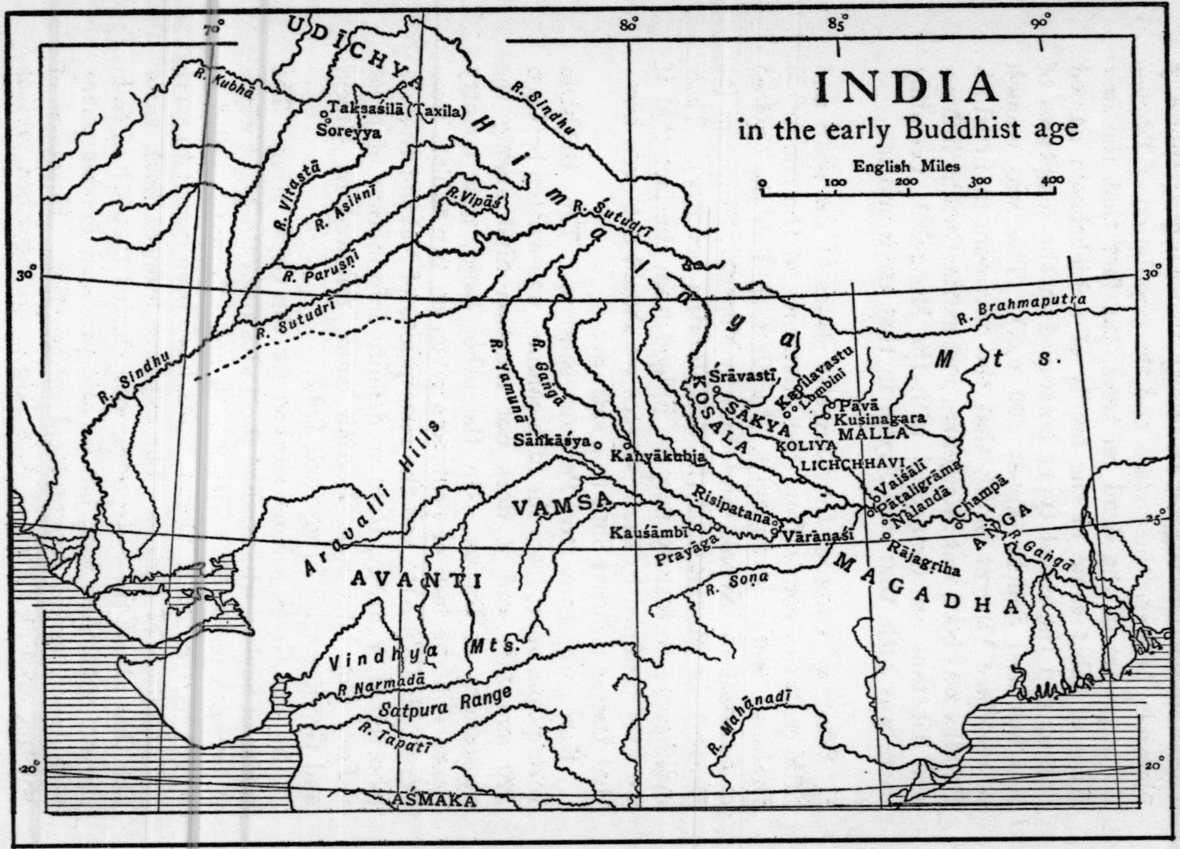

From *Men and Thought in Ancient India*, by R. Mookerji. Macmillan and Co., Ltd., 1924.

Page 28.]

peoples of Gandhara, the eastern border of Iran, and the upper Indus, but he started the mistake of identifying the Indians and the Ethiopians (end of the sixth century). A hundred years later (415–397) Ctesias of Cnidos, who was physician to Darius II and Artaxerxes Mnemon for seventeen years, described the races and products of the country, but was uncritical and retailed much nonsense. Herodotus (about 450), on the other hand, distinguishes what was fabulous and gives a very rational account of India as being made up of many peoples; unfortunately he had only heard of those lying nearest to Persia, and knew nothing of the Ganges or the country south of the desert beyond the Indus.

Persian rule lasted in Sind, varying in effectiveness, until the decline of the Achæmenids in the fourth century, but their sway ceased to extend after the defeat sustained by Xerxes (486–465) in Greece, where a corps of Indian infantry served. The men who saved Attica may perhaps have indirectly saved Gangetic India from invasion by the Great King.

We have little information about that India in the first century after the death of Buddha. Ajatasatru was succeeded by his son Darsaka (527–503, according to Smith), who is mentioned in the *Svapna-Vāsavadattā* of Bhasa, and his grandson Udayin or Udaya (503–470), who built Kusumapura on the Ganges, near Pataliputra. The Sisunaga dynasty ends with two princes of whom we only know the names, Nandivardhana and Mahanandin. Then a palace intrigue gave the throne to Mahapadma about 413; this king and his eight sons form the dynasty of the nine Nandas, whose wealth and glory are extolled both in the Purāṇas and by the Greek writers. They do not seem to to have belonged either to the priestly or to the noble caste, and this circumstance doubtless favoured the propagation of anti-Brahmanic heresies in a Magadha which grew ever greater, swallowing up its old rivals one after another. There was no sign of a reaction until, with the aid of his minister, Chanakya, of the Brahman caste, Chandragupta overthrew the last Nanda in 322.

CHAPTER III

Alexander. The Mauryas

I

THE CAMPAIGN OF ALEXANDER

THANKS to the information supplied by the Greeks—Arrian, Diodorus Siculus, Plutarch, Polyænus, Strabo—the expedition of Alexander appears to us as the chief event in the history of ancient India. Our point of view would be different if we were guided by native sources; we should hardly be told of an event which, though so astonishing, was of limited range and affected only part of India.

This expedition was the natural consequence of the establishment of the Macedonian power in Persia; it was as heir to the Great King that Alexander, carrying on the tradition of Cyrus and Darius, entered the Punjab. If the successors of Xerxes had been able to maintain their authority over the satrapies set up on the Indus by the great Achæmenids, the Western conqueror could have reached the land of the Five Rivers without striking a blow. Midway between the Greek and Indian points of view there is a Persian point of view, from which we should judge the events now to be described.

After the capture of Persepolis in 330, Alexander reduced Seistan and the Helmand valley and founded Arachosian Alexandria (Kandahar). In the rigours of the winter of 329–328 he crossed the mountains which lay between him and the valley of the Kabul. He was not yet aiming at India, but at Bactriana, the modern Balkh and Bukhara. To establish his power in that region on the ruins of the Persian sway, he founded military colonies on both sides of the Hindu Kush, which separates the Kabul River (Cophen) from the basin of the Oxus. The year 327 was spent in subduing the hillmen of the Chitral and Swat Rivers, which flow into the Kabul from the north. Alexander founded Nicæa in this semi-Indian country, which he made into a satrapy under Nicanor. When he came to the region of the Indus he had been for over a year in communication with Ambhi, the crown prince of the state which lay on that river.

So the crossing of the Indus on a bridge of boats above the confluence of the Kabul was effected without any opposition, and the army was well received at Takshasila (Taxila), the capital of the state, where Ambhi, on the death of his father, had just become king. Alexander confirmed him in his authority and assured him of his friendship. The first contact of Greeks and Indians was made and organized. Onesicritos the Cynic discussed Pythagoras and Socrates with naked ascetics.

On the other side of the Jhelum (Hydaspes), the westernmost of the five tributaries of the Indus, reigned a rival of Ambhi, belonging to the Puru dynasty. This " Puruid ", as a Greek would have called him, or " Paurava ", to talk Sanskrit, is the Porus of the Greek historians. He mobilized an army against the invader, but he found himself faced not only by the Macedonians but by native Indians, who were already vassals or allies of Alexander. The conflict which was about to take place can hardly be regarded as a war of Greeks against Indians. Greece Proper was only accidentally involved in the ventures of the King of Macedon, who was here acting as holder of the throne of the Achæmenids. The enemy, on the other hand, was only one of the many rajas of a country which was without any sort of unity, and could not regard himself as the champion of an Indian world inspired by a common patriotism. This Paurava, whose name we do not know, fought simply as the hereditary foe of the Rajah of Takshasila.

His army, according to Arrian, consisted of 30,000 foot, 4,000 horse, 300 chariots, and 200 elephants. At the beginning of 326 it concentrated on the Jhelum to prevent a crossing. The spring went by, while Alexander methodically prepared his advance, diverting the enemy's attention by various feints. When the day came, the Macedonian must indeed have seemed to come down like a thunderbolt, for a body of his troops suddenly crossed the river, at some distance from the main army, in a violent storm. The elephants, on which the Paurava had counted to create alarm among the enemy, were turned by the cavalry, 11,000 in number, led by Alexander himself. This cavalry, with the aid of archers from Central Asia, decided the battle; the infantry stepped in when the Indians were already thrown into utter confusion. Of the Indians 12,000 were cut down and 9,000 taken prisoner. Wounded nine times before he was captured, the Paurava claimed the treatment due to a king, and indeed Alexander restored him to his throne, but under his own overlordship.

Between the Jhelum and the next affluent of the Indus to the east, the Chenab (Acesines), lay the people of the Glausæ or Glauganicæ, who soon submitted. The army, proceeding along the spurs of the Himalaya, had reached the next river, the Ravi (Hydraotes), through the country of the Adhrishtas (Adræstæ) and a people whom Arrian calls the Cathæi. This last name stands for the Kshatriyas, who were, as we shall see, the noble, warrior caste in every Hindu society, not a particular nation. If it was recorded by the Greek historians, it was doubtless because a people in that district was ruled by a military aristocracy. Their capital, Sangala, was placed in a state of defence. This city, a traditional enemy of the Paurava king, was attacked by Alexander and his Indian ally, the latter of whom vented his destructive rage on such ruins as the Macedonian troops left. With more caution the Raja Saubhuti, whom the Greeks describe under the name of Sophytes as a remarkable administrator, received Alexander with gifts and honours.

At the fourth river beyond the Indus, the Beas (Hyphasis), the Greek advance was to come to a final halt. The commander's authority was faced by an obstinate determination on the part of his lieutenants that the conquest should be pursued no further. He shut himself up for three days in his tent and then decided to retire. But before giving the order he sacrificed to the gods of Hellas and erected twelve monumental altars on the west bank of the river. All that was lacking to the conquest was the last stage, the country leading to the Sutlej, the easternmost affluent of the Indus. For Alexander seems to have had no intention of attacking the states of the Ganges basin, about which he probably had no definite information.

The return commenced at the end of July, 326, across the states of the Paurava, now extended to the Beas. West of the Jhelum Alexander allowed three kingdoms to remain as his vassals—that of Ambhi between the Jhelum and the Indus and those of the Rajas of Abhisara and Urasa (Arsaces) in the upper valley of the river, in Kashmir. He ordered the Cretan Nearchos to get ready a fleet which, with Egyptian, Phœnician, and Cypriot crews, should descend the Jhelum and Indus to the sea. This last phase of the expedition, which was very hard, completed the conquest at the same time as it commenced the retreat. It was an achievement without parallel in the history of any country, the march of exhausted troops down an unknown river under a blazing sun between two deserts. On the two banks the divisions of Hephæstion and Crateros escorted the slowly-moving armada, fighting as they went. More than once the situation was saved by the action of the leader himself with his tactical genius.

As the army proceeded down the Indus it passed the mouths of the various tributaries, the upper waters of which it had recently conquered. It had started this part of its journey in November, 326. Ten days later it came to the Chenab. The troops marched through the country of the Sibæ, and then came, between the Chenab and Ravi, to the Malavas (Malli), who brought out a force of 100,000 fighting men. By quick manœuvring the Greeks extricated themselves from a nasty situation and slaughtered their opponents wholesale. Those of the Malavas who survived and the more prudent Kshudrakas (Oxydracæ), who lived between the Ravi and Sutlej, heaped Alexander with gifts—cotton goods, ingots of steel, and tortoiseshell. These wealthy tribes were annexed to the satrapy of Philip, which extended north-west of the Indus to the Hindu Kush (Paropanisadæ).

The first half of 325 was occupied in the descent of the Indus to Pattala, near Bahmanabad, where the delta began at that period. On the way Alexander had reduced "Musicanus", the chief of the Mushikas, to subjection without fighting; but the insurmountable hostility with which he met in these parts was inspired not by the warrior caste but by the Brahman priesthood, those strange "philosophers" who would not submit. The army was split into several bodies. One, led by Crateros, climbed on to the Iranian plateau and took the Kandahar road for

Seistan. The fleet left the river and sailed westwards across the ocean under Nearchos. Alexander founded various marine establishments at the mouths of the Indus, which were further north then than now, installed Apollophanes as Satrap of Gedrosia (west of modern Karachi), and then started across Persia for Mesopotamia. He reached Susa in 324, but died in Babylon in June, 323.

The importance of this Indian campaign of Alexander has been both exaggerated and under-estimated. It is true that it had no decisive influence on the destinies of India, for its results were short-lived. Yet the eight years of the Macedonian occupation opened an era of several centuries during which Hellenism was to be a factor not only of civilization but of government on the western confines of the Indian world. Direct contact was established between the Mediterranean civilizations and those of the Punjab and of Central Asia ; Semitic Babylonia and the Persian Empire were no longer a screen between West and East. These are facts of immense consequence, not only to Greek or Indian history but to the history of the world, which is the only real history.

II

CHANDRAGUPTA

In our eyes, India after Alexander is different from India before Alexander in many respects. Thanks to the Greek historians and to coins, there is less bewildering uncertainty about dates. The facts themselves become simple, as if, following the example of the huge Persian or Macedonian Empire, India itself sought to become united.

Magadha, as we have seen, extended its rule more and more over the Gangetic countries during the fourth century. About 322, roughly a year after Alexander's death, that state saw the beginning of a reign of twenty-four years, in which the first Indian empire was founded. A literary work of the fifth or seventh century after Christ, the drama entitled *Mudrā-rākshasa*, throws some light, though of an uncertain kind, on the palace revolution which set up the Mauryas in the place of the Nandas. Chandragupta, the

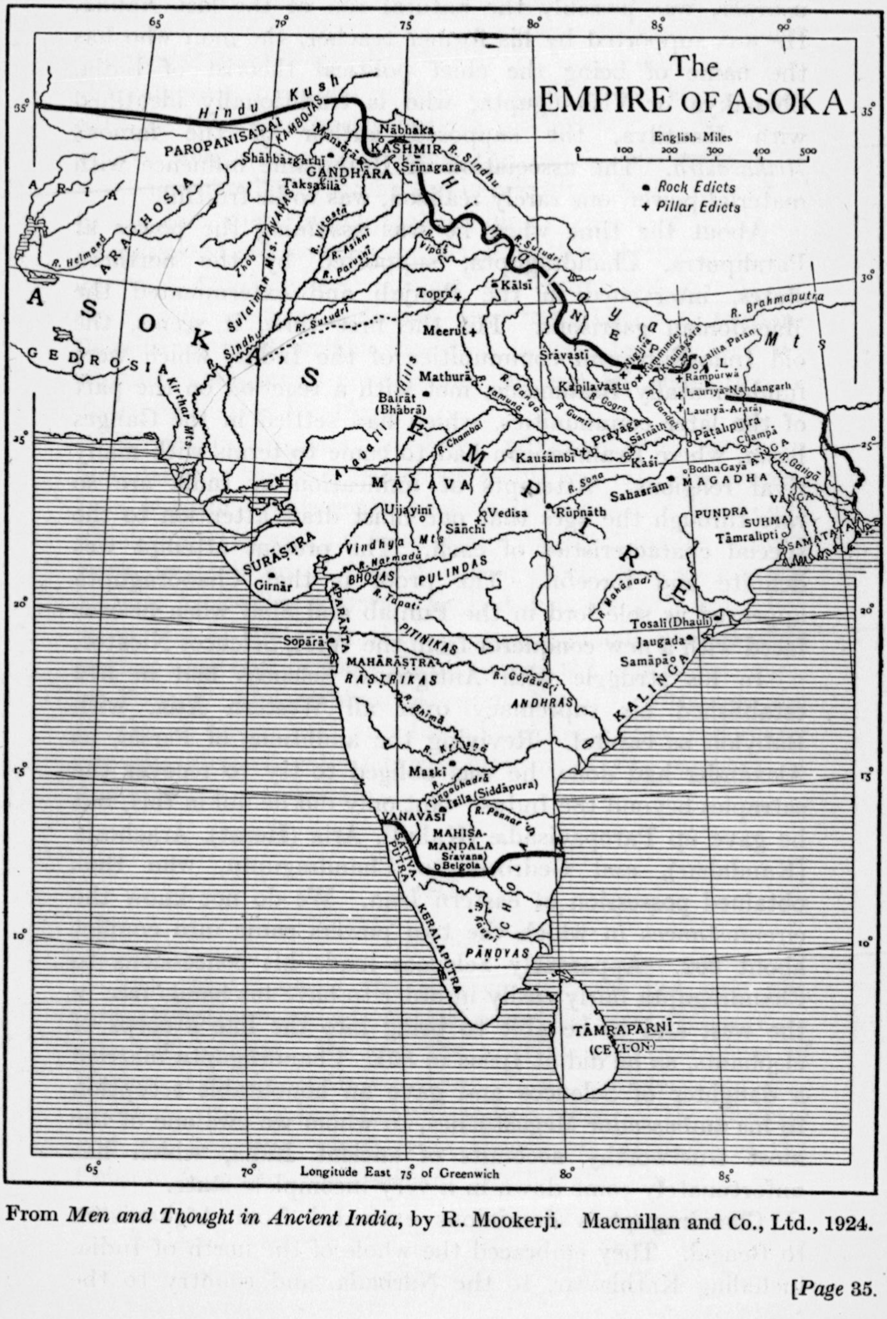

From *Men and Thought in Ancient India*, by R. Mookerji. Macmillan and Co., Ltd., 1924.

embodiment of his own time, and he comes before us as quite a modern figure. In the course of a long reign he achieved what seems to us to be a mere aspiration of the visionary: enjoying the greatest possible material power, he organized peace. Far beyond his own vast dominions he realized what has been the dream of some religions—universal order, an order embracing mankind.

Nor is this unique figure by any means legendary. Though it is wrapped in romantic and untrustworthy stories, the essentials, by a piece of good fortune unusual in history, are provided by epigraphic evidence whose genuineness is beyond dispute. At the four corners of India, rocks or stone pillars engraved with Prakrit inscriptions bear for all time the messages which the sovereign issued to his subjects, messages which tell an objective story without empty vain-glory, giving the rarest of biographies without emphasis.

The manner of thus addressing the people and posterity was inspired by the example of Darius. The architecture and decoration of the monuments which bear these inscriptions confirm the impression, for they definitely recall the style of Persepolis; one has only to look at the capital from Sarnath, now in the Lucknow Museum. The idea of a worldwide kingship in India was taken from the Persian Empire. Like the Achæmenids, Asoka took a passionate interest in the prosperity of his peoples. He founded Srinagar, the capital of Kashmir, and built five monasteries there. In Nepal he built Deo-Patan. In his capital, Pataliputra, he set up palaces of stone in the place of wooden buildings. He completed the irrigation-works started by Chandragupta. He established hospitals everywhere, provided with medical and pharmaceutical resources for man and beast. We must not regard all this as over-sensitiveness or exaggeration of religious scruple on the part of a sickly prince. His fight against suffering of all kinds bears the stamp of Buddhism and Jainism, but the determination to establish a universal order, regulated in its smallest details, for the safeguarding of all interests for which the King assumes the responsibility is the purpose of a "King of Kings".

All interests, moral or material, are regarded with the

same width of view and in the same detail. Just as a wide-awake government provides for the policing, financial affairs, and general economics of the country, so there are officials to enforce the reign of the moral law as well as of the purely legal. Tolerance, very different from what we conceive under the name, that is to say, allowing sects to worship as they wish provided that they do not injure internal peace, consists in active zeal on behalf of every religion. For each religion, like the royal power, is defined by the promotion of *dharma*, which is moral, religious, and civil law all in one. Even if this Law is the tradition of a particular sect or school, it does not menace the safety of the state if the state controls it ; and legislation, even if it comes from the King, is not regarded as " secular ", as we should say, or extra-religious, for the spiritual power and the temporal, which are divided between two castes, Brahmans and Kshatriyas, are not distinguished in the office of the sovereign. It was not, therefore, out of superstition, nor yet for the sake of syncretism, that Asoka, himself a convert to Buddhism, heaped favours on the Brahmans and gave such help to the Jains that he came to be regarded as one of them. Toleration here is not a makeshift intended to maintain peace, but " the very essence of religion ". " To foster one's sect, depreciating the others out of affection for one's own, to exalt its merit, is to do the worst harm to one's own sect." Asoka agrees with " ascetics and Brahmans " in prescribing " mastery of the senses, purity of thought, gratitude, and steadfastness in devotion " (Rock Edict VII), and " the least possible impiety, as many good deeds as possible, kindness, liberality, truthfulness, and purity of deed and thought " (Rock Edict II).

So, when he preaches, with his royal authority, what is ordered by the various religions in common, the King is doing the same organizing work as when he provides for the well-being of his peoples. This policy is expressed in the formula, " *Dharma* aims at the happiness of all creatures." This noble and simple rule, which is more susceptible of universal application than the Brahman tradition, is preached by Asoka throughout his immense empire as a medium of civilization which can be assimilated by dissimilar races, and he also makes it an instrument of union between the peoples beyond his frontiers. That was how he could become a Buddhist monk without his adhesion to the faith of Sakyamuni entailing any abjuration of Brahmanic orthodoxy ; at the very most he repudiated blood-sacrifice, following the precedent of Iranian Zoroaster. His attitude is that of a Great King in whose imperialism no distinction is admitted between spiritual and temporal.

The events of his reign show little sign of these magnificent principles of justice and humanity, at least after a certain date. Having ascended the throne at the age of about 21, about 273, Asoka became a Buddhist nine years later, but his conversion did not take full effect until after a war against the Kalinga country in 261. The war brought victory but great human suffering, for 150,000 were taken prisoners and 100,000 slain. The distress which the King felt over it determined the subsequent turn of his mind. Rock Edict XIII confesses his remorse and proclaims that he has finally taken refuge in the law of Buddha, and in the interests of Buddhism he summoned a council at Pataliputra, the Third Council of tradition, about 240. From then onwards the King strove for no victory but that of the Law, *dharma-vijaya*, and regarded all men as his children. By the missions which he sent out, he spread the renown of *dharma* as far as the courts of Antiochos, the grandson of Seleucos Nicator, of Ptolemy Philadelphos in Egypt, of Magas of Cyrene, of Alexander of Epeiros. Other missionaries reached the Tamil kingdoms of the Cholas and the Pandyas, and others established a connexion with Suvarnabhumi (i.e. Lower Burma). Under the conduct of Mahendra, a younger brother of the King, a form of Buddhism was planted in Ceylon (Lanka), where it endured ; King Tissa and his successors were to make Anuradhapura one of the great centres of that religion.

The death of the sovereign " dear to the Gods " occurred about 232—at Taxila, according to a Tibetan tradition. At once the Empire was divided between two of his grandsons, Dasaratha obtaining the eastern provinces and Samprati the western.

CHAPTER IV

INDO-GREEKS, INDO-PARTHIANS, INDO-SCYTHIANS. THE KUSHANS AND KANISHKA

DURING the century following the death of Asoka, interest centres on the north-western threshold of India, as it had done in Alexander's time nearly a hundred years before. The Mauryas grow weak and soon their rule is confined to Magadha. They vegetate until, about 185, a " mayor of the palace ", as Sylvain Lévi called him, Pushyamitra, sets up in their place his own family, known to history as the Sungas.

The decisive events which now took place in the west had their beginnings in the time of Asoka, about 250. The Seleucid Empire, ruled by Antiochos III (261–246), lost two provinces, Parthia and Bactriana, which emancipated themselves simultaneously. The Parthians, whom the Indians called Pahlavas, were related to the nomads of the Turkoman steppes and occupied the country south-east of the Caspian. The Bactrians bordered on the Parthians on the north-east and were settled between the Hindu Kush and the Oxus ; the number and wealth of their towns were legendary. These two peoples seem to have taken advantage of the difficulties of Antiochos and his successors, Seleucos II (246–226) and III (226–223) in the west to break away. The Parthian revolt was a national movement, led by Arsaces, the founder of a dynasty which was to rule Persia for nearly five hundred years. The Bactrian rising was brought about by the ambition of a Greek satrap, Diodotos, and represents an outbreak of Hellenism in the heart of Asia. There is no doubt that the formation of these enterprising nations on the Indo-Iranian border helped to shake the empire of Asoka in the time of his successors. One result, at any rate, was that India was conquered by Hellenism more effectively than in Alexander's day. This unexpected consequence is explained by the hold which Greek colonization had in Bactriana. We remember with what determination Alexander strove to take complete possession of that country, establishing garrisons and founding cities. Short-lived as were the victories gained by the conqueror, this part of his work had not been fruitless.

The Punjab, once a Persian satrapy and then a province of Alexander, was to find itself still more exposed to attack, now that smaller but turbulent states had arisen at its doors. After Diodotos I and II, the King of Bactriana was Euthydemos, who went to war with Antiochos the Great of Syria. Peace was concluded with the recognition of Bactrian independence about 208. But during hostilities Syrian troops had crossed the Hindu Kush and, entering the Kabul valley, had severely despoiled the ruler, Subhagasena. Demetrios, the son of Euthydemos, increased his dominions not only in the present Afghanistan but in India proper, and bore the title of King of the Indians (200–190). Between 190 and 180 there were Greek adventurers reigning at Taxila, named Pantaleon and Agathocles. From 160 to 140, roughly, Kabul and the Punjab were held by a pure Greek, Milinda or Menander, who left a name in the history of Buddhism. About 155 he conquered the whole of the lower Indus and Kathiawar, waged war in Rajputana and Oudh, took Mathura (Muttra) on the Jumna, and even reached Pataliputra. He was severely defeated by Pushyamitra, who was the chief defender of the Hindu world, although the termination of his name in *mitra* has caused some to suppose that he was of Iranian origin. It should be added that both in policy and in religion or literature this first Sunga stands for a definitely Indian reaction against every outside influence, and particularly for a Brahman opposition to Buddhism, which with its application to mankind in general had so strongly appealed to the greatest of the Mauryas.

Greek intercourse with India worked both ways. A Greek named Heliodoros, who was sent on a mission to Besnagar, near Bhilsa in Central India, by Antialciadas, King of Taxila, set up a column in honour of Vishnu Vasudeva, declaring himself his follower (*bhāgavata*). The monolithic pillar and inscription still survive, and their evidence agrees with that of plentiful coins to prove what interpenetration there was between Greeks and Indians at this time.

Bactriana was, at least in the north, a barrier between Parthia and India. India was therefore less exposed to attack from Parthia. Nevertheless, there was at least one Parthian ruler, Mithradates I (171–136) who annexed the country of Taxila for a few years, about 138. Indo-Parthians, like Indo-Greeks, are attested by coins even after the event which was to put an end to the independence of both Parthia and Bactria.

That event was a new invasion, resulting from a movement of tribes which had taken place far away from India, in the Mongolian steppes. About 170 a horde of nomadic Scythians, the Yueh-chi or Tokharians, being driven from Gobi, the present Kansu, by the Hiung-nu or Huns, started on a wild migration which upset the whole balance of Asia. They fell on the Sakas, who were Iranianized Scythians dwelling north of the Persian Empire, and settled in their grazing-grounds north of the Jaxartes (Sir Darya). The expelled Sakas fell on Parthia and Bactriana, obliterating the last vestiges of Greek rule, between 140 and 120. Then the Tokharians, being defeated in their turn by the Wu-sun tribe, established themselves on the Oxus, and after that took all the country of the Sakas in eastern Iran, at the entrance to India. That entrance was forced in the first century after Christ. It was the last Indo-European invasion of ancient India, for the Tokharians and Sakas were two offshoots of the Scythian branch, the most easterly branch of the Indo-European stock.

The conquest of India was the work of the Kushans (*Kushāṇa*), a dynasty which united the Yue-chi tribes and established their dominion both over their own kinsfolk, the Sakas of Parthia, and over the peoples of the Punjab. At this point great difficulties in dating arise. The accession of the principal king of this line, Kanishka, was placed at uncertain dates between 57 B.C. and A.D. 200. The excavations of Sir John Marshall at the site of Taxila have made it possible to reduce the range to about the end of the first century of our era. Chinese history also supplies some information. Communications between China and the valley of the Oxus were easy in the time of the Emperor Wu-ti, to whom the traveller, Chang-kien brought information about the West (120 B.C.), but they were suddenly interrupted at the beginning of our era, and were only restored by the victorious campaigns of Pan-ch'ao (73–102) against the Kushans. Kanishka seems to have become king after this defeat of the Yueh-chi, who had become an Indian power. Accordingly Vincent Smith, after first adopting A.D. 78, which appeared the most probable, finally chose A.D. 120, and we may agree with him that this date marks the beginning of the "Saka" period inaugurated by Kanishka.[1]

The order in which the chief Kushan kings followed is still doubtful.[2] It is generally agreed that Kanishka came after Kadphises I (Kujula Kara Kadphises) and II (Vima Kadphises). The former of these two, a Bactrianized Scythian, must, in Dr. Smith's view, have assumed power about A.D. 40. He seized Gandhara and the country of Taxila from Gondophares, the Parthian prince who, according to the apocryphal Acts of the Apostles, received St. Thomas. His son Vima (78–110) carved out a great empire for himself, embracing the Punjab and the whole western half of the Ganges basin. This seems to have been the empire the northern parts of which bore the shock of the Chinese armies led by Pan-ch'ao. Vima ventured to seek the hand of a princess of the Chinese court in 90, and the Chinese general, who had marched his troops as far as the Caspian, kept his envoy prisoner. The Kushan king, taking offence, sent 70,000 horsemen over the Pamir, but that enormous host was annihilated in descending on Kashgar or Yarkand. But this defeat, although it gave the Emperor Ho-ti Indian subjects, does not seem to have weakened the prestige of the Kushans inside India. In order to avoid the risk of error in this account, we should remember that it may have been Kanishka, not Kadphises II, who came into conflict with China, and that the Saka era may begin, not in 120 with Kanishka, but in 78 with Kadphises II.

But let us go on with our story, even if it is hypothetical. There seems to have been an interval of about ten years between Kadphises and Kanishka (? 120–? 162). The latter

[1] We should note that the Saka era began a hundred or a hundred and fifty years after the destruction of the Saka state of Parthia, and that it was the Yueh-chi who had destroyed that state. Saka dynasties continued to reign in a certain independence from the lower Indus to Kathiawar until the fifth century.

[2] A. A. Macdonell, *India's Past*, 1927, p. 265 : (Kanishka) "may possibly have preceded the two Kadphises kings ; in that case his date . . . would be A.D. 78."

was the son of one Vajheshka and no relation of his predecessor; he seems to have come from Khotan, not Bactriana, and indeed he spent the summer at Kapisi in Paropanisadæ and the winter at Purushapura (Peshawar). The axis of his empire was no longer in the middle of the Græco-Iranian country.

His warlike activity was displayed chiefly in the northern districts. He conquered Kashmir. He established his rule over the Parthians beyond the Pamir, in the Serindian regions where Kadphises II had been defeated, and it was now Chinese influence that retreated in those parts. It is a thing to be noted, that whenever a power extending to Iran or Serindia predominates in India, there is a recrudescence of Buddhism, and when a purely Indian dynasty comes to the fore there is usually a Brahmanic reaction. The reign of Kanishka coincides with a very great development of Buddhist propaganda.

Like Asoka, Kanishka called the Buddhists together in a council, but it was held in the recently annexed Kashmir. It was instructed to draw up definitive commentaries on the Canon and to engrave them on bronze. This laying down of dogma is an important fact in the history of the faith; a neo-Buddhism appears, in which the metaphysical element tends to prevail over the moral, and at the same time foreign factors are blended with Indian.

If we would see for ourselves, clearly and beyond possibility of doubt, the many elements which combined and conflicted in the Kushan Empire, we have only to examine the abundant coins of the period. The Persian title, "King of Kings," is found together with the Greek βασιλεύς, the Indian *Adhirāja*, and even *Devaputra*, the Sanskrit translation of the Chinese notion, "Son of Heaven." Coins bear the figures of Mithra, Siva, Buddha, and Heracles indiscriminately. The new Buddhism, which, in contrast to the old, was to be called the "Great Vehicle", grew up in a world scored across by the different influences which these names reveal.

The age of Kanishka was one of prosperity and magnificence. The great Asiatic routes which crossed the Kushan Empire made it wealthy. The inheritance of the Græco-Buddhist art of Gandhara was adapted to express native ideals. An extraordinary personality, Asvaghosha, Buddhist teacher and philosopher, poet and musician, opened many paths to the sacred and profane literature of later ages. The metaphysician Nagarjuna and the physician Charaka inaugurated great traditions.

But it was the destiny of India that no large part of the country should be united for more than two or three reigns, so that its culture could never be kept at the same level of brilliance for more than a few generations. The successors of Kanishka, like those of Asoka, almost at once allowed the Empire to fall into jeopardy. Of his two sons, Vasishka and Huvishka, who had shared the power with him, only the second survived him (? 162– ? 182). We know little more of him than his name, or of Vasudeva I. The power of the Kushans in the third century was reduced to Bactriana, with Kabul and Gandhara, and they fell beneath the yoke of the Sassanids.

CHAPTER V

The Deccan to the Third Century

THE history of the Deccan begins several centuries after that of Gangetic India and therefore still longer after that of the Punjab. The Indo-European conquest advanced eastwards before it moved downwards into the southern peninsula.

The conquerors worked along the coasts, and also went overland. We have seen that in Asoka's time Kalinga was conquered, on the Bay of Bengal (261 B.C.). Beyond Kalinga lay Telugu-speaking peoples, who occupied the deltas of the Godavari and Krishna (Kistna). Even before the death of the great Buddhist emperor this region, which Megasthenes already knew for its wealth, became the kingdom of the Andhras, which was at first tributary to Asoka and afterwards independent. It so grew in power that it even stretched beyond the Western Ghats, where its two rivers rose to the coast of the Indian Ocean, cutting right across the peninsula from east to west. So a rivalry arose between this kingdom and that of the Kshatrapas for the possession of the part of the west coast which was provided with ports and commercial outlets. The Andhra dynasty covers about four centuries, roughly from 230 B.C. to A.D. 225. At first the capital was at Amaravati on the lower Krishna, but about A.D. 100 Sri Pulumayi established his government at Pratishthana (Paithan) on the upper Godavari. The dynasty reached the height of its glory in the reign of Gautamiputra Yajña Sri, about the middle of the second century; he annexed the state of the Kshatrapas, but for a few years only. Possibly this king, who is also known as Satakarni I, was the inaugurator of the heroic Vikrama era, famous in native tradition; but in that case this Satakarni must be placed in the first century, and the era would begin in A.D. 58.[1]

[1] Not in 58 B.C., as was supposed by Vincent Smith (**LXXIVa**, p. 151).

Let us pass into the opposite camp, that of the Kshatrapas or Satraps. This title, which is Iranian, is borne by two dynasties founded by the Sakas who had been driven from their country by the Yueh-chi invasion. The first was established in Surashtra (Kathiawar). One prince of this line, Chashtana, seems to have held Malwa before the great days of the Kushans and to have become a vassal of Kanishka; he ruled over Ujjayini, which was the centre of a brilliant civilization. The second line, to which the name of Kshaharata is more particularly attached, was the hereditary foe of the Andhras; it ruled over Maharashtra, the country between modern Surat and Bombay. Menander, the Greek King of Kabul, had advanced as far as this in the middle of the second century B.C. The country owed its wealth to its many ports, which were all the more valuable since the coast became inhospitable further south. There were Bharukachchha (Broach) at the mouth of the Narbada, Surashtra (Surat) at the mouth of the Tapti, and Surparaka (Sopara). Navigation between India and Ptolemaic Egypt had increased since the first century after Christ, when the art of making use of the monsoons had spread in the West. It was this latter Saka state that was annihilated by Satakarni, and it was the former which avenged it, when Rudradaman, the Satrap of Ujjayini, conquered the Andhra king.

The antagonism between the eastern and western states seems to have been accompanied by a difference of ideals. The Sakas, like all the Scythians of India or Serindia, such as the Tokharians, retained from their foreign origin a sympathy for Buddhism, which was a universal religion, whereas the Andhras were keen supporters of Brahmanism. But we should not make too much of this antithesis. Ujjayini was a great Buddhist centre, but orthodoxy so developed there that the kingdom of which it was capital was the first to write inscriptions in Sanskrit instead of the old Prakrit.

In the extreme south of the peninsula there were several seaboard towns which were in communication with the China seas and with the West. From the Pandya country, for example, opposite Ceylon, a mission was sent which was received by Augustus in 20 B.C. The Chola kingdom was predominant on the coast of Coromandel, and that of the Cheras or Kerala on the Malabar coast, its chief ports being

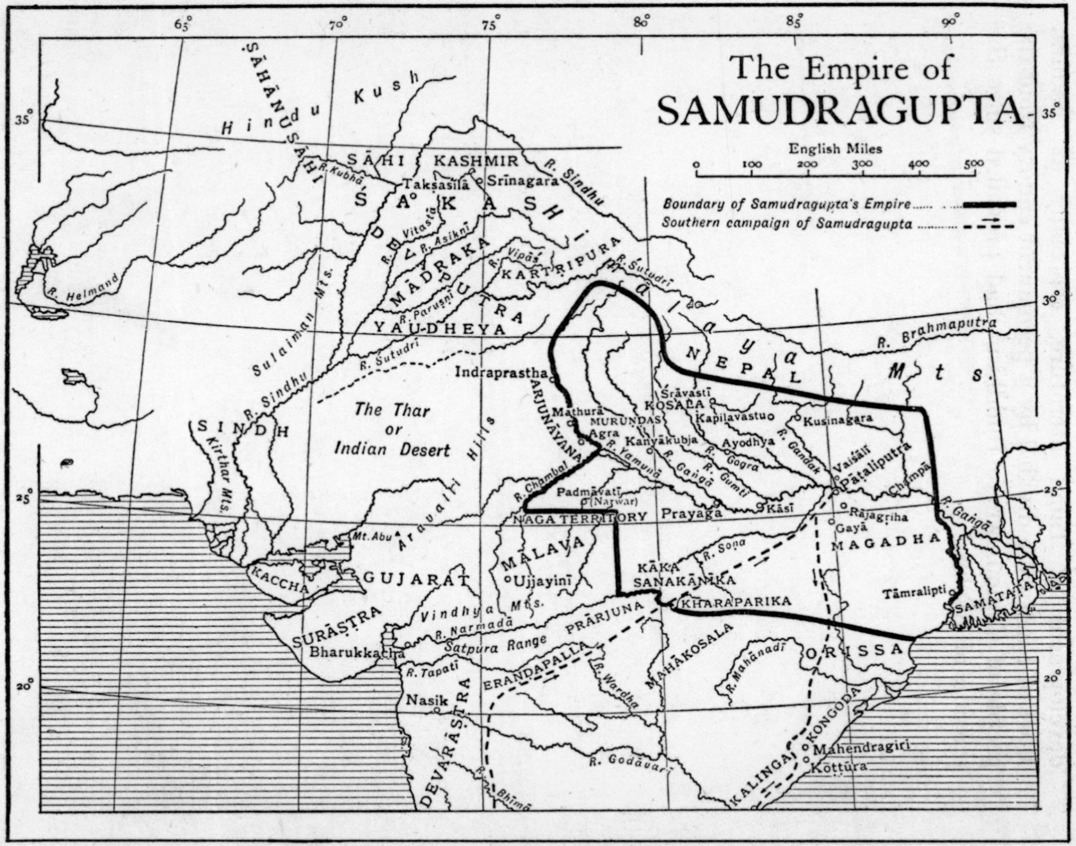

From *Men and Thought in Ancient India*, by R. Mookerji. Macmillan and Co., Ltd., 1924.

E

Muziris (Cranganore) and Bakarai (in Travancore). The nations of Coromandel reached a high degree of prosperity in the first three centuries of our era, as is proved by the development of Tamil literature, especially at Madura. Most of them were divided by a permanent enmity from the people of Ceylon, where Buddhism had prevailed since the mission of Asoka.

CHAPTER VI

The Guptas. Huns and Turks. Harsha

THE events of the third century are unknown to history, and we have very little information about the Kushan Empire. Daylight only returns in 318–19 when there arises in the old country of Magadha a new dynasty, this time really Indian, which revives the traditions of the Mauryas.

The very name of the founder of this line is a link with the past ; another Chandragupta takes the throne of Maghada. His ambition was furthered by a marriage, the memory of which was to be perpetuated by the coins of the period ; he married a princess of the house of the Lichchhavis, whom we have already met in the political surroundings of early Buddhism. Thereby Chandragupta I, the first of what historians call the Gupta dynasty, acquired not only Vaisali, but the ancient capital Pataliputra, and he even took in Oudh and Prayaga (Allahabad).

Samudragupta, his son (? 330–380), is an altogether outstanding figure ; in the gallery of Indian sovereigns he is the irresistible yet generous conqueror. We have a list of his great deeds in an inscription engraved on one of the pillars which Asoka had set up—that at Allahabad. It seems that somebody—doubtless his successor—wished to place the magnanimous warrior on the level of the peaceful emperor of glorious memory.

Samudragupta's conquests are described according to a conventional scheme by which they are directed towards the various cardinal points (*digvijaya*). First, there was a great expedition over the Deccan, passing first through the Kalinga country, in accordance with the tradition of Asoka, then following the east coast to Kañchi (Conjeeveram), cutting across to the west coast, and going north along it to the Chandragiri River, and returning by the inland side of the Western Ghats. The memory of this expedition lived long in the south. It was not quite a conquest, for the power of Samudragupta was hardly effective south of the latitude of the sources of the Narbada; yet it was more than a military promenade,[1] for in some parts the balance of the Deccan was upset by it. The fall of several thrones, even for a time only, must have furthered the ambitions of a southern dynasty which had a great future before it, the Pallavas, who were already masters of Kañchi when Samudragupta came there. The latter was content to pass through the country as the great overlord and to raise tribute among these distant peoples; he assumed the position of a "King of Kings" and, being unable to absorb such vast regions into his empire, he allowed himself the magnificent gesture of restoring the princes, once he had defeated them, under his own suzerainty.

The warlike ardour of Samudragupta was displayed in three other directions. He exterminated the immediate neighbours of his empire, particularly Ganapati Naga, King of Padmavati (Narwar in Gwalior), and rajas ruling between the Jumna and the Narbada. He reduced the Kings of the Jungle (Central India, according to Fleet) to bondage. He laid tribute on the frontier peoples east and west, from Assam to the republics of the Malavas, Arjunayanas, Yaudheyas, etc.—in other words, to the Punjab. To put the matter briefly, reducing the bombastic language of the inscription to positive statements, we may say that the true domain of Samudragupta embraced the whole of the Ganges basin but not more, and that in the Deccan and in the rest of India his overlordship was not asserted except when it was maintained by effective proof of his strength.

The Sakas of the north-west, with the Murunda portion of their kingdom, and the people of Ceylon are mentioned as distant satellites revolving round the glorious sun. In confirmation, we are informed by a Chinese source that two monks sent by Meghavarman of Ceylon (352–379) on a pilgrimage to Buddh Gaya concluded an agreement with the Emperor, by which the Cingalese were allowed to build a monastery in that holy place.

To proclaim and at the same time to consecrate his universal empire, Samudragupta had on his return from the Deccan performed the sacrifice of the horse, an old rite which none had dared to revive since Pushyamitra, the

[1] Jouveau-Dubreuil, CXX.

Sunga monarch. Geographically, Samudragupta may not have been the universal overlord, but he was so in the human sense. His magnificence was displayed not only in worldly glory but in liberality to all forms of worship. Although a follower of Vishnu, he was the patron of famous Buddhists, notably Vasubandhu. He had a talent for music and poetry; he appears on coins playing the *vīṇā*, and was hailed "King of Poets", *kavirāja*. The inscription describes him as "full of compassion and showing a tender heart . . . a true incarnation of goodness".

A happy era had certainly opened for India and the Indian spirit. The times had now come in which art, literature, Buddhist philosophy, and also orthodox speculation reached their height. Kalidasa was almost contemporary with Asanga. This expansion of culture could not fail to be encouraged by the exceptional succession of a number of remarkable monarchs, all on the whole wise and strong.

Indeed, the son of Samudragupta, Chandragupta II, is the ideal Kshatriya according to the *Bhagavadgītā*, reconciling, as he did, Vishnuite piety with a passion for war. He conquered the country of the Malavas (Malwa), Gujarat, and Surashtra (Kathiawar), overthrowing the twenty-first "Great Satrap" of the Saka dynasty of Ujjain. As a consequence of this very great extension westwards, he felt it necessary to move the axis of his empire in that direction, and made Ayodhya and Kausambi his capitals instead of Pataliputra. Then, adopting the traditions of Ujjain, where years were reckoned by the era of Vikrama (58 B.C. onwards), he took the title of Vikramaditya, "Sun of Power." It was in his reign (? 375–413) that the famous Chinese pilgrim, Fa-hien, in the course of his fifteen years of travel (399–414) spent several years visiting northern India from Taxila to the Bengalese port of Tamralipti, whence he proceeded to Ceylon and Java. His account brings up before our eyes the prosperity of the cities of the Ganges at the beginning of the fifth century.

Kumaragupta (413–455), the son of the preceding king, must likewise have sought military glory, since he celebrated the horse-sacrifice. The son whom he left when he died, Skandagupta, is the last great figure of the line (455–480).

It was not extinct yet, but henceforth it would rule only a shrunken, mutilated kingdom.

Since the foundation of the Indo-Scythian Empire and the Indianization of the Kushans, for three centuries and a half, India had lived free from foreign invasion. That does not mean that it had been shut off from other peoples ; on the contrary, relations with the West and the Far East were more frequent than ever before, but they were peaceful, and so far from hampering the Hindu genius they stimulated it. These favouring circumstances, combined with the creation of large empires, well-policed and strong, that of the Kushans and that of the Guptas, had raised all the potential qualities of native civilization to their height. For in that culture the development of one factor never entails the annihilation of a rival factor. So, although the dynasty of Kanishka had Zoroastrian convictions, it encouraged Buddhism ; although the Guptas fostered a brilliant revival of Brahmanic speculation, they assisted a great Buddhist expansion. Letters, arts, and general prosperity benefited likewise ; it was the Golden Age of India.

In the last years of Kumaragupta new Iranian peoples assailed the Empire, but they were kept back from the frontiers. Under Skandagupta the first wave of a formidable migration came down upon the same frontiers. This consisted of nomad Mongoloids, to whom India afterwards gave the generic name of *Hūṇa*, under which we recognize the Huns who invaded Europe. Those who reached India after the middle of the fifth century were the White Huns or Ephthalites, who in type were closer to the Turks than to the hideous followers of Attila. After a halt in the valley of the Oxus they took possession of Persia and Kabul. Skandagupta had driven them off for a few years (455), but after they had slain Firoz the Sassanid in 484 no Indian state could stop them. One of them, named Toramana, established himself among the Malavas in 500, and his son Mihiragula set up his capital at Sakala (Sialkot) in the Punjab. Once again Iran and Hindustan were governed by one power.

There was a temporary retreat of the invaders, with a revival of Malava independence, in 528. A native prince, Yasodharman, shook off the yoke of Mihiragula, who threw himself upon Kashmir. We should not fail to note, in this connexion, the increasing importance in the Indian world of the region intermediate between Hindustan and the Deccan, which extends from the Jumna to the Vindhyas and from Avanti to Kathiawar. Already in the fifth century Ujjain had been distinguished by quite especial brilliance, and had been coveted by the Andhras and seized from the Satraps by the Guptas. In the seventh century, in consequence of the weakening of Magadha, where the Gupta line was dying out, we find Malwa becoming the bastion of Hindu resistance. In the Kathiawar peninsula, at Valabhi, the probably Iranian dynasty of the Maitrakas founded at the end of the fifth century a kingdom which was to enjoy great prosperity and brilliant renown as a centre of Buddhism. Between these two centres, Ujjain and Valabhi, a tribe of Gurjaras, related to the Huns, squeezed itself in and settled at Bharukachchha (Broach) and at Bhinmal in southern Rajputana. From this last place, in the middle of the sixth century, one Pulakesin, of the Chalukya clan, emigrated, to establish himself at Vatapi (Badami in the district of Bijapur, Bombay Presidency); this was the beginning of a power which in the seventh century came to rule the Deccan.

The north-west of India had suffered severely. The last of the Kushans, driven out of Bactriana by the Huns and confined to Gandhara in the reign of Kidara, were compelled to leave Gandhara about 475 and to shut themselves up in Gilgit, in the hope that the hurricane would blow over. The Huns did indeed retreat in the middle of the sixth century, and the Kushans recovered part of Gandhara, which they kept until the ninth century. But frightful destruction had been done in the country. Many monasteries were in ruins, and the Græco-Indian tradition of sculpture was destroyed for ever.

Moreover, the expulsion of the Huns was not equally complete everywhere. A great many remained in the basin of the Indus. What is more, the damage done by the invasion outlasted the invasion itself. The country remained divided up into a confused multitude of states of medium or very small size. Vincent Smith rightly laid stress on the fact that the invasion of the Huns had put an end to a great number of political and other traditions, so that now, in the sixth century, India, where almost everything is traditional in character, found itself at an unusual and critical turning point in its development. We should add that the menace of new barbarian irruptions did not cease to weigh on it; shortly after the middle of the same century the kingdom of the Huns on the Oxus was absorbed into an equally warlike Turkish empire, which continued to be a danger to India until, a hundred years later, in 661, it in its turn fell before the armies of China.

At the beginning of the seventh century a power arose from the chaos in the small principality of Sthanvisvara (Thanesar, near Delhi). Here a courageous raja, Prabhakara-vardhana, learned the art of war in battles with the Huns and created a strong, organized kingdom, which showed its mettle against the Gurjaras, the Malavas, and other neighbouring peoples. Shortly after his death, in 604 or 605, his eldest son, Rajya-vardhana was murdered by the orders of the King of Gauda in Bengal. The power fell to a younger brother, aged sixteen or seventeen, in 606. This young man, Harsha or Siladitya, "Sun of Virtue," made a heroic beginning to a career which was to raise him to the level of Asoka. His life is known to us from the *Harsha-charita* of Bana and by another contemporary testimony, that of the Chinese pilgrim Hiuen Tsang.

As soon as he was elected by the Council of State, the King chastised the Bengali potentate in a lightning campaign. But then his own brother-in-law, the King of Kanyakubja (Kanauj), was killed by the King of the Malavas. Harsha seized Kanyakubja and made it his capital. So, supporting force with justice and justice with force, he gradually extended his dominions until they reached from the eastern border of the Punjab (exclusive) to the delta of the Ganges. Like Samudragupta, he held Malwa, Gujarat, and Kathiawar, and had the Narbada for his southern frontier. In addition he ruled Nepal. Influenced perhaps by the Gupta conqueror's example, he dreamed of striking a great blow in the Deccan against Maharashtra. In 620 he attacked the king of that country, Pulakesin II, of the Chalukya family, but obtained no great success in this quarter.

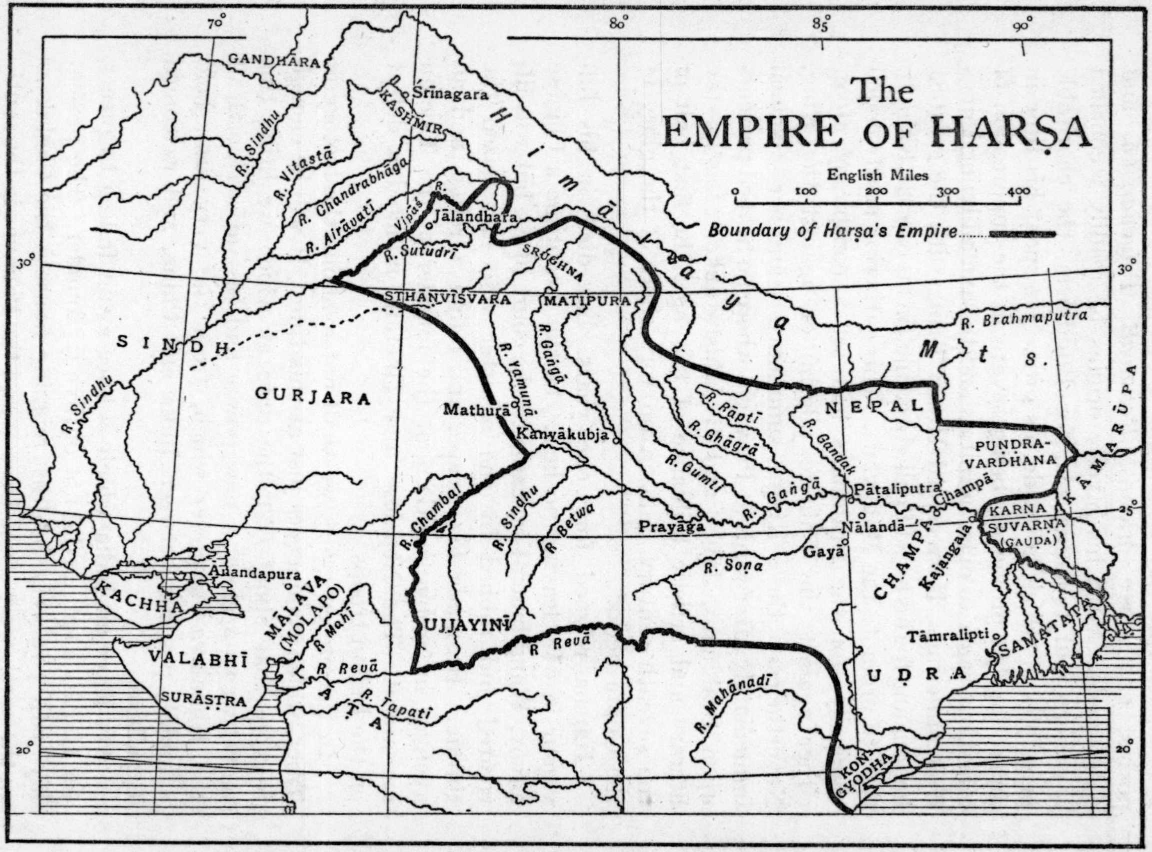

From *Men and Thought in Ancient India*, by R. Mookerji. Macmillan, 1924.

Page 57.]

Harsha was more than a glorious warrior. He, too, was a *kavirāja*. He is credited with a grammatical work, poems, and three dramas, *Ratnāvalī*, *Priyadarśikā*, and *Nāgānanda*. With his Sivaite origins he readily reconciled a sincere and touching zeal for Buddhism, the charitable principles of which he made his own. He spent his time in inspecting his provinces, being severe in the suppression of crime but eager to open hospitals and to save all living things from suffering. He received Hiuen Tsang with the greatest honour and for his benefit called a council in his capital (Kanauj, 643) to promote the Mahāyāna. This gathering nearly ended tragically, for the Brahmans had set a conspiracy afoot, either against the Chinese pilgrim or against the King. Nevertheless the King summoned another council immediately afterwards at Prayaga, where he heaped presents upon Brahmans, Jains, and Buddhists alike. Lastly, the literary and artistic brilliance of this age, the first half of the seventh century, falls in no way short of the glory of the Gupta period.

Harsha reigned forty-one years, but died in his full vigour in 647, leaving no heir. In the meantime a Chinese envoy, Wang-hiuen-t'se, came to the court (648), but was ill-treated and robbed by the minister who had seized the throne. He made his escape, and found a refuge and an avenger in Srong-tsan-Gampo, the founder of the Tibetan monarchy. The Nepalese and Tibetans inflicted a defeat on the Indian troops.

In the present work we shall not examine the history of Tibet, which commences just at this time. It will be enough to note that about 650, the date at which we bring this narrative to a close, a new power had just arisen north of the Himalaya—a power which, from the very first, held a middle position between India and China, and welcomed Buddhism.

We leave an India which is once again falling to pieces, for Harsha's empire did not outlive its founder. The present lay with two very healthy reigning houses—the Chalukyas in the north-west of the Deccan and the Pallavas in the south-east. The future would be with the Mongols, and in part with Islam, for the year 622 saw the Hegira.

In the twelve or thirteen centuries of history which I have just sketched, in the broadest lines and with many gaps, is there any kind of unity ?

That world of ancient India, we must repeat, is a chaos, because of differences of race and language and multiplicity of traditions and beliefs. Only in our own time have the reduction of distances by rapid communications and the imposition on all these alien peoples of a common tongue, English, given some homogeneity to the country. The chief unity which we find in the ages which we have so briefly described is that of the Vedic tradition imposed as Brahman orthodoxy by the Indo-European element. In politics the tradition of a King of Kings from time to time brings forth, in one place or another, a short-lived empire. But there is no local tradition to make such a power permanent. We have, indeed, seen interest centring on very different Indias in succession—the Punjab, the Ganges valley, the country of Ujjain, the Deccan.

Invasion from the north-west was an intermittent but chronic phenomenon. Sometimes it was new Indo-Europeans who came that way to reinforce the Aryans already settled in Hindustan, but sometimes it was Mongoloids, such as the Huns and the Turco-Mongols. Even in this latter case, no less than when the invaders were Greeks or Kushans, the new elements which attached themselves to the Hindu mass were, at least vaguely, Iranianized. In this way the invaders, even when not Indo-Europeans, continued and reinforced, and revived in unexpected forms, the ancient, permanent solidarity which united India to Iran. Without a doubt, we have here the most constant element in Indian history. From Iran came the claim to world-kingship, and there was a correlation between that supreme kingship and the favour shown to the only known religion which embraced all mankind.

Indeed, Buddhism rose to its greatest importance, not in India, but in the great Serindian spaces where it circulated from the Oxus to China. Græco-Parthians, Græco-Bactrians, Kushans, pre-Islamic Turco-Mongols, all the foreigners who set up their tents in Serindia before they established themselves in India itself, had more sympathy with an almost international religion than with Brahman orthodoxy, the social character of which was specially Hindu. That is why the great potentates belong to dynasties from outside, and why they combine with their temporal ambitions a devotion, the more sincere because it is interested, to Buddhism.

Lastly, we should note that the distinctions which we make in the West between antiquity and the Middle Ages, seen from the point of view of modern times, do not apply to Asia. Buddhism never brought in a new order, as Christianity did in the basin of the Mediterranean. In fact, it is one of the most ancient elements in the make-up of India, if we set aside Vedic prehistory, and it never conquered the whole of India, or anything like it. The invasions undergone by India and China did not introduce new institutions comparable to those which the Franks, for example, gave to Roman Gaul; much rather, they were remodelled in native forms. So there was no line between " antiquity " and " middle ages ". In a sense, one might say that Asia was in all historical periods in a state comparable to the Middle Ages among ourselves, in that Asia always lived according to a traditional order, accompanied by a scholastic science. It was partly in order to make that continuity clear that I have carried our story down to the seventh century. My other reasons lie in the fact that ancient India then showed its fullest development, and that at this time a factor came into play which none could have forseen—the expansion of Islam.

PART TWO

INDIAN SOCIETY

INTRODUCTION

WHILE it is true in general that among the various peoples the manifold functions of spiritual life, social or individual, only gradually break away from religion, it is particularly true of the civilization of India. Religion is, as it were, the common denominator, or the fundamental basis of all the factors which make up Indian life. In this second part we shall consider religion in its social aspect, deferring the examination of its individual aspect to the third part.

On the very threshold of the analysis of the religous institutions of ancient India which we have before us, we find once again the problems of the composition of the Indian world. We should be able to distinguish the Indo-European contribution from the earlier elements in which the Dravidian culture predominated. But to make this distinction, the materials are lacking.

Southern India, having been less thoroughly Aryanized than Northern, furnishes evidence about the Dravidian communities in the course of history and at this very day. But it would be very rash to venture to draw conclusions from it as to the social condition of the pre-Aryans who lived 1,500 or 2,000 years before our era. Lacking information about that non-Aryan India, we are reduced to the very arbitrary method of regarding as Dravidian those elements which are not drawn from the Vedic stock.

The Dravidians of antiquity, having left no written records, are only known to us through the Veda in the widest sense of the name. Since the Veda is, to a still greater extent, the basis of our knowledge of classical India, the time has now come to give a brief abstract of it, without prejudice to the study of it to be made later with reference to literary history.

The Veda, in the widest sense, is not a collection of texts, but the sum of *knowledge*, by which one must understand all the arts and sciences required by religious life (*dharma*). In a stricter sense the word means a certain literature, which at first was handed down orally. In the most limited acceptation it stands for four collections (*saṃhitā*) of hymns and formulas, the first foundation of Vedic literature.

The four collections are as follows: *Ṛigveda*, a corpus of stanzas (*ṛich*) praising some deity; the *Sāmaveda*, a corpus of tunes to which the hymns of the first collection are to be sung; the *Yajurveda*, a corpus of sacrificial formulas in prose, mostly later than the hymns of the *Ṛigveda*; and the *Atharvaveda*, a corpus of magical recipes. The form of this fourth Veda, which follows that of the hymns of the first, shows that it is a later production, but its foundation belongs to an extremely ancient order of beliefs.

A secondary stratum of Vedic texts consists of commentaries, ritual (Brāhmaṇas) or metaphysical (Āraṇyakas, Upanishads), respectively intended to govern sacrifice and to transpose it into abstract speculation. Each is attached to one of the Vedas; the *Aitareya Brāhmaṇa* to the *Ṛigveda*, the *Chhāndogya Upanishad* to the *Sāmaveda*, others to one or the other of the two versions of the *Yajurveda* (for example, the *Taittirīya* and the *Maitrāyaṇī Saṃhitā* to the Black and the *Vājaseneyi Saṃhitā* to the White), and so on.

The Brāhmaṇas, which are in prose, contain rules for sacrificing, drawn up by priests for priests. Their great number points not only to diversity of sacrifices but to multiplicity of schools (*śākhā*).

The Āraṇyakas, or "Forest Books", are intended for the use of hermits living far from the world in the forest. Remote from the conditions of human life, ritual religion becomes no more than the symbol of transcendental truth, and normally these works lead on to the philosophy of the Upanishads. The table given opposite shows the connexion between these various kinds of work. This is an actual connexion in the case of the *Aitareya Brāhmaṇa*, to which is attached an *Aitareya Āraṇyaka* containing an *Aitareya Upanishad*, and in the exactly parallel Kaushītaki and Taittirīya series. It is theoretic and artificial in other cases, for example in the connexion of many late Upanishads with the *Atharvaveda*.

VEDIC LITERATURE

Vedas	Schools	Saṃhitās	Brāhmaṇas	Āraṇyakas	Upanishads	Kalpa Sūtras
Ṛigveda	Aitareyins	Ṛiksaṃhitā	Aitareya	Aitareya	Aitareya	Āśvalāyana
	Kaushītakins		Kaushītaki (Śānkhāyana)	Kaushītaki	Kaushītaki	Śānkhāyana
Sāmaveda	Tāṇḍins	Kauthuma-Rāṇāyaniya	Tāṇḍya, Shaḍviṃśa		Chhāndogya	Lāṭyāyana, Gobhila, Khādira, Sāmavidhāna, Brāhmaṇa
	Talavakāras (Jaiminīyas)	Jaiminīya	Jaiminīya-Talavakāra		Kena	Jaiminīya
Yajurveda, Black	Kāṭhakas	Kāṭhaka	Kāṭhaka (partly in Taitt. Ār.)		Kāṭhaka	Kāṭhaka Gṛihya
	Taittirīyas	Taittirīya	Taittirīya	Taittirīya	Taittirīya, Mahānārāyaṇa, Śvetāśvatara	Baudhāyana, Āpastamba, Hiraṇyakeśi, Bhāradvāja
	Maitrāyaṇīyas, Kapishṭala-Kaṭhas	Maitrāyaṇī, Kapishṭala			Maitrāyaṇa	Mānava
Yajurveda, White	Mādhyaṃdinas	Mādh. Vājasaneyi	Śatapatha	Madh. Vājasaneyi	Bṛihadāraṇyaka	Kātyāyana
	Kaṇvas	Kaṇvīya Vāj.		Kaṇvīya	Iśā	
Atharvaveda	Atharvans				Muṇḍaka, Praśna, Māṇḍūkya	Kauśika, Vaitāna Śrauta

[*Page* 63.

A third stratum, comprising the six " limbs of the Veda " (*vedānga*) or sciences of exegetic interpretation—phonetics, ritual, grammar, etymology, metre, and astronomy [1]—consists of *sūtras* which are very brief mnemonic verses. This new literature, which is essentially scholastic, was learned by heart, and the prose explanations given by the master were intended to make the extremely condensed sentences intelligible. The Śrauta Sūtras give the rules for sacrifices; the Gṛihya Sūtras govern the sacraments (*saṃskāra*) which give a religious value to individual life from birth to death. These two classes of work together make up the whole corpus of ritual, Kalpa Sūtra, and are supplemented by manuals giving the methods of mensuration and geometry needed for the preparation of the place of sacrifice and altar, the Śulva Sūtras. Other Sūtras lay down correct conduct in legal, moral, and religious matters; these are the Dharma Sūtras. Here again reality corresponds to theory only in part. In the Kātyāyana series, for example, there are only Śrautra and Śulva Sūtras; in the Āśvalāyana series only Śrauta and Gṛihya Sūtras. Only the Āpastamba and the Baudhāyana series contain all four varieties of Kalpa Sūtra, the Śrauta, Gṛihya, Dharma, and Śulva Sūtras. In order not to complicate the table, these details are not given, nor those Sūtras which do not form part of the ritual (*kalpa*) properly so called.

[1] *Śikshā, kalpa, vyākaraṇa, nirukta, chhandas, jyotisha.*

CHAPTER I

The Family. Its Worship and Law

IN the Indian world the social horizon of the average man hardly extends beyond the rural hamlet. Individuals sprung from a common origin continue to live together according to certain rules, and the group consists in theory of kinsmen. *Janman*, the line of descent, is the same or almost the same as *grāma*, the village.

Yet the Aryan invaders, being nomads, had no villages, but only lines of descent, to which they clung all the more keenly because they found in this attachment to family traditions a means of preserving their specific character. To preserve the race (*kula*) unchanged was to them the great social duty, and classical literature is deeply stamped with that feeling. The Dravidians whose country they invaded, on the other hand, had long been settled on the soil, and they possessed agricultural centres and probably towns. So we find that the Dravidian religions continue through history to be local cults, and they imposed a religious village-life on Hinduism. It seems, therefore, that the identification of *grāma* and *janman* points to that mixture of population henceforward characteristic of the country.

The family rested on different foundations in the two racial environments. Matriarchy and polyandry must have existed in the original Dravidian element; traces or memories of them have survived. The Indo-Europeans, on the other hand, seem very generally to have maintained the agnatic principle in defining relationships, and they imposed it on later ages. Agricultural communities tend to give women a high social position, harmonizing with cults of natural fruitfulness, whereas conquering peoples need rather a masculine form of authority.

The Indian family of Indo-European type, composed of cousins and second cousins, corresponds to the Greek γένος and the Latin *gens*, and has the same name—*jana*, *janman*. The co-ordination of several lines in a wider group forms the tribe, *sabhā*, a union of villages. It is what the Southern Slavs call *pleme*, in opposition to *bratstvo*—a crowd as opposed to a brotherhood. Their *zadruga*, a family group smaller than the *bratstvo*, has an Indian equivalent, the *viś* or clan. A *jana* is divided into *viśas* as, in the vocabulary of Iran, the *zañtu* is divided into *vīses*, this last word *vīs* being identical with the Indian. We shall only go astray if we try to press similarities among the institutions of the many Indo-European societies, which are only approximate likenesses and are the result of long independent development. The three degrees, clan (German *Sippe*), stock or line (*Stamm*), and tribe (*Versammlung*), are distinguished to different degrees according to the environment, and on this point the discussions of the modern schools of sociology contain as much theory as history, if not more. The earliest Indian institution at which we can arrive is a social group, varying in size, of kinsmen or of juxtaposed lines of descent, and it does not much matter whether we call this group a "clan" or a "line".[1]

The criterion of membership of this group does not lie in consanguinity—what I have said of the kinsmen of the woman is proof of this—but in the practice of a common religion. Kinsfolk are those who pay the same honours to the same ancestor. They are *sapiṇḍa*, as in Greece the people making the same offering of milk to the same dead were ὁμογάλακτες. The social rather than biological character of kinship is well illustrated by the fact that when a husband was sterile he would obtain sons to carry on the family worship by the union of his wife with another man.

The father, grandfather, or great-grandfather is the head of the family, *pati*. There are also heads of clans, *viśpati*, and it is from among these, who in theory are all equal, that the military head of the tribe, the King, is chosen. His function is to maintain order, *rājati* (Avestic *rāzayeiti*). The power which elects the King is the association of lines which is called a tribe, *sabhā*, and that is how this term also has the meaning of "assembly". Such are the primitive rudiments from which later institutions were to develop.

[1] In the Brahman caste this group is the *gotra*, the members of which are supposed to be descended from a common ancestor.

I

THE WORSHIP OF THE FAMILY

The central point round which the Indo-European or Indo-Europeanized family is grouped is the hearth. The hearth makes its unity and dominates its worship. So through all the ages of India a prehistoric Aryan religion of fire is perpetuated.

There are as many fires as there are families. The fire, like the father, is the master of the house, *gṛihapati*, or the head of the village, *viśpati*, according to the size of the group. As once that fire, burning by the tents of nomads, kept away wild beasts, so, now that they are settled, it guards herdsmen and flocks, like a true pastor, *gopa*. It is essentially polymorphic and flames and crackles not only on the hearth but in the sky. It is the lightning and it is the sun. It is a formidable power and a friend of man, the thunderbolt which destroys and the heat which gives life. The divine, *deva*, is by its name heat and light ; it is over mortals as the sky is over them. But on the other hand nothing is more within man's reach than the hearth which cooks his food, serves for his rites, and presides over all the acts of his life. It springs not only from the cloud, as the Son of the Waters (*āpam napāt*), but from the wood of the *araṇi*, the fire stick and board. Therefore it can be produced. But blessed are those who do not allow the fire of the tribe to die out, and keep it up for ever. The most ancient Indo-Iranian priesthood is that of the *atharvans*, the fire-priests.

The handing down of fire is not merely symbolical of the maintenance of the ancestral line ; it is the same thing. The fire is equivalent to the " ancestor ", representing whom the father, grandfather, and great-grandfather, the *tripatores* of the Greeks, the *sapiṇḍa-pitaras* of classical India, have authority in the family. Just as the hearth now burning continues the fire of past years, so these " fathers " preserve to-day the sacred character which belonged to the mightiest of the dead, who still exist in a mysterious abode. The food offered to these dead is thrown into the fire, and so comes to them.

In virtue of this consubstantiality of the hearth-fire and

the line, the cosmic extensions of each are equivalent. Since there is fire also in nature, where the sky is luminous, the sky too is a father, *Dyaus-pitar*. This fundamental belief of the Indo-Europeans, familiar to us in its Græco-Latin form (*Zeus Pater*, Jupiter), marks the point at which cosmology and mythology link up with the most essential rites of the family. Communication is made with the heavenly beings or gods (*deva*) as it is with the ancestors, through fire, and among all fires that of the hearth keeps a pre-eminence which is very significant.

Every head of a family is a sacrificer. His religious duties are set forth particularly in the Gṛihya Sūtra, the book of domestic ritual, in which he is the sole or principal actor, but also, in part, in the revealed ritual described in the Śrauta Sūtra, which requires the offices of professionals. The fire of the hearth is sufficient in the first case; in the second, two other fires are needed, the *āhavanīya* and the *dakshina*, which stand respectively on the east and north of the household altar, but must both be kindled at the hearth. The altar is a mere patch of grass, strewn in a rough rectangle with incurving sides. On this the fires and the offerings are arranged, the latter being milk, butter, corn, meat, and fermented liquors. On this *vedi* the gods come and take their places. Such is the simple material apparatus of sacrifice, but the rites are highly complicated.

From morning to night the master of the house performs religious duties. The morning *sandhyā* includes various practices—bathing in running water, cleaning of the teeth, arranging of the hair, breathing exercises, and the recitation of the *gāyatrī*, the most sacred of all formulas,[1] and other Vedic texts. Then come five "great sacrifices" (*mahāyajña*)—offerings to the gods (*deva*), demons (*bhūta*), and ghosts of the dead (*pitṛi*), to men (*nṛi*) by the exercise of hospitality,

[1] "*OM, bhūr bhuvaḥ svaḥ.*
Tat Savitur varenyam
bhargo devasya dhīmahī,
dhiyo yo naḥ prochodayāt."

The first line contains OM or AUM, the mighty monosyllable, the Alpha and Omega of all reality, followed by the names of the three upper worlds, earth, atmosphere, and heavens. Then come three octosyllabic lines from the *Ṛigveda*: "That desirable glory of the god Savitar, may we possess it! It will awaken our thoughts!"

and to the Brahman by the reading of a Vedic text. This word " Brahman " will be explained later ; what we have here is veneration paid to scriptural revelation. After that, honour is paid to five idols of the home (*āyatana*), which are stones symbolizing the deities Vishnu, Siva, Durga, Ganesa, and Surya. Morning and evening there is an *agnihotra*, a sacrifice of fire in its three forms. At the midday meal food is thrown on the fire for the benefit of all the gods (*vaiśvadeva*). Then little heaps of cooked rice are placed inside and outside the house for the gods, the spirits, and the beasts. Then, and then only, do the men of the house take their meal, sitting on their hunkers ; the women, who serve them, do not eat till afterwards. At sunset there is another *sandhyā*. This simplified account hardly gives an idea of the number of the daily formalities by which the master of a house contributes to the universal order, promoting the movements of the sun by the regularity of his worship, nourishing the various kinds of spirits, including the gods and the dead, and keeping his group in harmony with the whole of nature. But one can see what a part fire plays in this religion of the household.

Now let us look at this religion in the course of the characteristic phases of individual life. Forty *saṃskāras*, or sacraments, should be enumerated, but we may be content to note those marking the principal epochs. Even before a child is born there are ways of facilitating the event, warding off evil influences, and obtaining the arrival of a male offspring (*puṃsavana*). The new-born baby is given ablutions and a spoonful of honey in a golden spatula, and speech and thought are breathed into his ear by the muttering of pious words. The constellation under which he was born is written down in a record of his birth (*janmapatra*), and this document will be consulted at the critical epochs of life. At the giving of his name (*nāma-karaṇa*), at least ten days after his birth, he receives an every-day name and another, which will be kept secret, which depends on astrological conjunctions. At the age of six the child gets his first solid nourishment (*annaprāshana*), which is rice. Between the ages of three and seven a boy is given his proper tonsure (*chūḍā-karaṇa*). Between eight and twelve he is taken as a novice or scholar by a teacher (*upanāyana*). This is the occasion of a second birth. Wrapped in an antelope's hide, he is invested with the sacred cord of the free man (*yajñopavīta*), and he is taught the *gāyatrī*, as an initiation into the Veda, which is all the spiritual nourishment which he will receive in his education. In theory he should serve an apprenticeship of twelve years for each Veda, or forty-eight years in all, but it is obvious that the exigencies of life, even for a man destined to the priesthood, make such a time impossible. Special rites emancipate the young adult from his studenthood and reintroduce him into the world (*samāvartana*). Marriage (*vivāha*) then becomes necessary; we shall see the forms which it takes presently. Now begins life as the head of a house, whose chief daily obligations we have just seen. It is recommended that at the age when a man has grown-up sons he should retire into the forest, or at least adopt the habits of a hermit, in expectation of the day when the funeral rites shall make him in his turn an ancestor. The ancestors at the start, the state of ancestor at the end, and the central part played by the father in the time between —that is the course of a cycle of family life based on the agnatic type. All the sacraments governing this evolution consist in prescribing a mode of life for a certain age, an action for a certain moment. The rite is nothing more than the suitable action required at the time, *kalpa*. It would be as idle to try to go on to a later time without performing the necessary rite as to hope to go from winter to summer without passing through spring.

In many of these *saṃskāras* there are sacrifices made at the hearth, or gravitating round it. When the young bride enters the house, she is accompanied by a special fire which indicates that a new element has been grafted on to the family tree.

Whether burned or buried, the dead live on in the existence appropriate to them, provided that they are fed by the offerings poured on the hearth. That hearth is plainly far more than the chief instrument in worship; it incorporates the essence of the family.

The Śrauta Sūtras lay down sacrifices requiring three fires and various categories of priests. We shall touch on them when we come to consider the priesthood.

II

THE LAW OF THE FAMILY

Dharma

The distinction of religion and law can be justified only from the European point of view; the two notions are one in Indian *dharma*.

But before going further we should note that, without losing their intimate connexion with religion, legal rules gave rise to a special literature. In the great age of the Brāhmaṇas, between the eighth and third centuries before Christ, thought began to concentrate on laying down legal relationships. This new interest was based, not on the Veda or on revelation (*śṛuti*), but on tradition (*smṛiti*).

The corpus of customs (*dharma-śāstra*) was drawn up in close connexion with the books of ritual. So far from setting forth codes which, in the European sense, have "the force of law", it defines a religious ideal of social order. It lays down duties much rather than rights—again two notions which in India are never opposed, but are enveloped in the intermediate notion of *dharma*. The books are drawn up like *sūtras*, but are full of maxims in verse. They bear the names of schools or traditions, like the ritual books.

The most ancient is the *Dharmaśastra* of Gautama, which is quoted as an authority by Baudhayana and Vasishtha; it is attached to the *Sāmaveda*. The *Dharma Sūtras* of Vasishtha, which belong to a northern school, cite *Dharma Sūtras* of Manu, which must have been the origin of the later *Mānava-dharmaśāṣtra*. The *Sūtras* of Apastamba, which are connected with a Black *Yajurveda* of Southern India, go back to about 400 B.C., a date slightly earlier than that of the composition of the *Sūtras* of Baudhayana, which have the same origin. These two works are the best preserved among the earlier legal literature. They quote the *Sūtras* of Harita, which belong to the same Veda but are of the Maitrāyaṇīya school.

Now we come to treatises which cannot have been written before 200 B.C. First there is the *Dharmaśāstra* of the Vaishṇavas, called the *Vishṇu-smṛiti*, which is founded on ancient Sūtras of the Kāṭhaka school belonging to the Black

Yajurveda. Next comes several other *Smṛitis*, the most celebrated of which is the *Manu-smṛiti* or *Mānava-dharmaśāstra*, known in the West as the "Laws of Manu". This new literature has much in common with the epic *Mahābhārata.* It is strongly marked by the influence of popular religions, and belongs to the centuries in which the epic was written (between 200 B.C. and A.D. 200); indeed, the epic refers to it (*Mahabh.*, bk. xiii). In character it is at once didactic, poetic, and philosophic, and has none of the dryness of the old Sūtras. The *Smṛiti* of Yajñavalkya, which dates from nearly the same time, is related to the Gṛihya Sūtras of the White *Yajurveda* of Eastern India. In expression it is more condensed, more systematic, and more lucid than the work of Manu, and therefore seems to have been written rather later. This late character is still more marked in the *Smṛiti* of Narada, certain interpolations in which (e.g. *dīnāra*, the Latin *denarius*) bear the stamp of the fourth century of our era. The *Smṛiti* of Brihaspati is, in substance, later than that of Narada, but it is presented as a commentary on Manu, definitely earlier than that of Medhatithi, the first of the classical commentators (ninth century).

These different works of "tradition" incorporate not only the early *Dharmaśāstras*, but very ancient maxims—the didactic aspect of a folklore diffused over Eurasia, no less than the semi-historical wisdom of the epics or the Purāṇas.

III

WOMAN AND MARRIAGE

We have seen that the preservation of the blood of the race, symbolized by the perpetuity of the domestic fire, is the fundamental idea of the Indian family. So the forms of conjugal union hold a central place in the law of the household.

Dravidian polyandry has left even in the epics a queer trace, which is a valuable historical record of bygone manners. In the *Mahābhārata*, Draupadi is the wife of the five Pandava brothers. But nothing could be more contrary to Brahman law, which is so strictly agnatic.

Polygamy is not forbidden ; it is even sanctioned by the various kinds of regular union, all equally lawful, which we shall consider. Yet the peculiar importance of the wife, who contributes, with the father, to the observation of the household ritual, and who is expected to produce sons to continue the worship of the ancestors, entails a sort of monogamy. Nor should we forget that on the whole India has, in every age, been a poor country. For the vast majority of men the maintenance of one wife is the utmost that can be borne, especially since sacrifices are very costly. In practice, only the nobles, if they are rich, can allow themselves the luxury of a harem.

In the Vedic ages woman seems to have had the power of choosing her husband (*svayaṃvara*), but that trace of a time and an environment in which her sex was predominant disappeared in the classical period. Far from a union being the result of elective affinities between individuals, it was normally arranged by the families and consecrated in the childhood of the future husband and wife. The *Dharma Sūtras* of Gautama already declare that girls should be married before puberty, and eventually children were married in their very early years, long before the girl, aged about eleven or twelve, went to live in her husband's house. In consequence, many women are widows when quite young, before the union has been physically consummated.

The same work allows a childless widow to remarry, but greater esteem is enjoyed by the woman who resigns herself to lifelong widowhood, even if her husband died at the age of three or four years of measles or whooping-cough. This feeling is so strong that a woman who loses her husband when he is grown up is encouraged to allow herself to be burned on his funeral pyre.[1] The *Atharvaveda* (18, 3, 1) already mentions the ancient custom of widow-burning. The custom was never enforced, but always highly commended. Belief in the next world, where the union of husband and wife is supposed to continue, justifies a practice in which it is hard for us to see anything but barbarity or pathetic self-sacrifice. We should remember, too, that the widow, being unable to return to her former family, to which she has ceased to

[1] A good monograph on the subject is Edward J. Thompson's *Suttee*, London, 1928.

belong, can no longer perform religious duties, whereas in following her husband, in the words of Sita in the *Rāmāyaṇa*, she rejoins "her god".

Be she daughter, wife, or mother, the woman is always a minor. "*Na strīsvātantryam,*" says Manu (xi, 1); there is never any independence for her. This subjection results from the absolute authority assumed by the head of the family in Aryan India. No doubt, in the previous age the mother could rule the family, but the exclusive capacity of the father to make offerings to the ancestors created patriarchy.

The transmission of name and clanship on the distaff side, of which there are vestiges in antiquity,[1] is the exception. The rule is that no man regards his wife's relations as being of his own family, and children do not regard their mother's relations as their own. This is an inevitable conception if marriage is the purchase of a woman, or rather of the children to be born of her; and it is equally inevitable if marriage is also regarded as the consecration of an abduction. The very principle of conjugal union requires that the woman should be a stranger to the family; for, while it is obligatory to marry in one's own caste, it is forbidden to marry a *sapiṇḍa* girl, that is, one whose father or brother would sacrifice to the same ancestors as the prospective husband. According to Gautama (iv, 1), a man cannot marry his kinswoman (*sagotrā, samānapravarā*) within six degrees on the paternal side, or within four degrees of his mother (as *sapiṇḍa* of the same *gotra* or family). This prohibition of incest is in marked contrast to the "sacred" marriages between close relations—parents and children, brothers and sisters—practised in the Iranian branch of the Aryans.

Manu (iii, 21) enumerates eight forms of conjugal union, which I shall give in order of dignity. It is a theoretical classification, in which the caste-spirit is displayed, but various principles can be discerned—mutual consent, real or fictitious purchase, abductions, or even violation. The term common to all these various modes is *vivāha*, which means etymologically a "carrying off", with or without violence; in any case a snatching of the girl from her parents' house. The four most estimable forms, which are really

[1] Przyluski, **XV**, Jan., 1927, p. 157.

orthodox, are suitable to the priestly caste, being of such a kind that the wife, on dying, obtains heaven, and the husband is then entitled to inherit his wife's property (*strīdhana*). These are *brāhma vivāha*, where the bride is given of her own will, *daiva vivāha*, where the bridegroom is a sacrificing priest (*ṛitvij*), *ārsha vivāha*, where the bride's father receives, fictitiously, two cattle, and *prājāpatya vivāha*, where the proposal of marriage comes from the man. The *āsura* form is suited to the Vaiśya and Śūdra castes, the merchants and craftsmen, for it is a purchase, though fictitious; the "hundred cows" which are supposed to constitute the payment are in fact given back to the husband. Lastly there are inferior forms, in which passion predominates—the *gāndharva* form, that of the spirits of the air, the love-match, which dispenses with the parents' consent (the privilege of the nobility); the fashion of the *Rākshasas*, which is devilish, namely rape, likewise characteristic of the warrior caste (*kshātra vivāha*); and lastly a contemptible form, that of the demons, *paiśācha*, which is a trap, violence suffered in a state of artificially produced drunkenness. Nobles may permit themselves this licence, but it bears the stamp of the low castes.

IV

PROPERTY

Common family life implies common abode, common meals, common religion, and common property. Indian law knows nothing of the will, so that if there is a division of property, it is done by the wish of the father, or by that of the sons with his consent. In theory, wives and daughters have no right to anything but their food and, only by tolerance, what they have received as gifts from relations. Yajñavalkya (ii, 123 and 115) allows the father to grant his wives a "son's share". But women have no right to inherit unless there are no male descendants at all.

There is no sign of village communism, even in the Vedic period, but one can see or infer both individual ownership and family communism. The head of the family is also the owner of the family property; but individuals can possess not only cattle, weapons, jewels, and slaves, but even land The terms *urvarāsā*, " one who obtains arable land," and *kshetrasā*, " one who obtains a field," are clear evidence of this. Besides, the Jātakas reveal a system of rural economy based on the ownership of the fields by the peasants. Landed property does not seem to have been marketable. The immense extent of the country and the fact that the Aryan conquest was never complete maintained certain survivals from early times in the classical period. " He who clears a piece of land," Manu says (ix, 44), " is the owner of it." Beyond a distance of 600 feet round a village begins a common zone, not that it belongs to the community, but because it is a " no man's land ".

From many signs it appears that the village community varied little from the earliest days of the Aryan conquest to the establishment of the British. André Philip describes it as follows [1] :—

" A typical village contains, according to the region, from fifty to two hundred families ; that is, a population of from 200 to 800 inhabitants. The houses, which are of wood or dried mud, consist of one or two rooms with a veranda, standing round a small open court, like the Roman atrium. Behind there is an open space where rubbish is thrown and which is used as a latrine. There are one or two outstanding houses with several rooms and perhaps two stories, with painted pillars by which one at once recognizes the home of an influential family, that of the head of the village or the accountant or the usurer. There are two or three parallel streets, each occupied by a special caste or trade. In the middle is the bazaar, where the whole collective life of the place centres, with a temple of Siva, Vishnu, or some other avatar of Brahma near by. A hundred yards away from the mass of houses stand the huts of branches and dried leaves in which live the untouchables, who are usually from 10 to 20 per cent of the population of the village. These huts contain only one room, often with no other opening than a narrow entrance, and in them human beings and domestic animals live all together in a state of disgusting filth. Most of the inhabitants of the village are agriculturists, and they usually belong to one single caste,

[1] CLVII, 14.

but they need a few craftsmen" who "belong each to a hereditary professional caste, and are the servants of the community, attached to the village and obliged to perform solely the duties considered indispensable to collective life. They are paid by the grant of an *inam*, or right to collect, in the place of the government, the revenues of a determined piece of land, and by a portion of the *baluta*, a determined amount of the produce of each harvest, which every peasant has to provide to the whole body of craftsmen."

In ancient India the land system was of the type now called *ryotwari*, "under which the peasants cultivate their land individually, making common use of the services of the craftsmen of the village and paying land revenue to the state through the village."[1] "No doubt there has always been a strong sense of unity in the village communities, but it does not seem to have been ever accompanied by collective ownership of the land. It seems rather that when India was invaded by the Aryan tribes the land was assigned to a certain number of families or of groups of families formed into clans. In exceptional cases a family constitutes a village, with common ownership of the surrounding land. Usually villages were founded by several families, each of which had its own land and cultivated it separately, while all remained collectively responsible to the sovereign for the payment of tax. But . . . what is the legal nature of the peasant family's right to its land? Is it a right of ownership, the land revenue being a tax, or is it not rather a mere right of occupation, the king . . . being the sole owner and collecting the rent of his land? The latter view has aways been preferred by the central power.

[1] Ibid., p. 31.

CHAPTER II

Caste

THE division of society into castes [1] is a peculiarly Indian phenomenon. In India itself it has been made the subject of theories which justify rather than explain it. European science has been hardly less active in theorizing. When an attempt has been made to go into the facts thoroughly, for example in the *Census Reports* of 1901 and 1911, the accepted hypotheses have been shown to be grossly inadequate and arbitrary. Nevertheless, those evolved by Indian thought, although they hardly correspond to reality, have this advantage over those of Europe as evidence, that they are part of the Indian state of mind. We must therefore pay due attention to them, even if we do not take them as an exact representation of the real state of society.

Let us first sum up the account given of caste by classical India. A caste is a group of persons traditionally given up to the same occupations, drawing their origin from the same human or divine ancestor, and bound in one body by determined rights, duties, and opinions, inherited from their tradition.[2] This group is called *jāti*, because a man belongs to it from birth ; it has this feature in common with the family, but it is stricter, for the family normally takes in individuals who are not related by blood, adopted children and wives.

The maintenance of unity of origin being regarded as essential, the marriage laws are the foundation of caste. Endogamy, the duty of marrying inside the group, is absolutely obligatory. To break that rule is the most certain and most scandalous of sins, the sin which overthrows the order of society. But there are other very strict rules in addition, regarding food and the manner of living. To take a meal with a man of another caste or to eat food touched

[1] The word comes from the Portuguese *casta* " race ", from Latin *castus*, and connotes purity of racial descent.

[2] Glasenapp, **CCXXVIII**, p. 318.

by someone of lower caste produces defilement, and so do travelling by sea and the neglect of traditional observances.

The maintenance of discipline requires authority. This lies with the most influential members, who belong to a special committee, *panchāyat*. A chief, chosen on hereditary principles from a certain family, presides over festivals and arbitrates in disputes.

Punishments are laid down for the many possible infringements of the rules, from a simple act of purification to expulsion. The court may order fines, or charities, or festivities for the benefit of the group. Loss of caste is the worst degradation; the excommunicated man loses all rights, has no protection against the various risks of life, and incurs universal reprobation. Renounced by those nearest to him, he is "dead to the world".[1]

The traditional plan of the social order comprises four castes. The first three comprise *āryas* or free men, and the fourth gives a legal standing to the masses in the Brahmanic organization.

The caste of the Brahmans, which has organized this arrangement and benefits by it most, assumes to itself the chief position in virtue of a great number of theocratic arguments. It is the depository of tradition and the heir to the revelation which was vouchsafed to the *ṛishis*, the mythical sages of prehistory. Not merely has it the monopoly of religion in that it controls the whole of Vedic worship; the same word, save for the accentuation (*brahmán*, masculine, *bráhman*, neuter), designates the priest and the Absolute of which he is the minister. The essence of the Brahman caste is one and the same thing as the holy, as the ultimate and first foundation of being. So the Brahman is literally a god among men. He is, in particular, a teacher (*guru*) for anyone belonging to the social order which one can call, in the strict sense, Brahmanism.

The caste immediately below, still of high rank, since it constitutes the nobility, is that of the Kshatriyas. War and temporal command (not spiritual) are its functions. From it the kings are taken. Its education is entrusted to the Brahmans, who take the greatest pains over it, for throne and altar need each other and combine to guide the rest of

[1] Abbé Dubois, *Mœurs*, i, p. 36.

mankind. Literature and philosophy are not the monopoly of the priestly caste; the nobility have excelled in them. As, for example, the Brāhmaṇas bear the stamp of the priest, the epics point to a feudal life.

The third caste, that of the Vaiśyas, is composed of the husbandmen and merchants. In the myth of the tenth book of the *Ṛigveda*, while the Brahmans and nobles were the mouth and arms respectively of the original cosmogonic Male, the Vaiśyas were his thighs. There was still something lower—his feet, which gave birth to the Śūdras, the people whose work consists in the humblest manual labours. But this fourth caste is composed of a mixed mass of non-Aryans, absorbed into the Aryan organization. Only in the first three does one find the "twice-born" (*djiva*), who at a certain point in their youth receive the initiation which makes free men of them, a real social birth added to their natural birth. That means that the Śūdras have no part in religious life. At the very most they perform certain rites of their own.

We must not forget that this organization is largely theoretical. The most rudimentary investigation of the facts shows us that, far from being confined to four, the castes have multiplied in swarms and are still doing so *ad infinitum*, assuming different characters according to the time and place. Thus the men who in actual fact obey the laws of the caste are not the whole body of Brahmans all over India, but a particular section of Brahmans in a particular region, practising a particular occupation. Even these sections are split up before our eyes, without their subdividings being subject to any strict principle. Migrations, the breaking-up of peoples at the time of foreign invasions, endemic scourges, wars, local economic rivalries, unequal blending with non-Aryan tribes, religious propaganda, and many other influences, the most effective of which were often the least general—these are the obscure but real causes, although they are usually beyond the ken of the historian.

Not only does the caste organization not form an unalterable structure, but that abomination of abominations, mixture of castes, happens every moment. The individuals born of these mixed marriages fall into lower castes or constitute new ones. So the theoretical rule of caste is an ideal rather than a fact, but in being an ideal it is a fact, maintaining, through the infinite diversity of real conditions, a few common principles, the chief of which is the prestige of the Brahman.

Various attempts have been made by Europeans to account for the facts of caste or the notion of caste. Sociologists and ethnologists have connected it with occupation or with race. Students of India, usually philologists, have searched the history of the country for literary evidence.

Nesfield maintained that the decisive factor was professional specialization. In his view, occupations are classed in order of rank—hunting or fishing, stock-breeding, agriculture, manual or servile labour, trade, priesthood. The abstract character of this conception is revealed by the assertion that a succession of stages like this is inherent in the whole of mankind. Senart's replies to the arguments of Nesfield and Ibbetson are insurmountable ; if the original bonds of castes lay in community of profession, those bonds would have preserved it from splitting up ; but the fact is that men who exercise the same occupation in the same district, and so should be united, belong to different castes, which keep them apart. One finds Brahmans practising all trades, save those which would make them lose caste. The rules which ensure the maintenance and perpetuity of the castes have no connection with occupation.

According to Sir Herbert Risley, caste is a matter of race. " It is scarcely a paradox to lay down, as a law of the caste organization, that the social status of the members of a particular group varies in inverse ratio to the mean relative width of their noses." [1] Even if the " nasal index " is significant in a certain part of the country, one may be allowed to remain sceptical. The population is inextricably mixed in an infinite variety of ways. Average types, with many gradations, are established, and there is always the possibility in individual cases of return to ancestral types, which new unions are as likely to restore as to obliterate. Besides, where in the world shall we find a people in which

[1] **XXXIX**, p. 29.

racial elements are not certainly mixed? But caste is a specifically Indian phenomenon.

Therefore the philologists were in a better position to obtain positive information on the subject. Unfortunately, it was mainly theoretical. More than on any other point, they were divided on the question of origins, according as they did or did not hold that the most ancient literary document, the *Ṛigveda*, attests the existence of castes among the earliest Indo-Europeans of India. Haug, followed by Kern, maintained, contrary to the current opinion, that the castes were accepted not only by the authors of the hymns but by the common stock prior to the Indo-Iranian separation. Their opponents have observed that clear mention of the four traditional castes is not found until the Purusha Hymn in the tenth book of the *Ṛigveda*, which is late, being probably of the same time as the first Brāhmaṇas. The truth is that the Aryans were divided into three social strata, which in Vedic India are named after the three abstract essences of which they are made, *brahman*, *kshatra*, and *viś*, and in Iran Atharvans or priesthood, Rathaesthas or warriors, Vastriyas-Fshuyants and Huitis, the mass of the people. But, Senart says, we still have to know if these are castes; what makes one doubtful is that the *pishtras* thus enumerated as making up the ancient population of Iran did not produce castes in that country. The development by which the notion of *brahman* gave rise to the Brahman caste, that of *kshatra* to the noble caste, and that of *viś* to the Vaisya caste is confined to India.

So Senart was led to his own theory, the essential idea of which is that the castes which make up Brahmanism were grafted on to ancient "classes"—those of the Vedic age and the original united Aryans. But there is a difference between class and caste. Class "serves political ambitions", while caste "obeys strict scruples, traditional customs, at the very most certain local influences, which usually have no connexion with class interests . . . The two institutions may, by the reaction of systems on facts, have become incorporated; but in essence they are independent" (p. 176). If "the existing system of castes was fitted into old divisions of race and class which were drawn for that purpose" (p. 152), it was under the influence of properly

Indian conditions. The fact that the Vedas make no mention of the Śūdras, and only speak of the mass of enemy Dasyus beneath the Aryan population, doubtless shows that the native masses were not yet assimilated ; their incorporation in the Aryan order of society was, indeed, afterwards expressed by admission into a fourth caste. Of the two terms used for caste, namely *varṇa*, properly " colour ", and *jāti*, properly " birth ", race, Senart holds that *varṇa* means the class, a group more or less clearly defined, vaguely hereditary, afterwards transformed by Brahmanic theory into those legal fictions, the four castes, whereas *jāti* would mean the real caste, strictly hereditary and obstinately exclusive, but very much more concrete than the alleged " four castes ". Legislation which was true and well-founded only for the *jātis* was, he thinks, transferred to the *varṇas* in accordance with an abstract conception which never corresponded to the reality. The fictitious unity, rigidity, and reality of the *varṇas* merely express the ambition of the Brahmans in favour of their own body and their quite unjustified exclusion of all the other classes from that pretension.

This explanation of Senart's is only one more theory added to many others. It supposes a distinct value for two terms which are in practice synonymous, *jāti* and *varṇa*. It has at least the merit of avoiding the exclusiveness of many earlier theories and of clearly marking the differences between Aryan and Brahmanic social divisions. As such, it is accepted, with some small reservations, by Iranian and Vedic scholars as well as by pure Indologists, by Geldner and Oldenberg as well as by Barth and Jolly.

We may adhere to Senart's view, holding that the way was prepared for the caste system by Aryan customs, but that the institution was the work of the Brahman priesthood. This is also, on the whole, the opinion of A. Barth and La Vallée-Poussin.

From comparison of Greek and Italic institutions, La Vallée-Poussin concludes that the Indian caste is constructed on the same pattern as the large family or phratry (brotherhood) comprising a certain number of γένη or *gentes*, with the double rule of exogamy for the *gens* and endogamy for the phratry. This endogamy, which is characteristic of the caste, distinguishes it from the totemic clan which may have existed in India before the coming of the Aryans, for the clan is exogamous.

On the other hand, caste, as a Brahmanic theory and system, affects the real society of India as an ideal pattern of every legally constituted society. In this respect it is an *a priori* canon or standard which advancing civilization tries to impose in all social matters. Whenever non-Aryan elements attach themselves to Hinduism they do so by taking the form of castes; the wretched refuse repudiated by the regular organizations, the casteless, are themselves grouped in special castes. Lastly, the professional corporations form castes. There is no more characteristic feature of Brahmanism than this type of organization.

CHAPTER III

The Political Order

I

SPIRITUAL POWER AND TEMPORAL POWER

ANCIENT India, so far as the Brahman caste presents it in its own literature, is a theocracy, in which no human power can rightfully counterbalance the authority of those living gods, the Brahmans. Nothing has been left undone by orthodoxy to provide an immovable foundation for the pre-eminence of the priesthood which holds the Vedic cult in its hands over the whole of Indian society.

This traditional point of view expresses a theory rather than the actual reality of things. Kshatriya literature and the popular religions offer a very different aspect of native society. The power, and not always the temporal power alone, is held at least as much by soldiers as by a caste of priests. But here we must be on our guard against the errors which we are in danger of making if we rely on our own political notions, developed with reference to our Western history.

No unit was ever established in the Indian world comparable to our modern states, or even to the ancient city in Europe. The country was too vast, the different parts of it too unlike, the peoples too heterogeneous, the non-Aryan masses too numerous. Even where the Aryans were masters beyond dispute, they felt that they were surrounded by neighbours who, if not hostile, were at least unassimilated, and therefore despised. This was the cause of the caste system, the essential object of which was to preserve the race of the people of Indo-European speech, the only " free " element. Such conditions perpetuated archaic institutions, petrifying the social system into comparative fixity.

We have already seen that law hardly emerged from its

primitive stage of custom, morals. There was an ideal, at the most a religious canon, but not a civil system based on a secular power. There was family tradition, infinitely variable, not a code of laws objectively laid down and binding without regard of persons. So authority is, as it were, extended downwards, in consequence of the sacred nature of family descent, not outwards, according to the territorial extent of a political power, as in the West. That is why all authority has so much of the characteristics of the family, both in the village, which is an enlarged family, and in the caste, which is a kind of endogamous family.

The temporal power exercised by the Kshatriyas is likewise modelled on that of the family. The small republics which are so numerous in Northern India in the first centuries of history are associations of families, all equal in theory, from among which the man who is to act as chief is chosen by election. The monarchies, great and small, which developed out of these republics or absorbed them achieved a sort of patriarchal despotism, established in a certain line by hereditary succession.

The power of the warrior and that of the priest were not always reconciled in the harmony preached, for instance, in the works of Manu. The fact that the Brahmans were so insistent in justifying their supreme position is fairly sure evidence that it was disputed or disregarded. A fundamental Brāhmaṇa, the *Śatapatha*, quoted by Senart, contains the declaration that nothing is above the power of the King, although priestly literature is full of assertions to the contrary, and in particular the royal unction is conferred by a Brahman rite. Even when we turn to the dogmas we find that in the historic period the Kshatriyas are frequently more powerful than the Brahmans, who need their protection.

The pre-eminence of the noble, the warrior, is everywhere implied in the epics. Buddhism, which emancipated itself from the prejudice of caste at the very beginning, makes Sakyamuni spring from a princely family ; it professes that religious excellence is the result of virtue, not of priestly birth. Now, among sections which are incompletely Aryanized and still less completely Brahmanized, the prestige of knightly courage continues to be very widespread and very tenacious. Free men or peasants employed in servile tasks, all need the help of him who "protects the land", *kshām trāyate*, the Kshatriya. That virtue composed of courage and loyalty, the honour of a soldier, is not the monopoly of a certain Indo-European class or caste; it belongs to every fighting clan, whatever its origin may be, aboriginal, Macedonian, Kushan, or Rajput. So the foreign conquerors contributed as much as the true holders of the Kshatriya tradition, not only to the political order of India, but to the classical theory of sovereignty.

II

ARTHA AND DHARMA

The divergence between this theory and the Vedic heritage, the patrimony of the Brahmans, may be measured by the distinction between *arthaśāstra* and *dharmaśāstra*. The gods Mitra and Varuna in the Vedas are the guardians, as a herdsman guards his flock, of an impersonal, objective order, inherent in the nature of things, *ṛita*. So, too, the *dharma* of the Brahmans goes by the proper duty of each man, according to the caste to which he belongs; it, too, results from the nature of living creatures. The Buddhist *dharma* is different in that it allows no differences between men and in principle is valid for all; but it still expresses the lawful, fundamental conditions of existence. On the other hand, temporal sovereignty is justified only by utilitarian motives—the interest of the community, or even the personal interest of the despot. Whereas *dharma* constitutes the very basis of the real, *artha* aims at an end and is therefore dependent on an activity; political opportunism has nothing to do with religious truth.

Indeed, the oldest known treatise on the subject, that of Kautilya or Chanakya—two names of the same man—is entirely secular in inspiration. The author, who is supposed to have been a minister of the Maurya king Chandragupta (last quarter of the fourth century B.C.), has no object but to serve the sovereign, without, however, seeing any difference between the King's good and that of his people. Moreover, J. J. Meyer, after a detailed analysis of the sources of this work, is of opinion that the author knew none of the *Dharmaśāstras* but that of Baudhayana.

So the inspiration of *dharmaśāstra* is plainly quite different from that of *arthaśāstra.* The Brahmans and their *dharma* certainly had not the hold on Indian society which priestly literature suggests. Politics, not theoretical but concrete, depended on the authority of the Kshatriyas, and also on an infinite variety of circumstances, much more than on Brahmanic ideals. If it were really true, as the religious books give one to believe, that the spiritual and temporal power were divided between two strictly separate and indeed rival castes, we should ask how the societies of India managed to live at all. In spite of the appropriation of *dharma* by the Brahmans, the Kshatriyas regarded themselves as the organizers of justice no less than as the possessors of physical power, and that is why the claims of the priests remained speculative rather than effective.

III

REPUBLICS

A very archaic form of state is revealed by the republics of the Punjab and the sub-Himalayan regions. I use the word " republic " only for lack of one more adequate to designate the non-monarchical government of an aristocracy. The Indian word which we shall agree to translate thus is *gaṇa*, meaning a group (*samūha*, *saṃgha*) of families (*kula*). The technical meaning coincides with the current use of the word in the sense of " crowd ", for here the state is simply the tribe or village, at least in theory.

Buddhism first arose in one of these states, that of the Sakyas of Kapilavastu. There were, perhaps, a million inhabitants, living in independence, though under the overlordship of Kosala. Public affairs were discussed in an assembly, the president of which (*rāja*) was elected by the people. In the same region similar states are found among the Mallas of Kusinagara and Pava and among the Vrijis. The confederation of eight states bearing this name included the Lichchhavis of Vaisali, from among whom the ambitious Chandragupta, the founder of the Gupta dynasty (end of the third century), took his wife. They had 7,707 senators (*rāja*), three archons, and nine ministers (*gaṇa-rāyāṇa*). In the sixth century the majority of the population of these states must have been Mongols, related to the people of Tibet.

Turning to the other end of Hindustan, we likewise find republics, doubtless more purely Aryan. It was these that Alexander found in the Punjab, and they were most of them destroyed, not by him, but immediately after his retirement by Chandragupta Maurya, hastening to create a native kingdom incorporating the regions which had been invaded by the Greeks. One might give a long list of these peoples, of which we often know nothing but the names given to them by the fellow-countrymen of Megasthenes. There were, for instance, the Malloi (Malavas) and Oxydracæ (Kshudrakas), who were rivals but had combined before the Greek menace, exchanging wives and troops; the Sabarcæ (Sambastai), who had three archons; the Nysæans, who were governed by a senate of 300 members. Diodorus remarks that the Pattalas, established at the top of the Indus delta, have, like the Spartans, two kings and a council of senators. The Greeks say nothing about theocracies in these Indian communities, but remark on the pride of the Kshatriya spirit. This pride was sometimes considered insolent or dangerous by the invader, and so the nobles of Sangala were put to death directly after the defeat of Porus. Memorable, too, was the conduct of the noble Agalassi, who, when defeated by Alexander, set fire to their city and saved the honour of their race by its complete extinction.

The occupation of Western India by the Yavanas, shaking the equilibrium of the states of the Indus and its affluents, prepared the way for great monarchies, Gangetic and Indo-Greek. The latter were inspired by the example of the Persian monarchy, for the Greeks did not come to India until they were established in their solid possessions on the confines of Iran—Parthia, Aria, Bactriana. It has been justly remarked that the same Macedonian imperialism was responsible for the enslavement of the cities of Attica and the Peloponnese and for the destruction of the republics of the Punjab.

A third group of republics is known to us from the *Mahābhārata*. These were distributed about the upper Ganges and the Yamuna, or between them and the Deccan. Such were the Yaudheyas, the Kunindas, the Malavas, the Sibis, the Arjunayanas. It is not easy to date them, for we do not know whether these peoples were still independent at the time when the epic was written, itself a very vague period, ranging from the second century before Christ to the second century after. We learn from this work that the Yadavas were a federation of small clans, each with its hereditary chief, and common affairs were managed by a body of elected senators. Here, it seems, each state is monarchic and the federation is republican.

KINGDOMS

Patriarchy furnished the societies of India with a prototype of monarchy, if we mean by that the government of one man by hereditary authority ; but it was doubtless practical circumstances that spread this form of state. To the invasions to which India was unceasingly subjected, groups of clans or alliances of independent peoples could not offer such a strong resistance as a large united kingdom. The empire of Alexander, at once a danger and an example, and the subsequent Greek kingdoms posed as the heirs of the Great King of the Persians. He was the archetype of the great maharajas, who claimed to be lords of the world. In this respect Aryan development in Iran had gone ahead of Aryan development in India. Zoroastrian monotheism was copied from the sole kingship of all Persia founded by the Achæmenids, and there the example came from the old Assyrian and Babylonian Empires.

There is nothing more remote from Aryan usages than hereditary sovereignty and extensive kingdoms. We have seen that the title of *rāja* does not at all imply what we call royalty ; it belongs potentially to every Kshatriya, even in a republic. The man who, in practice, governs, that is, who presides over the social order (*rājati*, from the same root as Latin *rex* and Gaulish *rix*), is chosen from among his peers (the *rājanaḥ*, his *sajātāḥ*) by election. The same customs prevail in this respect from Germany to India among peoples of Indo-European speech.

Originally the men who choose the King (*rājakṛitāḥ*)

are the nobles of the clan or tribe. Later the assent of the people becomes increasingly important. Very early the lower classes must have found that for protection not only against outside enemies but against abuses on the part of the nobles they needed an energetic king. Already the *Atharvaveda* contains the wish, "May the King become master of the princes!" (iv, 22). Unlike the warriors, the people, unskilled in arms, is at the mercy of anyone, and the chief reason for a king's existence is that he may make himself its protector. A sovereign is, therefore, *viśpati*, the lord of the lower caste, and he constitutes himself the guardian, the herdsman of these folk (*gopā janasya*), as a shepherd finds his justification in the protection of the flock.

Kingship, then, is a purely human institution, and claims no divine right. There is only an analogy between gods and kings and even then the comparison is only with Varuna, the Herdsman (*gopa*) of the World, and Indra, personified power. Yet a special ritual reveals the intention of the Brahmans to superimpose a religious consecration on the crowning Kings. The ceremonies of the *rājasūya* require a year of preparation. Various ritual gestures to be performed by the King must be interpreted as tests of capacity for his office. Skill in drawing the bow, the symbolic raiding of at least a hundred cattle, the symbolic taking possession of the four cardinal points, the execution of the Three Steps of Vishnu on a tiger-skin, and success in the game of dice show either that the new prince is approved by the gods or that he has the qualities needed in a monarch and that, consequently, the power is his lawfully.

Eminently characteristic of royalty, although only a king of the first magnitude can aspire to accomplishing it, is the sacrifice of the horse, *aśvamedha*. In an excellent monograph P. E. Dumont describes the bewilderingly complicated operations of this rite, which ensures that a sovereign who is already victorious and powerful shall have complete sovereignty and glory. The horse is turned loose, and its wanderings over the country indicate the unlimited extension of the King's power, and promote it. The symbolization of the sun by the horse is of the same order as the execution of the Three Steps of Vishnu in the *rājasūya*. Kingship has a solar aspect ; we shall see the mark of it in Buddhist mythology, and it was this that was exploited by the adulatory poets and artists of the *Roi Soleil* of France. A charm of fruitfulness accompanies the charms of universal dominion ; the King obtains sons from his wives, plentiful harvests from the earth, and regular seasons and prosperity from the whole of nature.

We have just contrasted the two extreme notions of Indian kingship—the simplicity of its origins, when the sovereign was elected by his peers, the nobles of the clan, and the grandiose claim to lordship over the whole human race and nature itself. Equidistant between these conceptions is the utilitarian theory by which the literature called *arthaśāstra* justifies the royal power.[1]

The *Arthaśāstra* of Kautilya presents a theory of sovereignty which is wholly rational, but reinforced by the belief, then become popular, in the divine nature of kings. Being devoid of any consideration of morality, it would subordinate religion to policy rather than policy to religion. The supreme end is the welfare of the state. The King, according to the precepts of Kautilya, is not afraid to say in front of his troops, " I am a mercenary like yourselves " ; he is the first servant of the community. But by that very fact all the elements of government are concentrated in

[1] The fundamental work of this literature is the *Arthaśāstra*, ascribed to Kautilya, who is said to be the same as Chanakya or Vishnugupta, the minister of Chandragupta Maurya. If this identification were authentic, we should have here the most exactly dated treatise of all Indian antiquity. But it is well known that the names of authors attached to ancient works in the East stand for a tradition, a school, not a historical individual. The very fact that *kauṭilya* means, if not " fraud " at least " crookedness ", and that in the work itself the author is never called Chanakya or Vishnugupta, is enough to make one dubious. But it is chiefly the pedantic, scholastic form of the work that deters one from placing it at the end of the fourth century B.C. The theories which it contains are much more systematized than those in comparable passages in the *Mahābhārata*, and therefore the work seems to be later, not earlier, than that epic. The affinities noted between it and the works of Yajñavalkya and Narada, and still more the likeness in composition to the speculative, logical, and other *śāstras* of the third and fourth centuries of our era, lead me to regard it as being not of the period just after Alexander, but of a time about seven centuries later. Moreover, a careful critic has noticed more differences than likenesses between the picture of Indian society given by Megasthenes and that of Kautilya, although the two men should have been contemporaries, and might have met at the court of Chandragupta, where the Greek was received as ambassador.

The sources of the *Arthaśāstra* accessible to us are the *Dharmaśāstras*, the Buddhist Canon, and later the Epics. Later political works are the *Nītisāra* of Kamandaka, the Purāṇas and Smṛitis, and many mediæval commentaries. The *Nītisāra* contains part of the *Arthaśāstra* of Kautilya in didactic verse.

him, and he can say, "*L'État, c'est moi*" (*rājā rajyamiti prakṛitisaṃkshepaḥ*). So the foundation of policy is the education of the sovereign; self-possession and voluntary discipline on the part of the master are the keystones of the whole state. Whereas the *Mahābhārata*, with its collection of less completely systematized traditions, confines itself to demanding three virtues of the King—noble birth, courage, and the power to lead armies (*satkula, śūratva, senā-prakarshaṇa* (i, 136, 35), the *Arthaśāstra* sets valour below mastery and mastery below reflection (*utsāha, prabhu, mantra*).

This theory of kingship deserved to remain classic. For it reconciled the good of the people with the personal interest of the King. The reason is that Kautilya does not set out to give a *rājadharma*, defining the ideal of the sovereign, like the parallel passages in the epic, but provides the King with practical directions, exactly like Machiavelli's *Prince*.

IV

THE ROYAL OFFICE

Between Vedic origins and the *Arthaśāstra* one suspects a great development of policy—great enough, certainly, for the latter work to fit the fourth century after Christ much better than the fourth century before our era. Those endemic scourges of India, invasion, the collapse of short-lived combinations, and anarchy, destroyed ancient manners, and although the village organization continued to monopolize the political activity of the free castes, the way was opened to monarchy, and even to the creation of vast though unstable empires. This was a movement further and further from the almost democratic spirit of the small units which we have noted between the sixth and fourth centuries B.C.; it was a tendency towards centralization, with the certain danger of falling into despotism.

Here we see the operation of two permanent influences, one or the other of which predominates according to the time and environment—the Brahmanic notion of *dharma*, which implies the special constitution of each caste and maintains a social order rather than it encourages the appearance of a political spirit, and the Buddhist notion of *dharma*, which aims at a law applicable to all mankind and makes for unlimited imperialism. The one conception stands short of monarchy, the other leaps beyond it and aspires to world empire. Chandragupta becomes a king, Asoka an emperor.

From its very beginnings, Buddhism was utilized by ambitious monarchs, because it made a clean sweep of castes and raised no theocracy against the royal power, and its spread was favoured by the development of the monarchic spirit. If its inspiration had been fully realized, it would have given to a power of Indian origin a character, abstract and not Indian, which one finds in the edicts of Asoka and in the patronage given to Buddhism by rulers of foreign origin, Greek and Scythian.

According to Brahmanic orthodoxy, the King—such, once more, as the Varuna of the Veda—confines himself to being the preserver of an order eternally pre-established. The *svadharma* of each caste, which he must both defend and respect, provides his reason for existing and his limitation. According to the Buddhist theory, it is the King himself who sets the Wheel of the Law (*dharma-chakra*) moving; he not only causes the Law to reign, he starts it and promotes it.

In the former case, *dharma* is natural and original; it made the blessedness of the Golden Age, which has not lasted. So Vishnu gave to men a first king, Viraja, and from him sprang a royal line of which Vena was born, a tyrant who made use of his power not for the benefit of the law but for his own profit. The *ṛishis* slew him and made sacrifice with his body, and from his arm was born Prithu, who swore to rule according to *dharma*. This legend, intended to inculcate the doctrine of the divine institution of kingship, comes in the end to extol constitutional monarchy.

In the Buddhist theory there is nothing primitive about *dharma*. The beginnings of mankind were mere anarchy. But men made agreements (*samayān*) to keep out and quell the unruly elements. This sort of Social Contract does not underlie Buddhism alone; it is echoed in an orthodox tradition recorded in the *Mahābhārata* (*Śāntiparvan*, ch. lxvii), which makes Manu the first king. Here sovereignty belongs fundamentally to the people, monarchy is a confessedly human institution, and law is the result of an agreement.

These are, it is true, theories rather than facts ; but they are theories which arose in different environments. The view of political institutions as artificial, which in India as elsewhere goes with free-thought and atomism, marks, in principle and if we neglect the attempted adaptation of it to Brahmanism, a reaction against orthodoxy. Buddhism which repudiates the castes, partakes of that conception, but it claims to go beyond it ; for, though it does not regard the *dharma* preached by the Buddhas as divine, it does not regard it as arbitrary. All these dissimilar elements, different in theory but based on real necessities, are amalgamated in the political thought of the classical age. It is agreed that in the simplicity of the earliest ages virtue and law reigned by nature. But it is also admitted that in the phase of the world in which we live the state of nature would be one of war of all against all ; *homo homini piscis*, India would say, not *lupus*, for the animal stage of mankind is there symbolized by the voracity of the fish (*matsya*), not of the wolf. Honour and obedience are due to the King who saves the weak from being devoured by the strong ; his reign is a sign both of a divine boon and of the triumph of a social convention. The aristocratic descent of the sovereign and his elective origin disappear from view. It does not matter whether he is a Kshatriya, so long as he protects all his subjects ; it does not matter whether he reigns by hereditary succession, provided that he uses his power for the good of his people. Regicide is lawful and commendable if the King makes wrongful use of advantages which are not given to him, but entrusted to him for the public weal.

So Indian politics consist, not in a doctrine of the state, but in an art of government, the keystone of which is formed by the education of the prince. The qualities required of this man are just as canonically defined as the characteristics of a god, a *bodhisattva*, or a fabulous spirit. A treatise on government has the same scholastic, *a priori* air as a treatise on æsthetics like the *Chitralakshaṇa*, or on eroticism like the *Kāmasūtra*, or on dramatic art like the *Nāṭyaśāstra*. Pedantic enumerations and distinctions forced on the facts rather than extracted from the analysis of them—these are the methods from which the Indian mind never would and never could free itself.

It would take long to describe " the " King. One can more briefly indicate the seven bases of government (*prakṛiti*), King, ministers, territory, forts, treasure, army, friendships (*Arthaśāstra*, vi); the six methods, peace, war, neutrality, capacity of taking the field at once, alliance, and doubtful attitude (vii); the many " thorns " on which a ruler who rubs against them pricks himself—miracle-mongers, coiners, highwaymen, healers, musicians, and dancers, all of whom are thieves in disguise (iv). Abstract as it is, this dogmatism is full of concrete details which make the *Arthaśāstra* the most attractive evidence on the social life of India that we have.

The *Mahābhārata* and the early Buddhist works, Sūtras and Jātakas, certainly give us something nearer the naked reality, untouched by the systematizing spirit. But the politics of which they transmit the memory are those of the feudal age after that of the Vedic clans, though earlier than the time of the great monarchies. That feudal system reigned from one end of Hindustan to the other at the time of Alexander's invasion, and that is a further reason against identifying Kautilya with the minister of the first Maurya. Chandragupta was one of the initiators of the policy of centralization which was practised for several hundred years, certainly from different centres, and culminated in the dogmatism of the *Arthaśāstra*. That, no doubt, is why tradition places the writing of the work in his time. But that elaborately perfected art of government, in which Indian political thought delights, is certainly the result of long experience, to which something was contributed by the rude energy and distrustfulness of Chandragupta, the interest in all mankind and the saintliness of Asoka, the imperialism of the Kushans, and, again, the warlike vigour of Samudragupta and Chandragupta II. Above all, let us bear in mind the great influence which the Persian monarchy had on the Mauryas and the Kushans. Not only by its architecture and its sculptured decoration did the palace of Pataliputra recall those of Susa and Ecbatana.

The wish to do good and to make *artha* coincide with *dharma*—that is what has become the meaning of politics in the inscriptions of Asoka. From this the classical *śāstra* has retained, to counterbalance its " Machiavellianism ", the very definite conviction that the justification of power is the good of the community. But from the great kings who had to use force and cunning to break the feudal lords it got the tendency to confuse policy with the right of punishing. In sharp contrast to the idealism of *rājadharma* there is the realism of *daṇḍanīti*, the art of punishment. The founder of the Maurya dynasty, to whom one always has to return, knew from experience that a strong power is established only by violence and maintained only by energy and elasticity. Having exterminated the heirs of the preceding line, he was cautious to the point of never spending two nights together in the same room. We need not be surprised to find counsels of cunning and regulations for the use of spies so highly developed in the *śāstra*. These teachings of experience, once they are codified, produce the theory that fear of punishment is the foundation of legal order, and that the King, the supreme judge, is by his nature exempt from every possibility of punishment (*adaṇḍya*).

V

ASSEMBLIES

The King's function as judge compels us to consider once more the successive phases of social evolution in ancient India. We now have to consider them in respect of the assemblies, which seem to have played an important part until autocracy came in.

Sabhā is the Indian form of an Indo-European word which has produced, among other terms, the German *Sippe*, and means an assemblage of kinsmen, family, clan, tribe. Of equal antiquity is the notion of a head of the *sabhā*, *sabhāpati*, the hereditary chief of a clan or the elected chief of a number of kindred clans. So this notion coincides in part with the ancient meaning of *rāja*. In the wide sense, *sabhā* does not so much mean, as Hillebrandt has supposed, a meeting-place, as every kind of meeting—a dicing party (*Ṛigveda*, x, 34, 6) no less than a political council or a judicial assembly.

Samiti, an expression often associated with *sabhā*, means the same thing in a vague sense. The assembly thus named elects the raja or approves his appointment. When he is crowned, according to the *Atharvaveda* (vi, 87–8), it calls upon him to show firmness, and after the ceremony a priest expresses the wish that the *sabhā* may be loyal to the prince. No doubt it is a gathering of free men (*saṃgati*, *saṃgrāmā*). Ludwig regards it as a more strictly defined body, the elected assembly of the representatives of the *viśes*.

We can only determine the special meaning of each of these terms if we can find in each a sense which the other does not possess. Now, *samiti* has a technical meaning, "order of battle." Doubtless the derivative meaning designates an assembly of a military character, like the Roman Comitia Centuriata, the members of which ranked according to their station in the army.[1] In the *Mahābhārata* the gathering of princes summoned for the *rājasūya* of Yudhishthira is called *samiti*; feudal etiquette must have been based on the order of rank determined by military discipline. Moreover, of all the meanings of the word *sabhā* only one is peculiar to it, that of "tribunal". A trite saying occurs in a Jātaka and in Narada[2] to the effect that wisdom belongs to the members of such a gathering. A fire burned in the midst of the *sabhā*, midway between gods and men, as protector of the law and the instrument of ordeals (Manu, viii, 116).

So, then, there are two types of assembly, which with time have grown more and more different, having started from an earlier mixed form—a council of war or general headquarters and a court of justice. In both the King, if there is one, plays an important part. It is possible that in the former the Kshatriyas alone have a voice, whereas the Brahmans, as depositories of the law, are supreme in the latter.

Sabhā and *samiti*, thus specialized, are very different from the *sabhā-samiti* of the primitive clans or early republics. They become mere administrative machinery. Far from the King being dependent on them, as in ancient times, they are dependent on him, for to him, standing at once under the sign of Indra and under that of Varuna, both justice and power belong.

A cross-section through the various social strata, one

[1] Bandhyopadhaya, p. 119. [2] Joshi, p. 81.

might almost say at any date in historical times, would show all the stages of this development in being at once, from the bottom upwards. The village assembly, *grāmasabhā*, never ceased to be a council of the *kulas*, families or lines. In a town, *pura*, there is at least differentiation between law-courts and assemblies of the guilds. In the capital, at the King's court, there are in addition the organ which decides military matters and the council of ministers, *mantrisabhā*. Let us look in turn, from the centre, which is the view-point of the King, at the army command, the organization of justice and the administration.

In mentioning *senā*, the army, after *sabhā* and *samiti*, we are following the practice of the *Atharvaveda* (xv, 8). The office of *senāpati*, the military leader and later the commander-in-chief, goes back to the earliest times. Traditionally the forces comprise four arms—foot, horse, chariots, and elephants. For those states which lay on a large river or the sea we must add the navy. Kautilya mentions a sixth branch, armament.

The foot-soldier carries a straight sword, slung from his shoulder by a baldric. He is armed as an archer, and shoots from a sitting position, bending his bow by pressing it with his left foot. He also has a javelin and sometimes a spear. His defensive armour consists of an ox-hide. The horseman has two spears and a shield. A large veterinary service looks after the chargers. The chariots, which seem to play a part intermediate between that of the cavalry and that of the elephants, by their weight and mobility, are drawn by two or four horses. Some are used for taking the couriers of the command or else idols to the fighting front. The others carry two combatants. The driver, the *sūta*, like the squire of the mediæval lord, enjoyed especial esteem in feudal times; according to Manu, he had to be the son of a Kshatriya and a Brahman woman. Many of these car-drivers were the bards who recited and in part improvised the epic legends. Lastly, the elephants, clad in coats of mail, are living fortresses, bearing at least three bowmen in addition to the mahout. The proportions in which these elements were combined in the army of Porus, according to Arrian, have been mentioned above. Nearly eleven hundred years later, in the middle of the seventh century after Christ, Hiuen Tsang says that his contemporary Harsha, having at first had 50,000 infantry, 20,000 cavalry, and 5,000 elephants, afterwards had 100,000 horses and 60,000 elephants. Vincent Smith suggested that if chariots are not mentioned, it is doubtless because they had ceased to be used in war.

The leaders, the *senāpati* and the *nāyaka*, come directly under the King. The cost of the upkeep of the troops is borne by the state, that is, the sovereign. Herein lies one of the strongest foundations of autocracy. There are, however, according to Kautilya, sections of quite different character in the army—a corps of what one might call hereditary Prætorians (*maula*), mercenaries (*bhṛitaka*), contingents furnished on short service by the guilds (*śreṇībala*), allies, and savage combatants, representing the non-Indo-European element of the population.

Strategy has its scholastic theory like politics and diplomacy. Every theoretically conceivable relationship between a power and its allies or enemies is classified. The various kinds of fighting are distinguished—in open country, in hollow ground, with missiles, by saps and trenches, by night and by day. Ruse is declared to be surer than force, and the most effective method is the best. It cannot be denied that there is something low in this ingenuity. We shall feel the same thing when we consider the æsthetics of India, which are too often more inclined to richness than to purity of form. Man's conscience in this country, which rises so high in religious experience and meditation, falls below the average, to our European eyes, in the domains which have been purposely kept apart from moral and transcendental ends (*dharma* and *moksha*). It is in the highest degree a reign or utilitarianism, *artha*, and this is particularly true of war, which in India is hardly ever ennobled by national feeling or selfless idealism. Here, again, the frequent comparison of Kautilya to Machiavelli is fairly just. That, perhaps, is why, in spite of valiant exploits and cunning treacheries, Indian troops have been so weak in battle against every foreign opponent—Greek, Iranian, Chinese, barbarian, and modern European. The real spiritual forces, in all except modern times, have lain elsewhere than in the armies. Only in our day is India becoming, for her own children, a country in the sense of *patria*.

VI

JUSTICE

Although the organization of justice and administration are in the sphere of *artha*, they are also in that of *dharma*. That is sufficient for an inspiration which, though equally pedantic and hair-splitting, is more elevated, that is, of more universal human application, to come into play.

Tradition distinguishes between two kinds of suit, those of civil law (*dhana-samudbhava*) and those of criminal law (*hiṃsā-samudbhava*). In the *Arthaśāstra* (iii) this distinction becomes one between the protective measures of law in general, *dharmasthīyam*, and penal law, or police measures, *kaṇṭaka-śodhanam*. In this sphere the King has a twofold function; he sees that the law is obeyed, and he takes the initiative in promoting new laws (*dharma-pravartakaḥ*). This second duty, which was expressly excluded by the original theory of kingship, is a sign of the advent of autocracy. The old idea of " setting the Law in motion " is no longer interpreted simply as an action intended to cause the laws to be respected; it means that the King can also make laws. So the impartial objectivity of *dharma* is in danger of being contaminated by the not always equally legal expediencies of policy and *artha*. The ancient legal writers of the *Dharmaśāstras* deplored this; not so Kautilya.

This change of principle, which was so favourable to despotism, found its pretext, or its justification after the event, in the mythical notion of regular, alternating periods, in which the Law reigns and fails in turn. This idea, in which we shall see a kind of translation into terms of cosmology of the law of transmigration, had the effect of accustoming men's minds to the absence of law. In these bad periods, in which the sense of justice and, as it were, of natural law, was lost, sacred law would be not only violated but unsuspected without the makeshift of laws made by royal decree. Police rule is better than anarchy; in the eclipse of law, punishments have their advantage. In the service of an autocrat the reign of law degenerates into a system of violence and penalties, *daṇḍanīti*. Every possible departure from the ideal order can be excused by the following principle, which in the letter is irreproachable and in accordance with the most august traditions : " If all the sacred laws disappear, the King is he who restores sacred law by safeguarding correct conduct in this world, which consists in maintaining the special character of the four castes and of the *āśramas*." [1] Thus, in one wise formula, the two poles of monarchy are reconciled—authority according to the ideal of Asoka, who declared himself the king of the Law (*dharmarāja*), and that of a despot.

In practice, and here scholastic ingenuity triumphs, these two poles are extreme cases. Careful examination of the real state of society reveals, by the side of *dharma*, three other kinds of case, which establish a certain continuity between *dharma* and *artha*. These (*vivāda-pada*) are *vyavahāra*, *charitra*, and *śāsana*. *Vyavahāra* seems to stand for contractual law ; sometimes it means trade, particularly purchase, which is a kind of contract, sometimes an agreement, a pact, and also a plaint, the accusation resulting from a presumed violation of the agreement. *Charitra* is usage, practice (*āchāra*). *Śāsana* is the royal decree.[2]

The ideal sovereign is imagined by native tradition as giving justice like St. Louis under the oak at Vincennes. He goes every day to the law-court of his capital, of which he is the head, if the chief justice is the mouth. So, too, in every royal fortified town there is a prætorium, orientated and adorned not only with statues or idols but with a crown and a throne. In the village justice is dealt out by a hereditary mayor, the *grāmaṇī*. In theory ten elements should go to the administration of justice—the chief justice, who pronounces the sentence ; the King, who punishes ; the judges, who examine the fact ; *dharmaśāstra*, *smṛiti* (tradition), from which the sentence proceeds ; gold, water, and fire, which are used for ordeals, the supernatural confirmation of the human judgment ; the accountant, who assesses damages and fines ; the scribe ; and the usher. When we come to study the origins of logical reflection, we shall see what it owed to the methods of trial and of pleading. Here we may merely note that the King, as being entrusted with the legal order, is liable, not to punishment but

[1] *Chaturvarṇāśramasyāyaṃ lokasyāchārarakshaṇāt naśyatām sarvadharmāṇāṃ rājā dharmapravartakaḥ* (*Arthaśāstra*, ed. Shama Shastri, p. 150, 4). On the *āśramas*, see below, pp. 240–1.

[2] Breloer, *Kautilîya Studien*, ii.

to religious penance for judicial shortcomings or errors—a day's fast for every guilty man not punished and three days' fast for an innocent man punished (Vasishtha, xix, 40–3). What a contrast between the astute monarch who has learned his lesson from Kautilya, and the ideal King of early Brahmanism, carefully informed, scrupulously respectful of the law of each caste, and referring in case of doubt to learned Brahmans ! [1]

VII

ADMINISTRATION

The basis of administration, let us say it again, is the organization of the village. The *grāmaṇī*, who has the authority, is responsible for the payment of taxes, and therefore sees to it that the work of the fields is done. In applying custom-law he takes counsel with the elders. Five or ten villages are combined under a *gopa* (always the same word, "herdsman," now the title of an official). This district is part of one of the four "quarters" into which the provinces are divided, just as the towns are divided into "quarters". The governor of one such section is called *sthānika*. Above him is the *nāgaraka*, and over all these various officials Maurya centralization placed a minister of the interior, *samāhartṛi*.

The first duty of these officials is fiscal. They establish the civil status of each individual, indicating his caste and his profession, and keep a register of his income and expenditure. Land-tax, taxes on irrigation, pastures, forests, and mines, customs and *octrois*, duties on commercial exchanges, on professions, on gaming-houses, and on passports, fines paid into the law courts—the money collected under all these heads found its way into the royal treasury through an administration which was as corrupt as it was pettifogging. So much of it as had not been diverted on the way was swallowed up by the needs of the court and the army, in salaries of officials, in pensions of the families of soldiers killed on service or of employees of the government who had died in office, and lastly in public works and charitable foundations.[2]

[1] Gautama, xi, 22–6. [2] **LXXIII**, i, p. 487.

The administration of the city is divided, according to Kautilya, into six sections, whose duties are the following: (i) The care of the artisans. Since their skill was regarded as an important part of the public wealth, a man who wounded them so as to diminish their capacity for work had a hand cut off or eye put out. The work done and the wages received by them were supervised. (ii) The control of foreigners. They were given lodging, allowed to dispose of their goods freely, and tended when ill, but their doings were watched. (iii) Recording of births, deaths, etc. (iv) Control of retail trade and exchanges: checking of weights and measures, collection of duties on sales, marking goods sold with an official stamp guaranteeing their genuineness. (v) Supervision and stamping of manufactured articles. (vi) Collection of the tenth on the amount of sales.[1]

Here we are on the edge of the economic domain, which we shall presently enter. But India does not distinguish between economics and politics as we do; the two are merged in that work of political economy, the *Arthaśāstra*. Our conclusion, as regards politics, will be that the advent of autocracy reduced them to mere administration. That administration gives proof of great assiduity in collecting and controlling; it is the masterpiece of Indian social science, just because it is a scholastic method in action. Whether we regard it as serving the state or serving the King, it is utilitarian, but, in our European judgment, destitute of ideas.

For all through the ancient history of India there is no sign of an aspiration to win what the Greeks called or what we call political liberty. The rule of caste, far from being resented as slavery, was felt to be the framework supporting traditional collective liberties; no individual Indian, in the past, wanted any other. A man who leaves his caste, far from becoming free, falls into abasement and loses every legal right and every protection which comes from belonging to a body of his fellows, unless he enters some sect, a religious order, or combines with others in the same case as himself to found a new caste. No doubt there is much to be said against a system which creates antagonisms between men; no doubt it was a very great merit of Buddhism that it preached compassion to all alike. Yet Buddhism was to

[1] **LXXIV**, p. 87.

be defeated by the defenders of the ancient rule, and it was to the ideal of caste that all India rallied.

The interest of a just prince never conflicted with the healthy independence to which the Hindu, fortified in the caste system, could pretend. The public good was made of the one and of the other. The rigidity of the social organization was even mitigated by the initiative of a realistic policy, while the *dharma* of the Brahmans raised insurmountable barriers against despotism. The only ruler who brought anything to government but pedestrian utilitarianism, Asoka, acted neither as a conservative nor as an innovator—words which in India would have no meaning—he behaved as a *bodhisattva.* As a *dharmarāja,* in the Buddhist sense, he was not a king, but a saint.

CHAPTER IV

Economic Life

A SCIENCE named *vārttā* is devoted to the study and management of the conditions of material life. Properly the word means both life and means of existence, professional labour. Brahmanism, according to the tradition of Manu, holds that the three sciences which make up human knowledge are *vārttā*, *daṇḍanīti*, the science of punishments, and *trayī*, the three Vedas or religious science. The materialistic tradition of Brihaspati recognizes only two fundamental sciences, *vārttā* and *daṇḍanīti*. Kautilya, in virtue of the etymology of *vārttā*, says that *artha* is the *vṛitti* of man, in other words, that it means the whole of human activity. The close connexion of the two lies in the fact that *artha* raises the question of ends and *vārttā* that of means. If the object of politics is the possession of land, or dominion, a well-filled treasury and a strong army are needed, and these imply abundant material resources. The idea of this connexion is expressed in mythology. The first human king, according to the Vedic legends, who is sometimes Manu and sometimes Prithu, is not only the first sacrificer, but a fire-bringing Prometheus and the inventor of agriculture.

I

WORK AND BUSINESS

The Workers

According to orthodox principles, economic life is the affair of the Vaiśya caste. If that caste, like the two above it, had a literature of its own, we should have valuable information, instead of being reduced to inferring the content of economic life from the form imposed on it by Brahmanic theory and the policy of kings. But it is idle to sigh for the impossible ; dedicated to work, the Vaiśya caste had neither the education nor the leisure to think about anything but accounts and output.

Yet the Vaiśyas were the aristocracy of the workers. Base and arduous tasks were left to the Śūdras, the slaves (*dāsya*), and all the dregs of the people who were kept outside the caste system. Of these, the slaves deserve special mention. A free man (*ārya*) might be a " temporary " slave—if, for example, he pledged his person because he could not otherwise pay a fine or the costs of a law-suit, or if he was carried off in a raid. Also, if a man left his caste to enter a monastic order and then left the order or never entered it, he became a slave of the King. We should note, too, that the King must liberate every free man reduced to bondage by violence, for he is, in principle, obliged to abolish or compensate every injustice, and the proverb says that slavery is not for *āryas* (*natvevāryasya dāsabhāvaḥ*. Kautilya, iii, 13, 65). The only case in which a free man who had become a slave could not buy himself off was where he had himself sold his person ; he then became like the permanent slaves. Of these there were four kinds—born in the house, bought, captured in a raid, and inherited. In all four cases the only legal duty owed by the slave to his master was obedience, the obligation to serve him in the matter of work.

Agriculture

The economic life of India is chiefly agricultural. The very name of *ārya*, in which the masters of the country pride themselves, means to them (root *kṛish*) the tillers of the soil, as opposed to the other occupants. Yet they came into the country as herdsmen, whose wealth lay in kine and horses rather than in crops. We must even, perhaps, suppose that the methods of irrigation on which the prosperity of the fields in the Indus basin depends were due not so much to these nomadic stock-raisers as to the settled Sumero-Dravidians, doubtless taught by Mesopotamian experience. However that may be, the Vedic Indians very early adapted themselves to the resources of the Punjab, rich in *yava* and sugar-cane.

At first *yava* means any grain, and later barley. It is often coupled with *vrīhi*, rice. This association summarizes the whole of agriculture, for rice, like millet, is sown in summer, and barley, like wheat, in winter. Sesame, beans, maize, and lentils are also important crops. From the earliest times cereals have been used to make *surā*, a fermented intoxicating drink.

Although certain regions are extremely productive, the country has always been poor and its inhabitants underfed. Famines, an intermittent scourge, were fought with magic formulas from the *Atharvaveda*; but Kautilya mentions more rational remedies, such as the creation of reserves, providing work for the poor, public assistance, and calling on allies for help. Usually the really effective remedy was improvement of the irrigation, so as to make the land give a regular return. But in case of war or floods these wise measures were useless. So, although Megasthenes gives India the credit of having kept down these endemic evils by wise use of the water, they were a constant danger.

The agricultural population lives in villages, surrounded by a fence and a ditch. Guards keep watch at the gates, and pits are dug to catch wild beasts. For in vast portions of the Ganges valley the jungle is quite close, with only a belt of pasture between it and the village, near which lie the paddy-fields. In the *Arthaśāstra* methods are sought for counteracting the disadvantages of the people living scattered over such great distances; there are special offices for centralizing the inspection of cattle, pastures, and forests. Distilling and salt-deposits are state monopolies.

Industry

Ancient industry is merely an extension of the exploitation of the soil, by using wool or textile plants or working clay, metal, or wood. The making of woollens goes back to the nomadic days of the Indo-Europeans. Once they settled in the country, cotton seems to have become the most typical material. Herodotus describes the Indian troops of Xerxes as clad in cotton, and Nearchos admires this vegetable wool, from which stuffs of dazzling white are woven. Tanning and dyeing are two equally ancient industries. Carpets, brocades, and embroideries mark advance in manufacture. Muslin is rivalled in fineness by silk, partly imported from China.

The earliest metal-workers wrought in a matter called

ayas. When no epithet is attached to the word, it seems to mean bronze in the *Ṛigveda*. But afterwards, with the adjective *śyāma*, " dark," it means iron, and with *loha*, " red," it means copper. The use of gold goes back to Vedic times. Tin, lead, and silver do not become common until the time of the Brāhmanas. Gems, to which magical values and superstitions were attached, in addition to their ornamental qualities, were prized in all ages.

The manufacture of chariots and waggons gave an importance, or rather a prestige, to work in wood and work in metal. For a long time only timber was used in architecture; religious edifices and royal palaces alone were sometimes built of stone. Delicate wood-carving and inlaid gold delighted the authors of the hymns. The wood-worker again came into request for building ships and boats.

Trade

Manufactured goods were exchanged or sold. The *Ṛigveda* speaks chiefly of exchanges, such as ten cows for an Indra. It was afterwards that the root *kri* gave the words *kraya*, *vikraya*, with the sense of " sale ". Yet the *Atharvaveda* (iii, 15) gives a spell for obtaining success in trade. No doubt, by the simple method of exchange (root *paṇ*, " to barter "), a certain social class, the *Paṇis*, had in Vedic times amassed fortunes which were considered scandalous. This type of man is odious in the eyes of the pious ancestors of the Brahman caste, the authors of the hymns; he is charged with rapacity, usury, and impiety. Perhaps the recognition of a legal standing for trade in the Vaiśya caste was one of the first concessions to the facts that the Brahmanic theocracy had to make in order to ensure at least a nominal supremacy for itself.

There is no certain evidence that markets existed in Vedic times. But towns and villages were already connected by tracks, with wells at intervals. The commercial centres grew up at the more important intersections of routes. This concentration of trade at fixed points must, however, have been long retarded by the itinerant business done by caravans, escorted by armed men. When studying the geography of the country we saw the natural routes by which India was entered from outside. Early Buddhist literature, especially the Jātakas, tells us of the internal roads. "From Maurya times onwards," J. Przyluski writes, "Pataliputra was connected with Gandhara by an imperial highway, drawn on the model of the great roads of the Achæmenids. It played a great part in the political and economic life of India. After the foundation of the Greek kingdom of Bactriana commercial intercourse became very active between the valleys of the Ganges and the Oxus. For caravans loaded with goods of Bactriana and Kashmir, Mathura was the first large city in Madhyadesa as one came out of the Indus valley . . . . From Pataliputra three great roads radiated to the frontiers of the Empire—the south-western to Barygaza by Kausambi and Ujjayini, the northern to Nepal by Vaisali and Sravasti, and the north-western, the longest, to Bactriana by Mathura and the upper valley of the Indus." [1] The care of the roads has an important place in the economics of Kautilya, who makes road-making a duty of the King. The provinces bore the cost of their upkeep. From the time of the Maurya dynasty pillars were set along the roads to mark distances.

In the same period much use seems to have been made of the waterways. We are too much inclined to forget that India was one of the greatest marine and colonizing powers of the past. One took ship for Ceylon not only at Tamralipti, the chief port of Bengal, but at Benares and Patna. Services which, it is true, were irregular and dangerous until knowledge of the monsoons became general in the first century, connected Bharukachchha (Broach), the ancient, more northerly, equivalent of modern Bombay, with Babylon on one side and with Suvarnabhumi (Lower Burma) on the other. Either through the Persians and Arabs, or direct, a connexion was established with Egypt by the Red Sea,[2] and the advantage of commerce with the east coast of Africa was not neglected. Shipping was, however, chiefly drawn to the Far East, where it linked up with Chinese trade after putting in at many ports in countries colonized from India. This expansion towards the south of modern Indo-China and the

[1] **CCVI**, p. 9.

[2] Pliny declares that the Roman Empire bought goods to the value of fifty million sesterces from India every year (**LXIX**, p. 68).

East Indian islands began, according to Ferrand, in the third or even the fifth century before Christ; Krom is of opinion that expansion to the islands did not start before the beginning of our era. Kaundinya, who started the Indianization of Fu-nan (southern Cambodia and Cochin-China), should be placed, according to Pelliot, in the second half of the first century after Christ at the latest. In the Champa region, still further away (Southern Annam), this process must have occurred a hundred years later. Sumatra, the Isle of Gold (Suvarnadvipa), and Java, the Land of Barley (Yavabhumi), were highly flourishing in Gupta times, when, for example, Fa-hien landed on the latter island.

This great radiation of Indian influence, extending from Madagascar to Tongking, was not merely an endeavour to acquire material wealth. It also aimed at religious ends. Vishnuism, Sivaism, and Buddhism all sought to take root in new soil, apparently without their rivalry giving rise to violent conflicts. The Indianization of the Austro-Asiatics and of the Malayo-Polynesians does not seem to have been the result of ferocious wars. Although these conquests were so far away, they were simply an extension of the policy by which the Deccan had been, though very unequally, subjugated.

In what we call India and outside it, every civilizing effort of the Aryans is of a colonizing character. One might say without paradox that the first colony of the Indo-Aryans was the Punjab and the second the valley of the Ganges. We know that, in spite of that sense of a vocation and that obstinate will, displayed over thousands of years, an immense amount of colonization has still to be done in India itself.

Indian trade was connected with that of Central Asia by a mountain track which ran from Kabul to the upper valley of the Oxus, east of Bactra (Balkh). Here it was crossed by the route which, running from west to east, passed round the north of the Hindu Kush, crossed the Pamir, and by the upper Tarim came to Chinese Turkistan, and so to Yarkand. North of the Pamir one could go from Maracanda (Samarqand) in Sogdiana to Kashgar on a tributary of the Tarim.

By these routes the silk travelled from China to Syria. By them, apart from the sea-route, Indian expansion and

Chinese expansion met, and came into conflict at the time of Pan-ch'ao's expedition to Persia between 73 and 102. From its beginnings Buddhist missionary enterprise had travelled along the trade-routes of Hindustan. Spreading to Bactriana and Kashmir, it reached Turkistan, and did more to unite India and China than economic needs had been able to accomplish. The relationships which were established between the two countries from the first century of our era onwards were subjected to various vicissitudes; from the fourth to the seventh century they were intensive, and the homogeneity of culture established by Buddhism from the north of Iran to the west of China could not but encourage commercial dealings.

Guilds

Economic organization seems never to have coincided with the abstract order of the castes. It involves special groups, the name of which is *śreṇi* (*seṇi* in Pali). This term, which in the Vedic period means a row, an alignment, takes in the Smṛitis the sense of a corporative association for all kinds of workers—tillers of the soil, herdsmen, sailors, artisans, traders, bankers, even Brahmans expert in Veda (Manu, viii, 41, commentary of Medhatithi). The *Mūgapakkha-jātaka* (iv, 411) mentions, among eighteen guilds not otherwise named, the wood-workers, metal-workers, leather-dressers, and painters. At the head of each corporation was a "deacon" (*jeṭṭhaka*), who acted as president (*pamukha*) and was an important personage at the King's court. It is characteristic of Indian society that a man standing alone counts for nothing. Just as the casteless sought to found pseudo-castes of their own, so there were *śreṇis* even to protect the interests of bandits, highwaymen, and ascetics.

Professional occupation is often handed down from father to son, like caste. Thus there were families of smiths, carpenters, potters, which were themselves grouped so as to form villages of smiths, carpenters, and potters. The powers of the guild were legislative, judicial, and executive. Order within the corporation was maintained by rigid discipline, and the King was strictly obliged to safeguard the customs of the guilds (Narada, x, 2, 3) and to accept their decisions.[1] The admission of new members and the expulsion of old ones required a decision by the assembly. The merchant guilds did not develop so far as those of the craftsmen. The latter did not all enjoy equally high consideration ; wheelwrights, basket-makers, potters, weavers, leather-workers, and above all barbers were regarded as men of inferior calling, as were butchers and fortune-tellers.

II

PROPERTY

Land

The production and distribution of wealth depend on the system of ownership. This, in primitive Aryan society, took the form of family ownership. The father had the right to distribute his goods among his sons, and land in particular (*kshetra*) might be distributed differently in successive generations. In the case of joint families, in default of the father his eldest brother took his place. Where the inheritance was divided up among the sons, all received a share, the eldest getting slightly more than the rest. Failing a son, the inheritance fell to the son of the daughter.

The type of ownership varied as the land was of one or another of three kinds—arable (*vāstu*), pasture, and forest. Arable land was the object of private ownership ; pasture was owned in common by the various families of the village ; forest belonged to whoever cleared it.

All this was changed by the institution of the castes and the introduction of monarchy. Only a free man can lawfully own property. For instance, there is no legal inheritance for a casteless man. Even the property of the lower castes becomes insecure. The Vaiśya is by nature a taxpayer, and it is very usual for him to be exploited by the nobles. The Śūdra is a serf, who can be dispossessed and slain at will. No doubt practice was less insane and barbarous than theory. There were Śūdras who amassed great fortunes in trade. In reality the position of the lower castes depended on the actual standing given them by the Kshatriyas more than on the regulations evolved *a priori* by the Brahman legal writers.

[1] Santosh Kumar Das, *The Economic History of India*, p. 251.

But the Kshatriyas, who in principle were the lawful owners of landed property, like the priestly class, gradually found their rights restricted as the power of the King increased. The whole of the land becomes, at least in theory, the property of the sovereign, and the proof of it is that all property which has no owner or loses its owner reverts to him. Therewith the nobles fall into the position of feudal lords, and the Vaiśyas to that of tenant farmers.

Revenues and Coinage

As government becomes more and more centralized, the King is no longer the holder of a vague overlordship, but the organizer and user of all property. Of the different kinds of agricultural produce, part is set aside for him by the mayor of the village or a state official, the proportion varying between a twelfth and a sixth. A tithe may also be exacted on human labour, in the form of corvées.

There is no doubt that the flow of wealth of all kinds, particularly of taxes, to the central government was simplified and also stimulated by the use of money. According to Arrian, the Hindus had gold coins before the invasion of Alexander—probably the *nishkas* with various types (*viśvarūpa*), of which necklaces were made, and the *śatamānas*, which weighed ten *kṛishṇalas* (the berry of *Abrus pecatorius*, a unit of weight) and, according to the Veda, were equivalent to a hundred cows. Another coin, about the value of which we have no information, was the *kārshāpana*, which was at first of copper and later of silver and gold. Under the Guptas the use of the word *dīnāra*, from Latin *denarius*, for a gold coinage points to Roman influence. It was generally allowed, about the Christian era, that money should produce interest, which was reckoned at 15 per cent per annum. Exemption from the tithe collected on income was enjoyed by " learned " priests, women, children under the age of puberty, Brahman students, ascetics, slaves, cripples, and sick persons.

State Socialism. The Poverty of India

The needs of the different states raised an infinite number of impediments to trade—duties to be paid on crossing frontiers, town *octrois*, customs dues, tolls, etc. Travellers had to provide themselves with passports, their declarations as to the value of the goods which they transported were checked minutely, and the tax-collector, the policeman, and the spy vied in zeal for the profit of their master, the head of the state. He, not only as King but as the manager of the national property, which, whatever its real size, was large compared with that of individuals, had a direct interest in the public wealth. Kautilya shows the extent to which economics contribute to politics, and advises princes to have superintendents to control mines, weaving, irrigation, stock-raising, and trade, all the sources of wealth. Business would have been subject to the most absurd red tape if the *Arthaśāstra* had ever had the force of law—checking of prices, the profit being laid down at 5 per cent for local trade and at 10 per cent for foreign goods, and increasing penalties in case of infringement of the regulations. All these are significant features of Indian society, which was developing under the influence of monarchy into a sort of " enlightened despotism ", which was practically state socialism.

But the development was theoretical rather than actual. The only political ideal of the countries of India was a wise administration, of which a few potentates of the first magnitude gave different models. But that administration was, let us say it again, an ideal much rather than a permanent reality. In spite of all its possibilities of opulence, India was and remained a poor country. Even more than by the treasury, the peasant is perpetually victimized by the money-lender ; for he is too ignorant, and often too far away from markets, to sell his own produce. " The money-lender therefore buys the whole available harvest at a price which he fixes by his own authority, pays the required amount of rent and land revenue to the state, and keeps all the rest as interest on his loan." [1]

This wretched existence of the immense majority of Hindus explains some of the forms of thought which we shall find when we study individual religion and philosophy. It created a melancholy pessimism, a hatred of life, at least among the unprivileged castes. It inspired, by the transposition of facts into ideals, the conviction that under-nourishment

[1] **CLVII**, p. 44.

and diminished activity were means to salvation. While the Brahman sets himself up as a god to whom honour and profit are due, the materialistic ascetic, who denies *dharma*, the Yogin, contemptuous of ritual, and the Jain or Buddhist monk, who as an individual owns nothing, will preach forms of religious life in which money does not matter. Sacrifices are very costly, and only possible for the rich. On the fringes of aristocratic orthodoxy sects of the non-possessors will rise in swarms, full of ardour and audacity. They will not aim at changing the social order, but they will take to themselves mighty compensations and incomparable reparations in the spiritual order. Not having enough property to win the favour of the gods, they will dispense with all worship, or they will teach that the only true sacrifice consists in knowing, or else in loving.

PART THREE

SPIRITUAL LIFE

Religions and Philosophies

RITES and institutions have introduced us to the religious life of India. We must now look at that religious life from within, from the point of view of men's consciences. For the very reason that the character of India was made up of a welter of different things, the elements of reflection were extremely heterogeneous, and one would say that there was all the more need for thought to concentrate in order to attempt some sort of unification. And indeed the collective efforts of meditation have nowhere been so intense and systematic as in India. Almost every activity was religious, and in the *élite*, among the races of higher culture, religion made sufficient appeal to personal reflection to deserve to be called philosophy. Speculative systems free of dogma and ritual existed from the dawn of historical times, and more than one of them afterwards gave birth to dogmas and ritual. Religious thought and free thought run into one another endlessly.

To divide the history of Indian thought into phases must needs be an arbitrary process of over-simplification. The religious life of the country, like its social life, is nothing but the confused total of local traditions, the history of which, far from being written, is hardly possible to write. From Kashmir to the Maratha country, from Bengal to Malabar, conditions vary very greatly, and in any one of these regions the many strata of the population are divided by insurmountable differences. An immense supply of notes on folk-lore, a searching examination of manners, a thorough clearing of overgrown jungles of literature, and an abundant booty of archæological finds would be necessary everywhere before a few inferences could be drawn. Treating of India in general, we are bound to be vague.

Nor is that all. In assuming *a priori* a development

in the world of Indian thought, we run against native sentiment. Let us admit that the impulse to look for development in every domain, even when the facts do not compel us to do so, may be a European prejudice. Let us draw a lesson from the dislike which the Hindu shows to sharing the principles of our " science " on this point. A custom or a belief may be much older than the earliest document attesting its existence. What does this mean, but that the very precautions of criticism may lead us astray, and that we have something to learn from those very peoples which Europe is instructing in historical method? When the Hindu rejects the explanations of the Westerner, he does so in virtue of a knowledge—vague, no doubt, but lively and direct—of the mentality of the people and the local conditions, which Europeans do not sufficiently take into account. Having made this reservation, we can and must attempt to look for changes in the course of the ages; and the less dogmatic we are the less we shall court disaster.

CHAPTER I

Origins

I

PRE-ARYAN ORIGINS

The Munda Element

THE barbarians who speak Austro-Asiatic tongues of Munda type form the lowest substratum of the population of India. Not only were they the original inhabitants, but vast reservoirs of " uncivilized " mankind still survive in the hill districts, away from the great roads and centres of culture. The Santals of Chota Nagpur and the Kols are at this stage to-day. Students of India were too long blind to the permanent influence of this factor, both racial and linguistic. It needed the curiosity of Sylvain Lévi, directed to place-names, to raise the question in all its bearings, and it needed the competence in Austro-Asiatic philology of his disciple J. Przyluski to produce definite results which are already very remarkable. It is established that the most ancient element in India is of the same race as the peoples of the Nicobar Islands and Malacca.

The religion of these tribes may be described as being based on totemism. The members of a group feel themselves to be one in that their life is the actual life of a vegetable or animal species. So the principle which animates them is at once immanent and transcendent ; and here we must recognize the first experience of an attitude from which many later metaphysical systems were to proceed.

Vegetable energy is very widely venerated. Eating offers a way of capturing this force by absorption of the spiritual principle. India was to keep the conviction that existence is a question of food, and of that axiom, based on elementary observation, it would discover many subtle applications. Moreover, to primitive man the spectacle of the vegetable world bears witness to the polymorphism of nature more clearly than that of the animal kingdom. That a tiny seed should produce masses of verdure, and that all that luxuriance should end in new seeds, which men can use or destroy, a fact to be seen on every side in the jungle which was the normal environment of man in India, no doubt planted in men's minds the notion of a mechanical, spontaneous evolution, which could, however, be arrested by human intervention. Even in its most abstract interpretations, this evolution would continue to be described in "vegetable" terms: the manifestations of existence result from seeds which ripen and fructify with a view to subsequent sowings without end, unless there is destruction by torrefaction.

The lower peoples of India were many of them cannibal. For them the best sacrifice of all was the consumption of the raw flesh and hot blood of human beings. This practice is in accordance with the principle of totemism, which finds the essence of universal life in the life of the species. These bloody rites are quite unlike Dravidian or Vedic sacrifices, and are doubtless the prototype of those exceptional rites, of which classical orthodoxy preserved the memory, in which the victim was a man.

Most of the features which Lévy-Bruhl has noted as characteristic of "primitive" thought are to be found not only among the less civilized peoples of India, but in a great many aspects of Indian thought in the syncretic form assumed by it in historical times. Such, for example, is the prelogical mentality, which never dies out, in spite of attempts almost as ancient as itself to set up a logical discipline. Such is the conviction of the efficacity of desire or thought. Such are the belief in continuance after death, and that in the power of an individual, living, dead, or divine, to be in more than one place at a time.

So it is one of the great differences between the West and India that the latter has always hoarded in her bosom, in the midst of highly refined cultures, elements which have remained, as it were, in their crude state. The "barbarian" invasions inflicted on her from outside were never as barbaric as some permanent factors in India herself.

Dravidian, Sumerian, and Semitic Elements

The Dravidian cults left on the religions of the classical period traces which, if not deeper, were at least more definite than those of the pre-Dravidian cults. One religious act in particular still bears their mark—*pūjā*, the veneration of an idol. To do worship to an image, to water it or scent it or hang it with garlands, is quite a different act from a blood-sacrifice. Flowers, scents, and the rest may, no doubt, be regarded as offerings, but they are attentions rather than gifts. Stone or wood, a statue is the symbolic object of a cult in that it is " cultivated ", rendered flourishing and prosperous, and therefore capable of radiating beneficent influences. The negritos who practise such rites are gentle creatures, very unlike the Kols with their bloody sacrifices.

In this religion grossness and ferocity are to be found in the gods rather than in man. Most of the deities are females, and this accords with the preponderant place held by women in matriarchal societies, from the Asianic peoples of Cappadocia to the dwellers on the seaboard of the Bay of Bengal. The hideous ogresses who still rule in the temples of the south-eastern coast of the Deccan perpetuate this form of divinity. There is no doubt that Kali the Black and Durga the Unapproachable would never have been brought into the Brahman pantheon if Dravidian goddesses with names ending in -amma had not stood as prototypes. It is even to be supposed that Krishna, the very much Brahmanized " black " demigod, keeps up some connexion with the primitive rites of the Dravidians especially when that mystic bridegroom of pious consciences assumes, and that too in the *Bhagavadgītā*, the aspect of a devouring monster.

So, then, the dark-skinned Indians were particularly alive to the maleficent and fearful attributes of the absolute, the *numinosum* which Rudolf Otto, following Durkheim, describes as one of the two faces of the sacred. They not only feared the gods, as did some of the contemporaries of Epicurus and Lucretius ; they were terrified of them. No doubt the caresses lavished on their images tended to make them inoffensive. When Hinduism coaxes the destroying god by calling him the Propitious or the Benevolent, Siva, it is acting in the Dravidian fashion.

The gluttonous, grinning goddesses rule the fruitfulness of nature. The masculine aspect of that fecundity is represented in an impersonal manner by many phallic emblems. This is the origin of the fetishism of the *linga*, so widespread in classical India, where, from the beginning, the name borne by universal spirit is the Man, Purusha. Here again the religion of Siva forms the bridge between Dravidian superstitions and orthodoxy, for the swallower assumes the character of the great generator; indeed, the chief contribution of the Dravidians to the abstract thought of Hinduism might well be the idea which had such a great future before it, though foreign to Vedism—that production and destruction come from the same principle.

We know nothing about the amalgam of Sumerian and Dravidian ideas which must have reigned in the Indus basin before the coming of the Aryans. But through it the religions of India are in part derived from the ancient religions of Mesopotamia. Animism, the belief in creation by the efficiency of the Word, and the worship of a Mother Goddess are very old Asianic and Sumerian convictions, and Iranian Ahura and Vedic Varuna are continuations of Anu, god of the sky, but also of rain and therefore of water, who was worshipped at Sippar and Nippur from the beginning of the third millennium B.C. The similarity of name between Ahura (Asura in Vedic) and Ashur, the eponymous god of Assyria, is striking, and we may add that the *apsu* of the Babylonians is probably equivalent to *apas* (waters) in the Vedas. Many Semitic legends, especially Assyro-Babylonian, were brought by the same road into the inheritance of India, such as the story of the Deluge, which must, in its most eastern form, have united with the myth of Manu. Lastly, Chaldæan astrology was also handed down to the Hindus.

II

THE RELIGION OF THE VEDIC ARYANS AND EARLY BRAHMANISM

The Vedas

In comparison with the religions of the other races of India, the primitive religion of the Aryans is one of which we can have some positive knowledge, for we have abundant evidence for it in its various forms. We must remember that the *Ārya*, the Indo-Iranian branch of all the peoples which speak Indo-European languages, can be studied in their Iranian aspect in Avestic literature and in their Indian aspect in the Vedas, and that the two series of works show very close affinities.

Here the difficulty lies in the interpretation of the documents. The two literatures developed independently, and it is rash to draw conclusions from their likenesses about the original phase from which both have come. The most ancient parts of the Avesta, the *Gathas*, preach the reformation of Zoroaster, which was not earlier than the second half of the seventh century B.C., and was a reaction against the previous cults. Many expressions survive from those cults, but only appear in the "late" Avesta, which was compiled in the second and third centuries of our era, and is therefore contaminated by elements a thousand years more recent. The *Ṛigveda* and *Atharvaveda* are on the whole more ancient than the *Gathas* of Zoroaster, but they already have an Indian, or at least a Punjabi character. And while we have much information about the use made by the Brahmans of the Vedas, we have very little about the rites practised at the time when the hymns were evolved, about 1,000 or 1,500 years before Christ.

The document which is earliest in inspiration, although it was compiled last of all the Vedas, is the *Atharvaveda*, a collection of magical formulas. In all probability, the original form of the religious act, *karman*, was a direct action by which a man, not yet a priest but the possessor of certain forms of words, could by the efficacity of those words bend nature to the achievement of his purposes. This fundamental conviction was to leave a permanent mark, but speculative inquiry would aim at an acquisition, *prāpti*, not the mere satisfaction of curiosity. What the Aryans of early India sought to obtain in this way was the goods of this world—subsistence, a minimum of well-being, even wealth, a full life, not cut off by premature death, and male descendants, who alone were qualified to continue after the father's death the offerings which supported the the life of their ancestors. Now, protection against evil forces—devils, the hungry dead, plague, human enemies, wild beasts—and the provision of descendants are both to be secured by direct influence exercised on things.

Rites and Magic. The Natural Order

What the formula needs, and all that it needs, to be successful is correctness. The Brahman word *satyam*, which is often loosely translated " truth ", simply means ritual correctness. This too was to become a permanent element in the thought of later times ; truth would be a matter of normality and propriety, not of conformity to an object. To know " in the right way "—that was the way to succeed in all circumstances.

The axiom implied in this magic, that the right formula is infallible, holds good both for what is in order according to nature and for what alters the course of events for the benefit of man, as an individual or as a group. In other words, formulas (*mantra*) ensure the normal order of natural events, such as the succession of the seasons, the fertility of the land, or the fruitfulness of animals, no less than the twist given to natural laws by a particular will. Here was another factor for all later Indian thought to retain. Nothing is effected save by a law in the sense of a norm, the average, regular order or the accidental, exceptional order. Afterwards the name of *dharma* was given both to natural existence and to legislation, to the order of objects and to the moral order. The Indo-Iranians had not yet constructed that supreme " category " ; they contented themselves with a word to designate the order of constitutive principles and of universal stability, the *asha* of the Iranians, the *ṛita* of the Vedas ; but they brought about that very order, like the order created by a particular will, by sacrificial formulas.

Sacrifice and the Gods

Ṛita as the basis and sacrifice (*yajña*) as the means, and the means to that same basis—such was the foundation of Aryan beliefs. From the idea that the world subsists by sacrifices the greater part of later speculative development sprang. When it was no longer possible to suppose that the mere action of an individual man could ensure the permanence of fundamental natural conditions, it was imagined that *ṛita* was the result of sacrifices made by certain gods, or by all the gods. It was even conceived that the world is a sacrifice. The Vedas, in the strict sense, stop short of this point. The authors of the hymns, less exclusively and crudely magical than those of the *Atharvaveda*, thought it advantageous to utter the praises of the gods in order to obtain from their favour the realization of human purposes; instead of themselves producing the desired phenomena, they left it to a "wished god" (*ishta devatā*) to satisfy their desires. Ritual correctness influences the gods, and influences things through the intervention of the gods.

This was not such a great change as one may suppose, for the gods are natural forces, most of them barely anthropomorphized. Although the theory that the Vedic pantheon had its origin in philological circumstances has been pressed too far, it is certain that a *numen* implies for a certain group of facts a *nomen*. A type exists when a word is found to give the data of experience a sign and an expression, which soon become their essence.

Ṛita never becomes a mere arbitrary institution, the work of a god. The gods themselves, entrusted with maintaining it in the universe, are only its keepers (*gopa*), as a herdsman has charge of his herd. This task falls on Mitra and Varuna. These two brothers, the first sanctioning contracts and ruling the friendships of men and the second governing the revolutions of the heavens and bearing witness to all actions, predominate over the earliest Indian reflection on the cosmic order, the social order, and their relations. The mainly "formal" character of their function makes them the most typical gods of India, which in every age, as we shall see, is inclined to define objectivity by correctness of operation, by canons of right practice. The other gods are merely personifications, often pale and abstract, of natural phenomena or instruments of worship.

Perhaps we should say, not "or", but "and". The naturalistic explanation of former times and the ritualistic explanation, more recent in Europe but classical in native

Brahmanism, might be interpreted more profoundly as systematized aspects of a single reality. *Agni* is the sacrificial fire as well as the element fire. *Parjanya* is the art of rain-making as well as the rain itself. *Ushas* is the delicate charm which drives away darkness and restores the light as well as the delicate dawn. *Soma* is the moon and also the sacrificial drink, for the moon, emptying and refilling without end, shows itself to be a cup of immortality. With regard to this we should note that in the Indian view an object is a force, and being is thought of only in reference to action ; it is important to observe this principle in operation at the very beginning of Indian thought.

In a domain where the spirit of system has given proof of its vanity we shall beware of believing in the value of one single explanation. Not all the gods in the Vedic pantheon are of this part natural, part ritual character. Underneath them we find the more ancient pair, common to the whole Indo-European stock of beliefs, of the Sky Father and the Earth Mother. Characteristic of the narrower range of Indo-Iranian beliefs is the honour paid to light in its various aspects. The gods (*deva*) are properly beings of light, shining or heavenly, and it was by an accident of history that the *dev* of the Avesta became anti-gods or demons. In sectarian and even Buddhist forms, a cult of the Sun continues all through religious development. In part it is derived from Vishnu in the Vedas ; his Three Steps symbolize his conquest of the three worlds. If we look for other sources, we may remember Savitri, the vivifying power of the sun's heat, and Pushan, the stimulant which causes plants and cattle to grow. Mitra himself is an aspect of Surya, the sun.

By the side of the metaphysical and moral god, Varuna, and the ritual god, Agni, the Vedas give a very great place to another deity, Indra. The books make these three figures, in turn or simultaneously, the very prototype of godhead. The storm which fertilizes the earth by pouring water on it, according to the myth of the liberation of the clouds in the form of cows, and blasts the demons which oppose that fertilization, is simply the aspect of Indra as a natural force. He, and he alone, has a very concrete human character ; he stands for the Aryan in his victorious war with

Dasyu, the dark-skinned first occupant of the country, who is symbolized by the demon Vritra. Force is his essence, and if, like all the gods, he owes his continued existence to ambrosia, he consumes it like a drunkard and glutton. Having won his celestial rank by his exploits, he has the air of a deified hero. Moreover, his connexion with the company of the gods is always uncertain; sometimes he is the son of Dyaus, and sometimes of Tvashtar. From the fact that he is invoked with Varuna as a witness of the treaty struck by the people of Mitanni in northern Mesopotamia (1400 B.C.), we may wonder if he is not more ancient than the arrival of the Aryans in India. Indeed, he is known to the Iranians, but, doubtless under the influence of the moral side of Zoroastrianism, he is placed among the demons, either because he is a *deva* or on account of certain unedifying passages in his story. None the less, he is the most Indian of all the gods. He is advised by Vishnu, the god of sacrifice, and combines with him in a dyarchy which is an anticipation of that of the Brahman and the Kshatriya.

Gods of secondary or still lower importance are numerous. Mitra and Varuna, coupled under the name of Adityas, are sons of Aditi, the Unlimited, the Indian form of the Great Goddess of Asia Minor. The Asvins, or Horsemen, also called the Nasatyas, are the Indian Dioscuri. Rudra, the Roarer, personifies all that cattle-owners fear—storm and plague. His sons are the Maruts, the hurricanes which descend from the mountains where he dwells. Since the protection of the living depends on him, he is supposed to have remedies for the pests which he lets loose. So Rudra is a first sketch of the destroyer whom men afterwards, to conciliate him, called the Propitious, Siva.

In the composition of the Indian pantheon abstract reflection can be seen at work in two opposite directions. We have seen how the pre-Indian gods Mitra and Varuna are concerned with contracts and the maintenance of order respectively; the latter watches in particular over the oath. Aryaman presides over marriage. In contrast to these old deities, others, already more Brahmanic than Vedic, are mere personified abstractions—Sraddha, Faith; Manyu, Anger; Prajapati, the Lord of Creatures.

The Exegesis of the Vedas

The confusion which we see, the different strata of religious life at which we guess, give the present-day reader of the *Ṛigveda* the impression of many serious discrepancies. But it has taken more than a century of Indian studies for these evidences to become manifest. The master-keys with which it was attempted to force the secret of the text were systems of etymology, language-study, mythology, or ritualism, and from Colebrooke to Bergaigne hardly anyone questioned that the content of the text was a systematic whole. L. Renou's objective examination in *Les Maîtres de la philologie védique* (Paris, 1928) gives an excellent account of the way in which exegesis, for a long time dogmatic, has advanced towards conclusions which are not sceptical, but relativistic. The mythology of the *Ṛigveda*, according to Winternitz,[1] is in a state of growth, and so is the text itself. Nothing could be more artificial than the arrangement of the most ancient part (books ii to vii), where the hymns are grouped according to the god praised and the number of lines. The later parts, the first and tenth books, border on the literature of the Brāhmaṇas. No doubt when a collection (*saṃhitā*) was put together by arranging already existing stanzas there were many interpolations. The stanzas themselves were already a mass of inconsistencies, some aiming at flattering a god or toadying to princes, others being used to accompany a sacrifice or a funeral, and yet others giving a dramatic dialogue or a philosophic reflection. Between the expositions of priestly ritualism, like those of the earliest Brāhmaṇas (of the sixth century B.C., for example) and the not merely Aryan but Indo-European inspiration (the Germans unjustifiably call it Indo-Germanic) of other hymns, we may reasonably place an interval of a thousand years. We must not, therefore, be surprised to find elements which are not Indian because they are pre-Indian side by side with others which are not only Indian but Hindu, that is, which already show a mixture of Aryan and aboriginal ideas.

Then we shall see why those who have specialized in the Veda from the beginning of historical times onwards have

[1] **CCLXXXVIII**, vol. i, p. 66.

failed to understand it. The explanations given by the earliest commentator, Yaska, about 500 B.C., are far from being concordant, and his collection of etymologies, the *Nirukta*, is hardly less disappointing, valuable as it is. But it gives more information than the paraphrase of Sayana, who wrote in the fourteenth century. What was already lacking in the sixth century B.C. was the prose commentary with which the singers, like the singers of the Avestic *Gathas*, used to accompany their recitation of the hymns. Moreover, the Brahman pundits looked in these books, which for the greater part they did not understand, for what they wanted to find there, namely hymns which could be used for their own sacrificial methods. In exactly the same way in China, Confucian tradition has been only too successful in transforming the love-songs of the Book of Verses into a treatise on morals and politics. In any case, it is obvious that the priestly scholasticism which already permeated the hymns encouraged the Brahmans in the illusion that their own scholasticism was a continuation of the same work.

Besides, mystery added to the prestige of the ancient poetry. Although lists of family traditions indicated, if not the actual authors of the hymns, at least their human origin, a metaphysical interpretation of the Veda became established as the immovable basis of Brahmanism. The hymns, according to the orthodox view, have an absolute reality, like the ideas in Plato. They are truer than empirical reality, they exist for ever and contain the secret not only of all wisdom but of all existence. They constitute a revelation, and a revelation by sound, which can be heard (*śruti*); to indicate exactly how far they have objectivity, they are said to have been " seen " by the first inspired bards, who, accordingly, are called *ṛishis*, the " seers " of the hymns.

The Brahmanic Cult

In the magic of the *Atharvaveda* and the verses of the *Ṛigveda* we have the whole of the origins of the Aryan religion of India. All that Brahmanism afterwards claimed to be was the inheritance of the Vedic tradition; certainly it was the exploitation of it, and exploitation by the priestly caste which came into being after the age of the *Ṛigveda.* It is an anachronism to regard the Veda from the Brahman point of view only, but that anachronism is the corner-stone of orthodoxy from the beginnings of history to our own time. The arrangement of the hymns in *saṃhitās* represents the first manifestation of Brahmanism. Other manifestations, akin to the first, were the development of the two supplementary Vedas, the Chants (*sāman*) and the Sacrificial Formulas (*yajus*). The Chants are almost all stanzas of the *Ṛigveda,* sung to music. The Sacrificial Formulas are shown to be much later than the Chants by the fact that they are written in prose, with or without a commentary (the White or Black *Yajurveda*). It was considered necessary to have as many collections of texts as there were priests in the sacrificial practice of the Brāhmaṇas ; the *ṛij* is recited by the *hotar,* the *sāman* chanted by the *udgātar,* the prayer of the *yajus* muttered by the *adhvaryu.*

The Brahmanic conception of sacrifice, which thus governs the way in which the Vedas are presented, is at once systematic and realistic.

It revels in abstraction. To speak in concrete terms, we should say that the magical operation of sacrifice creates or preserves the world. The authors of the Brāhmaṇas prefer a different language : the universe is a sacrifice. There is a cosmic giant, the Lord of Creatures, Prajapati, or the Man, Purusha, and the parts of the world are his members. Ever afterwards India would call the parts of a whole its members, *anga,* for everything that is consists of the members of the macrocosm. Prajapati is at once the sacrificer and the thing sacrificed. So this demiurge, so different from the Vedic gods, is equivalent to the personification of sacrifice.

Existences are classified in several strata of reality, which correspond to the senses and the intellect, so far as the microcosm is concerned, to the elements, to the Vedas, to the Vedic metres, to the principal gods, and so on. In each of the lists thus formed, any two principles stand in the same relation to each other as two principles in another list. This kind of intelligibility, based on analogies and orders of dignity, is both an ancient and a permanent feature of Indian thought. Any fact symbolizes a number of other facts, and all facts are at the same time governed by the act of sacrifice.

Brahmanic realism is like that which has been noted among many peoples described as " primitive ". It implies that abstractions, like Prajapati, have an objective existence, reigning over the whole universe or part of it. There are sounds which give birth to things—those of the ritual formula, Brahman, those of the voice, Vāch, those of the breath, Prāṇa, three terms whose meanings partly overlap. There are forms which are creative—gestures and drawings which have magical efficacy. By imposing names and forms on a chaos, Prajapati, like the Demiurge of the *Timæos*, introduces order and establishes the specific nature of beings. Thought, an operation of *manas* (the empirical mind and foundation of the five senses), is not a subjective double of the macrocosm, an accidentally individual disposition of representations ; it is a reality, not spiritual but vital, capable of going past the limits of the body by the sensorial orifices and wandering outside. Dreams, death, and the efficacity of wishes or purposes prove it.

The cosmic forces are catalogued by a kind of religious physical science, which is at once crude and subtle. They are impersonal like those just mentioned—ritual formula, voice, breath, thought. Men have a share in them, but they go from nature to man as well as from man to nature. In the latter case they are set in motion by the magical operation, but in the former they have a cosmogonic value. The chief of them are the following. *Mahas* and *aṇu* are largeness and smallness, growth and restriction. *Guṇa* is the characteristic quality of a being ; in the strict sense, it is kind, variety. Then there are various aspects, consequences, or conditions of life—*asu*, the vital breath ; *āyus*, both age and the normal length of life, the vital quantity imparted to each being ; *anna*, food as a means of subsistence. *Tanū*, a sort of humbler duplicate of the concept of *ātman*, which was to become so very important, is the self of each individual, and even of each thing, in both its material aspect (body) and its intelligible aspect (mind, essence). *Satya* is the truth of the real, the conformity of an individual to its type (an abstract extension of the primitive meaning of " ritual correctness "). The list includes principles endowed with partial expansivity, which, emanating from a centre, which may be the sun or a human energy, propagate as it were their vibrations through the whole extent of the *ākāśa*, the universal environment and condition of all movement. Such are *tejas*, the cutting, the piercing of a ray of light; *varchas*, luminous energy; *bhrājas*, brilliance; *śrī*, splendour, beauty, power and glory; *ojas*, energy. The neuter gender of many of these nouns shows that the principles which they designate are impersonal. We must add *enas* and *āgas*, crime and transgression, evil as a wrongful action, but also as the calamity which results from it; *pāpa*, misfortune ensuing from sin; *puṇya*, its converse, advantage ensuing from merit. The idea of activity is implied in these concepts, which are summed up in the notion of *karman*. This word, properly meaning "rite", covers every activity from sorcery (*yātu*, *māyā*) to the moral action, magical power and virtue being the two poles of religious activity. So the idea of *karman* is very wide, being at once very primitive and very capable of refinements, which in time to come would give expression to a reflection and a moral life, at first less gross and later more and more highly developed. But the notion of activity would keep some of its primitive characteristics, even if they were not properly understood. For example, asceticism (*tapas*), the superior acting of the man who has risen beyond action, properly means and originally meant "heating", the warmth which makes the demiurge sweat as he fashions beings or that which hatches the cosmic egg in the old myths.

Dharman, *karman*, *brahman*, and presently *ātman* stand in the front rank among these original classes, almost categories, distinguished by Indian thought. They all have neuter names, which will not produce masculine terms till later. They are all anonymous forces, of which existences are only the result. Schopenhauer shows a very keen understanding of the Indian mind when he says that in this domain, contrary to what happens in the classical antiquity of the West, *esse sequitur operari*. The rite being the origin of all speculation, action always stands at the beginning. These are the effective bases of philosophic reflection; they lie in a metaphysical theory of the rite much more than in a somewhat arbitrary mythology.

Metaphysical Mythology

Why arbitrary? Because most of the myths were made up in order to justify fanciful etymologies by which the theorists of sacrifice fathered their own lucubrations on the Vedic hymns. While abstraction, scholastic classification, and realism in respect of the forces connected with worship appear as the things which make up Brahmanism, there are signs of a variety of traditions and great vagueness in the legends. Take, for instance, the cosmogonic stories, the first specimens of which appear in the late tenth book of the *Ṛigveda*. The first being was a golden egg (*hiraṇyagarbha*), floating on the waters. From it came the vital breath of the gods (x, 121). But where would the waters and the egg come from? Then we are told that the universal demiurge, Visvakarman, has his foot and his foothold everywhere, it being understood thereby that the world is in him, not he in the world (x, 81). Generation began neither with being nor with not-being, but with the One, which was at once single and unity. This principle breathed without breath (x, 129), for its life required nothing outside itself. Like a germ in the void, it came to birth by the heat of its own *tapas*. Then it desired, and that desire was the germ of thought. Since the gods came after that first creation, nobody will ever describe the creative power, and even if there is some transcendent being who presided over this creation, does he know it himself?

The famous passage which I have thus summarized is alike contradicted and corroborated by similar passages in the Brāhmaṇas. The *Śatapatha* first says that thought, which was neither being nor not-being, existed, and, wishing to become an *ātman*, heated itself with that object, and so on (x, 5, 3, 1); and then that in the beginning there were the waters, and that they warmed themselves in order to produce the golden egg from which after a year, the beginning of time, Prajapati was born (x, 16, 1). Further on the same work brings in a Brahman, by name Svayambhu (which we may translate into Latin as *in se* and *causa sui*), who creates by sacrificing himself (xiii, 7, 1). The *Taittirīya Brāhmaṇa* sets forth that the world, not yet being, thought "I wish to be", and, heating itself, produced all things (ii, 2, 9, 1).

The corresponding Upanishad likewise holds that from not-being being proceeded, and made itself *ātman* (ii, 7). The very ancient *Bṛihadāraṇyaka Upanishad* already places at the beginning of everything an *ātman*, which says to itself " I am ", and is at first frightened and then bored by its solitude and therefore splits into a first pair (i, 4). It would be idle to seek for consistency in these gropings of philosophic explanation, when systematization reaches its height in the dogmatism of sacrifice.

It is in the course of the Upanishads, not in the Brāhmaṇas, that philosophic explanation becomes systematic, gradually shedding the character of myth and flowing into the moulds the sacrificial dogmatism. Two conditions led to this result. Thought became freer, less dependent on the interpretation of ritual formalism ; and the entirely new idea arose that meditation is a substitute for worship, and even an act more efficacious than the rite itself. This was a decisive turning-point in religious development. On the practice of rites there was superimposed a desire to understand the conditions of existence. The true and most operative sacrifice is to know, for it is by understanding more than by formulas that evil as well as error is eliminated. Knowledge (*jñāna*) tends to take the place of sacrifice (*yajña*). In this overturning of values *karman*, action, lost none of its dignity. It merely took on a different meaning ; it came less and less to mean a rite and more and more to mean acting in general, of which knowing is only one kind. Everything was ready for the advent of Buddhism.

This intellectual revolution was effected, and justified, by the equation of *brahman* to *ātman*, magnificently expounded in the Upanishads. To have set up as their watchword, among many others—Vāch, Prāṇa, Ākāśa—*brahman*, the Vedic Word, and to have made it the absolute, was the final achievement of the Brāhmaṇas and the triumph of the Brahmans. We must bear in mind that that entity, *brahman*, represented the essence of the Brahman caste, as *kshatram* did that of the Kshatriya caste. To raise that *brahman* to an absolute was to give a metaphysical justification to the necessary, eternal supremacy of the priesthood, the sole performer of the religious operations which preserve the cosmic order and the sole heir of Vedic knowledge (which was the same thing). I do not mean to suggest that to identify *ātman* with *brahman* was to depose that *brahman* and substitute a different absolute. If that had been so, the Upanishads, instead of being the great sacred texts, would have been heterodox. But the truth of the Upanishads was certainly regarded as being of a different order from that of the Brāhmaṇas, since it was considered to be secret, esoteric. According to that truth, every individual in principle partakes of *brahman*, and therefore has the absolute in himself. It reveals to every mind that the great cosmic god, by whom the gods of the Veda were as it were eclipsed, is consubstantial and identical with itself. " *Tat tvam asi*—Thou art that absolute ! " The *ātman* of each man is his self and at the same time his vital breath, but it exists only by participation in a universal life which also has its self. Except in size, if one may say so (although there are no degrees in the absolute), *ātman* is identical in the macrocosm and in the microcosm. A sort of pantheism, modified, indeed, by many limitations, became established in men's beliefs—a pantheism which to a remarkable extent lost sight of Vedic tradition and even of sacrificial dogma, a pantheism emancipated from the obsession of caste and apparently ascribing the same essence to all souls alike.

The Future Life

This meant a complete revolution in eschatological beliefs. All that the *Ṛigveda* wanted was that the pious man should live out his full life without premature death. After life the dead were received into abodes which were too indeterminate to be called either heavens or hells. The Brāhmaṇas, and, so far as they are continuations of them, the Upanishads, attempt a number of solutions of the problems of the next world. Sometimes the components of a human individuality go, after death, each to its natural place. Sometimes souls, with a subtle part of their body, travel across various regions of the world along routes strictly laid down according to the manner in which life has been lived on earth. But by the side of these theories of destiny, which indicate definite " ways " (*gati*), we find other solutions, which are simpler and more straightforward. A funeral rite feeds the ghost and prevents it from dying again or dissolving. Just as the offering of *soma* maintains the life of the gods, certain offerings secure for the dead " non-re-death " (*a-mṛita*), an expression which should not be translated as " immortality ", for the cult must be kept up for ever if the deceased are to continue to exist. The precariousness of this ritualistic solution contributed to the prestige of the purely metaphysical solution contemplated by the Upanishads. The sacrifice which is knowledge not only delivers the soul from error and sin; it reveals to it its true nature, its permanent, indissoluble consubstantiality with the absolute. It gives infinitely more than a means of prolonging existence in the next world; it causes each one of us to discover and experience, as Spinoza says, that we are eternal. This solution overshoots its mark, it is true, for it ignores the problem. Instead of securing that a man shall have a fate appropriate to the moral value of his actions, it transfigures his existence in proclaiming his identity with the absolute. All his human error is to think that he is a man, when he is a god. It is an immoral solution, for the rogue is *ātman* as much as the saint; or rather one still has to explain why, if at bottom we are the absolute, the relative, evil and illusion, exists. One might say that Brahmanic thought became too expert in a certain kind of dialectics in its efforts to adapt the hymns to the requirements of sacrificial methods, and therefore leapt too fast, in its advance from the Brāhmaṇas to the Upanishads, towards the most abstract ontology. A revision of the postulates on which these views were based, a loss of interest in being and a curiosity about becoming, and above all a turn of the helm which directed thought towards moral realities, were the correctives brought to bear on Brahmanic theory by the heterodox sects of the sixth century before Christ.

CHAPTER II

Early Jainism and Buddhism

I

THEIR COMMON CONDITIONS

THE attitudes taken by the heterodox sects, Jain and Buddhist, were partly a result of the development of Brahmanic thought, and partly a reaction against that thought in the form which we have seen it about to assume. But they were also the result of very different conditions, in which history and geography had a share.

Zoroaster's reform of the religion of Iran was in all probability one influence. That reformation replaced the old ritualism by a moral effort to struggle against error and darkness, to attain purity in the worship of a god very like the wise Varuna, who was adored in the days before the Indians and Iranians separated. Here there was a metaphysical simplification of religion, comparable to that made by Brahmanic thought in creating the conception of *brahman-ātman*, but with a fighting zeal of moral propaganda added. The reformation enjoyed special advantages because it went together with the unification of Iran under the Achæmenids. It is true that its triumph was not complete in the country of its origin, but that very fact encouraged it to spread into neighbouring lands, Central Asia and the borders of India.

Then Jainism and Buddhism arose, one a little before the other, and they developed in the same regions, favoured by the same circumstances, in an environment only slightly Aryanized and still less Brahmanized. The evolution of Brahmanism, the phases of which we have briefly surveyed, at least in their scriptural aspect, took place during the conquest of Hindustan by the Aryans, from their arrival in the Punjab to the time when they reached the Bay of Bengal. The beliefs expressed in the *Ṛigveda* were perhaps those of a people living on the fringes of Iran. The Saṃhitās of the hymns must have been put together in the Punjab. The Brāhmaṇas were the work of priests to whom the upper Ganges and the Yamuna were as familiar as the affluents of the Indus. But the holy land of the heterodox sects lies north of the lower half of the Ganges basin. If the first Jains and Buddhists showed little attachment to Vedic tradition and were very independent of priestly control, it was not because they were such free-thinkers as might be supposed, but doubtless because they were not yet to any great extent incorporated in the orthodox organization of society. In those districts, the Aryanization of which was still very incomplete, the noble caste probably had more influence than that of the Brahmans; and as it happens both Buddha and Jina were of princely, not priestly family.

The two new sects had in common a belief which was to direct religious life on to paths hitherto unforeseeable and to stamp Indian philosophy with a meaning which would distinguish it from every other philosophy. That was the belief in transmigration.

Transmigration

In works dealing with this belief *saṃsāra* is usually confused with metempsychosis, as if the Indian theory of transmigration were simply one of destiny. If this were so, the notion of *saṃsāra* would be Brahmanic and would be entirely derived from the eschatological theories of the Brāhmaṇas and the two earliest Upanishads, which are probably pre-Buddhist, the *Bṛihadāraṇyaka* and the *Chhāndogya*. Already in these works the fate of an individual depends not so much on what he has been as on what he has done. "By good action one becomes good and by bad action bad" (*Bṛih.* iii, 2, 13). And the deed depends on the wish (iv, 4, 5). The Brahmanic notion of *karman* takes, in a fashion, the first steps towards the Buddhist idea of transmigration, but it does not advance further.

What is new in the first heterodox teachings is that even in this life, and if one considers this life alone, man is plunged in a torrent of relativity in which he is in great danger of going down. This idea, which is common to Jina and Buddha, is very strongly emphasized in Jain teaching. As ardently as the first Christians expected the imminent end of the world, the Gangetic sects of the sixth century declared the instability of the human condition and the misery of existence. The soul sinks in the universal flux like a boat which has shipped water ; its destiny is to be carried along by the current not only without stopping but without belonging to itself. It is not, it becomes, and because it becomes and thinks that it is, it suffers. Not to belong to oneself is slavery. Suffering is equivalent to servitude. The Greek idea corresponding to Indian transmigration is not so much metempsychosis or palingenesis as the *Πάντα ῥεῖ* of Heracleitos.

Saṃsāra does not mean births and deaths without end, but " flowing with ", passing through a series of states. This rotation or whirling tyrannizes over the present no less than the future and the past.

Whence comes this belief in a universal flux ? From some Malayo-Polynesian or Sumero-Dravidian myth ? Possibly.[1] It does not fit at all well into the ideas of classical Indian orthodoxy or even of the heterodoxy which preaches it. Devices had to be used to adapt it to the ontology of *brahman-ātman*, which it contradicts, to the Buddhist theory of the act, which requires a soul sufficiently stable to transmigrate, and to the pluralistic substantialism of the Jains. Yet it very soon established itself in men's minds, and in almost all men's minds, although it brought with it a pessimistic conception of life. The history of mankind has seen other circumstances in which collective despair has produced immense upheavals. Perhaps societies, like individuals, are more accessible to negative suggestions, to suggestions of impotence, than to suggestions of courage in combined effort. Without doubt social causes of which we know nothing contributed to planting the idea of *saṃsāra* in the Aryan world, although it was incompatible with the optimism implied in the establishment of the Brahmanic cult, which offered satisfaction of all human needs. One

[1] The Semitic legends of the Flood reached the peoples of India and were merged with the tradition about Manu. One may also quote myths of Oceania ; many of the Polynesian islanders have believed that the dead set out over the sea towards the sun or moon for travel or residence among the stars, with which one may compare the " Ways " (*gati*) of the Upanishads.

may seek the cause in the frequence of invasions, in the long wars of the Aryans with the previous occupants of the country, or in the instability of the kingdoms. Or it may have been the support which the new beliefs offered to the ambition of new monarchies, in denying the validity of the caste system and tradition. For these implied a fundamental conservativism of the social order and an immovable permanence of cosmic reality, both maintained by one same *ṛita* ; and both are denied by the theory of the fleeting and inconsistent character of the universe preached by Buddhism.

The New Notion of the Act

The power of expansion of the new beliefs lay, no doubt, in the moral renovation which they preached. Not only do Jains and Buddhists disregard the gods of the Veda ; the contempt which they proclaim for every kind of cult and rite enables one to judge how little the circles in which they first preached were Brahmanized. *Karman*, to them, does not mean the religious operation, but the transmigration-producing activity which steeps us in relativity and misery. Instead of *karman* providing for our needs, it plunges us in boundless suffering, it creates our slavery. It prevents our ever being what by right we are, what we should be if we were preserved from its evil effects. But the tragedy of the situation is that this *karman* is not an external fate, but our very life. Our present state expresses and continues our past, as it binds and governs our future. Birth and death are comparatively unimportant episodes in the course of that continuous existence, that " vital urge " which would be freed only if it gave up being an urge or a life. Here the heterodox view agrees with the *Bṛihadāraṇyaka Upanishad* ; all evil comes from desire, and men bear the burden of their will to live.

The Aspiration to Deliverance

The preaching which gradually converted the minds of men in the sixth century thus incited them, not to secure a comfortable life by religious means, like Brahmanism, nor to rely on the absolute, like the esoteric doctrines, but to make their salvation. Henceforward the aim would be to untie the bonds of existence, to break out of the dungeon of passion or illusion, to escape from oneself and so from one's necessary suffering. Just as in other times and places man has regarded himself as being made through and through of the mud of sin, so he here regards himself as the author of his own misery and anxiously aspires to release from it. He wants deliverance alone, and he wants it beyond good and evil, which, both for the same reason, enslave him. For good deeds lead to transitory advantages and bad to transitory punishments ; fundamentally the former are not worth more than the latter, since, being deeds, they bring retribution after them. Liberation is obtained only by removing oneself from the necessity of later retribution, that is by ceasing to act. The way of salvation must, therefore, be sought outside morals and outside the current religion, outside the metaphysical pursuit of the absolute. All the more, then, is it opposed to the pursuit of interest. Deliverance (*moksha*) excludes *dharma* and *artha*. It requires an effort against the normal conditions of existence, an effort towards a transcendent end. Jains and Buddhists, as fanatical seekers after *moksha*, are from the point of view of nature or society pessimists, preachers of despair ; from the point of view of possible liberation, they are optimists and enthusiasts. Their kingdom is not of this world ; it is not of any world. As a result of their passionate preaching philosophies and religions came to lose all interest in this world.

One might suppose that all thought would be thereby condemned in principle, in favour of some blind asceticism. Just the opposite happened. Buddhism, in particular, condemns asceticism for the sake of asceticism, and allows it value only as a preliminary training. All the hope of the innovators is founded on knowledge ; it alone can win salvation. This knowledge must examine the conditions of existence, and therefore of misery, in order to undo the tangle of them and so liberate men. That is why heterodoxy, like the Reformation at the dawn of modern times in the West, gave an immense stimulus to philosophic inquiry and to what is called in Germany *Erlebnis*, the attempt to try new and sometimes barely conceivable experiences. Boldness in theorizing would tend to be touched with the fever of mystic ambition, but knowledge would always be regarded as the key to salvation. One cannot exaggerate the importance of this intellectualistic postulate in reference to the later thought of India.

The Influence of Yoga and the Sophists

The rapid success of the Jains and Buddhists is to some extent explained by the likeness of the morals and opinions which they professed to those of two types of men which were very active on the fringes of Brahmanism from the earliest historical times—the Yogins and the sophists. In both Jina and Buddha ascetic preparation for the understanding which brings salvation was copied from the methods of Yoga. At the same time the sophists, attacking the dogmatism of the Brahmans by their denials and their sarcasms, facilitated the advent of new dogmatisms, and the method of reasoning used by the preachers of both sects would be for many centuries a mere copy of that of the sophists.

The original Yoga is an *askesis* which aims at mastering organic life and endowing it with supernatural powers. By stubborn opposition to the normal conditions of life, the mind ceases to be the servant of the physiological functions and makes itself their master ; it concentrates itself, and so withdraws itself from natural vicissitudes. The discipline consists in governing the body by regulation of the motions of breathing ; the efficacy of this practice is to some extent confirmed by modern psycho-physiology, but it was chiefly inspired by a tacit definition of life as breath (*prāṇa*). In the end this gymnastic, prolonged by spiritual concentration, conquers the instincts, destroys, with desire, all capacity of enjoyment and suffering, and gives thought such a mastery that it can move through space, go back into the past, anticipate the future, and effect marvellous transformations of things and men. Herein Yoga is akin to Chinese Taoism, Shamanism, and many half-speculative, half-magical practices of an ascetic, mystic nature, which still survive. All Indian thought was deeply affected by the tremendous influence of the Yogins, who by their output of energy and the savage austerity of their manners achieved a sort of religious ardour very unlike the attitude of the priesthood. Yoga supplied the whole of India with the example of a practical method, and the heterodox sects of the sixth century in particular with the prototype of an obstinate will aiming at the liberation of the mind.

The sophists of India, like those of Greece and China in the same period, were wandering dialecticians, who sold their advice to private men and princes. While they attacked the traditional religion, they had no belief in the authority of moral rules. They revealed and exploited the relativity of things and of opinions, and they excelled at arguing for and against a case with equal skill. Some were merely rhetors; others were the ancestors of the logicians; others had metaphysical dogmas of a materialistic cast, such as the Lokāyatas, who, admitting nothing but what can be perceived, held the world of experience to be an absolute reality, and those who, making their belly their god, called themselves Gorgers (*Chārvākas*). They did not all present themselves as sceptics, but even those who proclaimed some things to be certain adopted the name of Deniers (*Nāstikas*), like the sceptics, in that they despised and scoffed at virtue and piety.

In very different times and places it has been possible for a most simple-minded person to be a great saint, and many Yogins were ignorant and dull. The sophist, on the other hand, was marked by critical agility. Jains and Buddhists were at once Yogins and sophists, in that they combined asceticism with dialectics. Against the Yogins they maintained that complete self-mastery is not an end but a means; against the sophists they held that there is a *dharma* which holds good for all mankind. But this *dharma* is different from that of the Brahmanic castes in that it does not consecrate rigid distinctions between men, and instead of aiming at governing life according to the world it aims at deliverance. The new sects were to take their stand midway between the anarchic individualism of the Yogins and sophists, who had broken away from the social organization and poured scorn on all order of dignity, and the orthodox regimentation of the different strata of the people in hereditary ways of life. They would found orders, which could only be entered on abandoning Brahmanic society, but which offered favourable conditions for the pursuit of salvation.

II

JAINISM

I have referred above to the discussions regarding the time at which one should place the founder of Jainism. His death has been assigned to different dates between 545 and 467 B.C., so that it is doubtful whether he lived in the sixth or the fifth century. It is almost certain that he lived chiefly in the sixth century, even if, though older than Buddha, he died some years after him. For another reason, too, Jainism represents a current of ideas characteristic of the sixth century: its origins are in part several generations earlier than the time of Mahavira.

The Nirgranthas. Jina

The most ancient name of the sect is Nirgrantha, a body of "tieless" men, emancipated from the bonds of *karman.* Their tradition goes back to one Parsva, who is supposed to have died 230 years before Mahavira, and whose school is marked by special features of its own. A man must observe four "vows"—not to kill (*ahiṃsā*), to speak truth (*sūnṛita*), not to steal (*asteya*), and to be chaste (*brahmacharya*). This pure life is possible, for our acts do not depend on a destiny within our own nature (the doctrine of the Svabhāvavādins), nor on an external, arbitrary fate (the doctrine of the Niyativādins), but are the result of our moral autonomy. Such distinctions show that there was in the seventh century, and perhaps before, a philosophic reflection independent of religion and already concerned with the problem of action.

The Nirgrantha, to whom the epithets of Great Hero and Victorious—Mahavira, Jina—were to be particularly applied, and who as such would be regarded by posterity as the chief champion of the sect, was named Vardhamana and belonged to the Jñatrikas (Jñatriputra), a Kshatriya clan of Kundapura, near Vaisali, north of Patna. His father, Siddhartha, who bore the title of Raja, had married Trisala, the sister of the Raja of the Lichchhavis. His family observed the rules of Parsva. He married, had a daughter, and then, since his elder brother, Nandivardhana, assumed the command of the clan, became a begging ascetic. He spent twelve years wandering over Bengal, among the semi-savages (peoples not Brahmanized) of the Ladha. After that, casting off all error, he took on the purity of absolute transcendence, or complete detachment (*kevala, kaivalyam*). The decisive point at which he began to approach this sublime condition is said to have been when, in addition to observing the four vows of the Nirgranthas, he abstained from all personal ownership (*aparigraha*). Henceforward victorious, he preached his gospel for thirty years through Kosala, Videha, Anga, and Magadha, residing during the rains in the cities of Vaisali, Sravasti, and Rajagriha. He died at Pava, near Patna.

In the legend he appears as a predestined Saviour, miraculously made flesh at the required time in the womb of Trisala. The period of his abode in heaven was ended, and the time had come to deliver mankind from increasing misery. To be an Arhat or Saint, a Mukta or Delivered One, or again a Siddha or Perfect One—such was his mission. Everything is accomplished according to the infallible canons which rule nature. The Master or Blessed One possesses eternally the characteristics which define him—thirty-four perfections, omniscience, impeccability, the splendour of the sun. " His body is symmetrical and regular in shape. His joints are firm as the diamond. His hair, black as kohl and thick and curling, is drawn back on the right and shines like molten gold. His head is set on his body like an umbrella, his glance is more radiant than the light of the full moon, and his breath is balmy as a lotus-flower. His neck, beautiful as a shell, corresponds harmoniously to the three parts of his face. His shoulders are strong and mighty as a lion's or a tiger's, and his chest, broad and full, recalls the doors of the gate which guards a great city. His waist is beautiful and bears a sign of happiness on the propitious place. His two arms hang like clubs, and the palms of his hands have all the favourable symbols, the sun, the moon, the wheel, the swastika, etc. His flanks are gracefully moulded and his hips are rounded like a warrior's shield. His navel is like a lotus-flower opening under the rays of the sun. The lower part of his body is as the shape of a fish; his knees are set close together, his legs round as a corn-stalk, and his feet as beautiful as a well-balanced tortoise, the soles bearing, like the palms of his hands, the signs of happiness." [1]

Let us return to the probabilities of history and philosophy. Mahavira or Jina must have preached with all the authority of a very stern asceticism and an extraordinary determination of selflessness and purity that man is the master of his acts, and that in any case he can make himself free. His view was that of a Kriyavādin, and he maintained it as such against the Akriyavādins who denied the moral independence of man. The two chief differences of opinion which broke out among his disciples during his lifetime were about the value of activity. For example, Jamali, his nephew and son-in-law, considered that an action is of no effect until it is completed, and so argued against Mahavira, who declared "Every action, as soon at it is being performed, is as good as if it had been performed". Gosala, the son of the disciple Makkhali, founded a separate sect, that of the Ājīvikas, whom he persuaded that responsibility has no meaning, for every man acts by necessity, by accident, by nature (*niyati-saṃgati-bhāva pariṇatā*), not of his free judgment.

The Community

According to the Kalpa Sūtra, the community already contained 4,200 monks when the Master entered Nirvana. No doubt there were still more of the faithful who remained laymen and practised less austere rules. Very soon nuns were allowed to form convents too, and becoming saints (*sadhvī*) could obtain deliverance like the men. The religious position of women is very much higher in these sects than in Brahmanic orthodoxy.

The monastery shelters a life which is outside the world and favourable to a speedy attainment of salvation. It is a hothouse in which *karman* must ripen quicker, without needing new nourishment. Fasting and mortification help

[1] Guérinot, **CLXXXIX**, p. 37.

the individual to live more and more according his spiritual side. By an old practice, earlier than even Jina's time, the Nirgranthas gradually reduce their food to a minimum, for starvation raises detachment to its highest pitch and precipitates deliverance. While aspiring to this end, the monk devotes himself to teaching and preaching. The novitiate which leads up to his consecration (*dīkshā*) is modelled on the life of the Brahman student, the pupil and servant of a *guru*. After ordination the monk comes under the jurisdiction of the hierarchy, and is subject to the authority of the doctors (*upādhyāya* among the Śvetāmbaras, *paṇḍita* among the Digambaras) and pontiffs (*sūri*). The most celebrated pontifical lines are connected with one of the Sthaviras, or Elders, that is, one of the *ganadharas*, the eleven favourite disciples of the Master, or an actual pupil of theirs.

The community grew rapidly. If we are to believe the tradition of the sect, Chandragupta Maurya, the great emperor, took the monastic habit in consequence of a famine and starved himself to death. A hundred years before Christ, Jainism was making progress from Orissa in the east to Mathura in the north-west, and in the second century of our era it influenced Tamil literature in the south. In Gujarat and Kathiawar the sect took a strong hold in the eleventh century.

The great event in the early history of the Jains was their division into Śvetāmbaras and Digambaras in A.D. 79 or 82. According to the *Bhadrabāhu-charita* (fifteenth century), the origins of the schism lay in the middle of the fourth century B.C. The pontiff Bhadrabahu, to relieve his people during a dearth, emigrated with part of the community to Mysore. The section which remained in Magadha, the better to endure the sufferings of famine, ceased to observe the rule of nudity. When the emigrants returned, they were shocked by the new manners adopted by their brethren, and called them the White-cloaks (*śvetāmbara*), themselves assuming the name of *digambara*, the Clad in Space. There must have been more serious differences in dogma or discipline beneath this quarrel about clothing. The truth is that the Śvetāmbaras carried on the inspiration of Parsva and the Digambaras the more austere asceticism of Jina.

The Canons

The schism is important because the two doctrines reappear in the canonical books. They seem to have been given a definite form, though still purely oral, at a council assembled at Pataliputra under the pontiff Sthulabhadra about 300 B.C., at the time when that part of the community which was to take the name of Digambara was away in the south. This council arranged the books theoretically in twelve sections, but noted that the sources regarding the Master's own teaching had been lost. The canon, thus limited, did not at all satisfy the Digambaras, who adopted another in A.D. 156, at an assembly over which Pushpadanta presided. The Śvetāmbara canon was finally laid down and established in writing at the Council of Valabhi in 527 according to the tradition of the sect, and in 467 according to Hemachandra. The chief part in this council was taken by the pontiff Devarddhiganin. The language is Ardhamagadhi, an ancient dialect of Magadha.

We must confine ourselves to the merest outline of the canon of the Śvetāmbaras. It comprises: (1) eleven sections (*anga*); (2) twelve sub-sections (*upānga*); (3) ten collections of miscellanies (*paiṇṇa*, *prakīrṇa*); (4) six books of statutes (*chhedasūtra*); (5) four fundamental books (*mūlasūtra*); (6) some unattached texts.

(1) *Angas*.—(i) *Ayāraṃga*: *āchāra*, monastic conduct; (ii) *Sūyadaṃga* or *Sūtrakritānga*, the distinction between true faith and false; (iii) *Thānaṃga* or *Sthānānga*; various subjects presented according to a numerical classification; (iv) *Samavāyaṃga*: a continuation of the preceding section; (v) *Bhagavatī Viyāhapaṇṇatti* or *Vyākhyāprajñapti*: detailed exposition, theory of beatitude; (vi) *Nāyādhammakahāo* or *Jñātādharmakathā*: edifying stories; (vii) *Uvāsagadasāo* or *Upāsakadaśāḥ*: decade for the use of laymen; (viii) *Amtagadadasāo* or *Antakṛiddāśāḥ*: decade (reduced to an ogdoad) of those who have starved themselves to death; (ix) *Anuttarovavāiyadasāo* or *Anuttararaupapātikuśāḥ*: decade of those who have risen to the highest heaven; (x) *Paṇhāvāgaraṇāim* or *Praśnavyākaraṇi*: problems and solutions; (xi) *Vivāgasuyaṃ* or *Vipākśrutam*: stories about the ripening and so about the retribution of acts.

(2) *Upāngas*.—(i) *Ovavavāiya* or *Aupapātika*: a sermon of Mahavira and explanations about the "obtaining of existences" in the twelve celestial worlds; (ii) *Rāyapaseṇaïjja* or *Rājapraśnīya*: the King's Questions about reincarnations; (iii) *Jīvābhigamasūtra*: classification of the living; (iv) *Paṇṇavaṇā* or *Prajñāpanā*: the same subject—two classes of men, Āryas and barbarians; (v) *Surīyapaṇṇatti* or *Sūryaprajñāpti*: knowledge of the sun; (vi) *Jambudvīpapaṇṇatti*: knowledge of the continent to which India

belongs, geography ; (vii) *Chaṃdapaṇṇatti* or *Chandrap.* : knowledge of the moon ; (viii) *Nirayāvalī* : description of the underworld ; (ix) *Kappāvadaṃsiāo* or *Kalpāvataṃsikāḥ* : description of the ten princes who reached their respective heavens ; (x) *Pupphiāo* or *Pushpikāḥ* ; (xi) *Pupphachūliāo* or *Pushpachūlikāḥ* ; (xii) *Vaṇhidasāo* or *Vṛishnidaśāh* : legends of the destiny after death of those ten princes, fallen in battle.

(3) *Païnnas.*—(i) *Chaüsaraṇa* or *Chatuḥśaraṇa* : the four refuges—moral observances, manual of confession, treatise on discipline ; (ii) *Āurapachchakkhāna* or *Āturapṛatyākhyāna* : on renunciation and the happy death ; (iii) *Bhattapariṇṇa* or *Bhaktaparijña* : preparation of monks for death ; (iv) *Saṃthāra* or *Saṃstāra* : the bed of grass on which a dying man should lie ; (v) *Taṃḍulaveyāliya* or *Taṇḍulavaitālika* : human physiology ; (vi) *Chaṃdāvijjhaya* : rules of morality at the various times of life ; (vii) *Deviṃdatthava* or *Devendrastava* : classification of the gods ; (viii) *Gaṇivijjā* or *Ganitavidyā* : astrology ; (ix) *Mahāpachchakkhāna* or *Mahāpratyākhyāna* : formula of confession ; (x) *Vīratthava* or *Vīrastava* : praise of the Hero, the Jina.

(4) *Chhedasūtras.*—(i) *Nisīhajjhayaṇa* ; (ii) *Mahānisīha* or *Mahāniśītha* ; (iii) *Vavahāra* or *Vyavahāra* ; (iv) *Āyāradasāo* or *Āchāradaśāḥ* ; (v) *Bṛihatkalpa* ; (vi) *Pañchakalpa*. These are six books of disciplinary rules (*kalpa*) ; the *Kalpa Sūtra* of Bhadrabahu is part of the fourth.

(5) *Mūlasūtras.*—(i) *Uttarajjhayana* or *Uttarādhyayana* : maxims, parables, dialogues, and ballads relating to monastic life ; (ii) *Āvassaya* or *Āvaśyaka* : the six observances obligatory to monks—abstention from all evil, exaltation of the twenty-four Jinas, respect for the *guru*, confession, penitence, and repudiation of bad deeds ; (iii) *Dasaveyāliya* or *Daśavaikālika* : ten chapters of maxims on monastic life ; (iv) *Piṇḍanijjutti* or *Piṇḍaniryukti* : morality.

(6) *Nandisutta* or *Nandisutra* and *Anuogadāra* or *Anuyogadvāra* : the total sum of knowledge, practical and speculative, required of a monk, and classification of the canonical texts.

The Digambaras reject the *angas*. Pushpadanta, in collaboration with Dharasena and Bhutavali, replaced them by three treatises (*śāstra*), the *Dhavala*, the *Jayadhavala*, and the *Mahādhavala*, all in verse, never published but preserved in a monastery in the Kanara country.[1] The sect also has four " Vedas "—the *Prathamānuyoga*, composed of *purāṇas* ; the *Karaṇānuyoga*, a corpus of cosmology ; the *Dravyānuyoga*, a philosophical collection ; and the *Charanānuyoga*, treatises on worship and customs. The works incorporated in these collections belong to various periods, chiefly in the eighth and ninth centuries. They are written in Sanskrit or in Sauraseni, the dialect of Mathura.

The Jains have also handed down a great mass of non-canonical literature, dealing with dogma, the sciences, and

[1] **CLXXXIX**, p. 82.

history or legend, besides epics, stories, and works on poetry. Almost all these works are later than the seventh century, the point at which we end our analysis of Indian life. The earliest philosophic treatises bearing an author's name are supposed to have been written by Kundakunda, who was pontiff from 8 B.C. to A.D. 44, and his successor Umasvati (44–85). But the works ascribed to them are much rather of about the fifth and sixth centuries—for example, the *Pavayanasāra*, attributed to the former, and the *Tattvārthādhigama Sūtra*, attributed to the latter.

Archaism and Realism. The Substances

The date of the Jain documents—the final edition of the canon and the composition of profane works—is therefore fairly late. But they often contain very ancient portions, especially in the verse parts, and the ideas which they express also frequently take us back to a very ancient form of thought, very much what must have prevailed in the seventh and sixth centuries before Christ. This archaism has left its mark on almost all Jain dogma.

What perhaps justifies us in making this assertion is the profound affinity between the philosophic opinions of the Jains and those contained in the other most ancient elements of Indian thought—the old materialism, the old Vaiśeshika, the first Sāṃkhya, the earliest Buddhism. These various systems, the origins of which lie very far back in the past, even if they were not codified till late, have a common foundation, namely atomic or at least materialistic principles to explain nature, and sometimes even certain psychic functions. Here we must see a survival of the old ontology which constituted Indian thought before the belief in transmigration turned philosophy into a pursuit of salvation.

Further certain evidence of the antiquity of Jain dogma is furnished by the primitive simplicity of its materialism, side by side with an equally simple spiritualism. We should add the very special meaning which it gives to certain terms such as *dharma* and *yoga*. Still more, we should place its gross theory of *karman* at the very beginning of the new trend taken by speculation in the sixth century B.C. We shall see that certain later conceptions of *karman*, for instance in the Buddhist works, represents a more subtle attempt to solve the difficulties encountered by the Jains.

The realism which we have observed in the Brahmanism of the Brāhmaṇas is found in its entirety in the substantialism of the Jains. Briefly, it comes to this. There are two kinds of substance (*dravya*), animate (*jīva*) and inanimate (*ajīva*). But among inanimate things there are some which we should call forces, or manners of being, or points of view, not substances—spatial extension (*ākāśa*), the principle of movement (*dharma*), the principle of rest (*adharma*), matter (*pudgala*). These realities are " places " (*pradeśa*) in which are situated simple elements (literally, small, *aṇu*, or extremely small, *paramāṇu*), which may be called atoms, although neither extension nor infinite smallness nor indivisibility defines them. These last are Greek notions, which we have no right to apply in the case. So there are different manners of being—the simple, the complex or the molecule, which is an aggregate of simples (*skandha*), the entrance of simples of one kind into aggregates of another kind, such as that of matter into spiritual aggregates, and the expansivity of an aggregate, greater or less according to its movement and rest, which makes it possible for the soul to gather itself together or to spread through the body and even outside it. This physical theory contains the key to the explanation of facts and to the moral or religious effort to be undertaken.

The Soul and its Salvation

The misery of existence is due to the fact that the spiritual (*jīva*) does not know itself as such because it allows itself to be invaded by matter and entangled in it. Just as, according to modern medical science, we suffer from arthritis because uric acid crystals collect in our joints, human ills are the result of the residue left by former acts. *Karman*, which is wholly material, consists in this obstruction. Our personality is cramped in bonds (*bandha*) ; this last word was to remain in the Indian vocabulary, which would retain the notion of servitude as a being tied fast. Not only is our purely spiritual initiative (*vīrya*) hampered ; our intellect is darkened and loses itself. So, when ignorance has become too dense, a guide, a saviour, must reveal us to ourselves.

We shall see that the sixth-century doctrines of salvation must have been modelled on the medical theory of the same period; are not salvation and health parallel notions? The discovery of an ill implies that of a remedy. The theory of phenomenal existence and the desire for salvation are concerned with one single *fact*, which must be *undone*. When one knows how a knot has been made, one knows how to untie it. The physical theory of *karman* and the process of deliverance are absolutely inverse, but they imply the same conditions. Liberation is the inverse of slavery.

To prevent new *karman* from encumbering our fundamental freedom and to dissolve and eliminate the *karman* accumulated in it—that, then, is the way to salvation, the cure for suffering. The "warmth" of asceticism hastens the ripening of the residues of *karman* and effects a "cleansing" which, returning each substance to its place, restores us to our native purity.

In this anxiety to preserve the original nature of man entire there is some affinity with the doctrines of Zoroaster. Another common feature is the scrupulous respect for all life, the horror of hurting any animal (*ahiṃsā*). In after ages Jains would place a piece of linen or a fine strainer over their mouth for fear of inhaling a midge. The dualism of the spiritual and the material, and even the Śvetāmbaras' preference for white clothing, further increase the likeness to Zoroastrianism.

Self-mortification as an antecedent means and understanding as the ultimate means of deliverance make up the programme, negative rather than constructive, of Jain austerity. Buddhism, even that of the Small Vehicle, will present more stuff, more colour, more subtlety, and in the Great Vehicle it will admit of unlimited philosophic developments. Dry Jainism never produced a Mahāyāna; it would remain, beneath its dogma and its discipline, little changed through the ages, a permanent survival of very ancient opinions and beliefs. That is why a knowledge of it is of such value to the analyst of the Indian intelligence.

III

BUDDHISM

Buddhism makes its appearance as a younger brother of Jainism. It had its origin in the same parts, it developed in the same circumstances, and its inspiration was always fundamentally similar, although its breadth and influence were far greater. It is possible that in the early years the Buddhist apostles imitated the Nirgranthas, but in later centuries it was rather Jainism that modelled its legends and dogmas and rules of life on Buddhist forms, whose reputation and power of attraction were far greater.

Buddha

He who was to become the Buddha, the Illuminated, was born at Kapilavastu on the borders of Nepal, of a "royal" family of the Sakya clan. We should remember that, according to the dating most usually accepted, his birth and death probably occurred in 560 and 480. His biography is composed of a mixture of elements which may be historical with varying amounts of legend, even myth. The most rationalistic accounts are not necessarily the most likely to be true. They may be further removed, if not from reality, from truth, than accounts containing a large proportion of legend; for that legend is an integral part of the facts, and contributes potently to the rise of the beliefs from which it is itself derived. We may safely say that, to understand the religious mission of Buddha, we must take into account the solar myth described by Senart, largely on the strength of Mahayanistic documents, no less than the traditions of the purely human sage which we learn from the Pali *suttas* and their interpreter, Oldenberg. It would be foolish not to make use of them. The oldest documents which speak of the Blessed One tell us not so much about the life and opinions of Gautama, son of Suddhodana, as about the way in which his life and opinions were imagined in the early centuries of the Buddhist community, and every later age evolved biographies after its own mind. We need not be too much surprised to be told by some writers that the Master evangelized Mathura and Kashmir, or by others that he, who was delivered while alive, was more than a god—an eternal principle.

Here, in outline, is the ancient framework, into which myths and fables were introduced in quantities. Queen Maya-devi (one is tempted to translate the name, " Divine Illusion ") conceived, in the form of a tiny elephant which entered her side, a supernatural being, who was born in the garden of Lumbini, his arrival being proclaimed by various prodigies. He was called Gautama, after the section of the Sakya clan to which he belonged ; his personal name was Siddhartha, like that of the father of Jina. Maya died seven days after the birth of the child, but her sister (whose name is equally mythological—Mahaprajapati) reared him, and he grew up as if he had been called to rule the world, amid wealth and happiness. As a young man the prince married his cousin, Yasodhara, who bore him a son, Rahula. This happened at the turning-point in his life. A god had just revealed to him, in four different visible forms in succession, the aspects of human misery, of which he had hitherto known nothing. Going out of the palace, he had met an old man, worn with years, an incurable invalid, a funeral procession, and an ascetic. These four visions had troubled his mind ; he had now seen the slavery that results from suffering and the desirability of liberation. So, when he learnt that a son was born to him, instead of rejoicing, he thought to himself, " Now I am bound by a new chain." Then he decided to break them all. He fled from his home by night, his heart torn by the attitudes of his sleeping wives, rode off alone, and bartered his rich clothes and ornaments for the plain dress of an ascetic. He was twenty-nine years old.

He sat at the feet of two Yogins, Arada Kalama and Udraka Ramaputra, whose teaching did not satisfy him at all. He went through Magadha and practised the hardest austerities at Urubilva, now called, in memory of what happened there, Buddh Gaya (Gaya of the Illumination), south of Patna. Here the complete understanding, the full and entire illumination (*samyaksambhodi*) which he has sought for seven years, came to him at night as he was meditating under a fig-tree. Henceforth he was a Buddha. Unavailing were the temptations of the Evil One, Mara, the god of love and death, who offered him the dominion of the world and its joys. The ascetic had not only passed beyond the capacity for pain and pleasure, he had discovered the secret of all being and stood above good and evil, gods and demons. Gods and men must pay honour to this shower of the Way which leads to deliverance.

Buddha commenced his preaching by the sermon at Benares, where " the Wheel of the Law was set in motion " (*dharmachakra-pravartana*). That is the memorable phrase by which the declaration of the conditions of salvation is likened to the institution of the Brahmanic *dharma* by the King in the capacity of judge, and also to the regular revolution of the sun, the orderer of all life ; for the wheel, a solar emblem, is also a symbol of kingship. Thus the first preaching is made equal to the essential attribute of a king and to the efficience and glory of Vishnu, the sun-god. To complete the likeness, later ages ascribed to the child Buddha the Three Steps which make Vishnu a principle co-extensive with the whole universe.

Coming to Rajagriha, the Master there converted the two disciples who were to have a very great influence on the community, Sariputra and Maudgalyayana, and after them his two cousins, Ananda and Devadatta, and then Anuruddha and Upali. These two last are revered as the respective founders of *abhidharma*, which we may provisionally call metaphysics, and *vinaya*, or monastic discipline. Ananda was the favourite disciple, the St. John of Buddhism, and it was in his arms that the Master died. Devadatta, on the other hand, is the Judas. He tried to involve the Blessed One in the bloody plot by which Ajatasatru dethroned his father Bimbisara, and, a more serious and perhaps a more historical act, he brought discord into the community by founding a sect in which asceticism was more rigorous.

Forty-three years of preaching and wandering, except in the rainy season, constituted the " Buddhist career " for Buddha. It ended very simply. Near Kusinagara the Master, at the age of eighty, was entertained by the smith Chunda ; the old man's death was brought on by indigestion caused by eating boar's flesh, and he attained Nirvana, repeating to his followers, " Yes, I tell you, all passes. See to your salvation." In later ages the community kept of these words only their metaphysical meaning. Far from allowing that the Master had " passed ", they came more and more to declare his permanent transcendence ; not only had he entered on the way of salvation in the course of his human life, but his thought, at once as a " wish " and a " grace ", formed the unchangeable foundation of universal spirit. A second way, still more Indian, of raising the Blessed One to a cosmic principle was to make him the Buddha of the present phase of mankind, and so to make him one of an infinite series of other Buddhas, past and future, all co-eternal but incarnate each at the time determined by the rhythm of the world and the law of transmigration.

The Buddhist faith consists in recognizing the supreme excellence of three " jewels " (*ratna*), which are three " refuges ", Buddha, his Law (*dharma*), and the Community (*Saṃgha*). The point of view of the historian differs from that of the dogmatist ; instead of regarding these three principles as of equal worth, he places the *Saṃgha* first, for the biography of the Master and the structure of his teaching express without any doubt the opinion of both formed by the body of the faithful in the course of the ages.

The Community. Councils. Sects.

This community, like the Jain, includes laymen and regular clergy. The former must observe five rules : not to kill, not to steal, not to lie, not to get drunk, and not to fornicate. They are recommended to provide for the maintenance of the clergy and to take part in their feasts. The monk must abstain from all sexual intercourse and possess nothing, save his yellow rags, a belt, a rice-bowl, a razor, a needle, and a strainer to prevent him from killing little beasts by swallowing them when he drinks. He must never take money, at least as an individual. He lives on what he gets by begging. Although the clergy dress in rags, they must keep fairly clean, shaving themselves at the two feasts of the month and caring for their teeth and nails. As spiritual heirs of the Brahmanic Āraṇyakas, they should, properly, live in the forest ; but in practice, since they have to mix with other men in order to propagate the Law, the forest becomes merely a park or garden which the faithful provide for their use. There were no monasteries at the beginning, but they developed from the *viharas,* at first temporary, where the monks spent the rainy season, when movement was impossible. With this early scattered existence went an absence of any order of rank or centralization, the result of which was an extreme diversity of traditions and, later, of opinions. The title of Sthavira or Elder does not stand for a definite office, but merely for the special dignity conferred by age. Such distinctions as are allowed are metaphysical rather than social. The neophyte is a *śrotāpanna,* " entered in the stream " to reach Nirvana ; the *sakṛidāgāmin* is one who must be born on earth once more ; the *anāgāmin* is " he who will not return ", since he will obtain deliverance in his present life ; the Arhat is one who is delivered while alive, a possessor of sanctity.

Anybody regardless of caste, can enter the community, except the sick, criminals, and serfs, who are not free to dispose of themselves. Marriage and every other social tie are dissolved for one who enters orders. The ceremony called *pravrajyā* consists in leaving worldly life to take the equipment of a monk, or rather mendicant (*bhikshu*), and declaring that you place your refuge in Buddha, the Law, and the Community. After a noviciate, by a second consecration (*upasampadā*), the neophyte " arrives at " the state of monk ; before a large number of monks he makes vows, which are not, however, eternal, for a *bhikshu* can leave the community. From the time of the Blessed One, women have been admitted to the religious life as nuns, with a code of rules exactly corresponding to that of the men, but the monks have a right of disciplinary supervision over them.

The cult practised by these monks and nuns disregards the gods of the Veda and those of the sects, and therefore Buddhism has been described as an atheistic religion. The phrase is an exaggeration, for the Master never denied the gods ; he merely expected nothing from them, and his Nirvana made him incommensurable with the divine beings who dwell in the paradises. But it is fair, if it means that the pursuit of salvation has nothing to hope from theology, popular or esoteric. The essential part of the cult is the celebration twice a month, at the new and the full moon, of the *upavasatha*. At this gathering the whole community of the district must appear for the reading of the *pratimoksha* and a public confession of sins, which are thereby remitted. In spite of the entirely moral aspect of this piety, many practices border on popular superstitions—the recitation of formulas, intensified by the use of praying-mills, the adoration of relics or holy places rendered illustrious by the Master or some Arhat, pilgrimages, to *stūpas* which commemorate some event of a spiritual nature, and so on. Beginning as moral and eschatological fanaticism, Buddhism was to develop on the one hand into pure metaphysics and on the other into a religion which grew more and more like Hinduism.

Recent works of Sylvain Lévi and his pupils, particularly Louis de la Vallée-Poussin, followed by Tuneld and Przyluski, have entirely revised our knowledge of the Buddhist councils. We are no longer content with the traditional account, according to which the discipline was laid down at Rajagriha shortly after the Master's death, and then at Vaisali a hundred years later, and the canonical books were finally established at Pataliputra in 245 B.C., under Asoka. We are beginning to suspect that Buddhist traditions vary very greatly according to the place and time, and to realize that one council or another, without being a mere myth, is presented in a legendary aspect. Not only are the accounts incomplete, or late, or fanciful; they are biassed, being intended as the defence of a particular tradition. Only the critical dissection of a vast mass of Indian, Chinese, Tibetan, and Serindian literature will make it possible to throw some light on those early ages of Buddhism, whose air of rationalistic simplicity led the first Western historians who studied them so far astray.

J. Przyluski has noted how, as council followed council, the Buddhist centre of gravity gradually shifted westwards, and this fact, as he interprets it, seems to him to be very informative. The first great manifestation of the sect, like the first attempt to set up a great monarchy, takes place in Magadha and the surrounding countries, which, as we must once again recall, were little Brahmanized in the sixth century. One feels that the caste system was not likely to be propitious to politics on a grand scale or to a religion embracing all mankind. Vaisali marks a first stage in the westward movement, but the account of the assembly supposed to have been held there " can only have been written at a time when Mathura was already the seat of an influential community ".[1] But that city, the centre of a truly Brahman district, was a centre of Sanskrit literature. The Mathura stage therefore marks the adaptation of Buddhism to the intellectual civilization of the Brahmans, its incorporation, not indeed in the orthodoxy, but at least in the classical thought of India. As for the Pali canon, which was to reach Ceylon, it is found in a school which is almost unrelated to that of Mathura, namely the school of Kausambi, whose influence extended to Ujjayini in the south-west. Lastly, the council summoned by Kanishka, at which Asvaghosha was instructed to draw up a gloss explaining the dogma (*vibhāshā*), was held in Kashmir, away in the north-west, in countries subject to many western influences, Iranian or transmitted through Iran.

The Buddhist legends, no less and perhaps more than the real facts, reflect the rivalries of sects. If, for example, a book tells us that Madhyantika, the apostle of Kashmir, converted Upagupta, the saint of Mathura, let us regard the statement as an anachronistic and nonsensical claim of a later church to be senior to an older church. So, too, the innocent expositors of the past did not see what lay beneath the veneration of a particular saint in a particular place. A church invoked the inspiration of Ananda, Upali, or Mahakasyapa, according as it set most store by *dharma* or discipline or metaphysics. Ananda is the religious type of early times, full of moral inspiration and compassion; Anuruddha is the superhuman, supernatural Arhat.

The Council of Rajagriha, when viewed in the light of this new and searching criticism, becomes a legend embroidered on a wholly pagan canvas, the seasonal myth of Gavampati, the god of drought, losing his power at the beginning of the rains.[2] It is very likely that arrangements had to be made when, for the first time after the Master's death, the weather compelled the *Saṃgha* to gather together,

[1] CCVI, p. 10. [2] CCVII, p. v.

but there is more of folklore than of history in the story of the gathering. An assembly like that which took place every year at the same season and was marked by a popular festival evidently seemed a great event, at any rate to those interested in regarding it as such, namely the clergy who wanted to distinguish themselves from the community in the wider sense, including the laymen (*mahāsaṃgha*). When the texts have been taken to pieces in the same way for the other councils we shall perhaps be more sceptical of the genuineness of the accounts, but we shall have more correct notions of what it is most important to discover, the life of the many sects.

They seem to have evolved from an unorganized, semi-democratic state of things, in which no permanent hierarchy was possible, to an oligarchy in which the Elders (Sthavira) have authority, while the saints become patriarchs. So a monastic system grows up in which the rules of discipline (*vinaya*) become more and more important compared with the Law (*dharma*). The clergy are less interested in the edification of the faithful than in forming a nursery of Arhats, whose merit will presently be judged by gnosis or efficience rather than by punctual observance of the rules. But all generalization is rash, so different are local communities.

From the most ancient tradition, that of the Mahāsaṃghikas, in which there was least differentiation between layman and cleric, the eastern churches sprang. In the west two stocks were to flourish particularly. The Sthaviras of Kausambi established the Pali scriptures in Ceylon, and the Sarvāstivādins of Mathura spread to Kashmir, where they founded a sect which claimed to conform to the original spirit of that tradition, and therefore called itself the Mūlasarvāstivādins. Since the Sthaviras and the Sarvāstivādins travelled to opposite ends of India, the former introducing Pali texts where they went and the latter Sanskrit, they have in Europe until recently been superficially contrasted as Southern Buddhism and Northern Buddhism.

A great deal of critical examination of the evidence is still necessary to disentangle the confused mass of sects. The question is of importance, for the canon varies according to the sect or tradition. Certain works have only been preserved in the version of one school; others are found, at least in bits, in different districts, and therefore in very different languages. The student of Buddhism must be in a position to draw on other than Indian sources—Tibetan, Chinese, and Serindian or Iranian as well as Sanskrit, Pali, and Prakrit. As a result of the fruitful collaboration of Sylvain Lévi and Édouard Chavannes and the marvellous French and German discoveries in Central Asia, it has been possible for Gauthiot with his penetration and Pelliot with his vast erudition to bring to the exploration of the Buddhist canon, or rather canons, a mass of archæological and linguistic evidence which daily grows more varied and voluminous. Thanks to Minaev and Scherbatski in Russia, to Grünwedel, von le Coq, Walleser, and Leumann in Germany, to the Belgian L. de la Vallée-Poussin, and, quite recently, to the Italian Tucci, to Bunyiu Nanjio and subsequent Japanese lexicographers, Buddhist studies are one of the most thriving branches of the humanities. Here the first rank is still held by Sylvain Lévi, who has an unequalled mastery of the whole subject and has inspired researches beyond counting. The army of pupils which he has raised keeps the spiritual heritage of Burnouf alive and flourishing in France. The French School continues to take a special interest in Northern Sanskrit Buddhism, in contrast to the preference shown by scholars like Rhys Davids and Oldenberg for the Pali canon.

The Canon

Let us draw up the scheme of that canonified Buddhist literature. In theory every work should, allowing for variants, appear in Pali, Sanskrit, Tibetan, and Chinese.

The whole corpus, the Tripṭaka or Threefold Basket, is divided into three sections—the Baskets of Vinaya or Discipline, of the Sūtras or Stories, and of Abhidharma or the Essence of the Law, that is metaphysics.

(1) Vinaya.—*Suttavibhanga*, explanation of the *sūtras* or articles of the *prātimoksha; Khandakās*, " sections " on the daily life of monks and nuns; *Mahāvagga*, the " great division ", and *Chullavagga*, the " lesser division "; *Parivāra*, a late collection of unconnected texts and canonical tables.

(2) Sūtras.—Five collections (*nikāya*): the long collection, *Dīgha* (34 *sūtras*); the medium, *Majjhima* (152 homilies or dialogues); the composite, *Saṃyutta* (56 groups of *sūtras*); the numerical, *Anguttara*, in which each section contains one piece

more than the preceding ; and the least, *Khuddaka* (shorter texts). This last contains works of great importance ; (i) *Khuddaka pāṭha*, short texts ; (ii) *Dhammapada*, the Law in maxims : (iii) *Udāna*, the " spiritual " aspirations ; (iv) *Itivuttaka*, utterances of Buddha ; (v) *Sutta nipāta*, sections of less amplitude ; (vi) *Vimānavatthu* and (vii) *Petavatthu*, tales of divine palaces and ghosts ; (viii) *Theragāthā* and (ix) *Therīgāthā*, verses of the monks and nuns ; (x) *Jātakas*, stories of previous births of Buddha ; (xi) *Niddesa*, partial commentary on the *Sutta nipāta* ; (xii) *Paṭisambhidāmagga*, a work of *abhidharma* ; (xiii) *Apadāna*, " Feats " of holiness ; (xiv) *Buddhavaṃsa*, legends of twenty-four Buddhas prior to Sakyamuni ; (xv) *Chariyāpiṭaka*, thirty-five Jatakas showing how Sakyamuni came to possess the ten perfections.

(3) Abhidharma.—(i) *Puggalapaññatti*, the theory of individuality ; (ii) *Dhātukathā*, an exposition of the elements or factors which condition psychical phenomena ; (iii) *Dhammasangaṇi*, an enumeration of phenomena ; (iv) *Vibhanga*, fragments of the same kind as the preceding section ; (v) *Paṭṭhāna* ; (vi) *Yamaka*, questions asked in positive and negative form ; (vii) *Kathāvatthu*, a manual of controversy for the use of monks.

Such is the gist of the Pali canon. Its more ancient parts are the first two Baskets. The *Abhidharma*, a " supplement ", an extremely subtle inquiry regarding the Law, came later as a more profound development of the doctrine implied in the Suttas (Sanskrit, Sūtras). Thus the *Kathāvatthu* is supposed to be the work of Tissa Moggaliputta, a doctor of the third century B.C. Most of the works mentioned above must have been in existence at that time, particularly in the reign of Asoka, when the Emperor called the great Buddhist assembly of Pataliputra. It was then that " abidharmic " theory took definite shape, to be a special Basket henceforward.

There is a great mass of literature, still in Pali, but outside the canon, which is a continuation of these texts and in great part a commentary on them—the *Milinda-pañha*, or Questions of King Menander, which is so characteristic of the speculative activity of the Indian sophists of the second and first centuries B.C. ; the *kathās* (the *Aṭṭha* and the *Nidānakathās*), which are explanations of the Jātakas ; the glosses of Buddhaghosha, the great commentator of the fifth century of our era (*Visuddhimagga, Samantapāsādikā, Sumangalavilāsinī, Papañchasūdani, Sāratthapakāsinī, Manorathapūranī*) ; two Cingalese chronicles, the *Dipavaṃsa* and *Mahāvaṃsa* ; and many other works.

The Literature of the Mahāyāna

Let us now run through the names of the chief non-Pali works, chiefly Sanskrit, which have often been attributed to a supposed Northern Buddhism, as if the Sanskrit and Pali literatures were fundamentally and originally opposed like the north and south of India. Most of these books belong to the Mahāyāna, the Great Vehicle, or mark the transition from it to the Small Vehicle, the Hīnayāna. None is earlier than the first century of our era.

The *Mahāvastu* and the *Lalita-vistara* are legendary biographies of Buddha. The former is the work of the Lokottaravādin Mahāsaṃghikas of the first century and the latter belongs to the Mahāyāna Sūtras. The corpus of these Sūtras contains a number of texts in which myth and metaphysics are combined—*Saddharma-puṇḍarīka*, the " Lotus of the Good Law " (beginning of the third century) ; *Kāraṇḍavyūha*, which is fundamental for the worship of the *bodhisattva* Avalokitesvara ; *Sukhāvatīvyūha*, a defence of the paradise of the Buddha Amitabha ; *Gaṇḍavyūha* or *Avataṃsa-kasūtra*, an eulogy of the *bodhisattva* Mañjusri ; *Karuṇapuṇḍarīka*, the " Lotus of Compassion " ; *Lankavatara*, an account of the supposed visit of Sakyamuni to Ravana, King of Ceylon ; *Daśabhūmīśvara*, an account of the ten " lands " through which one travels to the condition of a Buddha ; *Samādhirāja*, the " King of Concentration " ; *Suvarṇaprabhāsa*, the " Splendour of Gold " ; *Rāshṭrapāla-paripṛichchhā*, the question of Rashtrapala, being explanations about the state of *bodhisattva*.

Most of these works were translated into Chinese from the fourth century to the beginning of the seventh. At the beginning of the Great Vehicle stands the literature of *prajñā pāramitā* (first and second centuries), the " Highest Degree of Knowledge ", which opens the way to the great philosophies, that of the Mādhyamikas (Nagarjuna, followed by Aryadeva, between 150 and 250) and that of the Yogāchāras (fourth to seventh century), before which comes the great figure of Asvaghosha (second century).

This immense output of religious and philosophical works is spread over at least eight hundred years after the days of Buddha. It rises in Bengal, in the form of a moral apostolate ; it spreads to Brahmanic India of the Upper Ganges and all the west, from Gujarat to Kashmir ; and at the dawn of the Mahāyāna it has its centre in the far north-west, in contact with Iran, Persian and Serindian.

Its advance to the Far East and its penetration of Tibet, and on the other hand its exportation to the colonies in Indo-China and the East Indian Islands confirm that the thought which animated it was at least as universal as Indian in its appeal. The conquest of China and Japan by that thought was to be one of the mightiest manifestations of humanism recorded by history.

The only Buddhism which we should discuss in this chapter is that of the earliest centuries down to the beginning of the Christian era. Here the Pali canon is our principal source.

Dogma

The corner-stone of the doctrine consists of four "Noble Truths" (*āryasatyāni*), which, according to the sermon at Bernares, form the Law.[1] They are: (1) All that exists is subject to *suffering*. (2) The *origin of suffering* is in human desires. (3) The *suppression of suffering* comes from the suppression of the desires. (4) The *Way* which leads to that suppression is the "Noble Eightfold Path": rightness of intuition, of will, of speech, of action, of life, of aspiration, of thought, and of concentration. That Path led the Master "to rest, to knowledge, to illumination (*bodhi*), to Nirvana". So the doctrine is presented as founded on experience; the Blessed has discovered, not an aspect of being, but a way, and he dedicates himself to pointing it out. The simple believer will set out on it on the word of Buddha, and will thus travel to salvation, but deliverance properly so called can only be won as the Master won it, by the same act of understanding as made him an Illuminated One. Also, the *karman* accumulated must be exhausted; illumination wins Nirvana by right, but is not enough to achieve it in fact.

Przyluski is of opinion that the very earliest Buddhism promises heaven (*svarga*, *brahmaloka*), not Nirvana.[2] The chief argument for this view comes from an edict in which Asoka speaks of *svarga* as a future reward of the faithful. This very mundane evidence hardly seems convincing. A monarch speaking to the mass of the people may neglect the niceties of an exceptional metaphysical experience.

[1] *Mahāvagga*, i, 6, 17–29; *Saṃyutta*, 56, 11.
[2] **CCVII**, pp. 368, 371.

Besides, the *Gītā* tells us that access to *brahma* is a Nirvana [1]; for there is extinction of our individuality in that fusion with the absolute, just as in the properly "Buddhist" experience. One thing does seem certain: the most ancient notion of Nirvana has a moral content much rather than a metaphysical. To have done with slavery, it is necessary and it is sufficient to extirpate selfish desire. That must have been the constant theme of the earliest preachings.

At Mathura or elsewhere new-born Buddhism must very soon have come into contact with Brahmanic thought, and to defend itself against it it had to provide itself with anti-Brahmanic dogmas. It discovered that the denial of egoism is an *an-ātmatā* which denies the *ātman* of the pundits. It had to attempt to explain the structure of existences, about which it was at first content to say that they are pain through and through. It had to look for a physical theory of phenomena, the methodical dissociation of which would be equivalent to the attainment of salvation. The philosophy thus constructed was, needless to say, ascribed to the founder of the sect, and it was alleged that, to enjoy supreme illumination, the Sage of the Sakyas had performed a prodigious feat of speculation.

That metaphysical exploit is the famous argument of the twelve conditions (*nidāna*), which connects misery with ignorance by ten intermediate terms deemed to be necessary and to prove the case. In the Upanishads there are many arguments for the connecting of terms which are presented in the same fashion—a cascade of conditions governing each other in a certain order. Moreover, the idea of connecting suffering with ignorance is not without precedent in early Brahmanism. What is new is the demonstration of the theme by a piece of reasoning whose logical force is regarded as absolute.

Suffering (*duḥkha*), age (*jarā*), and death (*maraṇa*)—these are the state of facts, the starting-point of the intense reflection in which Buddha engaged. Why do we die? Because we are born (*jāti*, birth). Why are we born? Dying and being born are two alternative modes of being (*bhava*) or, better, coming into being. Why do we come into being? Because we feel a holding fast (*upādāna*) for what maintains

[1] *Brahma-nirvāṇa*, v. 24.

our existence. That is how the physical or psychic aggregates, (*skandha*) of which we are composed are maintained; for, having nothing substantial, our existence, as a mind or as a body, is nothing but instable groupings of phenomena. Why do we tend to appropriate external things to ourselves? Because we have a thirst (*trishṇa*) for life. Whence comes that desire? From the fact that, being endowed with feeling (*vedanā*), we seek pleasant sensations. Whence comes sensation? From a contact (*sparśa*) between our organs and objects, a contact between our six senses (the usual five plus *manas* or intellect) and six objective "fields of operation" (*āyatana*). How does this duality of organ and object come about? Because every individual is name and form (*nāmarūpa*), that is, composed of a subjective or conceptual element and another, objective or corporal. How are names and forms possible? By discrimination (*vijñāna*), which is at once the cognitive act and the principle capable of knowing. Whence does discrimination come? From residues of our past experience, which at the same time form anticipations of our future experience; these are the *saṃskāras*, a word which embraces what we in Europe call habit, memory, heredity, innate faculties, subconsciousness. And to what are these latent dispositions to be ascribed? To ignorance (*avidyā*). They come from the fact that we think that we are, a sovereign error, a moral and a metaphysical sin, whereas we merely become and there is nothing consistent or lasting in us. We suppose ourselves to be an *ātman*, an absolute, when we are steeped in relativity.

This laborious analysis of phenomena is full of obscurities for us Europeans, and is hardly less difficult for an Indian intelligence, for it took unparalleled concentration on the part of Buddha to make it and, besides, it can only appear decisive to a mind matured for complete understanding by having advanced through many lives. The historian of philosophy, less ready to be struck with wonder, sees in it a kind of sorites in which Indian logic is trying to take its first steps. But the argument is of immense importance in Buddhism. Working from the twelfth term to the first, it proves the misery of man; from the first to the twelfth, it reveals the sole means of salvation, it delivers by knowledge. Knowing how desire is kept alive, one knows how to destroy it, and pain with it. So in the night of the Illumination Buddha sits in the attitude of bliss, with the triumphant half-smile which the sculptors have glorified, and delights in meditating on the saving formula in both directions.

This theory of the "conditioned production" of phenomena (*pratītyasamutpāda*) appears in many different forms in the books, but it always establishes the connexion of suffering and ignorance. It always bears witness to a phenomenalism, a relativism, which remind the European of the doctrines of David Hume. The determination to exorcise substance, material or spiritual, and to admit no causes except antecedences in relation to sequences, is certainly as resolute in this system as in that of the illustrious Scot. Bent on following a "middle path" between realism and nihilistic dogmatism, Buddha refuses to recognize or to deny an absolute of any sort, thing or soul. In his eyes our existence is made up of assemblings, always instable, of phenomena which unceasingly appear and unceasingly vanish, and these are of five kinds—material forms (*rūpa*), pleasant or painful impressions (*vedanā*), perceptions (*saṃjñā*), discriminations (*vijñāna*), and tendencies (*saṃskāra*).

Thorny discussion at once arose, to reconcile with the essential morality of Buddhism this philosophy, which perhaps goes beyond the object for which it was constructed. If there is no substantial human soul, what is it that transmigrates from body to body, from life to life? Is it a "relative", not absolute, soul? Or a stock of *karman*, instable by definition, since it both disappears by exhaustion and forms again by action? Or, again, the effect of the last thought, which would thus set some future existence going beyond death? All these solutions, and others too, were attempted in their time. Early Buddhism purposely abstains from taking a stand on such questions, which are idle because they have nothing to do with human conduct. A decided agnosticism in respect of ontology counterbalances the equally decided intellectualism which bases deliverance on a certain knowledge, that of the conditions of slavery.

CHAPTER III

Brahmanism as Hinduism, from the Fifth Century B.C. to the First Century of Our Era. The Religions of Vishnu and Siva

THE Brahmanic literature of the ages when the Buddhist canon was constituted no longer presents the crude simple-minded realism which prevailed in the Brāhmaṇas and the two oldest Upanishads. It assumes a completely classical character, like the Sanskrit in which its inspiration is expressed. The religious or philosophic thought which it contains presents a very great variety of aspects, reflecting an immense enrichment of culture. Although kept at arms' length as being heterodox, the Jain and Buddhist sects contributed to this renewal of the spirit. In orthodoxy itself they sowed the belief in transmigration and a notion of *karman* similar to their own, and they compelled orthodoxy to regard the problem of deliverance as one of the first importance.

Not only Buddhism had an effect, if only by contrast, on Brahmanic thought. A factor which had hitherto lain outside classicism won its place there, and a highly important place—the popular religions. While the *Brāhmaṇas* were especially the production of the Brahmans and the epics of the Kshatriyas, the masses, a mixture of Vaiśyas, Śūdras, and non-Aryan peoples, had, if not their literature, at least their beliefs, cults, and traditions. All these were elements which, in an adapted form, came to be incorporated in a syncretic type of Brahmanism to which, in our day, the name of Hinduism has been given.

The Upanishads of medium antiquity on the one hand, and the *Mahābhārata* on the other, furnish the chief documents for this orthodox eclecticism. But similar themes are to be found in Manu (his *Dharmaśāstra*), the *Rāmāyaṇa*, and the older parts of the Puranic books.

The ancient theory of sacrifice becomes less and less important in the Upanishads. As a result of the curious belief that the sacrifice of sacrifices is knowledge, the science of ritual tends to be eclipsed by a gnosis (*jñāna*, or *prājña*, which presently becomes *prajñā*). A beginning was made when it was admitted that intelligence is a means of salvation, because it distinguishes between the relative and the absolute, appearance and reality. This went parallel with Buddhist intellectualism. But eventually everything, relative and absolute, was regarded as being inside the function of knowing, and so a gnosis was formed, just as that of Syrian Alexandrianism proceeded from the Peripatetic postulate that *νοῦς* is, in a fashion, all reality.

The classificatory type of intelligibility of early Brahmanism was gradually replaced by an evolutionary conception connecting the various cosmic or intellectual principles by one same dynamism. The whole theory of nature in the Sāṃkhya system was to be stamped with this evolutionism. Nothing could be more contrary to the static hierarchies of the Brāhmaṇas and the materialism, often atomistic, of early physics. And, just as in the West the hypothesis of evolution owed its success to the importance attached to the idea of life, so in India the same interest produced a series of pantheisms, always renewed, and that among many more non-pantheistic elements than have usually been supposed, since Deussen's time, to have existed in India.

In these pantheisms, which are haphazard rather than systematic, orthodoxy found a means of defence against Jain or Buddhist heresy. The principle of those heresies was a pessimistic valuation of life, in the assertion that a man's act breeds a sort of original sin. Against these gloomy beliefs orthodox esotericism produced the serenity of a philosophy according to which the relative differs from the absolute only as appearance differs from reality, and therefore, provided that we substitute knowledge for ignorance, deliverance cannot escape us, since we were never enslaved except in appearance. But we must bear in mind that the heterodox and the orthodox did not take their stand on the same ground, and that therefore we cannot dismiss them as arriving at opposite conclusions. The Buddhists will have nothing to do with ontology, and indeed deny the absolute; the Brahmans of the Upanishads, in their passion for the absolute, base life and knowledge alike on being. In German terms, the former are *Erkenntnistheoretiker*, the latter *Dogmatiker*.

The already Hinduized Brahmanism which flourished at the beginning of the Christian era differed from the old in that it was no longer confined to an exposition of the Vedas. That task henceforward fell to a special discipline named Mīmāṃsā, which we shall discuss later. The new orthodoxy was wholly penetrated by the influence of a strange asceticism, Yoga, which had not yet become a philosophic system, but claimed to obtain the realization of the absolute by a certain manner of living. Since organic life is explained by the circulation of the breath, certain breathing-exercises are the key to salvation. This is how: to govern inhalation and exhalation enables one to concentrate the mind, both by emptying it of the content which it has received from sensuous experience and by making the voluntary attention supple. When the mind is concentrated and, in the words of the metaphor, has become dense and hard and cutting like the diamond, it breaks loose from physiological conditions and so finds itself as it should be, omniscient, or omnipotent, free, and able to create at will—in short, the possessor of efficiences which to the vulgar seem to be supernatural powers. Although this contraction of the thinking principle had, in principle, nothing in common with Vedic science (*vidyā*), every later Indian conception of knowledge bore the indelible mark of Yoga, insomuch as knowledge will always imply, in the most realistic sense, a capacity of realization.

Theism. Siva, Vishnu, Krishna, Rama

The combination of Vedic tradition and Yoga led, in the middle Upanishads, to the sacrificial fire and the breath being compared and even identified. So individual morality became, properly, a sacrifice, and the physical theory of the cosmos became an ascesis. This was quite new and revolutionary. Hitherto the notion of salvation had had no meaning save for the individual consciousness; henceforth it would have one even for the universal consciousness. Great Purusha, the cosmic giant whose limbs are the parts of the world, becomes not only a blissful, serene *ātman*, but a great Yogin, the guide and support of souls struggling for deliverance.

He transcends nature (*prakṛiti*) and his spiritual spontaneity, like the human soul, can transcend biological functions. The absolute does not merely exist; it enters into sympathy with human endeavours. Thereby the way is opened to two things characteristic of Hinduism—the belief in a metaphysical first principle periodically becoming incarnate in saviours of the human race, and a pious devotion which connects the relative with the absolute not by knowledge but by sentiment. That which is the universal substance, the universal origin, the universal end, takes on the character of a God, in the Jewish and Christian sense of the word. The neuter *brahman* is transformed into the masculine Brahmā, and into more concrete divine forms, having a personality. The religious bond tends to become an intimacy between soul and soul, instead of being a reabsorption of the individual in the unindividualized.

It was under the banner of Yoga that these changes took place. The ascetic practising that discipline, the *yukta*, was in the strict and original sense " joined " with himself by the mastery of his vital functions, as a wheel is joined by the insertion of the spokes in the nave. A secondary and later sense is " united ", not to oneself but to a higher principle; in other words, in communion with God. From then onwards, it is by " union " with God that the soul acquires its " unity "; it aims not so much at realizing the absolute as at reaching it and fusing with it. Yoga becomes theistic, and towards theism it gradually draws, if not the philosophies, at least the religions.

The great ascetic god is Siva, in whom his worshippers recognize a " lord ", Isvara. His origins are partly Vedic, for he is derived from Rudra, who slays cattle but also preserves them, a principle of destruction capable of deserving his euphemistic names of the Benevolent (Siva). *Bhakti*, the confident worship which is henceforward a means of salvation in Yoga, is paid to Siva (as we find in the *Śvetāśvatara Upanishad*) before being addressed to Vasudeva Krishna, as in the *Gītā*. While mysticism, using its favourite pastoral symbol, attaches the worshipper to his divine master as a herd (*paśu*) to its herdsman (*pati*), popular eroticism is chiefly alive to the generative aspect of God, whom it adores in the form of the phallus (*linga*). We must accustom ourselves to contrasts like this when we examine vast religious monuments to which very primitive and more civilized societies have contributed. The classical figure of Siva is perhaps the result of a combination of a native, non-Aryan god of natural fruitfulness and the Vedic Rudra. The Indo-Greek period, which certainly did not last so long as the Hindu mixture, reveals a confusion between Siva and Dionysos. This first god who was God, Mahādeva, in contrast to the many divine figures of India who are merely limited aspects of nature, may for that very reason be represented at the same time as an obscene Priapus and as an austere Digambara. The dancing Siva, who creates magic by his rhythm, stands half-way between the simple natural energies symbolized by his wives and the severe purity of a transcendent spirit.

By his original destructive function and by his secondary form as a rigid ascetic, Siva represents the terrible aspect of godhead. Its lovable aspect is embodied in various demigods who are gradually combined in a single figure, that of another Mahādeva, Vishnu. Kshatriya inspiration predominates in the legends of this cycle, which have their scene in the north-west of Hindustan, at any rate further west than the countries where the Jains and Buddhists made their appearance.

Panini, who probably lived in the fifth century B.C., mentions Vāsudevakas and Arjunakas, sects worshipping the heroes Vasudeva and Arjuna, whose deeds are celebrated in the *Mahābhārata*. In the first years of the second century B.C. the column of Besnagar, in the south of Gwalior, was erected in honour of the same Vasudeva by the Greek Heliodoros of Takshasila, who had been sent to that country as ambassador. At Ghasundi in Udaipur, an inscription of about 150 B.C. mentions an edifice built in honour of Samkarshana and Vasudeva, two heroes, the former of whom was the elder brother of the latter. Now, Vasudeva is simply another name of Krishna. About the same date, Patañjali in his *Mahābhāshya* quotes a line which runs, " May the power of Krishna, accompanied by Samkarshana, increase ! " So there was in the second century and earlier a cult of demigods, whose worshippers, according to the monuments of Besnagar and Ghasundi, declared themselves Bhāgavatas, sectaries of the

Bhagavat, which term is translated the Lord, or the Adorable, or the Blessed.

An older name than Vasudeva applied to the same person is Narayana. It is the name by which the *Śatapatha Brāhmaṇa* describes the supreme soul, Purusha, as the common foundation of men (*nara*). To give it to Vasudeva is to make an absolute of him.

The name of Krishna is associated with many legends. One of the Vedic *ṛishis*, who is supposed to have "seen" the seventy-fourth hymn of the eighth book, bears this name, which was passed on to a Brahman *gotra* mentioned by Panini (iv, 1, 99) as Karshnayana. The Krishna who is the hero of the *Mahābhārata* must have been derived from this source. In the course of the epic, he develops from a human being into a god who is both immanent and transcendent. Even more explicitly than the *Bhagavadgītā*, or *Gītā* of the Blessed, the *Harivaṃśa* makes Krishna a god who has become man. But even that work (3808) shows him refusing to join in the worship of the Vedic god Indra and crying, "We are herdsmen roving in the woods. Our gods are the kine, the mountains, and the forests!" Is it an Aryan herdsman or a Dravidian cattle-owner speaking? The question cannot be answered, but one is the more tempted to ask it because *kṛishṇa* means "black", perhaps in the sense of "negro". Does the magnanimous hero of the epic belong to the same race as the "white" Arjuna? In any case, there seems to be no connexion between the account of Krishna taking part in the war as the ally of the five Pandavas and other stories of how Krishna Vasudeva was saved from Kamsa, the tyrant of Mathura, at his birth, was reared by the herdsmen and loved by the herd-girls, and finally triumphed and delivered his city. The pretty-pretty "childhoods" and the tales of the amorous youth of the young cowherd (*gopāla*) seem to belong to an independent cycle alien to the Kshatriya inspiration of the epic and later than the beginning of our era.

We are reduced to conjecture when we try to determine how this confused, involved worship of Krishna became connected with the tradition of Vishnu. The *Taittirīya Āraṇyaka* (x, 1, 6) regards Narayana, Vasudeva, and Vishnu as three phases of the same god. Already the Brāhmaṇas give the first place among the gods to him who conquered the three parts of the world by his Three Steps and sits in the ultimate abode (*paramam padam*). The Purāṇas make him the supreme spirit. On the way he as it were absorbed the demigods of the popular cults and the heroes of the feudal romances. No doubt the Brahmans hoped to safeguard orthodoxy by annexing many widespread myths to the tradition of a Vedic deity, the solar Vishnu who reigns in the height of the heavens.

Rama is a later subject of legend than Krishna. According to the *Harivaṃśa* he is his brother; in the epic of which he is the central figure, the *Rāmāyaṇa*, he is the son of Vishnu, although in the natural order his father is Dasaratha, King of Ayodhya. For his strength, his courage, his generosity, and his love of his wife Sita, he is one of the dearest ideals of the Indian soul. As the slayer of Ravana, the hideous despot of Ceylon, he belongs to the line of giant-killers. The first and last books of the *Rāmāyaṇa*, which were obviously added later as a framework to the legend of the hero, present him as a god come down to earth.

The Avatars. Eclecticism

This phrase, "come down to earth," which is so familiar in our language, expresses fairly exactly the notion of the *avatāra* or "descent" by which Vishnu is believed by India to partake of humanity at intervals. This notion is like the belief that there is a Jina or a Buddha especially connected with each cosmic age. Prophets and Messiahs are not the monopoly of the Hebrews, nor even of the Semites. This type of semi-divine man first appeared in Iran, with its Assyro-Babylonian inheritance, if only in the person of Zoroaster, and Zoroaster's example had a very wide and profound influence on India and on Central Asia. The Indian fashion of justifying the providential saviour, the shower of the way, is to present him as brought forth by the law of universal *karman*, not to make him an emissary of God or the announcer of a future order.

The most important avatar is that of Krishna, who has even been compared to the Judæo-Greek Christ on the strength of an apparent likeness of name. The only fundamental similarity is the immense love underlying the two cults. The *Bhagavadgītā* has spoken to men's hearts no less than the *Imitation of Christ.* The value of an act does not lie in its content, but in the intention of pleasing Bhagavat. If every act, every thought, makes Bhagavat its end, salvation is certain. It does not matter if the Kshatriya comes to it by his own function of warlike violence, or the Brahman by his sacrifice and science, or the slave by his obedience; all *dharmas* are of equal worth, provided that they are accomplished in order to please Him who is the origin and end of everything. To see God in everything and everything in God is to know. To refer every action to Him alone is, in full confidence, to worship.

Yet it hardly seems that we should see here any actual contact between Christians and Hindus. It is true that the story of *Barlaam and Josaphat* was introduced into Buddhism. Perhaps we shall never know how much truth there is in the tradition that the apostle Thomas evangelized the kingdom of Gondophares and won the martyr's crown at Mailapur. It is possible that Christians, especially Nestorians, went through Serindia at an early date, but there seems to be no reason to follow Grierson in ascribing the importation of pious devotion to Christian colonies established in the southern ports, when we have evidence that Bhāgavatas worshipped Vasudeva, or Narayana, or Krishna, in the north-west about two hundred years before the Christian era. Although *bhakti* forms no part of early Brahmanism it seems to be a purely native phenomenon.

In allusion to a conception of the fifth century after Christ, it has been said, and too frequently, that Hinduism worships three divine forms regarded as equal—the *trimūrti* of Brahma, Vishnu, and Siva. Brahma seems a very pale figure beside the two great gods of the rival religions, Vishnuism and Sivaism. The ultimate prototype of the Brahman caste remains a faint abstraction by the side of deities so rich in content that their inconsistency misleads one and so laden with social efficacy that they serve as rallying points to two sects.

Apart from Brahmanic orthodoxy, which in any case is a system rather than a reality, the religious life of India resides in the sect, a free group in which individuals are united without any consideration of caste or profession. This community is animated by a religious tradition, a social conviction, and it may split up *ad infinitum* according to the developments of the faith or local circumstances. The same process of disintegration which we have seen in the caste reappears in the sect. The followers of Siva or Vishnu, far from forming two solid, homogeneous bodies, break up into a multitude of groups. Nor is there anything to prevent one man from belonging to several groups. Thus the same men were often patrons of the Jains and of the Buddhists, or adherents of a religion of Vishnu and of one of Siva. What prevents Brahmanism from being a sect is its adherence to the dogma of caste; but the Hinduism which is its successor is a chaos of sects, vaguely dominated by the heritage of the Vedic religion, which is the monopoly of the Brahmans. A man can quite well belong to a caste and to one or more sects, although many sections of the people belong to sects without having any caste.

It is a mistake, then, to look for unity in the beliefs or manners of the worshippers of Vishnu in his many avatars and of Siva. For like reasons, we must not be surprised at the attempts made to bring the two great Hindu cults together, to make them parallel and to some extent equivalent. The determination to harmonize them is clearly seen in many passages in the *Mahābhārata*, whereas the two inspirations often divide the Upanishads between them. The allegory is transparent in the *Harivaṃśa* (*adh.* 184–190), where it describes a fight between Siva and Vishnu, and terminates the episode by bringing in Brahma, who reconciles them, declaring their fundamental unity. Unity of dogmatic syncretism going with infinite diversity of concrete life is altogether normal in India.

The Philosophy of the Epics

The philosophic attitudes covered by the general name of Brahmanism at the period which we are considering are extremely varied, like the religions; indeed, religion and philosophy can hardly be distinguished from each other, and are both a matter of sect. A philosophy, like a religion, is a collective tradition regarding salvation and the pursuit of it. The *Mahābhārata* gives a very lively picture of the conceptions, of various degrees of orthodoxy, prevailing in the last centuries before our era.

The old sacrificial dogma is eclipsed by bold speculations for which the way has been prepared by the irreligion of the materialists, the sophists, the sceptics. Most of the reflections which will serve as a basis to the various systems which will take shape later already appear in an atomism which anticipates the Vaiśeshika, in an illusionism which forms a pre-Vedānta, and in a Sāṃkhya and a Yoga which are already very explicit. These last two systems have not yet their classical structure; they are presented as equivalent, the Sāṃkhya giving in theory the same teaching as Yoga in practice. Such as they are, they dominate all philosophic thought.

The countless translators of the *Bhagavadgītā* have made the West familiar with the notion of an "epic" Sāṃkhya—that is, such as it is expressed in the epics. As its name indicates, it is a doctrine of the enumeration of the ontological principles in order of dignity. At the bottom is *manas*, the empirical mind or *κοινὴ αἴσθησις* which collects sensible data; above that is *ahaṃkāra*, the function of the self, the "I think"; higher still is *buddhi*, which judges and decides. These three faculties belong to nature (*prakṛiti* or *pradhāṇam*); their operation belongs to the material order and they are governed by an evolution. Pure spirit, Purusha, dominates them. In the classical Sāṃkhya it will float in absolute transcendence (*kaivalyam*, isolation) outside and above matter. At the present stage, although transcendent, it is also immanent, and the *guṇas* or qualities of nature are regarded as being at the same time its qualities. It puts them on, it sets them working; cosmic reality is its play, its manifestation, as it were its creation, not a pure illusion as in the Vedānta or part of a wholly secondary and opposite principle, like the nature of the later Sāṃkhya.

The epic Yoga is also different from the classical Yoga. The meaning of the word is bewilderingly elastic; every practice or method is called a *yoga*. In the strictest sense, it means breathing exercises and concentration of thought, after its diversities and fluctuations have been checked.

So, in practice, one attains to that pure spirituality which the Sāṃkhya defines as a detached Purusha, abstracted from all contamination by nature. Nevertheless, the Sāṃkhya and Yoga must have been very different in their prehistory, for it to be so necessary for the syncretic epics to declare that they are fundamentally the same. Nothing could be less theistic than the Sāṃkhya as finally established, in which the transcendence of spirit is asserted in the most uncompromising fashion—nothing, except primitive Yoga, which tried to realize the absolute by doing violence to human nature without any divine assistance. Yet the characteristic feature of the Sāṃkhya and Yoga of the epics is that they agree in a devout theism ; such was the influence of Krishnaite sentimentality in that period.

The philosophies which most frankly bear the mark of the age are the Sivaite Pāśupata and the Vishnuite Pañcharātra or Bhāgavata. According to the former, the effect, which is the world, must be distinguished from the cause, which is at once the Lord and nature (*pradhānam*). According to the latter, the supreme spirit, decked out in its qualities (*guṇa*) and its forms extended in space (*vyūha*), supports and sustains all things. These metaphysical systems would remind us of certain pantheisms of the European Renaissance, if their dogmas were not submerged in a confused *bhakti*.

The Transformation of Orthodoxy

The decline of Brahmanic orthodoxy is manifest in every respect. The less the Vedas are understood, the more they are replaced by gnosis or devotion. Jainism and Buddhism are reprobated, but their substitution of the eschatological problem for the ontological is adopted. Since the popular religions cannot be excluded, they are accepted, being given a faintly Vedic aspect either by the device of the avatars or by means of imaginary lines of *ṛishis*, pundits, and *gurus*, traced back to the mythical days of infallible certainties, the Golden Age. The more that strange novelties are consecrated as authentic, the more " Purāṇas " are composed, in which the new is linked to the old by quite unfounded " ancient histories ".

Without a doubt, a place would have been found in

orthodoxy even for the Buddhists, if they had not scorned caste and disputed the divinity of the Brahman. The epics give the impression of a hotch-potch, in which all the different elements of a chaotic civilization have been heaped together, to be saved when invaders, Parthian or Saka, entered the country. So too the Brahmans, to preserve their pre-eminent position, were compelled to set the stamp of orthodoxy wholesale on many religious or social elements which were as alien to the matter of the Brāhmaṇas as to that of the Vedas. That simply means that, as Brahmanism came to cover, in addition to the content of the Brāhmaṇas, more and more " Hindu " elements, it was more and more reduced to a form—we may even say a label.

CHAPTER IV

The Great Vehicle

FROM the first century before Christ to the sixth century after, the great initiative in Indian speculation was taken by Buddhism, which gives proof of a marvellous effort in philosophy. The movement was led by a comparatively new Buddhism which, about the second century after Christ, came to be distinguished from the old by the name of Mahāyāna, the Great Vehicle, as opposed to Hīnayāna, the Small Vehicle. These two forms of Buddhist thought would react one on the other until, the heresy being eliminated from India itself, the Small Vehicle was confined chiefly to Ceylon and certain colonies (Siam, Burma), while the Great conquered Central Asia and the Far East.

Political and social events contributed to this change in teaching. It was not by mere chance that the north-west played a chief part in the advent of the Mahāyāna. We know that this was the side by which foreign elements could always enter the country easily, and there was a connexion between the appearance of the new Buddhism and the assembling of a great council in Kashmir under Kanishka. Greek, Semitic, Iranian, and perhaps Chinese influences created from Sind to the Pamir a peculiar environment, into which would come a Buddhism which had just assimilated on the upper Ganges what it could borrow from Brahmanic classicism.

At the very time when the *dharma* of the sect was becoming less " Indian " because more universal in its appeal, it was becoming more " Hindu ". The contradiction is only apparent. The popular religions, which we vaguely classify under the heads of Sivaism and Vishnuism, were tending to creep into the dogma of Buddha as into that of the Brahmans, and we have seen the part played by these same north-western districts in the formation of the cult, for instance, of Vasudeva. Vishnu, a sun-god, had close connexions with the metaphysics of light which had always flourished in Iran. Amitabha would be, as it were, a light-god, and Senart has shown very convincingly to what extent the legend of Buddha was affected by a solar myth. The Great Vehicle was not only to encourage abstract ontology; it would welcome a mass of fables and superstitions of the Hindu admixture in all their confusion. In short, Buddhism would have its Tantras and, in a fashion, its Purāṇas. We have only to compare the biography of Sakyamuni given in the *Lalitavistara* and the much more rationalistic (but not necessarily more historical) life contained in the Suttas.

In different conditions and environments, speculative interest shifts. As the age in which the Master had preached receded into the distance, the community sought to determine the Law less by his direct example or teaching than by abstract thought about fundamental principles. So a "Basket" of *Abhidharma* appeared and grew on, the top of those of the Sūtras and Discipline. *Abhidharma*, a refinement on *dharma*, increased steadily until its preponderance in theory was consecrated by the Mahāyāna. In other words, the moral teaching of the early ages dropped into the background and the front place was taken by metaphysics.

Many have observed, following Sylvain Lévi, that the notion of holiness had changed as the Mahāyāna came into being. Personal deliverance was no longer regarded as a sufficient ideal. In its unending war on selfishness, an effort which it afterwards made its whole purpose, Buddhism here took another step forwards. Individual salvation has no absolute value unless it contributes to universal salvation. The Nirvana of the Arhat is to be condemned as a shameful exaltation of self, if it is merely a cowardly flight by which an individual escapes from misery. But it represents the end of ends if it confers on him who enjoys it an infinite capacity to shed grace and blessings on the whole of nature. Like Christianity, Nestorianism, and Manichaeism, this Buddhism, which is Asiatic rather than Indian, stands for a zeal for all mankind, which, by the laws of transmigration, is one with the whole world.

The methods employed by the new forms of speculation have attracted less attention than their dogmatic content. They, too, aimed at obtaining results of universal effect. There are two chief methods—a certain dialectic, and a sort of concentration inspired by Yoga.

Dialectic. Nagarjuna

From its beginnings Buddhist preaching was akin to the methods of reasoning employed by the dialecticians of whom we find echoes in many epic works, the best known of whom is the Nagasena of the *Milinda-pañha.* In order to convince their hearers, both for the propagation of the Law and for the refutation of Vedic tradition, the early Buddhists needed a certain dexterity in argument. It is agreed that the Law is not established by authority, nor by revelation, but by understanding. The backbone of their logic, in which the methods of the apologist and of the rhetor are combined, is the application, indefinitely extended, of those chains of conditions of which we have seen a short example in the famous argument of the Twelve Causes. The logic of the Buddhists discusses facts or conditions, establishes or contests sequences.

In the first century B.C. the wordy dialectic of the Suttas gave place to a philosophic literature which very skilfully argues the relativity of the *dharmas*, that is, of the factors of existence or psychic phenomena. But this relativity is not interpreted, as in the previous teaching, in a dogmatic, constructive fashion, in mutually connected determinations, which taken all together make up knowledge. It is now interpreted in a negative, nihilistic fashion, to lead to the everlasting contention that a notion is not a notion and a sign is not a sign. There is no permanent or constitutive character in any notion—for example, in those of self, being, and phenomenon, nor yet in those of not-self, not-being, and not-phenomenon. Therefore all ideas are of equal value in complete insignificance and emptiness. Everything is empty, characterless, indifferent (*śūnya, animitta, apraṇihita*). A huge mass of literature repeats over and over again that to perceive this is the Supreme Knowledge, *Prajñā Pāramitā.* Such is the logic set up as a " diamond-cleaver ", Vajrachchhedikā, to pulverize the reality, even phenomenal, of phenomena. Its aim is exactly opposite to that of the Vaiśeshika system in Brahmanism, which sought for specific determinations, or to that of our own classical metaphysicians, who recognized and determined " essences " as the foundation of " existences ". Among ourselves, it is true, many have thought that there is a point at which science should halt and the field be left to faith, but Buddhism could hardly allow this, for in India faith is never considered in contrast to intelligence, and for Buddha in particular true salvation is not possible except by comprehension. In this case what delivers a man is the conviction of universal vacuity.

One of the two chief schools of the Mahāyāna returned to this negative dogmatism in Southern India between A.D. 150 and A.D. 250. It claimed to follow the "Middle Way", the *madhyama pratipad* which, in early Buddhism, consisted in refusing to affirm and deny and in deliberately clinging to ontological agnosticism. To show that it proceeded from that inspiration, it declared itself the Mādhyamika on the ground that it said neither "Yes" nor "No". None the less, *śūnyatā*, the argument of universal vacuity, was an invention of the Great Vehicle, for the Small Vehicle confined itself to treating "Yes" and "No" as equal and maintained the reality of phenomena, which was expressly denied by the new dialecticians, Nagarjuna and his disciple Aryadeva. These last go so far as to declare that even the notions of slavery and deliverance are futile, and their definition of salvation consists in the paradoxical equation of *saṃsāra* and *nirvāṇa*.

Concentration. Asvaghosha, Asanga, Vasubandhu

The other direction to which the Great Vehicle turns is that of Yoga. Those who followed it set out to behave as Yogins, and were accordingly called Yogāchāras. They founded a method by which the asceticism of the Yogins was carried beyond regulation of the vital functions into spiritual concentration. Control of the breathing by itself gives a mastery over the attention. What will be given by an attention which aims not at the extension of knowing, as in European psychology, but at the simplification of the mind? For we must not forget that the point from which the Yogin starts is the stopping of empirical and utilitarian thought (*chittavṛittinirodha*). Attention of this kind is an attempt to change the psychic energy into a kind of perforator, and the more concentrated and fined down it is the sharper and more piercing it will be. By a process of boring, one will come down to deeper and deeper strata of the universal spirituality, freeing oneself from the contingences of space and time. That is what Yoga gave, when transposed into a metaphysical method—power rather than knowledge, and a penetration and so a utilization of the cosmic life to make it produce more harmonious worlds, in which the mind no longer feels itself a slave, but free and a master. This made immense philosophic developments possible, thanks to an action which in this case does not enslave but, on the contrary, frees and creates. For Europeans this is an appalling conception of metaphysics. Only the most lyrical and futuristic of the German Romantics have come near it, such as Novalis, who, turning round on modern rationalism, says that the novel is truer than history, and poetry truer than science, and would deliberately turn philosophy into magic.

After the beginning of the Christian era the history of thought is marked by a few names of men who are not wholly mythical. The period in which the Great Vehicle took shape is dominated by Asvaghosha, who was a contemporary of Kanishka and took a leading part in the council which met in that emperor's reign. He is one of the most representative figures of India, a musician, a founder of Sanskrit poetry, and a Brahman born who became a Father of the Buddhist Church. He was certainly not the author of all the works ascribed to him, but at least some of them, such as the *Mahāyānaśraddhotpāda*, the "Awakening of the Mahayanist Faith", are connected with his influence. If he were only the author of the *Buddha-charita* and the *Sūtrālaṃkāra* it would be enough for him to have left a deep and permanent mark.

The *Sūtrālaṃkāra* shows a new spirit—the intention of giving literary form to the matter of the Buddhist Sūtras in order to spread the Buddhist faith among the Brahman *élite*. The *Buddha-charita* is a biography of the Blessed One in the form of a philosophic poem. In both works the themes of the Great Vehicle appear. They are presented much more systematically in the *Mahāyānaśraddhotpāda*, which does not seem to have been composed before the third century. Deepening the notion of an eternal Buddha, as a metaphysical reality underlying phenomena, this work introduces an ontology into Buddhism, a quiddity (*tathatā*), the place in which existences succeed one another (*dharmadhātu*) and the womb of providential beings, the saviours of the world (*tathāgatagarbha*). This *Urgrund* or *Weltseele* contains, as the "containing consciousness" (*ālayavijñāna*), the germs whose developments are the *karman* of the many minds. We must regard this metaphysical theory as a Buddhism adapted to the Brahmanic doctrine of the absolute, just as the works authentically ascribed to Asvaghosha reveal a desire to make the Law of Buddha intelligible and acceptable to minds whose education is traditional. All the same, the author of the *Vajrasūchi*, who may be Asvaghosha himself, declares that one is a Brahman by wisdom, not by birth. Everything in his works, genuine or supposed, tends to bring orthodox and heterodox together.

In the fourth and fifth centuries, in Gandhara, a region which had been Hellenized and was still subject to Iranian influence, the Yogāchāra doctrine spread. Its chief exponent was Asanga, the founder of a philosophic movement as powerful and of as widespread influence as that of Plato and Aristotle. The idealism introduced by his *Mahāyānasūtrālaṃkāra* (a title inspired by the work of Asvaghosha), his *Dharmādharmatāvibhanga*, his *Uttara-tantra*, and his *Saptadaśabhūmi* not only took a predominant place in the Great Vehicle, but provoked considerable reaction on the part of Brahmanism and conquered China and Japan. Transforming the asceticism of Yoga into a spiritualistic dialectic with infinite possibilities, he regards liberation as a progressive conquest of "lands" (*bhūmi*), as a series of approximations to absolute Mind, coming closer and closer to it. This metaphysical flight starts from the statement that every phenomenon (*dharma*) exists only as an operation of thought (*vijñaptimātra*). This argument was popularized in various works by his brother Vasubandhu, once he was converted to the Mahāyāna by Asanga. Vasubandhu is not so original, but he played an extremely important part, for as an adherent of the Small Vehicle and afterwards as a preacher of the Great he composed many treatises which became classics. The best known are the *Abhidharmakośa*, a complete account of the Hīnayāna philosophy, and the Mahayanistic *Viṃśikā* and *Triṃśikā*, which are demonstrations of absolute idealism.

The Sects

The new Buddhism and the old contended in an extremely confused rivalry. The Great and Small Vehicles embraced a swarm of sects, the enumeration of which would take long and would be intelligible only if their history could be outlined. We are far from being able to do that. The list varies not only according to the period but according to the school. The tangle cannot be straightened out until the various canons have been methodically cleared up.

The Mahāsāṃghikas, who believe in the Great Community, that is, in the competence of both clerics and laymen, represent a schism which has been imputed to each of the three councils of tradition, those of Rajagriha, Vaisali, and Pataliputra. They are opposed to the Sthaviras, the Elders, who trace their tradition back to Buddha's own teaching. They belong to Eastern India.

The Sarvāstivādins of Mathura and the Mūlasarvāstivādins of Kashmir are two varieties of one sect, which prevailed in the north for centuries, whereas the Sthaviras were strong in the south and Ceylon. The Kashmir branch call themselves " genuinely, thoroughly " (*mūla*) Sarvāstivādins, and so admit that they sprang later from the original stock. Being exposed to Western influences, they contributed greatly to the Mahāyāna.

When we add to this list the Sammitīyas scattered about the country, we have the four chief schools which dominated the eighteen sects described by the Chinese pilgrim I-tsing in 692. They have their traditional books, their favourite patriarchs, and their own views on discipline and dogma. With the development of *abhidharma,* divergences of opinion increased. Thus the *Vibhāshā,* the commentary on *abhidharma* undertaken at the time of Kanishka's council, gave rise to the Vaibhāshika school, who are chiefly Kashmiris. A masterly commentary on their doctrine is given in the *Abhidharmakośa* of Vasubandhu, admirably translated by L. de la Vallée-Poussin. The Vaibhāshikas are opposed by the Sautrāntikas, a sect founded by Kumaralabdha in the second century, who are more faithful to the spirit of the Sūtras.

Apart from questions of discipline (*vinaya*) these schools differ in giving a more or less phenomenistic interpretation of the *dharmas* (varieties of existence or facts of consciousness), and in their conception of Buddha. In consequence they have different notions of Nirvana.

The New Metaphysics

The general postulate which distinguishes a Buddhist from a Brahmanic doctrine is the denial of all substantiality (*an-ātmatā*), both of corporeal things and of mind. There are, therefore, only incohesive phenomena, incessantly forming or disappearing, governed by the law of causality, or rather by a universal relativity. This philosophy excels in discouraging desire, since nothing exists in the absolute sense of the word, and egoism, since the ego exists neither in itself nor by itself. But it perhaps goes too far, for the very theory of *karman* requires that a certain continuity should connect the successive phases of a consciousness in one same life and through successive lives; one must allow some sort of a soul, if not substantial, at least phenomenal. That being granted, certain theories, realistic in different degrees, of existence and perception can be conceived. The Pudgalavādins allow a certain reality of the individual (*pudgala*) as an aggregate of phenomena. Almost all the Hīnayāna is atomistic; not that it believes in substantial atoms like those of Democritus or Epicurus, but it believes in relative atoms, groups of intermittent forces. So, too, there are many shades of idealism or realism in the existence allowed to the *dharmas*, lists and classifications of which appear in the Hinayanist treatises on *abhidharma*. While the Sarvāstivādins proclaim a "complete realism", the Vibhajyavādins, "discriminalists," say that nothing exists except the present and so much of the past as has not yet fructified; the rest of the past and the future do not exist at all. With regard to perception, the Vaibhāshikas stand for realism, whereas the Sautrāntikas hold that outward objects are inferred, not apprehended. These fragmentary indications are enough to show to what intricacies and infinite shades of dogma the proliferation of sects gave rise, and how far Buddhist philosophy always was from being homogeneous.

Between the pseudo-historical Buddha, the human sage who discovers and reveals the secret of existences, and the Buddha of the Mahāyāna, ever coming closer to an ontological absolute like that of the Brahmans, there is a whole scale of " soteriologies ", which approximate in varying degree to the popular " theologies ". There was a " Docetism " of Buddha as there was of Jesus, Son of God, and the Sakyamuni who set the Wheel of the Law in motion was infected by the characteristics of Vishnu, the mover of the wheel of the sun. The *abhidharma* of the Small Vehicle assigns to the Blessed a function of universal salvation ; that of the Great Vehicle makes his thought the place of minds and the support of the cosmic order, and yet more—the instrument of a mighty magician. The advance from one of these notions to the next is effected in the theory of the Three Bodies (*trikāya*). According to the eminence of the disciple, as he is an Arhat or Śrāvaka, a Pratyekabuddha (a Buddha for himself, not a preacher, not yet devoted to the good of the world), or a Saṃyaksambuddha (completely illuminated), the Master expresses himself in three degrees of the same teaching. In these, to use the phrase of Malebranche, he makes himself participable to a variously adequate extent. These more or less subtle ways of preaching the Law (*dharma*) are equivalent to more or less subtle creations of phenomena (*dharma*) ; for deliverance would have no meaning without the production of these appearances which constitute the world. To preach and to create are two complementary aspects of the work of Buddhism. Thereby *saṃsāra* and *nirvāṇa* are intimately connected, like the two sides of one thing. He who saves at the same time deceives, and he who deceives saves. Fundamental truth being ineffable, all preaching is only an approximation, and therefore, at least to some extent, deceit. Nevertheless, the utterances of a Buddha, the *nirmāṇa* which corresponds to the *māyā* of Varuna and to the *yoga* of Krishna, are of value not only as phantasmal creation but as grace, since they guide creatures to their salvation. Nirmāṇakāya, Sambhogakāya, and Dharmakāya are three kinds of supreme truth or reality.

Mythology

The infinite multiplication of Saviours, consequent on the now abstract and ontological conception of Buddha, is a feature of the Great Vehicle. The Small Vehicle had been content to allow plurality of saints (*arhat*). Another consequence of the abstract character assumed by " Buddhaship " is the increasing importance of the notion of the " him whose nature is *bodhi* ", the *bodhisattva* who possesses illumination but not yet Nirvana, and therefore is acquiring the rarer and greater perfections while at the same time, being still, if one may say so, of this world, he radiates virtues and beneficences in it. Sakyamuni having attained to Nirvana five hundred years or more ago, the authors of the Mahāyāna conceived the notion of other beings, all embarked on the glorious road of final deliverance, and these became the chief patterns of the " career of a Buddha ". After a quasi-theism, the doctrine was invaded by a quasi-polytheism.

Eternal Buddhaship, what the Buddhas, fundamentally identical, have in common, became a sort of metaphysical essence lying behind everything, Adibuddha, the primal Buddha. This notion was developed into that of a number of particular Buddhas set alongside of Sakyamuni, such as Amitabha and Amitayus, Infinite Light and Infinite Duration, who are duplicates of each other, and Maitreya, the Buddha of the Future, who is at present still a *bodhisattva*. These august beings have each his paradise, to which their followers aspire just as in the old Brahmanism pious souls might aspire to the heaven or world of Brahma. Since the last thought at the moment of death decides the fate of the soul, devotion, with all the sentimentality and illogicality which it entails, takes the place of the intelligence of the unavoidable *karman*. Thus these forms of Buddhism are in great part new religions, less Indian than Iranian and Asiatic. The Far East took to them eagerly, for they required less adaptation to the Indian spirit than the intelligence of classical Buddhism. By the second half of the second century the Chinese had a translation of the *Sukhāvatīvyūha*, the basis of the worship of Amitabha.

Buddhist mythology is still further complicated by late

systematization. The concentration (*dhyāna*) of Adibuddha produces, as gnostic hypostases, five Buddhas of concentration (*dhyānibuddha*)—Vairochana, Akshobhya, Ratnasambhava, Amitabha, and Amoghasiddhi. The " human " Buddhas (*mānushibuddha*), who are simply the magical transposition of these into our world of illusion, are Krakuchchanda, Kanakamuni, Kasyapa, Sakyamuni, and Maitreya. In addition, from the meditation of the *dhyānibuddhas* emanate *dhyānibodhisattvas*, and in the same way there are *mānushibodhisattvas*. In this hierarchy of abstractions the spiritual position of Sakyamuni is as follows :—

Adibuddha = Tathata = Sunyata

Amitabha (dh.-bud.) — Sakyamuni (m.-bud.)

Avalokitesvara (dh.-bodh.) — Ananda (m.-bodh.)

The best commentary on this endless multiplication of abstractions is to be seen in the decorative sculpture which afterwards covered huge buildings with statuettes in thousands, each representing some blessed Saviour.

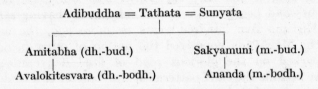

To understand the subjects represented by the plastic arts one needs some knowledge of these abstract myths. The *Mythologie asiatique illustrée* published in Paris in 1928 (Librairie de France), may be taken as a starting-point, but it must be remembered that all these types are derived from the original Greek models introduced in India by the Gandhara school. The decisive influence of that school, steadily advancing over the eastern half of Asia, has been demonstrated in masterly fashion by A. Foucher. Until Hellenizing artists interpreted Sakyamuni as a god of Olympus, he was never represented by an image. After that the Indo-Iranians working for the Kushans established the various characteristics by which, according to strictly laid-down canons (*pramāṇa*), a Vairochana, an Amitabha, and so on should be recognized. Then the Chinese, Japanese, Tibetans, and Khmers adapted these conventional types to their own spirit. The most astonishing of these transformations was that by which Chinese piety turned the *bodhisattva* Avalokitesvara, the charitable saint who refrained from passing into Nirvana in order to devote himself for ever to the salvation of others, into a Madonna named Kwan-yin.

On the notion of deliverance, lastly, the tenets of the Great Vehicle differ from those of the Small. The Hīnayāna, tempted at first to define deliverance as illumination which saves, had as it were duplicated the notion of Nirvana by saying that when the Master died his *karman* attained to "complete extinction", this final Nirvana being *parinirvāṇa*. When, in the Mahāyāna, Buddha becomes, by a sort of tacit return to Brahmanism, an eternal quasi-*ātman*, Nirvana is presented as a permanent characteristic of that absolute. Therefore to obtain deliverance is the same thing as to join Buddha, and that can be expressed in terms of piety as a ravishment in the divine love or in terms of eschatology as admission to a paradise, the Pure Land. Thus, instead of salvation consisting in casting off all sensibility by rejecting selfishness, as in the early ages of the Buddhist religion, it is contaminated by sentimental devotion and degenerates into a pursuit of happiness. Only the austere abstraction of the great metaphysical systems counterbalances the crass superstitions of the popular cults. In fact, the Mahāyāna ushered in a third Vehicle, the Vajrayāna, which is sheer Buddhist Tantrism.

CHAPTER V

Philosophy at its Highest Development

I

THE BRAHMANIC SYSTEMS (A.D. 100–500)

THE Buddhist heresy had adapted itself to classical Brahmanism by providing itself with a Sanskrit literature with which to confront the epics, Purāṇas, Dharmaśāstras, and Upanishads. To counter a Buddhism which had become learned and literary, Brahmanism found it necessary to codify its tenets, hitherto unorganized, in finally established systems. Indeed, the orthodox systems are drawn up parallel to the Mahāyāna. It is true that many of them were of much earlier inspiration, but they were now set down authoritatively in *sūtras* which are as condensed and rigid as possible—a form so abstract and succinct that these works at once required commentaries. More than ever Brahmanism took on a scholastic aspect. Thereby it was the better able to combat heresy.

Six principal systems are regarded as orthodox—the "Views" (*darśana*).

Pūrva Mīmāṃsā

Although the Vedic age now lies far back in the darkness of time, the tradition of the Vedas continues, at least in principle, to be the source of Brahmanic culture and the standard round which it rallies. That is the cause of the permanent interest of an exegetic system called the Pūrva or Karma Mīmāṃsā, the First [1] Inquiry, or Inquiry about Rites.

The *sūtras* of the Mīmāṃsā, which are ascribed to the legendary Jaimini, cannot be earlier than the second century of our era, but their foundation is older and in vocabulary and manner of argument agrees with the work of the grammarian Katyayana, dating from the fourth century B.C.

[1] In opposition to the Second Inquiry, *Uttara Mīmāṃsā*, i.e. the Vedānta.

There are commentaries on them in a *vṛitti* of the fourth century of our era and the *Bhāshya* of Sabara, which is about a hundred years later. We may here note that the chronology of the *sūtras* of the six *darśanas*, though still full of uncertainties, has been determined approximately by comparison with Buddhist literature, through the combined efforts of Jacobi and Scherbatski, scholars to whom Indian studies owe much.

The Mīmāṃsā is an analysis and a legal code of Brahmanic *dharma*. The pursuit of deliverance does not come into it any more than into the Vedas, for the only *karman* which comes into question is the ritual act. The authority of the Vedas is sufficient to itself, and does not need to resort to any faculty of knowing or any reasoning. The correct execution of the injunctions (*vidhi*) of the Vedas produces a force " non-existent before " (*apūrva*), which brings the individual his reward here below or in heaven. This notion gives something not unlike the *karman* of the Buddhists and Jains, but merit and demerit are not regarded as creating slavery except in the late Mimamsists Prabhakara and Kumarila (between 650 and 750), the outcome of whose arguments is that this system is simply a *darśana* like the others, conceived like them with the object of procuring deliverance, which in this case is the cessation of the union of the soul to a body.

Vaiśeshika

The *sūtras* of the Vaiśeshika system are doubtless of the first half of the second century ; they seem to be the oldest of the philosophic *sūtras*. The author to whom they are ascribed belongs to the domain of myth ; he is Uluka the Owl, commonly called Kanada or Kanabhuj (Kanabhaksha), the Grain-eater, in allusion to his atomistic doctrine. Among the Jains and in the Hīnayāna we have noted this atomism as a feature of very early Indian physics. But in the present case the atoms are not all homogeneous, as in Jainism, but differ in qualities, and they have an absolute existence, not a relative, as in Buddhism. There are four kinds of atom. Those of earth are qualified by scent, those of water by taste, those of fire by colour, and those of wind by tangibility. We must not be misled by the Greek word "atom"; these corpuscles, which are more like those of Epicurus than those of Democritus, are not of an absolute hardness, but are extremely tenuous (*paramāṇu*). Two primary atoms added together make a *dvyaṇuka*, or combination of two, and three of these together make a *tryaṇuka*, or combination of three.

Motion is explained by various principles. First, there are *ākāśa*, which is ether rather than space, and *kāla*, time—two dynamic factors rather than two empty media or two abstract frames. Above all there are merit and demerit (*dharma*, *adharma*), that is, an invisible power, *adṛishṭa*, analogous to the *apūrva* of the Mimamsists, which makes and unmakes the aggregates. This body-creating power resides in souls. It has no intentional efficacity, and yet cannot be called a blind fate, for the Vaiśeshika doctrine professes, if not the freedom of the soul in the European sense, at least its independence in its acts (*kriyāvāda*). True freedom, in the sense of deliverance, consists in freeing oneself from the body, not in moving it. This is how. Normally a man, *qua* mind, is composed of an *ātman*, which in principle is absolute and infinite, to which is joined an atomic *manas*, the function of which is to perceive and act by means of the bodily organs. Let the *ātman* recognize that it is other than the *manas* and the body and it will be delivered.

The result of this is a theory of knowledge which comprises a doctrine of categories and a doctrine of criteria.

In this realism, the categories are not types of judgment, but headings under which things are distributed (*padārtha*)—substance (*dravya*), quality (*guṇa*), action (*karman*), commonness (*sāmānya*), singularity (*viśesha*), inherence (*samavāya*). The first three concern objects (*artha*); the next two exist in things but are relationships apprehended by the intellect (*buddhyapeksha*); the last designates a connexion, not accidental but intimate and necessary. The Vaiśeshika is a philosophy which looks for specific properties (*viśesha*) in everything. Even deliverance depends on the recognition of a specific character, that of our *ātman*.

The doctrine of criteria became established, with the modifications suitable in each case, in every system. It consists in a statement of the correct modes of knowledge (*pramāṇa*). They are two—perception (*pratyaksha*) and inference (*anumāna*), the former being direct apprehension and the other mediate, as it were, by transparence through a perceived datum. *Śabda*, sound, was a correct mode of knowing for the Mimamsists, whose whole philosophy was based on the heard revelation of the hymns; it is not one in the present system, or at least it is included in perception. The original name of inference is *laingikam*, and it means a conclusion from a sign (*linga*) to a thing signified. It takes various forms as the relationship consists in causality, contiguity, opposition of extremes, or intrinsic coincidence.

These theories of nature and of knowledge were incorporated in the succeeding system as soon as its *sūtras* were put together. The Vaiśeshika and Nyāya systems were regarded as complementary and were merged in the eleventh century, starting from the *Saptapadārthī* of Sivaditya.

Nyāya

The *sūtras* of the Nyāya, which are supposed to set forth the teaching of one Akshapada Gautama, a legendary figure, belong to the first half of the third century. They give an art of reasoning. A man who can argue avoids false knowledge, vice, action, birth, and pain—a chain of terms recalling the Buddhist series of the Twelve Conditions. So the art of reasoning liberates the mind, that is, it frees it from transmigration.

The modes of knowing are like those described in the Vaiśeshika. *Ātman* can only make intelligence pass from power to action by using its organs, which are *buddhi*, thought, and *manas*, the *sensorium commune*, but in doing so the soul becomes enslaved. One must therefore distinguish two efforts, working in opposite directions and each aiming at understanding. One of them chains the mind, because its effect is to make it serve life; the other frees the mind, because it detaches it from life. It is in the order of knowledge that this enslavement or purification of the spirit takes place. Both the theory of the empirical consciousness and the doctrine of salvation entail, each in its own fashion, the necessity of being able to reason.

Here perception and inference are not the only correct modes of knowledge (*pramāṇa*). One must add analogy (*upamāna*), which likens an unknown object to one already known, and testimony (*śabda*). Inference is of three kinds. It may be *pūrvavat*, drawn from antecedents, as when, having previously seen fire where there was smoke, one again supposes fire in the present case where one sees smoke. It is *śeshavat*, drawn from the consequence, when, having observed that one grain of rice has been cooked, one induces that all the other grains in the pot have been cooked too. It is *sāmānyato dṛishta*, drawn from a common character, when, having admitted that in man change of place implies a principle of motion, one supposes that there is such a principle in the sun because it changes its position from east to west. On the other hand, it does not follow from the fact that a people has a king for its support, that states of consciousness have a soul for their substratum, for the connexion of the thinking principle with phenomena is not an object of experience.

This attempt to define exactly the intrinsic force of logical connexion produced a type of reasoning which is not unlike the syllogisms of Aristotle. The Jains had already, with a great apparatus of theses, antitheses, analogies, objections, scruples, and reservations, constructed an argument in ten members which deserves notice in a history of logic but was clumsy and cumbersome to manipulate.[1] The Naiyāyikas (adherents of the Nyāya) invented a briefer argument in five propositions :—

There is fire on the mountain (*pratijña*, assertion) ;

Because there is smoke on the mountain (*hetu*, reason) ;

Everything which contains smoke contains fire ; for example the hearth (*udāharaṇam*, example) ;

But it is so here (in the case of the mountain) (*upanaya*, application to the particular case) ;

Therefore it is so (*nigamanam*, result).

This reasoning is a web of observations regarding facts, not a deduction regarding ideas, and that is enough to distinguish it from the syllogism. The difference will be more evident when we have contrasted this reasoning with that which the Buddhist logicians of the fifth and seventh centuries

[1] See my *Philosophie comparée*, 1st ed., p. 120.

set up in opposition to it, although even this latter, in spite of appearances, is no nearer to the Greek type. The common characteristic of the Nyāya and Vaiśeshika systems is their realism. It made it possible for them to adapt themselves to each other in order to join forces to resist the idealistic principles of Buddhist epistemology.

Vedānta

The second Mīmāṃsā (Uttara), otherwise called Vedānta, or " Completion of the Veda ", is the most famous of the systems among which Indian philosophy is divided. Not only has it been made known in the West to such an extent that it has been quite wrongly regarded as summing up the whole of Indian philosophy, but it was the principal heir of all the orthodox systems ; it even owed part of its inheritance to Buddhism, from which it retained all that could be incorporated in orthodoxy.

The central theme of the Vedānta is simple, and indeed remarkably narrow. It is no more than the opposition of the relative or illusion (*māyā*) to the absolute, the *ātman-brahman* of the Upanishads. This conviction forms the unity of all the successive Vedāntas which have arisen, from the old Brahmanism to the Indian thought of our day. But one must consider the manner in which that conviction is presented, and the manner differs according to the time, the environment, the school. Although P. Deussen made the philosophy of the Vedānta familiar in the West, it is far from being properly known among us in its historical stages. With that follower of Schopenhauer, European students have too often regarded the Upanishads, the *Brahma-sūtras*, and the commentary of Sankara as all containing the same matter.

Among these three kinds of work, the *Brahma-sūtras* of Badarayana hold a middle place, both in time and in character. The criticism of Buddhism which they contain shows that they were composed about the beginning of the fifth century of our era. We know that the classical Upanishads belong to the last six centuries B.C., the two oldest being doubtless pre-Buddhist. On the other hand, Sankara, the most celebrated of the Vedantine commentators, was a contemporary of Charlemagne. If we note how much the interpretation of the Vedānta varies from the eleventh to the sixteenth century, in the philosophies of Ramanuja, Madhva, Nimbarka, and Vallabha, we must gather that it could vary greatly in the course of the fifteen hundred years or so which lay between the end of the " Vedic " era and the time at which Sankara lived.

The oldest Upanishads do not contain " a " philosophy, but the seeds of the various philosophies and of the Vedānta. Those which are exclusively Vedantine bear the stamp of a late date, several centuries after the beginning of our era. Such is the *Māṇḍūkya*, with its commentary the *Gauḍapadīya Kārikā*, probably of the seventh century. In declaring that it is not dualistic (*advaita*), the Vedānta tries to make a complete break with the Sāṃkhya, from which it barely differed in the epics and the *Maitri* and *Śvetāśvatara Upanishads*, and by which it was again affected after Sankara. The various degrees of non-dualism, more or less strict, are seen in the position given to *māyā*, which is the magical power of a demiurge in early Brahmanism, the veil of illusion from Sankara onwards, and in the interval a sort of " nature " like the *prakṛiti* of the Sāṃkhya. This *māyā* does not develop from a real phantasmagoria to pure illusion until it is influenced by the Buddhist *avidyā*, which is an integral part of a system which rejects the belief in substantiality as the worst error. In view of this change, the system of Sankara came to be condemned as " disguised Buddhism ".

So, at the point in Indian history at which this book stops, the Vedānta was turned towards complete monism. Phenomena, which are manifold and various, are real in so far as they are founded on the absolute *ātman-brahman*, and false and non-existent if taken apart from it. To suppose them to be what they seem is to commit the error of the man who takes a rope for a snake. Deliverance consists in judging right, in not letting oneself be duped by appearances ; one may say that it consists in seeing the absolute in everything and, so far as it is possible, in being equal to it oneself. In reality, servitude and transmigration exist only by illusion, and our salvation is only conceivable because we were never truly enslaved. We thought that we were, and right knowledge undeceives us. It can be seen to what an extent Brahmanic orthodoxy, when presented thus, adopts the Buddhist principles of *tathatā* and cosmic emptiness. Buddhism might be rooted out of India, but it had made great conquests over its conqueror.

Yoga

I have already shown (p. 142) the part played by the Yogins in the first centuries of Brahmanic thought. In the Upanishads the orthodoxy of the priests seems to endeavour to assimilate their theory and their discipline of the vital breaths, by identifying those breaths with sacrificial fires. I then showed the influence of Yoga on the thought of the epics (p. 177), and afterwards on the school of the Yogāchāras, which was of such importance within the Great Vehicle (p. 183). Thus, in a variety of ways, the practice of the Yogins was transformed into a method by the most different religions and philosophies.

The *Yoga-sūtras*, reputedly the work of a Patañjali, who may be another man than the grammarian of the second century B.C., are roughly of the fifth century of our era. They criticize Vasubandhu's idealism. The oldest commentary on them, ascribed to Vyasa, must have been written between the seventh century and the ninth.

The equivalence of Yoga practice and Sāṃkhya speculation, already proclaimed in the epics, is postulated throughout the *Sūtras* of Patañjali. The mind according to nature must efface itself before the transcendent mind, which is the only true mind. A commencement is made by the suppression of all activity of the thinking principle (*chitta*)—*chittavṛittinirodha*. Then the mind gives itself up to operations which concentrate it more and more, gradually abstracting it from the outside world, but thereby giving it the greater mastery over itself and the world—fixation (*dhāraṇā*), meditation (*dhyāna*), supreme absorption (*samādhi*). So one realizes transcendence of the *purusha*, otherwise called its isolation (*kaivalyam*). The mind recognizes itself to be outside all that is not it, which in this philosophy is the *chitta* and in the Sāṃkhya, *prakṛiti*. What it is, is light (*dīptiḥ*), and therefore knowledge. But as it exerts its capacity of concentration in one direction or another, it obtains marvellous powers, which are not, however, as they are too often called, supernatural, for it is, on the contrary, the property of the mind according to its true nature to possess these. Nothing can oppose it, not time, nor space or distance, nor the resistance of bodies. One might say that concentration has made it hard and sharp so as to have a perforating power; one might say that the more deeply it penetrates into itself the further in time or space are the strata of material or spiritual reality which it can reach. "Second sight" and magical action are justified.

Whereas the old Yoga realized the absolute in the ascetic himself, in so far as he became *yukta*, joined in all his parts, classical Yoga is theistic. It holds that salvation is obtained not only by the concentration of *samādhi*, but by devotion to the Lord, Isvara. The whole effort which empties the soul of its empirical content on the pretext of realizing pure spirituality comes in the end to enabling it to assimilate itself adequately to an objective absolute. Doubtless this change took place under the influence of that piety, that passive self-abandonment to the divine love (*bhakti*) which, starting in the popular religions, spread in the course of what we call the Middle Ages to most of the philosophies of India.

Sāṃkhya

That the Sāṃkhya and Yoga, the one theoretical and the other practical, are parallel, of equal value, and complementary, is a principle asserted from the remotest antiquity to modern times. Even if the correspondence is the result of an artificial, syncretic adaptation, the two systems are, all through the historical period, adapted one to the other. The principle which they have in common is the complete antagonism between the life according to nature and the life according to the mind, and consequently the achievement of salvation by an absolute transcendence, in which the mind confines itself to contemplation. What does it contemplate? Nature or empirical thought, in order that it may recognize itself to be quite different from it, thoroughly alien to it. So we get the myth of the Raja and the Dancing-girl; all that the latter has to do is to "be seen" in her many movements and postures, and then to vanish from the stage, away from the King in his splendid isolation.

So dualism constitutes the fundamental postulate of the Sāṃkhya in its quite explicit form. As a matter of fact, just as the monism of the Vedānta was seldom very strict, the dualism of the Sāṃkhya often yielded to a tendency to monism. At first Mind (*purusha*) has a pre-eminence over Nature (*prakṛiti*) in reality as well as in dignity, for it is sufficient to itself, whereas nature exists "for Mind", if only to permit it to become aware of its perfect spirituality, its complete independence of things. Later, in more than one Upanishad and in the epics, we come upon a Sāṃkhya in which *purusha* is held as it were to produce nature by evolutive emanation, and a Yoga in which the ascetic process is supposed to advance by a continuous effort, without break or dualism, from empirical thought, which is a diluted, loosely-knit existence, to the concentrated thought, dense as the diamond and sharp as the lightning (both are what India calls *vajra*), which realizes the absolute. In spite of everything, both systems in their classical form tend to dualism, and therein they stand at the opposite pole of Indian philosophy to the Vedānta.

The *Sāṃkhya-sūtras* were only composed in the fifteenth century, but what the *sūtras* of other philosophies did in fixing their classical form, as has been described above, was done for this system by the didactic verses (*kārikā*) of Isvarakrishna, which were translated into Chinese by Paramartha in 546 and were probably written in the fourth century. The story that the system was originally founded by the sage Kapila is doubtless only a myth, corresponding to no historical fact.

The Sāṃkhya theory of nature is a qualitative one, which gives place to the idea of evolution. Nature is analysed into three elements (*guṇa*), which are in everything, unequally combined. *Sattva* is, literally, "the fact of being *sat*, what is"; but this etymology, which connects the concept with the earliest Brahmanic ontology, is more misleading than informative as to the essence of this principle. *Sattva*, far from being the same as the absolute, the *sat* or *brahman* of the Brāhmaṇas, is merely one aspect of becoming—that of luminosity. As such, it is akin to knowledge; in fact, although nature has nothing in common with mind (in the classical form of the system), there is in nature something which " imitates " the spiritual, which is, one might say, the foundation of the " mental ", that fallacious approximation to true mind.[1] We shall, indeed, see that nature possesses a collection of " mental ", if not spiritual, functions. The two other qualities are *rajas*, a principle of movement which effects transition between the clarity of *sattva* and the opacity of *tamas*, and *tamas* itself, the principle of heaviness and darkness.

Properly, the Sāṃkhya is presented as the " enumeration " of the stages of which nature is made up. (i) Five coarse elements: *ākāśa*, wind, fire, water, earth. (ii) Five subtle elements (*sūkshma*), that is, unmixed (*tanmātra* = being this alone and nothing else at the same time): sound, contact, shape, taste, scent. (iii) The organs of knowledge: hearing touch, sight, taste, smell; and of action: voice, feet, hands, and the organs of generation and evacuation. Both elements and organs are concerned with a function which is already " mental ", the *ahaṃkāra*, the " maker of self ", and this is connected with the *mahat*, the " great ", that is, the whole of the physical world, synonymous with *buddhi*, the discernment which, to use a Greek formula, is all things potentially—in short, intellect (iv, v). Lying one inside the other, these forms of existence, appearing by unfolding, are what is evolved, the *vyaktam* (vi), as opposed to the raw material, the *Urgrund* of nature, *mūlaprakṛiti*, the unevolved (*avyaktam*) (vii). In all there are twenty-four principles, rising, as it were (without ever reaching it) towards the twenty-fifth, Mind, of which one may almost say that, like the God of Aristotle, it moves or draws as an object of love, by the attraction of its finality. This is the explanation of the evolution which goes on all through nature and causes it to produce an activity which resembles mind, although it is not mind in any degree but is merely " empirical thought " (*chitta*).

[1] *Esprit* is translated " mind ", " spiritual " being the adjective associated with it. (Trs.)

II

THE PHILOSOPHIES IN THE SEVENTH CENTURY

In the middle of the seventh century, the period at which our brief analysis of Indian history comes to an end, speculation reached its highest point, both in Brahmanism and in Buddhism, and as a result of a fruitful rivalry between the two inspirations.

Orthodox Commentators

Most of the *sūtras* were by now composed, resuming in a form which claimed to be final at least a thousand years of thought. Since a *sūtra* is so laconic that it can only be understood if explained by a gloss, the age of the commentators begins as soon as the texts which are intended to be authoritative are established. A scholasticism comparable to those of the West, Christian, Jewish, and Mussulman, developed in every tradition. Thus, among others, the Mīmāṃsā gave rise to the commentaries of Sabara-svamin in the fifth century and Prabhakara in the seventh; the Vaiśeshika to those of Prasastapada and Matichandra in the fifth and sixth; and the Nyāya to those of Vatsyayana in the fifth and Uddyotakara in the seventh.

Jainism

Jainism was at the height of its expansion. In the second half of the fifth century Umasvati, the author of the *Tattvārthādhigama Sūtra*, had already set forth the exact tenets of the sect, and in the sixth the Śvetāmbara canon was not only composed but written down. Siddhasena Divakara opposed Kundakunda the Digambara, whose teaching was continued in the following century by Samantabhadra.

Buddhism

Buddhism made an extraordinary advance, both in theory and in practice. The Hīnayāna, although duplicated by the

Mahāyāna, was as full of life as ever. In the fifth century, perhaps in the fourth, Vasubandhu wrote a summary of it in the *Abhidharmakośa*, and the Pali school of Ceylon produced a great commentator in Buddhaghosha, a former Brahman of Magadha.

In the Great Vehicle, the Mādhyamika school, of southern origins, and the northern line of the Yogāchāras vied in activity. The former split in the fifth century into two groups—Buddhapalita and Chandrakirti with his Prāsangikas (seventh century), who were adepts in the *reductio ad absurdum* (*prasanga*), and Bhavya, the master of the Svātantrikas, who stood for an "independent" method of reasoning. So the passion for dialectic survived in this line until the teaching of the Yogāchāras influenced Santideva, a Prāsangika of the end of the seventh century, who wrote on the "Career of the Bodhisattvas", *Bodhicharyāvatāra.*

The Yogāchāras reigned at the University of Nalanda, and their influence spread over the Far East as well as over India. Dignaga came from the south, Buddhadasa from the west, Sthiramati from the east, and Sanghadasa from Kashmir. Here the fifth century shows an astonishing productiveness. Whether the spread of absolute idealism (*vijñaptimātra*) was due to the genius of Asanga or, as a certain Japanese school now maintains, to Maitreya, a historical person rather than a *bodhisattva*, in any case that exuberant metaphysical theory found in Vasubandhu, possibly a brother of Asanga, its first scholastic exponent of doctrine and in Dignaga its dialectician. The logic of Dignaga, revived in the seventh century by Dharmakirti, the author of the *Nyāya-bindu*, is comparable to that of Aristotle in its originality and in the fact that it spread over the whole eastern half of Asia. In no part of the world and in no age has the power of the philosophic spirit had a vaster development.

Some explanations are necessary about this logic, which was the outcome of such a volume of speculation. It differs from Aristotle's in that it deals not with concepts (for no Socrates or Plato persuaded India that man thinks in generic essences), but with objective realities. Yet the absolute idealism in which this logic had its birth distinguishes it from the empiricist logic of the Nyāya. The objective realities whose relations are considered by Dignaga, the immediate disciple of Vasubandhu, and by Dharmakirti are realities *thought*, not merely inferred by the relation of the sign to the thing signified as in Brahmanic orthodoxy. There is a natural connexion (*svabhāvapratibandha*) between the proving reason (*sādhana*) and the inference proved (*sādhya*). The best authority on the subject, Scherbatski, has with great penetration noted in these idealistic logicians a kind of presentiment of what Kant was to call synthetic *a priori* judgments; only necessities inherent in human thought in general can be the foundation of universal and necessary relations.

From the practical point of view the development of Buddhism is attested by historical evidence of certain date. Sooner or later after their composition, the books of the Great Vehicle were translated into Chinese and spread to the Far East. Full of emulation, Indian missionaries and Mongolian pilgrims went to and fro between the two centres of humanity, carrying with them documents which had with great pains been brought within reach of non-Hindu peoples. In the second and third centuries the exchange was chiefly carried on by Parthians, Sogdians, and Yueh-chi. In the fourth, the Tartar kings encouraged the introduction of Buddhism in Shansi. The beginning of the fifth century saw the Chinese translations of Kumarajiva and of various religious writers of Gandhara and Kashmir, Fa-hien came to Magadha in 405, and in 431 Gunavarman settled in Nanking. In the sixth century the practice of *dhyāna* (*ch'an*), preached by the more or less legendary Bodhidharma, reached southern China, which was already to some extent prepared by its Taoism to accept Buddhist ideas. Paramartha landed at Canton and settled at Nanking in 548. The doctrine of the Lotus of the Good Law (*Saddharma-puṇḍarīka*) was established in the monastery of T'ien-t'ai through the zeal of Che-yi. In the seventh century, Hiuen Tsang stayed in India from 630 to 644 and I-tsing from 673 to 685. All this mutual visiting and translation of books and erudite enthusiasm for a religion which was in principle universal, all this intercourse between two civilizations which had hitherto been separated by almost impassable barriers, is one of the greatest facts in "humanism" recorded by history, and its sole direct cause was the propagation of Buddhism.

The introduction of Indian influence in Tibet was also due to that religion. The consequent advance in civilization and the translation of the Buddhist canon into a new literary language are events which lie outside the limits of the present work. But we may just note the incident by which they were started—the despatch by the creator of the Tibetan power, Srong-tsan-Gampo, of his minister Sambhota to Magadha to study Buddhism about 632.

So, great as were the efforts made by the Brahmans to bring the sectarian cults into the orthodox fold and to reply to the developments of heretical thought by a philosophy, or even by several philosophies, the expansion of Buddhism is the great fact of the seventh century. No doubt, it was an expansion which brought exhaustion, for in the very next century signs of decay are to be seen, and Buddhism was destined to disappear from the country of its birth and to see its Indian empire limited to Nepal and Ceylon, at the opposite ends of the peninsula. No doubt there was never more than a very small minority of Buddhists in the mass of the Indian people, and the select few who adhered to the Law, sterilized by the monastic life as soon as they were recruited, could not produce a large progeny. No, doubt, too, Buddhism was bound to perish by its very triumph. It had provoked an intensely energetic reaction on the part of the Brahman caste. It had caused a great part of its convictions to be absorbed into the dogmas of that caste—transmigration, universal emptiness, compassion for all creatures. It had set up an ideal of life too un-Indian for India to grasp, and of such a generally human appeal that all the shiftings of peoples in Asia—save the expansion of Islam—helped to propagate it. Like the dancing-girl of the Sāṃkhya, it might withdraw, once its part was played.

III

THE CHARACTERISTICS OF INDIAN THOUGHT

India's contribution to the culture of mankind is twofold. There was her effort at civilization, aiming at raising to a higher level the native populations of India itself and of all the countries to which the Hindus spread, from Africa to Oceania and from Iran to Manchuria. There was also the result of her reflection on human problems—a reflection which, being pursued continuously from the dawn of historical times, at an early date produced a mental type very different from the Mediterranean or Western type and from the Chinese. We must try to say exactly what are the specific characteristics of that product of a special development, the Indian mind.

Indian Science

In its pride in its own creation, "science," the West is over-ready to blame India for having contributed little to this most valuable of all the conquests of man. But we should note some distinctions. What was called science in the West before the sixteenth century was cultivated with enthusiasm by India; but India knew nothing of mathematical physics, mechanistic biology, or the objective analysis of human affairs by history. None the less, India produced mathematics, and physics, and biology, and history.

The *Śulva Sūtras* of Apastamba are a treatise on practical geometry, applied to the erection of altars. They cannot be safely placed before the second century B.C. They include the construction of right angles, squares, and rectangles, and Pythagoras's Theorem.[1] The influence of Paulus of Alexandria and, indirectly, of Ptolemy appears in the *Paulīśa-siddhānta* of Varaha Mihira, composed about 550. This work gives a table of sines and two trigonometrical rules. Aryabhata, born in 476, gave a value of π and a rule for the solution of simple indeterminate equations, a subject also treated by Brahmagupta (born 598).

We have no exact dated information about ancient Indian astronomy. It must have owed something to Chaldaean science and to Chinese. "The most ancient source which can be discerned in it, the lunar zodiac, seems to be rather an adulteration . . . of the system of the *siüs*."[2] The sun-worships

[1] See A. Rey's analysis in **CCLXXVIII** and in *La Jeunesse de la science grecque*.
[2] Rey, **CCLXXVIII**, p. 408.

held in such esteem by the Indo-Iranians do not necessarily imply a system of astronomy.

Mythical cosmogony was enormously developed by Brahmans, Buddhists, and Jains. The aspect taken by physics is qualitative rather than quantitative, not only in the case of *guṇas* constituting nature, as in the Sāṃkhya, but even where a kind of atomism suggests mechanistic principles to us Europeans. Several types of atomism appear. In Buddhism there is a sort of atomism of time, duration splitting into discrete instants, besides a material atomism which is purely relative, since this philosophy allows no substantiality. With the Jains and Vaiśeshikas, there are minute corpuscles, which are neither infinitely small, vanishing quantities, nor solids having an absolute hardness. To use Greek terms, India is concerned rather with the dyad of the large and the small than with atoms like those of Democritus, or even with partially qualitative atoms like those of Epicurus. *Aṇu* and *paramāṇu* mean " small " and " very small ", not, like our " atom ", " uncuttable."

In Vedic times vegetable species must have been treated for the manufacture of sacrificial fermented liquors or magical drugs. Then Brahmanism set up a science of life (*āyurveda*), based on a classification of the breaths (*prāṇa*). These quasi- πνεύματα circulate in tubes known as *nādi*, which include both the nerves and the blood-vessels. They are controlled by various nervous centres, namely the " lotuses " which are disposed along the dorsal column, rising in importance as they are nearer the top. With the theory of the five elements goes a corresponding theory of sensation, literally of " taste " (*rasa*). The fundamental work on chemistry and medicine is the *Saṃhitā*, which is attributed to Charaka, a Kashmiri contemporary of Kanishka, but appears to date from the second century of our era. The *Suśruta*, which contains an art of surgery and is ascribed to Nagarjuna, seems to be hardly later.

Whereas in the West biology has, slowly and painfully, become mechanistic, in the East it was vitalistic. The former point of view, which is now firmly established in our convictions as to method, is far from gaining the acceptance of all Hindus who study our science. Bose, for example, partly owes the original idea of his discoveries, which show such a rare penetration, to the postulates of his native tradition. So, even if mechanistic intelligibility is henceforward the very condition of science, intuitions of another kind may have their value. The knowledge which is at once most objective and most satisfactory, not only to Europeans but to all mankind, will doubtless have in the future to take into account the spirit contributed to it by non-Occidental minds, which are more sensitive than ours to certain aspects of reality.

It is above all in psycho-physiological research, which has been pursued there since time immemorial, that India has very valuable experience. No doubt that experience is often vitiated by the theoretical explanations, often incorrect, which are attached to it. There is myth all through the chemistry, the physiology, and even the anatomy of the Hindus. But a tradition of thousands of years of practice cannot be wholly fallacious; the power is often greater than the knowledge. Just as Leibniz found gold in the dung-heap of scholasticism, a science yet more critical than our own will one day extract the ingredient of genuine success and true data from the asceticism of a Yogin or the magic of the Tantras.

Ancient India has no Thucydides, nor even a Herodotus, nor a Ssu-ma Ch'ien, and that is why our knowledge of it is so uncertain that hardly a single date can be determined without Greek or Chinese evidence. The interest which this civilization takes in its ancestors is not that of dispassionate curiosity but that of loyalty. Just as Indian patriotism hardly consists in imperialistic pride and egoism, but is manifested in depth, in the consciousness of carrying on the *kūla* or family line from the age of the semi-divine *ṛishis*, so attachment to the past is entirely traditional. Kingdoms, sects, and schools of thought find their titles to glory in their genealogies of heroes, patriarchs, and saints. This is the only way in which the individual is honoured—as a point in a line. This is what gives history its particular form; it is a collection of separate histories, and never attempts to bring together a number of these series and to set forth their manifestations synchronistically.

The Indian mind, then, is interested in annals, but very few of these are older than the seventh century. The genealogies doubtless contain much that is arbitrary, due to pious frauds or biassed devices of policy. Nevertheless, when a large number of traditions have been subjected to impartial criticism, results will no doubt be obtained, provided that the way opened by Pargiter is followed. It will then be possible to set aside the epic or lyrical ingredient in the accounts and to discover, for example in those " Antiquities ", the Purāṇas, solid historical information mixed up with farragoes of stuff about " the old days ". At this date we cannot help seeing how normal it is for peoples to record their past only in terms of praise or blame, the stories being intended to lead to action or to promote interests, not to establish facts. The cult of truth, like art for art's sake, is a very modern and purely European interest.

The Problems of India

It is idle to reproach India for having such a different attitude towards the knowable from our own, and we should rather inquire what circumstances have led to the adoption of such attitudes there and here. We should recognize that the intellectual problem and the social problem of Indian civilization go together.

The social problem, as we have seen, is that never-ending task—the Brahmanization of a chaos of peoples which was never completely assimilated by the conquering Indo-Europeans. The intellectual problem consists in preserving and promoting an orthodoxy in the midst of the most bewildering amalgam of traditions and methods.

That is why the task of speculation was wholly scholastic, as in the Confucian, Jewish, Christian, and Islamic civilizations, in which likewise, an orthodoxy based on traditional teaching sought to set up the system of acquired knowledge as a rigid protective framework. What distinguishes Indian scholasticism is the fact that it is the property of a caste and that the theoretical problem on which its efforts centre is to obtain deliverance in respect of transmigration. The pursuit of transcendent ends, quite outside the natural order, and often contrary to nature, doubtless helped to divert men's minds from interest in facts. So true does this seem to be, that even when India created arts and sciences with no transcendent object, such as sculpture, economics, legislation, medicine, or eroticism, it proceeded by *pramāṇas*, that is, by rather *a priori* canons, not by objective investigation seeking the laws of facts in the facts themselves. This is still normal in mankind in general, for the positive spirit is quite recent and very limited.

The problem of deliverance, central as it was, never emerged from the speculative domain, and awoke no aspiration to what we should call greater social justice. The total ignorance of the mass of the people barred them from the material power and religious sentiments which might have brought their liberation. There is no attempt, all through history, to win political freedom. Neither individuals nor groups strive for wider rights than those given to each man by his birth. The liberty of each individual lies in his rights, no doubt, but also in his duties; *dharma* stands for both ideas without distinction. The only injustice is the confounding of *dharmas*, that is, the mixing of castes; but a man is free in enjoying his own *dharma*, and that implies that he respects the *dharma* of others. So it is fidelity to tradition that guarantees liberty. No progress is conceivable beyond the maintenance of order, which takes into account the nature of men. One may improve the administration of public affairs; one cannot seek a better ideal or new forms of society.

The only real slavery, in Indian opinion, lies in not knowing the true nature of the mind. So apart from the preliminary training of asceticism, it is by the intelligence alone that one can obtain emancipation. If faith has a part to play—in Brahmanism as confidence in a rite, in Buddhism as refuge in the Triple Jewel—it always implies a fully reasonable assurance, it never harbours a doubt or requires any free assertion. Not only would India refuse to say "*Credo quia absurdum*"; it would never admit, as Europe has done, that sincerity of adhesion may make up for obscurity of knowledge. The Asia which we tax with confused mysticism would have regarded as madness something which we in Europe have often accepted—the notion of an irrational belief which is good and necessary, although irrational.

The Indian Conception of Mind

The examination of the religions and philosophies and of the psychological vocabulary of the Hindus reveals a conception of mind very different from ours. It is an eminently dynamic conception, as against the passive attitude which we have learned both from the idealist Plato, for whom the intellect reflects eternal intelligibles, and from the sensualist Epicurus, for whom our senses receive images emanating from things.

India knows no " states " of consciousness. The phenomenon, objective or subjective, is *vṛitti*, " whirl " ; in fact, the operation of the demiurge, of the king, and of the Buddhist is to set the Wheel of the Law rolling, the wheel which, according to the direction in which it revolves, produces slavery or deliverance, existence or salvation. The phenomenon is also called *saṃskāra* or *saṃskṛita*, " concocter " or " concocted ", names which indicate the continuation and combination of antecedent factors in a present existence.

The root *as* (*asti* = ἐστι = est), which corresponds to our notion of being, was not developed at all. On the other hand, the root *bhū*, " to become, to come into being," gave rise to a wealth of terms, in which being appears, if one may say so, and has various senses according to complexities of grammar, in the active, passive, causative, desiderative, intensive.[1] Thus becoming has a great many shades of meaning, which make it quite unlike the inert τὸ ὄν or τὰ ὄντα to which the Greek tradition has accustomed our philosophy.

The mind as represented by the Brahmans and Buddhists does not reflect like a mirror, but shines like a lantern. By the organs of the senses it sheds its own light outside and perceives what it illuminates. Sensation is not receptive, but apprehensive (*grahana*) ; the whole mind takes part in it. Images do not come to us from outside, but are spontaneous. One has the perceptions which one has deserved. What we take for an object is the residue of our experiences, the accomplishment of the act for which we construct the thing.

As there is no difference between sensation and intelli-

[1] *Bhavati*, he becomes ; *bhūyati*, he has become ; *bhāvayati*, he causes to become ; *bubhūsati*, he wishes to become ; *bibhāvayisati*, he wishes to cause to become ; *bobhāvīti*, *bobhavati*, *bobhoti*, *bobhūyate*, etc., he is accustomed to become. Adjectives and nouns sprouted in profusion on the various branches of this verbal stock. See my communication of March, 1929, to the Société française de Psychologie in *Journal de Psychologie*, 1930.

gence, so there is none between imagination and intellect. The imagination is not, as with us, a receptive function. Instead of being a fancy capable of both error and flashes of genius, it has at its command norms, which we ascribe to reason. I am here referring to certain images of *pramāṇa*, rightly produced, which serve as models to logic and to æsthetics. There is no prototype of the true but perception done well; there is no prototype of the beautiful but literary or artistic creation according to the rules. This is neither realism nor idealism, but right practice. These images are in no degree arbitrary or infected with individuality; their value is the greater, the more traditional and impersonal they are in character. Although subjective, since they are not received from outside, they possess universality or necessity, because every Indian mind, as such, brings them about. Factitious does not mean arbitrary. The canons, the criteria, are, as Taine would have said, true hallucinations.

India has not our prejudice, due to Socrates and Plato, that man thinks in general concepts or ideas. The rich philosophic vocabulary designating the operations which break up and those which combine, by the use of the prefixes *vi-* and *sam-* respectively, offers nothing equivalent to induction and deduction, to analysis and synthesis dealing with concepts in the Peripatetic fashion. One can join, construct, without generalizing; one can dissociate, dissolve, as an acid would do, without passing from the more general to the less. Reason as a " place of ideas ", or as a system of the principles which, spread through the cosmos, make the laws of the world, is without doubt only a Greek fiction, for nothing like it is to be found in Indian philosophy.

Nor do the Hindus distinguish understanding and will as we do. The words *kalpanā* and *saṃkalpa*, which are often translated by one or the other of these terms, stand for an aspect of thought prior to the distinction into discerning and wishing—a sort of project or intention which may become concrete as an intellectual " determination " or as an act of voluntarily " deciding ". It is no doubt partly because the East does not separate will from intelligence that it does not contrast belief and science as two almost opposite terms. Although it does not hold that there is freedom in the sense of free will, it regards knowledge as entirely active. Doubtless Europeans have distinguished understanding and will simply because, regarding intelligence as wholly passive, we have been compelled to recognize, as a correlative and complementary capacity, a pure activity.

The higher functions of the mind do not consist, as among the Greeks, in speculation, that is, in contemplation. According to "normal" psychology, which aims at the direction of our body and our interests in accordance with common experience, the highest faculty is *buddhi*, which is a synthesis of perceptions and actions, a power both of discerning and of determining. If, on the other hand, the mind does not place itself at the service of life, but aims at transcendent ends, the ultimate operations are *dhyāna* and *samādhi*, those forms of absorption in which the thought by concentration obtains irresistible power, once it is emptied of egoism and relativity. It would be a mistake to suppose that these powers are acquired apart from complete knowledge; knowledge and power are one.

That is the true keystone of Indian philosophy. The acts which make a man a slave are those which he does outside perfect knowledge. Those which he does with that knowledge, being purely spiritual, not only do not enslave him, but effect his freedom by efficience. So, in her philosophies as finally established, it is not true that India merely sought deliverance, negatively; she seeks to achieve liberty, positively. The mind only knows by doing, and then it makes itself. Those of its acts which rise beyond utilitarianism and dialects are operations of magic as much as of intelligence.

This conception of mind, so unlike the European, is the result both of metaphysical systems and of intimate experience. The most certain result of any comparative study of philosophy is that convictions express mental structures, and that mental structures come from traditional convictions. There are no facts except as the result of theories, and theories are themselves facts. Human types are the realization of opinions. In this sense, the religions and philosophies of India brought about the Indian mind, and the analysis of that mind, as it becomes more and more complete, not only adds to our knowledge of man, but enables us to perceive how much is relative in our own mind. The lesson which India teaches us is that which she taught herself—that to understand better is to free oneself.

PART FOUR

AESTHETIC LIFE

BOOK ONE

The Literature of India

INTRODUCTION

I

THE LANGUAGES OF INDIA [1]

The Aryan invaders of the Punjab spoke an Indo-European language.

The name of Indo-European is given to every language presenting a phonetic and morphological system analogous to that observed in such tongues as Greek, Latin, and Celtic. As soon as the ancient books of Indian literature were known, it was observed that Old Indian showed similarities to Homeric Greek, Latin, and other languages of Europe. Franz Bopp, who studied Sanskrit under Chézy in Paris in 1812, was struck by these likenesses, and published in 1816 a small work in German, entitled "On the System of Conjugation of the Sanskrit Language in comparison with Greek, Latin, Persian, and Germanic". From that moment we had an Indo-European family of languages. It is divided into several groups—Indo-Iranian, Greek, Italo-Celtic, Germanic, Balto-Slavonic, Armenian, and Albanian. Indo-Iranian, or Aryan, is the branch which advanced furthest to the east of the region formerly occupied by these tongues. I say "formerly" because Indo-European languages are now spread all over the earth—English, French, Portuguese, Spanish, and the rest of them.

In the country which Aryan was to occupy, it found Dravidian already in possession. The Dravidian group does not seem to be especially related to any known speech. An attempt has recently been made to connect it with

[1] **XXXVIII**, J. Bloch.

Uralian.[1] The Dravidian now spoken as a living language in Southern India comprises Tamil, spoken by over eighteen million souls, in the south of the peninsula and northern Ceylon ; Malayalam (six to seven million), a western dialect of Tamil, but having a literature of its own; Telugu (twenty-four million) on the east coast north of Madras, to about 20° N. and 77° E. ; and Kanara or Kanarese (ten and a half million), found in parts of the west coast.

Each of these tongues has its literature. The most ancient, belonging to the first centuries of our era, is that of the Tamils, which does not fall behind Sanskrit literature in richness. The Tamil, or Tamul, language has also spread outside the peninsula, having been taken as far as South Africa by emigrants.

Dravidian languages are still to be found sporadically north of the Deccan. These are islands, steadily dwindling, of Gondi, the language of a fallen nation, Kolami and Bhili, which are also threatened with extinction, and Kui, which is of rather more consequence.

Dravidian seems to have once occupied a larger area. It may possibly have been spoken all over India and even beyond its frontiers. In Eastern Baluchistan it has left a dialect of its family, Brahui, which is spoken by barely 200,000 persons. Indian and Iranian tongues are encroaching more and more on this dialect. Brahui is interesting as evidence of the former expansion of Dravidian. Was it a temporary expansion, due to a conquest, or a permanent state of things ? The latter hypothesis seems fairly likely.

Dravidian, which is now retiring before the advance of the Aryan languages of India, had itself once driven back Austro-Asiatic tongues.[2] Remnants of these survive [3] in the shape of the so-called "Himalayan" dialects (about 100,000 speakers) and the Munda dialects in the east, in Bengal, spoken by about three millions. Through these Munda languages the linguistic history of India is connected with the Mon-Khmer group of Indo-China.

The language brought into India by the Aryan tribes

[1] Cf. *Zeitschrift für Indologie und Iranistik*, 3, 1 ; O. Schrader, *Dravidisch und Uralisch*.

[2] On the Austro-Asiatic languages, see J. Przyluski's articles in *Journal Asiatique* (1925) and in **XXXVIII**.

[3] *Id.*, ibid.

conquered the peninsula. It has passed through three historical stages—Old Indian, Middle Indian, and Modern, or New, Indian.

Old Indian is, firstly, Vedic, the language of the hymns of the *Ṛigveda.* It is still so like the Iranian of the sacred books, of the *Avesta,* that if one knows Vedic one can soon understand Avestic. Vedic is not a perfectly homogeneous language. It shows signs of a long process of development, and one notices innovations and influences from outside. Some of the hymns are very archaic, while others, such as the whole of the tenth book, are in a perceptibly later language.

To the stage of linguistic development represented by this tenth book belong the other Vedas, the Brāhmaṇas, the Āraṇyakas, the Upanishads, and some of the Sūtras. In these last, the *mantras,* which are formulas taken from the *Ṛigveda,* still represent the old linguistic stage.

About half-way through the fourth century B.C. the language was codified by the celebrated grammarian Panini. It became the Sanskrit or "perfect" language (*saṃ* ; here *saṃs* + *kṛita* means "adorned, arranged"), the sacred language by the same right as Vedic and, still more than Vedic, the means by which the higher intellect of India could express itself. It was never the speech of the people. Students learned it from Brahman scholars (*śishta*), by repeating the words of the master. The upper classes spoke Sanskrit, the others only understood it. It was one of the privileges of education. So, in Indian dramas, the chief characters, the King, the Brahmans, and, of the women, the nuns and the courtesans, speak Sanskrit, while the others use the popular speech. Sanskrit is also the language of the great epics, one of which at least, the *Mahābhārata,* is of popular origin. From this we may infer that, even if the people did not speak Sanskrit, there was a time, before it was made into a learned language, when it was hardly different from those in current use.

Accordingly Old Indian is usually divided into Old Indian properly so called, or Vedic, and later Old Indian, or Sanskrit.

The language of the Brāhmaṇas, etc., is also called post-Vedic. In Sanskrit itself strata of different dates are distinguished—the Sanskrit of Panini, and Epic and Classical Sanskrit, the language of post-Paninian literature.

Vedic is sometimes called "Vedic Sanskrit". The expression is convenient from the point of view of unity, but it can be misleading, for it suggests that Sanskrit was a continuation of Vedic in a direct line. This it was not. The grammatical forms of Sanskrit are based on a dialect which is like Vedic but not the same.

By the side of Vedic and Sanskrit, which were the languages of the hymns and invocations, sacred and learned languages, there developed on the Aryan foundation popular, or Prakritic, languages, from which the sacred language itself sometimes took manners of pronouncing and expressing itself, as the cultured classes often do under the influence of the masses. Moreover, when Vedic, having become ancient and hardly understandable, yielded its place as the learned language to Sanskrit, the Prakrits themselves arrived at a certain maturity and formed Middle Indian.

Certain new literary languages came into being in this way. The most important is Pali, at present the ecclesiastical language of the Buddhists of Ceylon, Burma, and Siam. It is not known exactly where and when it was spoken before it was used in the preaching of the disciples of Buddha and the composition of the Buddhist canon. Since Buddha came from Magadha, the prototype of Pali has been sought in the Magadhi language, but it is more probable that it is based on the dialect of Ujjayini, which the Master may have used in order to make himself understood by all his hearers.

Part of the Buddhist canon was written in Sanskrit. Certain works and certain fragments of verse inserted among the prose are not in pure Sanskrit, but in a tongue approaching to Middle Indian, which Senart has called "Mixed Sanskrit".

The Jains also made use of Middle Indian to set forth their doctrine. Jain Prakrit, the language of the Jain canon, is distinguished from Jain Maharashtri, the language of the commentaries and secular works of the sect.

In addition to these two great ecclesiastical languages, there are the Maharashtri of the Maratha country, which has produced a fine literature; Sauraseni, a dialect of the neighbourhood of Mathura, and also the language of noble ladies in the dramas; Magadhi, the speech of the lower classes in the dramas; and Paisachi, spoken there by the lowest of the people. The Indians said that Paisachi was the language of the demons called Piśācha, but it was simply the language of a subject people which had been Aryanized. It, too, is a literary language. A very remarkable work, the *Bṛihat-kathā* of Gunadhya, is written in this dialect.

Lastly, a whole class of Prakrits, some still living and some only known from the dramas, in general everything which departs at all from Sanskrit, is called *apabhraṃśa*, "what is detached, fallen from," that is, detached from the main stem, which is the sacred language.

The modern languages derived from the same Aryan source are many. Among the chief of them we may mention Sindhi, Gujarati, and, in part, Hindi, forming the western group, and the eastern group, comprising Bihari, Uriya, Assami, and, the most important of them, Bengali. In the south of India, Marathi is chiefly spoken; in the north, Kashmiri and Naipali. The language which is common to almost all the people, or at least is very widespread and therefore useful to the traveller, is Hindustani or Urdu. This is the Hindi of the camps of Mahommedan soldiers concentrated in the neighbourhood of Delhi in the twelfth century. It contains an admixture of Persian and Arabic and is written in Arabic script; from the sixteenth century onwards it served for the expression of a fairly considerable literature.

II

WRITING

When the Aryans entered India they already had a literature, but it was oral. For a long time the tradition was maintained of confiding literary works to the memory without writing them down. Even to-day, although the Indians have learned European science and methods of research, they prefer to learn orally from the teacher's lips. An educated man is called *bahuśruta*, "who has heard much." Their reading was hearing, and their writing was keeping in one's own memory or passing on to that of others. We are still surprised at the ease with which they learn by heart. Story-tellers go into the villages and recite whole poems for hours to audiences as unwearied as themselves. Rhapsodes used to visit the courts of princes and chant endless, involved tales of the deeds of Rama or the Pandavas. We do not hear of books, *pustaka* ; the word is not found in the old texts. It seems to come from the Iranian *post*, " skin " [1] ; sacred texts of the *Avesta* were written on calf-skins prepared for the purpose. The more usual *pāṭhaka*, now " reader " or " teacher ", originally meant " reciter ".

The Indians maintained that their sacred works were better preserved by memory and ear than by manuscripts. It was even thought to be a profanation of the divine word—and the greater part of their ancient literature is the word of Brahma—to reveal it to anyone who could read. The Vedas were only written down very late, at the end of the eighteenth century and the beginning of the nineteenth, under the influence of the Europeans and by the " treason " of certain Brahmans. The enormous literatures of the Brahmans and Buddhists were produced, preserved, and spread abroad without the aid of writing. For long periods in the monastic life of Buddhism, when a community lacked a text, it would borrow a learned monk from another community, just as we now borrow scarce editions from old libraries. The monk came and recited his " book ", and the text was reprinted on the minds of his hearers.

This does not mean that there was no writing in existence. The earliest dated inscriptions are of the time of Asoka (third century B.C.). If the King could address his people in writing, the people must have been able to read, and therefore, in most cases, to write. Only the use of writing was not preferred to other methods of teaching.

The most ancient Indian script, Brahmi, so called because it was dictated by the god Brahma, is based on the Semitic alphabet. Merchants trading with Babylon, or even with the Phoenicians, doubtless introduced it very early, about 800 B.C., for their commercial use. From them it passed into the chancellories of kings, and the Semitic signs were added to and altered to render Aryan sounds.

Another alphabet, Kharoshthi, shows its Aramaic origin more clearly. Here the vowels are barely indicated, and the words are written from right to left. Kharoshthi, introduced into north-western India in the sixth century as a result

[1] Cf. R. Gauthiot, *Mém. Soc. Ling.*, xix (1915), quoted in B. Laufer, *Sino-Iranica.*

of Persian rule, was fairly widespread in Chinese Turkistan under the Kushans, in the first and second centuries of our era.

The alphabet most generally used is Nagari, the " urban " writing, or Devanagari, the " urban and divine " (or royal) writing, derived from Brahmi. It is a syllabic script. Thus, for example, if we see the signs *k d l*, we shall read, from left to right, *kadala,* " banana-tree," for if there is no special sign indicating another vowel one always reads *a*.

So, then, very little writing was done, and that very late. Only some hundreds of years after Christ do we find books—rare, it is true—exhorting good men to transcribe works of study and to spread them abroad. The habit was to keep knowledge to oneself as a personal gift and a caste privilege. A man who wished to acquire it had only to go to a reputed teacher. But he had to belong to the upper class. The Brahmans defended the doors to knowledge jealously. " If a Śūdra," we read in an old collection of laws, " listens to the Vedas, let his ears be filled with molten tin . . . If he dares to recite them, let his tongue be cut off." Even if the practice was not always so cruel, the prohibition expressed in such terms proves that every opposition was made to the spread of knowledge to the lower classes. Therefore it was not entrusted to writing, which was accessible to all.

The danger was not very great, for writing-materials were fragile. For a long time writing was done on birch-bark, and even after paper was known palm-leaves and wooden tablets were used. In the damp climate of India manuscripts deteriorate very quickly. They keep better in the dry climate of Turkistan. In 1900 Sir Aurel Stein discovered five hundred tablets covered with writing in the sand of the desert of Taklamakan. But as a rule the manuscripts are not old. We have none earlier than the twelfth century. Most documents are written on paper, which the Mussulmans introduced into India in the thirteenth century. Metal plaques were also used, the value of the metal varying according to the importance of the document, and people even took the pains in the twelfth century and later to carve whole dramas on rocks ; strangely enough, it was not the best works that were thus placed on permanent record. But the Mussulmans of the neighbourhood took the stones for building their mosques.

III

THE STUDY OF INDIAN LITERATURE IN EUROPE

Our earliest information about the Sanskrit language and literature came from the missionaries. The Austrian Carmelite friar, Paulinus a S. Bartholomæo, utilizing the works of his seventeenth-century predecessors, Abraham Roger and the Jesuit Hanxleden, and his personal knowledge of India, published a Sanskrit grammar in 1792 and a work on the religions and languages of India in 1798.

At the end of the eighteenth century France lost interest in India. Great Britain turned its attention to the country, and the East India Company's little Fort William became the nucleus of the future Indian Empire of the British Crown. Whatever may be said of the misfortunes which the bad policy of the Company brought upon the Indians, one must recognize, to the honour of the British, that they wished to know their new subjects. They had fairly urgent reasons, for the customs of India made the task of the foreign colonizers difficult. Warren Hastings, the first Governor of Bengal, caused a practical code of law to be extracted from the Sanskrit collections and translated into Persian, and this version was finally translated into English (1776). It was not yet possible to translate direct, for the British knew no Sanskrit and the Brahmans knew no English.

To know Indian law, then, was one of the first concerns of the British administrators. Sir William Jones, a judge at Fort William, courageously learned Sanskrit in order to translate the ancient collection of laws attributed to Manu. At the same time, in his enthusiasm for India, he founded the Asiatic Society of Bengal, which has done much to make India known in Europe. But of greater importance for the general literary public were the translations of the masterpieces of Sanskrit literature. The drama *Śakuntalā*, translated by Jones in 1789, and the *Bhagavadgītā* and the fables of the *Hitopadeśa*, translated by Charles Wilkins in 1785 and 1788, awakened a somewhat romantic interest in India. Goethe himself was filled with admiration, and his famous elegiacs on *Śakuntalā* are only too well known.

The true founder of Sanskrit philology was Henry Thomas Colebrooke. He was not a poet or a literary man, but a born seeker after knowledge, and he directed his researches to almost every domain of Indian thought, beginning with the translation (1797) of a collection of laws on inheritance and contracts prepared by the pundits (*paṇḍita,* " learned man "). He had not the enthusiasm of Jones or Wilkins, and Max Müller, who in later years was introduced to him in England as a young man of talent, made fun of his dryness. But by his works and by the acquisition of a great collection of manuscripts in India Colebrooke created scholars.

Presently the French took part in the movement. In 1801 and 1802 Anquetil Duperron published his translation of the Upanishads from Persian into Latin, and, though criticism was not lacking, it created a great impression.

But Duperron did not know Sanskrit. A. L. de Chézy, the first Professor of Sanskrit at the Collège de France, had learned the language alone, without a teacher and without going to India, with the help of the English works and the manuscripts of the Bibliothèque Nationale.

The Bibliothèque Nationale had about two hundred manuscripts, which were catalogued about 1807 by A. Hamilton and L. Langlès. Hamilton, on his way back from India, where he had learned Sanskrit, happened to be in Paris in 1802, when hostilities were renewed between Napoleon and Great Britain, and he had to remain there some years. He taught Sanskrit to Friedrich von Schlegel, who was the promoter of Indian philology in Germany and largely responsible for the enthusiastic fancies about the ancient wisdom of the Aryans, the Golden Age of the Veda, and the *Muttersprache.* These ideas were still in vogue fifty years later.

Chézy had given Germany its first Professor of Sanskrit. This was his pupil, August Wilhelm von Schlegel. Another of his pupils was Franz Bopp, the author of the first comparative grammar based on Sanskrit. The Schlegel brothers, Bopp, and Wilhelm von Humboldt introduced Indian studies into the scheme and courses of German scholarship, while the poet Rückert revealed Indian poetry to the intelligent masses of Germany, although he transformed it into a romantic echo of European ideas of the Orient.

At the beginning of the nineteenth century students dealt only with the classical literature of India. They had at the most a very faint notion of the Veda and knew nothing at all of Buddhism. It was Eugène Burnouf, Professor at the Collège de France (died 1852), who founded the critical study of the Veda, as he founded that of the *Avesta*, of the Pali language, and of Buddhism. Burnouf's teaching, cut short too soon, was an epoch in Indo-Iranian philology.

Among Burnouf's pupils was Rudolf von Roth. He started Vedic studies in Germany, while Friedrich Max Müller, Burnouf's other great pupil, introduced them in England and brought out a complete edition of the hymns of the *Ṛigveda* with Sayana's commentary.

The impetus given by Burnouf still continues, and it would take too long to enumerate even the more important of the many workers and works. We may, however, mention the *Catalogus Catalogorum* of Theodor Aufrecht, the fruit of forty years' labour, a list of the Sanskrit manuscripts in all the great libraries of Europe and India, and the great Petersburg Dictionary, in seven volumes, published (1852-1875) by Otto Böhtlingk and Rudolf von Roth.

At the present day "Indian studies" cover a domain so vast that the life and strength of one man are no longer sufficient to cope with it. So specialization increases, and works come out every year in greater numbers. Moreover, the subject now involves a knowledge of Central Asia, the Far East, and even, since the Hittites have come to the fore, Asia Minor. It had already long been bound up with the study of Iran. Soon the term "Indian studies" will be as vague as, for instance, "Western European Studies" would be. But the vague name covers a number of strictly scientific branches of learning.

Old problems, for a time neglected, come under the examination of scholars anew. The question of the Vedas, treated in a new fashion since Burnouf's time by Bergaigne, comes to the fore again. This is the day of checkings, doubts, and resumptions of research on unforeseen bases and in new directions. We are passing through a time of bold and unwearied activity.

IV

THE LITERATURE OF INDIA

Indian literature is at least three thousand years old. It has grown up in an area two-thirds the size of Europe. It extended from Central Asia to Japan and from Tibet to Indonesia.

Its character is essentially religious. That is doubtless due to the nature of the Indians, but also, and still more, to the fact that the ancient works have passed through the hands of Brahman editors. Besides, the first monument of that literature, the *Ṛigveda*, continued to be a model and laid its mark on all later writing.

Nevertheless, the Indians have cultivated every literary form. In one domain they have distinguished themselves especially—that of grammar. India was the first—and until the beginning of the last century the only—country to be able to think its language philosophically. In this study it reached a very high degree of unbiassed, clear, exact observation.

Although the Prakrit and non-Aryan languages of India produced fairly rich literatures, we shall here confine ourselves to works in Vedic and Sanskrit. We cannot, however, entirely neglect Pali literature. It is too intimately bound up with all that is of popular origin in the Sanskrit works and too much rooted in the thought and traditions, not only of India, but of the Aryans, for it to be possible to ignore it in a general picture of the Indian spirit.

It might, then, be said that we are about to discuss profane literature. But this word cannot be used of India. That the most ancient works have come down to us only in the form of religious hymns, in which a little history is sometimes mingled, is not surprising; it happens elsewhere. But that the whole of literature seems to proceed from the priestly circles, or at least to bear their impress, is a fact peculiar to Hindustan.

I propose to describe the development of Indian literature from the earliest times to the Mussulman conquest.

The most ancient phase is Vedic and post-Vedic literature. It consists first of the Vedas, and secondly of the Brāhmaṇas,

Upanishads, and Sūtras. It is hard to say when this period began. It is regarded as having ended some centuries before Christ, although works proceeding from the same inspiration and subject to the influence of the same language may have appeared fairly late. This is true especially of the Upanishads, and also of some of the Sūtras and Brāhmaṇas.

To the same period belong those Indian *Gesta Deorum* known as the Purāṇas, popular tales of half-historical, half-legendary deeds, the theme of the great epic poems and the prose epic fragments. The *Rāmāyaṇa*, a conscious work of art, was already, according to Indian belief, known as a complete work before the time of Christ. The *Mahābhārata*, a more popular and more chaotic work, does not seem to have received its final form until early in our era (the third or fourth century).[1] Of the Purāṇas parts are as old as the Vedic age, but they were put together fairly late, and works of the seventh and eighth centuries after Christ are still called by this name (*purāṇa* = " what happened in old days ").

Contemporary with the epics and Purāṇas are the fables and tales. Buddhism has left the Jātakas in Pali, which are popular tales illustrating the successive lives of Buddha previous to that in which he became the possessor of absolute truth. These Jātakas already existed, if not in collected form, at least in fragments, in the third century B.C. Scenes from them were carved on the pillars which Asoka set up at Bharhut and Sañchi. In Sanskrit there were beast-fables, intermingled with aphoristic verse, in two closely related collections named the *Hitopadeśa* and the *Pañchatantra*. We do not know when these works were first compiled, but one of them was already well known in Persia in the sixth century of our era, and doubtless before. On the other hand, the development of the romance or novel was due to the artistic effort of poets, seeking to please the refined and cultured nobility under Harsha and monarchs of his type.

The last form to develop was the drama, which falls entirely within the Christian era. The drama, the lyric, which was cultivated early but did not really reach its full

[1] S. Lévi, **XV**, v (1915).

flower until later, and the romance of adventures are the glories of the period called the Indian Renaissance, which commences under the Guptas at the beginning of the fourth century, although the ground was prepared by contact with the Hellenic world.

CHAPTER I

VEDIC AND POST-VEDIC LITERATURE

I

THE AGE OF THE ṚIGVEDA

REFERENCE has already been made in this work to the difficulty of dating the *Ṛigveda*. Whereas Müx Muller was of opinion that the year 1000 B.C. was the latest possible date of its compilation, shortly afterwards knowledge of the language of the *Avesta*, which is very like that of the *Ṛigveda*, caused the latter to be brought some centuries later. Now that the comparative antiquity of the *Avesta* is coming into favour, the age of the *Ṛigveda* is benefiting by it. Besides, there have been discovered in the Vedic hymns memories of a life which may have been led very far away from Hindustan, far in time and in place, for it seems to contain Asianic elements intermingled with Indian. Scholars are inclined to throw certain parts back to the period of the Hittites in Asia Minor.[1] Nor should we forget the bold contention of H. Jacobi,[2] nor that of Bal Gangadhar Tilak of Bombay.[3] These two views were put forward at the same time, independently of one another, and they present the most astonishing conclusions. Jacobi, in virtue of an examination of the Indian calendar as it is found in certain Vedic chants and of a comparison of these data with those of the Brāhmaṇas, places the age of the Veda over four thousand years before our era. Tilak places it six thousand years before Christ. Doubt is still permissible ; were the observations of the heavens recorded in the texts correct ?

Jacobi's hypothesis is corroborated by another passage in ancient Indian literature. The Gṛihya Sūtras, which are

[1] Cf. Wust, in **XXVII**, 34 (2).

[2] Jacobi, " Über das Alter des Ṛig-Veda," in *Festgruss an Rudolph von Roth*, Stuttgart, 1893.

[3] Tilak, *The Orion, or researches into the antiquity of the Vedas*, Bombay, 1893.

collections of family rites, describe an impressive marriage-ceremony. The bridal pair, arriving at the end of the day at their new home, sit in silence on a bull's hide. They remain thus until the stars appear. Then the husband, pointing to the pole-star, says to his wife something like this: "May you be as constant as it, and happy in my house!" The name of the star is *dhruva*, "firm, constant," and its faithful appearance, always in the same quarter of the sky, symbolizes the wife's fidelity to her husband. But in our time the pole-star is scarcely visible, and it is hard to think of it as striking the imagination. Two thousand years ago it was still so far from the pole that it revolved round it with the other stars and could not be regarded as immovable. It is therefore probable that the custom in question referred to another and brighter star, which may, at a very remote time, have been so near the celestial pole that it was the pole-star for the people of that age. This was the case with Alpha Draconis in the first half of the third millennium before Christ. But the *Ṛigveda*, which is much more ancient than the Sūtras, makes no mention of this custom, and therefore seems to be earlier than the third millennium.

However, the only conclusion which we can at present accept is that the Vedas and Sūtras contain memories of civilized life in a very early state. The final compilation of these collections may have been done in a comparatively late period, which we cannot determine exactly.

II

GENERAL FEATURES OF THE RIGVEDA

The *Ṛigveda* is a collection, put together late, of remnants of old legends, of chants of an epic kind which never formed a complete epic, of incantations, and, more rarely, of lyrics. All this was adapted to the purposes of sacrifice and consecrated by tradition. The authors delight in repeating the same similes, the same metaphors. One is confronted by stock phrases which show that before the work was put together there was a vague period of literary production. At times one comes on intense religious enthusiasm, and elsewhere are fragments vibrating with hatred of the enemies of the Aryan people. The pictures of festivals, particularly of chariot-races, the portraits of the gods, and the descriptions of natural phenomena are astonishingly rich in colouring. But it is all the result of work spread over centuries and not in the least spontaneous, the fruit of an aristocratic and warlike civilization, already well organized and divided into classes; it is the creation of later generations, a mosaic rather than a picture, laborious and sophisticated, in no way reflecting the supposedly happy and virtuous primitive society. These people fight more than any other ancient race, to judge from the documents, they enjoy life in the most violent way possible, and the beautiful simplicity of their religious faith is proved by many passages in the hymns not to have been the general rule. There are many flashes of irony or scepticism at the expense of the gods.

The language of the hymns shows a good deal of borrowing from the Prakrit languages.[1] This shows that the popular speech was at one time not separated from the ritual language by an absolute barrier.

Varieties of style can be seen in the different parts of the *Ṛigveda.* This fact seems to be due to difference either in the dates of composition or in the authors, who might live in very different regions from each other. Tradition ascribes certain books to Brahman families, whose names it gives. It may be that the descendants of a sage, the real author, shared with him the glory of having conveyed the divine words to men; or perhaps certain families of priests claimed to be the sole repositories of the hymns which were especially adapted to their functions as *hotar*, *udgātar*, or whatever they might be.

This diversity of detail is accompanied by uniformity of versification. The prosody of the *ṛich* is syllabic; no attention is paid to quantity except in the last two feet of each line. Indeed, one should not speak of feet with reference to the Indian stanza, for except the four, or, rarely, the five last syllables the whole beginning of the line is free. Of course when it contains only five syllables, as in the stanza named *virāj*, each has its definite quantity. A line is called *pāda,* which means "foot" and also, and preferably, "quarter." Three *pādas* of eight syllables with an iambic

[1] Wackernagel, *Altindische Grammatik*, i.

ending form the *gāyatrī* stanza, which is the most usual in Vedic and is intended to be sung. Less frequent in Vedic, but afterwards employed generally and forming the true epic stanza, *śloka*, is the *anushṭubh,* four lines of eight syllables. Other stanzas, such as the *trishṭubh* or four *pādas* of eleven syllables with a cæsura after the fourth or fifth syllable, or the *jagatī,* four lines of twelve syllables, ending in a troche, are found alternating with much more elaborate and complicated metres. This is another proof that the composition of these poems was far removed from popular creation. An elaborately worked-out metre has always been favoured by Indian poets, but in the age of the Veda and the Brāhmaṇas metre had a sacred and symbolic value. One finds in Indian expository works, some centuries before Christ, long speculations on the mysticism of metres and their part in ritual, which was a magical and very potent part. The inspiration of the poet and the enthusiasm of his listener became a support of the liturgy and its explanation.

Let us admit that we are still far from understanding the whole of the *Ṛigveda.* At every step one comes upon difficulties. The Indians themselves had long lost the tradition of it when the great Sayana (fourteenth century of our era) set himself to comment on those ancient books. Modern scholars are not agreed as to what is of Indo-European origin and what is purely Indian. The slow formation of the hymns in the course of very remote ages and the late date at which they were assembled in collections are great obstacles to Vedic exegesis.

The 1,028 hymns (*sūkta*) of the *Ṛigveda* are divided into ten circles (*maṇḍala*). The principles on which this division is based are very rough. Hymns are classed together sometimes by the name of the *ṛishi* or sage who wrote them; sometimes by that of a family of chorister-priests with whom they are associated by tradition; sometimes by their subject. Thus, Books II–VII are known as belonging to certain families; the ninth deals with the cult of Soma; the tenth is latest in language and ideas; the first is the least like the rest, having been added later to the original collection. But, just as one finds hymns of comparatively late language side by side with others of undoubted antiquity, so in the names of authors (some of them women) the principle of unity is not strictly observed.

III

THE OTHER VEDAS

The Sāmaveda, Yajurveda, and Atharvaveda

The *saṃhitā* of the *Sāmaveda* is simply a collection of tunes to which to sing the sacred hymns. Yet it contains no musical notation. All that it says is something like "This should be sung to the air of such-and-such a stanza". This is followed by a line or a few words from the beginning of a hymn which was well enough known to serve as a model. The tune, according to the Hindu idea, was fitted to the stanza, and indeed sprang from it; the stanza was the "womb" of the air.

Only long afterwards did music begin to be indicated by means of special signs, first by syllables and later by figures, from 1 to 7, which correspond to our scale from *fa* downwards to *sol*. Since all teaching was done orally, the master was there to give the signal with his hand and indicate the notes with his fingers.

Singing was of very great importance in worship, and therefore there were many modes of singing. A late writer mentions as many as eight thousand.[1] The practice of magic, which has such a great place in India, was accompanied by special chants, and the *Sāmaveda*, outside its ritual use, became the favourite Veda of sorcerers. There is even a text-book of sorcery, the *Sāmavidhāna Brāhmaṇa*, which says what melodies (*sāman*) should be used to make the spell efficacious. So the very sound of the *sāman* filled people with terror, and although the *Sāmaveda* was one of the sacred books, the Brahmans interrupted the recitation of the *ṛich* and the study of the Vedas as soon as the sound of the *sāman* mingled with them. Only officiating priests could handle that dangerous weapon with impunity.

From the literary point of view, the *Sāmaveda* is of no interest. It repeats the stanzas of the *Ṛigveda*, especially of the eighth and ninth books. A few dozen lines added

[1] **CCLXXXVIII**, p. 146, n.

by the authors of the *Sāmaveda* are quite worthless. It was intended for the use of the *udgātar*, the priests whose office it was to chant prayers during sacrifice. For the phrases to be recited in a low voice or murmured by the *adhvaryu* priests there was another collection, the *Yajurveda*. The *yajus* were short invocations in prose or verse. They were composed on the model of the stanzas of the *Ṛigveda*, of which some of them are merely copies.

We know two recensions of the *Yajurveda*, the Black and the White. The Black is the older, to judge from the language and the imperfect nature of the exposition. It is called " black " (*kṛishṇa*) in the sense of "obscure, dark", for its formulas are mixed up quite unsystematically with the exegetic explanation or *brāhmaṇa*. It was taught by four great schools of expositors, and four *saṃhitās* of it are known —the *Taittirīya*, *Maitrāyaṇī*, *Kāṭhaka*, and *Kapishṭhala-Kāṭha Saṃhitās*, the last being fragmentary.

The White *Yajurveda* is called the *Vājasaneyi Saṃhitā*, because a famous teacher, Yajñavalkya Vajasaneya, is mentioned in it. Two recensions are known, those of the Mādhyaṃdina and Kaṇva schools, but they are just like each other. The *Vājasaneyi* contains only the formulas. They are clearly and systematically arranged, and the compilers evidently took pains. But the last fifteen sections out of forty are of later origin, and although they are connected with the ideas already set forth in the tenth book of the *Ṛigveda*, their mysticism betrays the influence of the Upanishads. In the older portion one finds, among other things, traces of very ancient rites, interesting for folk-lore—the King's sacrifice and the horse sacrifice. Both ceremonies are described in detail in the *Śatapatha Brāhmaṇa*, which we shall discuss later.

It would be a mistake to suppose that the *Yajurveda* is homogeneous in thought all through. By the side of very simple prayers which merely name the god to whom the offering is made, and others, equally straightforward, to the effect, " Give this or that to me who give thee so-and-so," one finds incantations in the form of litanies, and endless lists of the names, epithets, and attributes of a god, intended solely to exert pressure on him and compel him to favour the worshipper. Nor are secular elements lacking, and these are of great importance to the historian. They tell us that society included craftsmen of all sorts, from cartwrights to goldsmiths, etc., and that the Brahmans already formed a privileged guild, if not a caste. In places, too, curses and spells are mingled with prayers of an elevated tone. Elsewhere we find exclamations in which the words, incomprehensible to us, have a mystic value for the Hindu. This is not only true of the syllable OM. Every act is merely the symbol of another act not revealed to our eyes, every object is the symbol of a secret power, every word has a hidden meaning. One is surrounded by mystery. The common man is always exposed to dangers, the least of which is that his prayers will be ineffective. A word mispronounced, an altered stress, may let loose magical, hostile forces upon him. But he "who knows thus" (*evaṃvid*), he who understands the symbolism and mysticism of objects or sacred formulas, alone can handle them with impunity, for his own benefit and to the detriment of his enemies.

For a long time only three Vedas were recognized. The books speak of the Triple Science (*trayī vidyā*), the liturgical knowledge contained in the *Ṛigveda*, *Sāmaveda*, and *Yajurveda*. At a fairly late date the fourth Veda was added, the *Atharvaveda*.

This collection is not itself more recent than the others. Its very title proclaims its ancient origin, for *atharvan* is the fire-priest, the *atar* of the Avesta. The word is of Indo-Iranian origin, dating therefore from the time when the two peoples were one, and it is preserved in Old Indian only in the name of *atharvan*, "sorcerer-priest." The complete and oldest title of the *Atharvaveda Saṃhitā* is *Atharvāngirasaḥ*, meaning *The Atharvans and Angiras*. The former are wizards who perform good spells ; the latter make destroying spells, black magic. Thus, while the *atharvans* heal the sick, give protection against misfortune, etc., the *angiras* send sickness and misfortune to enemies and rivals.

The best known recension is the *Śaunaka Saṃhitā*. Its twenty books contain seven hundred and thirty-one hymns, some of which are very short, being incantations of one or two lines (Book VII), while others are several dozen lines long (XVII and XVIII). The systematic arrangement of the hymns, which is entirely formal and based on a mechanical principle, is evidence of its late composition. Thus in the first book the hymns are almost all of four lines, in the second of five, in the third of six, and in the fourth of seven. After that the outward arrangement is allowed to slide a little, but the thought seems to matter more. Prose, too, is mixed with the poetry.

In general the language and prosody of the *Atharvaveda* are those of the *Ṛigveda*, but one finds later passages, "written" under the influence of the popular languages. The foundation of the *Atharvaveda* is likewise popular and without doubt very ancient; it draws on the grossest superstitions of an uncivilized people which is as passionate and uncontrollable in its hates as in its desires. Yet the place and time are not the same as in the *Ṛigveda*. The tiger is mentioned, so the Aryans must have already come near the jungle of Bengal. Much is said in these hymns of the Brahmans, of the honours which are due to them and their material interests. This proves not only that the *Atharvaveda* had undergone Brahman editing, but that society was moving towards the supremacy of the Brahmans. That supremacy, which, if not altogether unknown, is at least little emphasized in the Vedic period, makes itself clearly felt in the post-Vedic Brāhmaṇas and Sūtras.

IV

THE BRĀHMAṆAS [1]

As time went on, the Vedas ceased to be clear, their language became incomprehensible, and the tradition of the cult was in danger of being lost. Accordingly experts in ritual composed liturgical treatises for the use of Brahmans who officiated during sacrifice. Above all it was necessary to explain to the officiant the relationship between the formulas which he murmured or the hymns which he sang and the various ritual acts and consecrated gestures which he performed. These treatises are called *brāhmaṇas*, "explanations." Every discussion on a point of exegesis is named thus, and so are collections of the teachings of the Brahmanic schools.

[1] S. Lévi, CLXXIX.

The explanatory passages in the Black *Yajurveda*, mingled with the *mantras*, are the first *brāhmaṇas*. The language and ideas developed after the Vedic period.

The Brāhmaṇas are in prose, the usual form of scientific literature. There was, of course, some prose in the Vedas, but in the main they were poetic. In the Brāhmaṇas the proportion is the other way round. The Vedas may stupefy the reader by the chaotic mixture of their matter, but the Brāhmaṇas surpass everything in stark aridity.

If, however, we embark on an examination of them, we shall find much information about the past of India, the expansion of the Aryans in the Ganges valley, ancient customs and the formation of a philosophy. For geographical and historical information and ancient legends, the Brāhmaṇas are an inexhaustible mine, but everything is mingled with a farrago of explanations which are as detailed as they are artificial, defying all logic. Etymologies of surprising puerility are used as arguments in the solving of abstract problems. The identification of objects or phenomena which have nothing in common and symbolism pressed to the wildest lengths, together with an attempt to bring all things down to fundamental unity, reveal a speculation which is on the road to becoming philosophy but is at present only a feeble stammering.

Each Veda has its Brāhmaṇa. This was not so from the very beginning, but as exegetic literature grew, new treatises were composed on the same questions, and they were attached to the parts of the Vedas which lacked them.

One Brāhmaṇa of the *Ṛigveda*, the *Aitareya*, tells an interesting story connected with the abolition of human sacrifice.

> King Harischandra, of the line of the Sun and the race of Ikshvaku, wished to have a male child, and to obtain him he presented him in advance to Varuna. But when the god came to claim his due, the King, on various pretexts, caused the date of the sacrifice to be put off until the boy should be of age. He then bought from a poor Brahman one of his sons, named Sunahsepa, to offer up instead. Just as the victim, decked with flowers and tied to the post of sacrifice, was about to be slain, the gods, summoned by his lamentations, intervened, and Varuna showed mercy.

What strikes one in this legend is the wretched condition of the old Brahman who will sell his son for a herd of cows and cut the lad's throat himself. This may be an echo of a change which had taken place in the mind of the Vedic Indian, which had led to a respect for human life and the replacement of human sacrifice by that of animals, the latter of which soon gave way in part to the peaceful offering of Soma.

The most important and also the latest of these works is the "Explanation of the Hundred Ways" (? of sacrifice), the *Śatapatha Brāhmaṇa* of the White *Yajurveda*. It is placed about the fifth century B.C.; in any case, Panini, who must have lived in the fourth century at the latest, seems to be acquainted with it, although not perhaps in its final form. This *Brāhmaṇa* is intended for the use of the *adhvaryu*, the priest who performs all the technical offices of the sacrifice, accompanying them with *yajus*. It explains the *yajus* and their connexion with the ritual acts. It is a didactic and expository work, and is written in the dryest and most concise manner possible; its use of adjectives, participles, and substantives as epithets makes its elliptical style inimitable. The brief words must have been supplemented by gesture and voice-production on the part of the master. Fortunately, its discussions are occasionally interrupted by an *itihāsa* (literally, "In truth it was so"), *ākhyāna*, or *purāṇa*; these are "stories", sometimes historical and sometimes fabulous.

In it we find the very ancient legend of the Deluge, but the identification of the Indian story with Semitic legends is not established.

> One morning water had been brought to Manu that he might wash, "as is still the custom among men." While he was washing his hands, a little fish threw himself into them. "Save my life, and I shall save yours," he said. "From what will you save me?" "Great waters will come, and they will carry away all living things." "From what and how am I to save you?" "I am small, and large fish can devour me. Keep me in a pot. When it becomes too small for me, dig a ditch for me, and when that is too small, throw me into the sea." Now, this fish was a *jhasha*,[1] and he grew enormous. At last, going away, he said, "The great waters will come soon. Make yourself a boat and wait for me. I shall come and save you." At the appointed time, the great rains came on. The water rose on every side. Manu went into his boat, and the *jhasha* came to him, made him tie the boat to his own horn, and swam beyond the northern mountains. There he bade Manu tie

[1] A mythical fish, not identified.

his boat to a tree and then, as the water fell, loose the rope and drift carefully with the stream. The place where he came down is called to this day the Descent of Manu. Thus Manu was the first man of the new creation. With his daughter Ida he begot the human race, and when Ida, hiding herself from her father to escape incest, turned herself into a cow, a she-goat, and other creatures in turn, Manu, taking on the shape of the same beast, begot with her the animal world.

Very beautiful, like the echo of a melancholy song, is the legend of Pururavas and Urvasi, which the *Śatapatha* tells in continuation of some stanzas preserved in the tenth book of the *Ṛigveda.*

The nymph (*apsaras*) Urvasi loved King Pururavas. Marrying him, she made him accept three conditions, one of which was that she should never see him naked ; " for such is the custom of us women," says the text. A year went by, and Urvasi already bore within her the child of Pururavas, but the Gandharvas, the heavenly musicians, companions of the nymphs, wearied for her. " It is long that this Apsaras stays among men," they said one to another. They devised a trick to bring her back. Urvasi had two pet lambs, which she tied to her bed at night. The Gandharvas stole one of them, and the next night they took the second. Then Urvasi complained that she had been wronged " as if there were no man in the house ". Pururavas rushed after the Gandharvas, but they sent a flash of lightning and Pururavas was naked in front of his wife. At the same moment she vanished.

The *Śatapatha* contains many cosmogonic legends.

For example it relates that at the beginning nothing existed but Prajapati (" lord of creation ", *prajā* meaning " posterity "). " That I might multiply myself ! " he thought. By mortifying himself, he created Fire, Agni. He brought him out of his mouth, and, on account of his origin, Agni " eats ", that is, devours, the offering. But since there was nothing to consume, Agni turned, with flaming mouth, against his creator. Prajapati then hastened to create plants and trees, milk and butter, and to institute the sacrifice. In this way he escapes destruction and also multiplies himself in his creations.

The conclusion is that sacrifice is a divine institution, and he who makes it with full knowledge escapes destruction and multiplies himself in his progeny. Such is the reasoning of the Brāhmaṇas.

Would you know why the mountains cannot fly ?

They had wings once, and transported themselves from one place to another.[1] But the weight fell heavy on the earth, and it

[1] *Maitr. Saṃh.*, i, 10, 13 ; L. v. Schroeder, *Indiens Literatur u. Kultur.*

sank under the impact of their descent. The god Indra found a remedy for its distress. He cut off the wings of the mountains and made them immovable (*achala*). The wings became clouds, and that is why we see the clouds going so much to the mountains.

The work from which this legend is taken, the *Maitrāyaṇī Saṃhitā*, which is composed, as we know, of formulas (*yajus*) followed by explanations (*brāhmaṇa*), tells the exquisite story of the creation of night.

Yami mourned the death of her brother and lover, Yama. The gods could not console her. To make her forget her beloved, they created night, which covers everything with its veil. When on the morrow the day broke, Yami had forgotten her brother.

Sometimes the exegesis contains a dash of fun.

The gods were in conflict with the Gandharvas, who had stolen the Soma from them, and they sent Vach, the Voice, a young and beautiful woman, to them. She turned the heads of the Gandharvas and took back the Soma. But they demanded in compensation that she should return among them. "Good," said the gods. "Let us have a contest, and let her choose." The Gandharvas, contrary to their true nature, wished to appear serious beings, and to win the lady by knowledge. They recited the Vedas to her. "See how learned we are!" they said to her. But the gods created the lute, and played and sang. Vach ran to them. That is why women are so charmed by dancers and singers.

Like the Vedas, but even more so, the Brāhmaṇas indulge in fanciful etymologies. They justify a rite by explaining its name, or rather by glossing it by another which resembles it.[1] Thus the name of Indra is derived from the root *indh*, "burn." This would give Indha, and that must be the real name of the god, hidden under his ordinary appellation. Why should it be hidden? "Because the gods love mystery." Plants are called *oshadhayah*. Why? Because they appeared after Prajapati said, "*Oshaṃ dhaya*," "Wood, while you burn," when he was pouring the libation into the fire. Agni, Fire, was created first, *agre*; it is as if he were called Agri.[2] Likeness of sound is enough to identify words, and the identification of words identifies ideas and causes them to be symbolized by the most different objects.

There is an astonishing mixture of sophisticated speculation with simple and often gross analogies and proofs. Sexual brutality is mingled with liturgical acts.[3] The act of

[1] Oldenberg, *Vorwissenschaftliche Wissenschaft*.
[2] *Ś.B.*, ii, 2, 4, 2.
[3] Cf. **CLXXIX**, for all this.

procreation is frequently called in to explain the details of sacrifice, and is itself merely the image of sacrifice, the woman being the altar. All phenomena and the whole life of the universe are explained as symbolizing one another and being merely the various appearances of the sacrifice which men make to the gods and the gods make to themselves. Unity proved, or supposed to be proved, by the juxtaposition of images is the principal idea of the Āraṇyakas and Upanishads.

V

THE ĀRAṆYAKAS AND UPANISHADS

In the age of Middle Indian, the post-Vedic period, the priestly caste, now completely organized, is established in its privileges. It never forgets, in the Brāhmaṇas, to remind others of its superiority. But new ideas soon come to the fore, and laymen take part in the controversies of the doctors. Even from the priesthood free spirits spring, who deny the efficacity of the cult and of liberal gifts to its representatives. They seek for other ways of salvation and other bases for their speculations. The products of this very intense intellectual movement are the Āraṇyakas, "Reflections in the Forest," and the Upanishads, "Secret Teachings," which were only communicated to a limited number of disciples.

There is no sharp break between the Brāhmaṇas and the Upanishads. At first the latter form part of the former. Thus, the Great Upanishad of the Forest, the *Bṛihadāraṇyaka*, is included in the *Śatapatha*. Only in the course of time does production diverge, on the one side into *sūtras* and on the other into "free" teachings, speculations about the absolute (*ātman*), which are given the name of Upanishads. They are also called Vedānta, the "Completion of the Vedas", for they close the Vedic period. The Āraṇyakas are the fruit of solitary meditation, of a hermit life which was always familiar to the people of the Ganges valley. The Brahmans even instituted the theory of the four *āśramas*, or phases of life for a noble or Aryan.

The first stage was that of *brahmachārin*, or Brahman student, the time of study under a Brahman teacher. The young man owed complete obedience to his master; he had to act as his servant and beg food for him. In return, he was allowed to repeat the words of the Vedas after his teacher until he knew them by heart. Then he gave his master a present and, being released with his blessing, returned home to marry and found a family. This *āśrama* was that of *gṛihastha,* or master of a house, the age of social and religious activity. Then, when all duties had been done, children reared and married, and the continuance of the family ensured, the devout Indian might, if he wished, renounce the world and retire to the wilderness to worship the gods or to meditate on the problems of existence, the mystery of sacrifice, and so on. But sometimes this life as a *vānaprastha,* "forest-dweller," did not satisfy the sage; or else, feeling his end draw near, he ceased his pious exercises and only meditated on union with the absolute. In that case he was called *saṃnyāsin,* "renouncer of everything." The *saṃnyāsins* sometimes became wandering ascetics or went on pilgrimages to the holy places or the distant hermitages of the Himalaya. In the end they allowed themselves to die of hunger and fatigue, indifferent to everything. But most usually the hermitages were little colonies far from the towns. A thinker or a man renowned for piety or wisdom brought together disciples, who came to follow his teaching and share his penances. A school grew up. The reflections of the sages, collected by their disciples, gave birth to the Āraṇyakas and after them to the Upanishads.

The Upanishads were for the most part formed outside priestly circles. Philosophic speculation was no longer the exclusive privilege of a caste. Thus, Janaka, King of Videha, surpasses the Brahmans in sacred knowledge, and the famous Yajñavalkya, the head of a Brahmanic school, goes to the King for instruction. Other kings and nobles are mentioned fairly often as teachers. Even women take part in the *brahmodyas,* or Brahmanic contests. It is therefore natural that, as new elements of society enter the domain of philosophy and religion, they should introduce new intellectual elements. Under this influence, the Upanishads develop the doctrine of the absolute as the sole reality, a doctrine of pure idealism. Thanks to the elasticity of Brahmanism, this doctrine, which was diametrically opposed to the old Vedic religion, was incorporated in what is called by the general name of Veda.

The most ancient Upanishads are the *Bṛihadāraṇyaka*, *Chhāndogya*, *Taittirīya*, *Aitareya*, *Kaushītaki*, and *Kena*. But the creation of Upanishads has not yet come to an end. Every mystical treatise can lay claim to the title, which means a "secret doctrine" which the teacher confides *rahasyam*, "mysteriously," to his disciple. *Upa-ni-shad* means "to sit close beside", as if to hear a secret.

The subject of these works, as I have said, is the absolute, *ātman*. But by the side of the metaphysics there are delightfully simple and picturesque passages.

Here is a scene of a Brahman contest.

> The King promised a herd of a hundred cows to whoever should answer three questions which he asked. "Bring out the cows, my child!" the sage Yajñavalkya calmly bade his disciple, before even entering on the discussion. "Ho, Yajñavalkya!" other Brahmans cried. "Do you not think that we too might wish to win cows?" But they were soon defeated by the learned doctor.
>
> Another time Yajñavalkya advised the Brahmans not to measure themselves against King Janaka. "For," he said, prudently, "if you win, people will say that it is quite natural, for he is a Kshatriya, a warrior, and does not concern himself with knowledge. But he might be the victor, and then what a cry there will be, 'The Kshatriya has defeated the Brahmans!'"
>
> When this sage wished to leave the world, he shared, his goods between his two wives, Katyayani and Maitreyi. "Shall I be immortal, Lord," said Maitreyi, "when I have riches?" "No," answered the doctor, "you will live like rich folk, but that has nothing to do with eternal life." "Then what would you have me do with these goods? Teach me, Lord, rather the knowledge which you possess." And the sage proceeded to expound to her the doctrine of *ātman*, one without second, outside which nothing exists, which is the only reality and the only life.[1]

A little poem, the *Kāṭhaka Upanishad*,[2] contains a pretty story of Nachiketas.

> He was a youth who, seeing his father give alms to the monks, asked him, joking, "And me, your own son, to whom will you give me?" "I give you to Yama" (the god of death), replied the father impatiently. "What will Yama do with me?" Nachiketas asked himself sadly. But he obediently went to the underworld. Yama was not there, and Nachiketas waited for him for three days without receiving the honours prescribed by hospitality. When Yama returned, he hastened to repair the omission, and offered Nachiketas three favours, at his choice. The young man wished to return to his father and find him happy, and secondly to be happy himself; and then, when he had to choose the third gift, he thought, and said, "When a man goes away

[1] *Bṛihadāraṇyaka*.
[2] Published by Apte, Poona, 1889.

from this world, some say, 'He is there; he lives,' and others say, 'He is nowhere; he no longer exists.' Answer me, Yama, what is the truth. You alone can resolve my doubts." Yama tried to evade the question. It is too difficult, and the gods themselves used to hesitate about it. "Ask something else, Nachiketas.[1] Choose great herds, horses, and elephants. Take gold and silver, take broad lands. I give you greatness and power, long life and posterity. See my fair Apsarases sitting in ornamented chariots, or playing harps and dancing. Be happy with them, but do not ask me about death!" Nachiketas refused everything. What are joys worth, what is even the longest life worth, if death comes to break off all? He wished to know what there was afterwards. At last Yama, defeated by so much insistence, taught Nachiketas the theory of immortality in *ātman*.

Even feminism could find a place in the Upanishads. One of the later ones says that truth could not be found by the great saints and sages. A simple woman, Uma,[2] found it on her path as she walked. But she was judged worthy of it through her virtues.

VI

THE SŪTRAS

A. *The Kalpa and Gṛihya Sūtras*

While the style of the Upanishads is lively and easy, the Sūtras are the dryest and most condensed works produced by India and are at once the least pleasant to read and the easiest to learn by heart. They consist of short, chopped sentences, composed almost entirely of substantives, abstract for choice, and adjectives, without verbs.

Sūtra means "thread, clue, rule". The name is given to collections of precepts accumulated in the course of ages and transmitted by oral tradition. Those dealing with ritual have the general name of Kalpa Sūtras. Some describe the practices of the "official" cult, represented by great sacrifices, which are usually long and costly; these are the Śrauta Sūtras. Others, the Gṛihya Sūtras, teach the worship of the household, and are important to one who wishes to know the life of the orthodox Hindu. Rites and prayers, or rather utterances, suited to every occasion, accompany the Hindu from his birth, and indeed from his conception, to his death. These

[1] Cf. *Ś.B.*, xi, 5.
[2] She also appears as the wife of the god Siva.

texts show India to be closely connected by its customs with the civilization of peoples now dwelling far away, such as the Slavs and the Finno-Ugrians.[1] For although the Sūtras were collected in books in the post-Vedic period, and some of them quite late, they contain reminiscences of a very distant past. They prove the unity of Indo-European civilization and add their testimony to an already considerable quantity of evidence that the original habitat of the Indians lay a long way from their present country.

With the Gṛihya Sūtras are connected the Dharma Sūtras, which are precepts regarding morality—the whole duties and rights of the individual and the laws which govern his existence. Each caste has its own *dharma*. Morality consists in being faithful to the obligations, religious, social, and other, of your state in life and the circle in which you move.

B. *Vedānga*

While the Brāhmaṇas and Upanishads are sacred books, the Sūtras are not regarded as revealed scriptures. With other similar works they form the Vedānga, the " sciences connected with the Vedas ". Besides ritual (*kalpa*), these sciences are phonetics, grammar, etymology, prosody, and astronomy.

Phonetics, or rather the teaching (*śikshā*) of the recitation of the hymns, dealt with the proper pronunciation and accentuation of the Saṃhitās. For the very syllables and accent of the word contributed to the magic of the sacrifice. A wrong intonation might release forces contrary to those which were being invoked. The legend of Tvashtar[2] is eloquent testimony of this. He was a demon, who was performing a magical rite against Indra. At the culminating point, he made a mistake; instead of saying *indraśátru*, " enemy of Indra," he pronounced it *indráśatru*, with the emphasis on *indra*, meaning " who has Indra for his enemy ". The spell turned against him and killed him.

So at a very early date there had been *Saṃhitā-pāṭhas*,

[1] Cf. L. v. Schroeder, *Die Hochzeitsgebräuche, etc.*, Berlin, 1888; M. Winternitz, *Das altindische Hochzeitsrituell nach dem Āpastambīya-Gṛhyasūtra, etc.* (*Denkschr. d. K. Ak. d. Wiss. in Wien, phil.-hist. Kl.*, xl, 1892); W. Caland, *Über die Totenverehrung bei einig. der indogermanischen Völker*, Amsterdam, 1888, and **CXXXII**.

[2] *Śat. Br.*, i, 6, 3, 8 ff.; *Taitt. S.*, ii, 4, 12, 1 ff.

works in which the lines were pronounced in their entirety according to tradition, and *Pada-pāṭhas*, in which the same lines were broken up into separate words. The *Pada-pāṭhas* of the *Ṛigveda* were attributed to the sage Sakalya, one of the doctors of Brahmanism.[1]

The most ancient collections of phonetic rules are the *Prātiśākhyas*, which are indications adapted to the recensions of the various schools or " branches " (*śākhā*) of the Vedas.

To the domain of grammar and, in part, of etymology, belong the *Nighaṇṭus*, or lists of Vedic words classified according to meaning. Alongside of a list of different words their chief synonyms are set down. Thus, under " earth ", we find twenty-one names used for it in the Saṃhitās and one hundred and twenty-two verbs for " walk ", and so on. The most celebrated commentary on these *Nighaṇṭus* is the *Nirukta* ascribed to the scholar Yaska,[2] of whom we only know the name. But according to tradition Yaska was the most brilliant exponent of the Veda, and five hundred years before our era his name was spoken as that of an ancient teacher.

The correct recitation of the sacred hymns required a knowledge of prosody. The cult demanded that sacrifice should be performed at certain times, at the solstices and according to the position of the stars. So the Brahmans had to have some notions of astronomy. Treatises on prosody and astronomy must have existed at an early date, although those which we possess are late.

What is the age of the Sūtras ? Examination of the text only allows one to say that they came after the Brāhmaṇas and Upanishads. The period of the Brāhmaṇas came to an end with the advent of Buddhism, that is, before the middle of the fifth century B.C. The first Upanishads were already in existence. The Kalpa Sūtras, probably the earliest of the Sūtras, may have been compiled about the fifth or fourth century. Sūtras continued to be produced very late, being gradually superseded by didactic treatises called *śāstras*, a name which appears in the title of many works on morality and politics. Moreover, even late works, whenever they were in the form of aphorisms, were often called *sūtras*. Such, for instance, was the *Kāmasūtra*, the " Precepts

[1] **CCLXXXVIII**, iii, p. 620.
[2] Ed. *Bibl. Indica*, Calcutta, 1892.

of Love ", a book in which, three or four centuries after Christ, the learned and pious Vatsyayana described, defined, and classified the practices of purely sensual love.

The Sūtras of Panini

It is in *sūtras* that the grammar (*ashṭādhyāyī*, " eight [chapters of] rules ") of Panini is composed. The Indians have the merit, which is very great in the history of civilization, of having at a very early date applied their philosophic spirit to observing the facts of language. They ascribed a mystic force to words, and Vach, the Voice, is a divine being. Even the syllables of a word (*akshara*) contributed to the magic of the sacrifice, and each has a special meaning and virtue.

The study of the Vedas gave birth to grammar, *vyākaraṇa*, literally " analysis ", or, according to Wackernagel,[1] the " separation " of words into their component parts. The *Prātiśākhyas* are first attempts in this direction. The Brāhmaṇas, by the side of their clumsy and childish etymologies, reveal a tendency to analyse words. Yaska already distinguishes the parts of speech. Here the Indians were far ahead of the Greeks. Purity of speech was very highly esteemed. Young Brahmans went to the universities (Brahmanic schools) of the north, where the best speech was to be heard. The earliest manual of Old Indian grammar which has come down to us, and the most perfect, is that of Panini. Panini had had many predecessors, but their names, save that of Yaska, have been forgotten. Of his successors none attained to his glory.

We have very little information about this grammarian. Legend relates that he acquired his knowledge by a revelation of Siva, who was moved by the asceticism of a young man who had hitherto not been particularly intelligent. His mother's name was Dakshi and he came from North-western India, from Salatura, where the Chinese pilgrim Hiuen Tsang saw a statue of the great scholar a thousand years later.

Panini's date has long been a matter of controversy.[2] He used to be placed in the fourth century B.C. It would

[1] *Indische Grammatik*, i. [2] **CCLXXXVIII**, iii, p. 383.

be more correct to suppose him to be contemporary with the infancy of Buddhism, that is, not much later than the beginning of the fifth century.[1] He uses abbreviations and words invented expressly to designate grammatical forms; they are a kind of algebraic signs of grammar. With these word-signs he lays down, clearly and briefly, real rules of linguistic algebra. For example, the notion "If the vowels *i*, *u*, *ṛ*, and *ḷ*, short or long, stand before a vowel, they become *y*, *v*, *r*, and *l*," is expressed in three words, *iko yaṇ achi*,[2] where *ik* stands for *i*, *u*, *ṛ*, and *ḷ*, *yan* for *y*, *v*, *r*, and *l*, and *ach* for the vowels in general.

Memory plays an important part in the study of grammar. To understand a rule, you must remember all the preceding rules and know by heart the *Dhātu-pāṭha*, or "List of Verbal Roots", and the *Gaṇa-pāṭha*, or "List of Word-groups", that is, of words which behave with reference to a rule like the first of them, which alone is quoted as an example. Only by means of this ingenious system of abbreviations and references, which was doubtless invented before Panini, could the whole of the language, differences of dialect being taken into account, be described in one small volume.

The Grammarians after Panini

Thanks to Panini, we know the language of the Brāhmaṇas, the Upanishads, and the Kalpa Sūtras. That of the Vedas, *chhandas*, is only recalled by him incidentally; it was already a dead language in his time. Katyayana, the author of the *Vārttikas*, probably of the third century, discusses certain of his famous predecessor's rules and adapts them to classical Sanskrit, then just beginning. A commentary was written on the *Vārttikas* themselves by Patañjali in his *Mahābhāshya*, or "Great Commentary", in the second century.[3]

After these two grammarians hardly any addition was made to Panini's work, and scholars were content to make his *sūtras* more accessible. Of these refashionings, the clearest is the *Kāśikā Vṛitti*, the "Commentary of Benares", composed in the seventh century by Jayaditya (Books I–V) and

[1] Liebich, *Pânini*, Leipzig, 1891.
[2] *Pâninis Grammatik*, edited, with translation and indices, by O. Böhtlingk, Leipzig, 1887.
[3] **CCLXXXVIII**, iii, p. 389 n.

Vamana (VI–VIII). I-tsing, who visited the Buddhist sanctuaries towards the end of that century, is full of praise for this commentary. While the study of grammar usually required twelve years,[1] the *Kāśikā* could, he says, easily be understood in five !

In the seventh century after Christ, Bhartrihari wrote a commentary on the *Mahābhāshya* which won the approval of the pundits. The Buddhists, from Ceylon to Tibet, adopted the Sanskrit grammar, named *Chāndra-vyākaraṇa,* of Chandragomin,[2] and the Pali grammar of Kachchayana.[3] For the Jains, Hemachandra, at the bidding of King Jayasimha Siddharaja, compiled a grammar of the dialect in which their sacred books are written. Lastly, the Prakrit dialects, which were old popular languages which had become literary, were at an early date codified by Vararuchi Katyayana.

All these treatises followed the lines laid down by Panini. New paths were, however, sought. The result was a grammar by Sarvavarman entitled *Kātantra.*[4] It doubtless met the needs of the day, for it was used as far as Central Asia, and in the south it served as a model for works on the grammar of the Dravidian tongues.

VII

BHĀSHYA

The *sūtras* were learned by heart, but to be understood they had to be supplemented by less concise explanations, the *bhāshyas* or "commentaries" (from *bhāshā,* "speech," ordinary speech as opposed to the Vedic language). Scientific literature developed the *bhāshya* style, which is different from that of the *sūtra.* A start was made by the commentators of Panini. Katyayana still uses the old form, adding brief remarks in verse (*ślokavārttika*) alongside of it, but for Patañjali the age of the *sūtra* is the past and he writes in the new manner.

A studied prose takes the place of aphorisms. This style, developed in cultivated circles in the discussions of scholars

[1] *Hitopadeśa,* introd.
[2] Published by Liebich, Leipzig, 1902.
[3] Published and translated by Senart, in *J.A.*, 1871.
[4] Published by J. Eggeling, in *Bibliotheca Indica,* 1874–5.

and commentaries of scholiasts, is a little dry, but not wearisome, being often interrupted by similes and rules, *nyāya*, examples.

Some centuries before our era, we witness the development of a very skilful use of prose for dialectical and scholastic purposes. Prose was to continue to be like this to the present day, and when Sanskrit had been relegated to the pantheon of dead languages (we must remember that it was never alive except in the Brahmanic schools) it would serve as a pattern to the modern tongues of India.

At the same time, the practice of writing in verse spread. Scientific works were composed in *ślokas*, stanzas like the old Vedic *anushṭubh*. This is the form of the *kośa*, which is a lexicon carrying on the tradition of the *nighaṇṭu*. But whereas the *nighaṇṭu* refers to some passage in the Vedas, the *kośa* is intended to provide poets with a supply of words. Sanskrit, not being spoken by the people or even ordinarily by the upper classes, could not keep alive.

Dictionaries of synonyms are distinguished from dictionaries of homonyms. The latter were extremely useful to people who no longer knew the language thoroughly and wished to show their cleverness in the form of poetry. The most celebrated *nāma-lingānuśāsana*, " teaching of names and their genders," is the work of Amarasimha, one of the " Nine Jewels " of the court of King Vikramaditya (this may be the name of several sovereigns). It is entitled *Amara-kośa*,[1] and it was composed after the sixth century of our era. It was followed by a great production of lexicons.

[1] Published by Loiseleur Deslongchamps, Paris, 1839, 1845.

CHAPTER II

Epic Poetry

INDIA had epic legends at an early date, but it did not produce an epic poem.

The *Ṛigveda* has it *ākhyānas*, " stories " ; there are *itihāsas* (*iti* + *ha* + *asa* = " it was so ") or legends in the Brāhmaṇas ; there is a whole literature of Purāṇas, tales " of old days ". India is full of echoes of great happenings. In its literature they are watered down in lyricism or, worse, in didacticism.

There are few peoples so fond of listening to the story-teller. During the great sacrifices which went on for months and months (the horse-sacrifice lasted over a year) bards came and sang the great deeds of the dead and the virtues of the living. On days of mourning the family met to hear some tale of good omen. Heroes ill-treated by fate are consoled by the stories related to them by a compassionate sage. A special caste, that of the Sūta, the son of a Kshatriya and a Brahman woman or of a Vaiśya and a Kshatriya woman, exercised the function of court poets, or rather of reciters. The Sūta was at the same time the King's charioteer, who accompanied him to war or the chase and saw his prowess. He also handed down the epic traditions from generation to generation. Itinerant bards (*kuśīlava*) made poems written by true poets known among the people. Indian working-men, wearied with the toil of the day, are capable of spending the whole night seated in a circle round the fire listening attentively to a drama of three thousand years ago.

Nevertheless, no trace has been found of a popular epic. What has become the national epic is a collection of songs composed in different ages by many authors and refashioned by many editors, but gathered round a nucleus of ancient heroic legend.

I

THE MAHĀBHĀRATA

The "Great Epic of the War of the Descendants of Bharata"[1] consists of a central theme, on to which a multitude of subsidiary stories are grafted in a more or less artificial or episodic manner. The main theme is summarized by G. Courtillier as follows.[2]

Pandu, King of Hastinapura, was slain hunting on the Himalaya, and his elder brother, Dhritarashtra, who, being blind, had had to cede the throne to him, returned to power. He had many sons, the Kauravas, whom he caused to be reared with his five nephews, the Pandavas. In spite of the justice of the King, discord soon sprang up between the cousins. The Pandavas so excelled in all exercises that Duryodhana, the eldest Kaurava, was jealous, and caused them to be driven into the forests. After some time, the five brothers came to the King of the Pañchalas to ask for his daughter Draupadi in marriage. One of them, named Arjuna, was victor in the trial of the bow, and, in the mountain fashion, Draupadi became the wife of all five. Strengthened by this alliance, they made their cousins give them back part of their father's inheritance and settled at Indraprastha (Delhi).

But they did not keep it long, for the eldest, Yudishthira, was more boastful than brave, and was a great gamester. Duryodhana artfully provoked him to play at dice, and by trickery caused him to lose his kingdom, his brothers, his own person, and their wife. Draupadi was cruelly insulted. With the aid of their uncle, the Pandavas were able to escape with her to their forests for a long time. At the end of their time of hardship, they asked for their portion once more, and, when their enemies refused it, war began. This time the Pandavas, likewise using trickery and treason, were victorious, and the Kauravas, in spite of prodigies of heroism, were destroyed almost to the last man. Dhritarashtra gave up the throne to the Pandavas and retired to the mountains, where he presently perished in a fire. The Pandavas returned to Hastinapura and there ended their days with various fortunes.

One object of the editors was to make Yudishthira stand for law. He is the son of Dharma, the god of justice, and he is surnamed Dharmaraja, "King of Justice, Morality." His dual character is the result of the twofold nature of the poem, with its popular origin and heroic legends mingled with Brahmanic influences. The Pandavas, who were rough and unscrupulous warriors, whose only virtue was their courage, have been transformed into pious Brahmans, very careful in their formal observation of the "law". But the

[1] Bibliography in **CCLXXXVIII**, i, p. 273 n., and iii, pp. 623 ff.
[2] **LXVIII**, p. 96.

rough edges of the old epic have not always been polished away by the files of the editors, and we catch glimpses of social conditions very different from those which the Greeks, often mentioned in the poem as Yavanas (Ionians), could observe in India, and, still more, of an age very different from that of the stone houses and complicated government of the fourth century B.C.,[1] when the poem finally arrived at the state in which we know it.

The more learned developments are chiefly found in the twelfth book, *Śāntiparvan*, the "Book of Pacification" (politics and philosophy), and the thirteenth, *Anuśāsanaparvan*, the "Book of Teaching" (law). Philosophy is mingled with psychology and worldly wisdom, and there is no strict system. One is surprised to find the dualistic ideas of the Sāṃkhya side by side with strict monism and the latter beside the principles of Yoga, the whole being adorned sometimes with fine poetic parables and metaphors, but most often spread out in unnecessary and wearisome verbiage.

The thirteenth book is a fairly late addition. Its author or authors, knew the collections of laws made since antiquity well, but laid great weight on the *dharma* of generosity to Brahmans.

The *Mahābhārata* is a mass of repetitions and contradictions, which show that its composition covered a long period. One comes to the same conclusion if one examines the metre and language. The chief epic metre is the *śloka*, a stanza of two lines, based on the old *anushṭubh*, which consisted of four hemistichs of eight syllables each, with two iambi at the end of each line. But one finds other metres. all of Vedic origin. There are also passages in prose, sometimes rhythmic and sometimes alternating with verse. This is an ancient and popular phenomenon.

It is the same with the language. It is sometimes called Epic Sanskrit, but this implies a homogeneity which does not exist. The language fluctuates between that of the Veda and that of the sophisticated poetry of the Indian Renaissance. It also reveals popular ingredients. This language has given rise to controversy. Some will not allow that it is the tongue in which the original was written, and maintain that the *Mahābhārata* was composed in Prakrit and translated into

[1] Cf. S. Lévi, in **XV**, 1915, p. 122, quoted **CCLXXXVIII**, iii, p. 623.

Sanskrit long after, for the use of the upper classes, who had been won over to Brahmanic culture. A. Barth [1] makes an eloquent defence of this position : " . . . A poetry which, in its borrowed garb, one still feels to be full of the national, popular sap, and the subject of which does not belong to the old Brahmanic foundation," could only be expressed in a language of the people. This view has now been abandoned.

Attempts have been made to reconstruct the original *Mahābhārata*.[2] They were bound to fail, for even the story of the war of the cousins has come down to us in a much changed form, and it is hard to pronounce in favour of one version, and still harder to select one expurgated according to our modern tastes.

The whole work is strongly tinged with asceticism. Here we find King Sibi purchasing the life of a dove with a pound of his own flesh. Here, too, Janaka of Videha cries, "Infinite are my riches, for nothing is mine. Even if Mithila [3] burned, nothing would burn there which is mine." In the twelfth book, that of " Pacification ", there is a pathetic story which sets forth the Hindu idea of causality, the idea of *karman*.

> The only son of a widow dies of a snake-bite. But the snake is not to blame, for he was only the instrument of *mṛityu*, death. Nor is death guilty ; it was sent by *kāla*, time or fate. And what is fate ? Our acts and their consequences, the results of our previous lives, our *karman*. So the poor widow sees that evil is inevitable, for it is we ourselves who create it, and none can remedy our suffering except ourselves—in a series of existences.

The old gods of the Veda have lost some of their majesty in the *Mahābhārata*. This is especially true of Indra. Above the gods stands the ascetic, and above human society stands the Brahman. Yet the poem contains some allusions to a war, or rather wars, of bygone days between Kshatriyas and Brahmans. In the end the Brahmans won the moral prestige and made the Kshatriyas accept it as their duty to defend them ; but it must have cost them many a struggle first.

There are many fables in the *Mahābhārata*, in great part the same as in the Buddhist Jātakas. I may tell that of the man in the pit.

[1] **III**, vol. ii, p. 398.
[2] A. Holtzmann, *Das Mahâbhârata u. seine Theile*, 4 vols., Kiel, 1892–5 ; Joseph Dahlmann, *Genesis des Mahâbhârata*, Berlin, 1899, and *Das Mahâbhârata als Epos u. Rechtsbuch*, Berlin, 1895.
[3] His capital.

"A Brahman, losing his way in a forest, fell into a pit. As he fell, he caught hold of the creepers on the edge, and hung 'like a ripe fruit', while at the bottom of the pit a monster opened its greedy mouth to devour him and at the root of the creeper two mice, one white and one black, gnawed at the feeble support. As if this were not enough, a black elephant with six heads and twelve legs came up to crush him. But in the hollow of the tree which stood by the pit bees had made honey, and the sweet stuff fell in thick drops within reach of the hand of the hanging man. Then, forgetting the near danger, the Brahman stretched out his hand and ate the honey greedily."

We are all that Brahman. The forest is the circle of existences, the monster below is inevitable death, the creepers are the life which is given to us for a time, the six-headed, twelve-legged elephant is the year with its six seasons and twelve months, the mice are the nights and days, and the drops of honey are the joys which we succeed in snatching.

The hundred thousand or so *ślokas* of the *Mahābhārata* do not seem to have been enough for the poets who, in different periods, erected these bizarre constructions on the top of the edifice attributed to Vyasa. They found it necessary to write sixteen thousand supplementary stanzas, containing cosmogonic legends and the equally miraculous genealogies of the house of the Sun, from which King Ikshvaku sprang, and the house of the Moon, to which Pururavas belonged (above, p. 238).

This supplement is a very unequal work, often of doubtful literary value and heterogeneous in composition, in three books, the second of which, the *Harivaṃśa*, has given its name to the whole. Hari is one of the many names of Vishnu, and *vaṃśa* means "genealogy". It is the story of Vishnu in his incarnation as Krishna. We have here, so to speak, a third Krishna. We must be on our guard with the various heroic or divine figures designated by this name. Sometimes Krishna is the chief of a clan of sub-Himalayan herdsmen and friend of the Pandavas; sometimes he is the charioteer of Arjuna, who is an incarnation of the supreme god Vishnu, the sole god of the *Bhagavadgītā*, an episode in the epic; and sometimes he is the boy Krishna of Hindu legend, the beloved god, to this day passionately adored by his many followers in the Deccan. As a young man of marvellous bravery and strength and unquenchable gaiety, he is the god whom Megasthenes described to the Greeks as the Indian Heracles. He has outlived other gods of the pantheon, and in modern Hinduism Siva is his only rival; indeed, more usually the two are combined in a single god, Vishnu-Siva. That there is no connexion between these three Krishnas, in spite of what the *Mahābhārata* says to the contrary, is unnecessary to prove. But the theory of avatars provides a very convenient, if not convincing, explanation for it all.

There are points to be noted in the birth and childhood of Krishna.

> He was the eighth child of Devaki, the wife of Vasudeva. According to the prophecy of Narada, the messenger of the gods, he would kill his wicked uncle, King Kamsa. So Kamsa had all his nephews slain as soon as they were born. When Krishna was born, his parents at once gave him in exchange for the infant daughter of the herdsman Nanda and his wife Yasoda. Like the low-caste woman who perished for the Pandavas with her five sons, the little girl paid for Krishna's life with her death. The young prince was brought up among the herdsmen, and soon distinguished himself by his great strength, uprooting trees, kicking a chariot into the air, and so on, and by his noble deeds, slaughtering demons, vanquishing the King of the Snakes, and humbling Indra. Naturally he also killed Kamsa.

The later part of the legend of Krishna shows him sometimes as the young herd, beautiful and sportive, the despair of love-lorn maidens, and sometimes as the god Vishnu in his incarnations. As a boar, he pulls the earth out of the sea as it is about to sink into the abyss, thrust down by the demon Hiranyaksha ; as a lion-man he rends the impious Hiranyakasipu ; as a dwarf he wins the earth and the sky from the Asuras by means of his Three Steps.

The *Harivaṃśa* stands on the boundary between the mythological poem and the planless narrative, wandering about at the author's will and stringing unconnected myths and traditions together, as is usual in the Purāṇas. It belongs to religious literature, and the songs inserted in it were doubtless used in worship, the chief characteristic of which was the passionate, amorous adoration of a god.

II

THE RĀMĀYAṆA [1]

While the *Mahābhārata* is still popular literature, the *Rāmāyaṇa*, although older, is a conscious work of art. First

[1] H. Jacobi, *Das Râmâyana, Geschichte u. Inhalt*, Bonn, 1893 ; A. Baumgartner, *Das Râmâyana u. d. Râmalitteratur der Inder*, Freiburg i. Breisgau,

we must consider this matter of age. The roots of the *Mahābhārata* go deep into a very distant past, but it was put together after the *Rāmāyaṇa*, which is often mentioned, in the *Mahābhārata*, if not as existing in its present form, at least as a complete story, and appears in an abridged form (*Rāmopākhyāna*) in the third book. To console Yudishthira for the abduction of Draupadi, the sage Markandeya tells him how Sita was carried off by the demon Ravana and how Rama, with the aid of the army of monkeys, rescued his wife and brought her back to his kingdom.

Although the *Rāmāyaṇa* is a comparatively sophisticated work, it is not lacking in popular elements of a naïvely fabulous kind. Numerous interpolations have extended the poem, which was originally much shorter, into a work of 24,000 *ślokas*. None the less, it is a single work, harmoniously constructed, and written, for the most part, in a language which bears witness to a high literary and æsthetic culture. Naturally, the Indian love of exaggeration and profusion is gratified only too generously, and it is full of marvels to overflowing, but the technique reveals a poet conscious of his art. For it was written by one single poet. The name of Valmiki, the author of the *Rāmāyaṇa*, is mentioned in the *Mahābhārata*, and even has a legend attached to it ; Valmiki committed the unpardonable crime of killing a Brahman and was a brigand in his young days, but the worship which he vowed to Siva purified and ennobled him. The existence of such a legend indicates that the *Rāmāyaṇa* is old, since the facts about its author had had time to pass into the stage of almost mythical tradition which cannot be confirmed or disproved by investigation.

The poem is divided into seven books, of which the first (*Bālakāṇḍa*, the hero's boyhood) and the last (*Uttarakāṇḍa*) were composed long after the " true " *Rāmāyaṇa* (Books II–VI). Yet the form of the whole seems to have been quite established by the second century after Christ, when the *Mahābhārata*, the nucleus of which belonged to a much earlier time, was still in process of formation.

The dramatic story of Rama is, like that of the other

1894. It has been translated into French by Hippolyte Fauche, 9 volts., Paris, 1854–8 ; into Italian by G. Gorresio, from the Bengali recension, 5 vols., Paris, 1847–1858 ; and into English by M. N. Dutt, Calcutta, 1891–4. For bibliography, see **CCLXXXVIII**, i, pp. 404 ff., nn.

great epic, placed in Madhyadesa, the "Middle Land" between the Himalaya and the Vindhya. But whereas the rivalry of the Kauravas and the Pandavas took them to Kurukshetra, in the west of the central region, the adventures of Rama happen further east and north-east, towards Bengal, on the fringes of the Himalaya, and even take him to the far south, if the fabulous isle of Lanka can be identified with Ceylon.

Again I take G. Courtillier's summary of the poem.[1]

> Pursued by the jealousy of a stepmother, Rama, son of the King of Ayodhya, was obliged to fly to the forests with his wife Sita, unaccompanied save by his brother Lakshmana. For all his prudence, he allowed himself to be drawn off in chase of a magic gazelle, leaving Sita unprotected. The lovesick Raja of the Rakshasas, who had put up the delusive quarry, sought to seduce Sita and carried her off by force, taking her in his flying chariot to the island of Lanka, where he kept her shut up among his women. Rama, after giving himself up to grief and despair, started off in search of the ravisher. The monkeys placed themselves at his service and showed him the way. The cleverest of them, Hanumat, leapt over the wall with one spring, came to where Sita was, and comforted her. Presently the army of monkeys, led by Rama, arrived under the walls of Lanka. There was a battle; the ravisher Ravana was slain, the Rakshasas were vanquished, and Rama, after subjecting Sita to the ordeal of fire, brought her back to Ayodhya.

Barth [2] has believed it possible to see traces of an agricultural myth in the figure of Sita and even in Rama. Sita, "Furrow," is a daughter of Earth; Rama, otherwise called Ramachandra, "Shining Rama, Moon-Rama," is sometimes identified with the Moon which rules the world of plants.[3] So they would be the deities who preside over the sowing. In that case, in a heroic and elegant epic (for the latter term applies to the account of the court of Ayodhya, with its zenana-intrigues), we come upon traces of a distant past, conceptions already obsolete in the Brahmanic period. There is another curious thing to notice. *Rāma*, which means "charming", also means "black", and in fact Rama is imagined as being so, like Krishna. Are they both incarnations of Vishnu? The characteristic of one might have been transferred to the other.

[1] **LXVIII**, p. 97.
[2] **III**, i.
[3] Cf. the principal Brāhmaṇas, e.g. the *Śatapatha*, when they speak of plants.

The *Rāmāyaṇa* contains allusions to a conflict between the Brahmans and the Kshatriyas. In the first book there is an interpolated passage about Parasurama, " Rama of the Axe ", a Brahman who has vowed boundless hate against the Kshatriyas. With his dreadful axe he slays them almost all, until at last Rama checks his bloody fury. But, knowing that he has to do with a Brahman, Rama dares not take his life, and only compels him to retire into the underground world where he will live in bliss " merited by his former penances ".

The legend of Parasurama and its interpolation in the poem are puzzling. Parasurama is the sixth avatar of Vishnu, according to the tenth book of the *Mahābhārata* ; if so, he here meets his own seventh avatar in the person of Rama. It is better to suppose that the two passages in question represent two independent traditions.

It is also from the first book that we learn that Ganga, the River Ganges, came down from the sky. There, too, we find legends that have appeared in the *Mahābhārata*, such as those of the churning of the ocean to produce the drink of immortality, the incarnation of Vishnu as a dwarf, the seduction of the young ascetic Rishyasringa by the king's daughter, etc. Although the *Rāmāyaṇa* is much better constructed than the *Mahābhārata,* in its first and seventh books it is, like the *Mahābhārata,* an encyclopædia of mythology.

Like the *Mahābhārata,* the *Rāmāyaṇa* is composed in " Epic Sanskrit ", Sanskrit of a somewhat popular kind, less refined than the classical language. A. Barth,[1] as we have seen, is of opinion that both poems were at first composed in a popular dialect and only later translated into Sanskrit. In spite of his lively presentation and solid defence of this theory, it is hardly justified. We must remember that Sanskrit was from very early times the literary language. No doubt it was not usually spoken in daily life, but everybody understood it, and the poets ordinarily used it even when they were treating popular subjects. It is true that the inscriptions of Asoka (third century B.C.), which are addressed to all his subjects, are in dialect, in " Middle Indian ", a common language ; but from that we can draw no certain conclusion save that in Asoka's time the royal chancelleries had not yet

[1] In xxvii and xlv, quoted in **CCLXXXVIII**, i, p. 436.

adopted Sanskrit for their official documents. That happened much later and has nothing to do with the literary practice, which even Buddhism, which addressed itself to the masses, did not completely abolish.

To this day the *Rāmāyaṇa,* translated into the living languages of modern India, is the favourite work of the Hindu, and Raam is his favourite hero. In Hinduism he shares the honours with Krishna, the other incarnation of Vishnu, and in the popular imagination he surpasses even Arjuna, the most brilliant of the Pandus. Temples were dedicated to Rama. Some of them survive, such as the grandiose building in the Dravidian style, Ramesvaram, erected on a small island of that name between India and Ceylon. At Ellora the rock-hewn walls of the Kailasa are adorned with scenes from the *Rāmāyaṇa,* and north-west of Allahabad, where the hill of Chitrakut rises, pilgrimages are held in honour of the place where Rama and Sita lived so happily in the first time of their exile. The statue of Hanumat is rarely lacking at the entrance to a temple of Vishnu. On the site of the ancient city of Ayodhya, where Buddhist sanctuaries succeeded Brahman altars and were replaced in their turn by mosques, themselves now fallen in ruin, there still rises the imposing structure of a temple of Hanumat. It is very common to see, in places of pilgrimage, troops of monkeys fed at the expense of the community. They say that these monkeys do no damage in the fields, and they seem to be familiar with civilized life.

Beyond India properly so called, north, south, and east, Rama is held in honour, and his epic, in the original Sanskrit, in adaptations, or merely in imitations, finds enthralled hearers. No work of literature has spread over such a vast area as that poem of knightly honour, self-denial, and love of husband and wife.

While the *Mahābhārata* was a mine of subjects for later writers, the *Rāmāyaṇa* became simply a subject. Great poets like Kalidasa and Bhavabhuti owe their finest works to the legend of Rama, and as late as the sixteenth century Tulsi Das, on the basis of Valmiki's poem, wrote in Hindi a moral and religious epic which is the Bible of the ninety million Hindus dwelling between the Himalaya and the Vindhya, between Bengal and the Punjab.

Sometimes the story taken from Valmiki was used for purposes which had nothing to do with poetry. Thus the poet Bhatti, in the eighth century of our era, composed a veritable epic on the death of Ravana in twenty-two cantos; but the strange thing (quite normal in India) is that his poem was intended for teaching grammar and the theory of poetry. The sentences are examples of the rules of Panini and of an unknown text-book of *alaṃkāra*. For instance, the last part of this *Rāvaṇa-vadha* ("The Slaying of Ravana") teaches the use of tenses and moods. The moment when Rama repudiates Sita happens to come in the chapter on the imperative. Accordingly, Rama repulses Sita in a succession of imperatives, and in imperatives Sita protests her innocence. The effect would be comic if Bhatti were not a poet. Fortunately, in spite of his didactic intention, he has succeeded in producing a fine work—at least to the Indian mind—but the labour of the artist is too evident and the effect too deliberate.

III

THE PURĀṆAS

I have said that parts of the *Mahābhārata* and *Rāmāyaṇa* are Puranic in character, that is, that they heap old legends together without plan or logical order. There are works which are called just Purāṇa, meaning "a tale of old times".

It is hard to determine their date. The foundation is ancient, and so was their first form, but that in which they have come down to us is, on the whole, of the seventh century after Christ. Moreover, the name of "Tales of Old Times" is often given to late works written in imitation of the old manner.

The Buddhist scholar Amarasimha (between the sixth and eighth centuries), who wrote that admirable lexicon the *Amara-kośa*, defines the notion of *purāṇa*. A true work should treat of five subjects: the creation of the world, its periodic destruction and recreation, the pedigree of the gods and mythical sages, the periods of the life of the world, over each of which a new Manu, or First Man, presides, and the pedigrees of the kings of the lines of the Sun and of the Moon. These rules of the type are rarely observed. Most of the Purāṇas are dedicated to the worship of Vishnu or Siva, and particularly to the cult of the "female godhead",[1] Sakti, personifying the energy of the god.

They yield historical information in the form of allusions and of prophecies regarding future ages, which are really memories of the past. Thus the last age, which will be followed by total destruction, is called Kaliyuga, a sort of Age of Iron in which barbarians rule and morals decay. Historians, including Vincent Smith,[2] suppose that the invasion and savage rule of the Huns, of dreadful memory, inspired the "prophecies" of the terrible time of Kaliyuga.

"Of the eighteen principal Purāṇas," Barth writes,[3] "not one is dated, they almost all quote each other, and the time of their composition may perhaps cover a dozen centuries." With rather more probability one might set the beginning of the collections in the third century of our era.[4] In the eleventh century the Arab traveller Al-Biruni already knew the same number of them, eighteen, but new works continued to be written.

The Hindus ascribe the composition of the Purāṇas to Vyasa, the legendary author of the *Mahābhārata*. That would place their origin very far back. They are regarded as sacred books of the second order, intended for the middle classes and preserved in the Sūta caste of bards who are not Brahmans but know Sanskrit. They bring together the legends of the popular heritage. To the old mythical and cosmogonic foundation they add ritual information, historical memories, hymns, and even entire poems in honour of a god or goddess, the whole being accompanied by a short exposition of the Sāṃkhya philosophy or, still more often, of Yoga. The result is that this literature is known at this day by every educated Hindu, even if he has not read the Vedas. The Purāṇas are to the Hindu what the Bible is to the Protestant, and pious families read portions of them every day.

It is a much more extensive literature than the *Mahābhārata*. The *Padma*, the fifth on the list, contains 50,000 *ślokas*, and the *Skanda*, according to contemporaries,

[1] Barth, **III**, i, p. 178.
[2] *Early History of India*, 1904.
[3] Barth, op. cit., i, p. 167.
[4] R. G. Bhandarkar, in **XVIII**, 1900, p. 403, quoted in **CCLXXXVIII**, iii, p. 631.

had 500,000 lines. This immense field has not been sufficiently cleared. F. E. Pargiter has done much work on it, seeking for historical certainties in the lists of kings.[1] His conclusions have been much disputed.

One of the most important and earliest Purāṇas is the *Mārkaṇḍeya*, ascribed to the sage of that name, the man who, in the *Mahābhārata* tells Yudishthira the story of Savitri. Here he relates to his disciple the creation of the world, the epochs, and the genealogies. Since, all through this portion, the supreme gods are still Indra and Brahma, or even, from a more distant time, the deities of the Veda, it is supposed that these chapters were composed before the cult of Vishnu or Siva had grown up. That would be at the beginning of our era, if not earlier—probably about the time when the twelfth book of the *Mahābhārata* was taking shape.

The Purāṇas display a rather crude and simple-minded attempt to moralize. It has been said that they were popular reading with women on account of the marvels and the piety which they contain. None the less, historians, philosophers, and above all mystics have found much to glean from them.

The most famous of them, the favourite book of the Bhāgavatas who worship Vishnu-Krishna, is the huge *Bhāgavata Purāṇa*, in twelve books of 18,000 stanzas altogether. It was known in Europe in the eighteenth century. Eugène Burnouf translated it into French. According to Pargiter,[2] this Purāṇa is not earlier than the eighth century, and it contains much later portions in which Colebrooke, Burnouf, and Wilson have seen the work of the thirteenth century. But by that time the *Bhāgavata* was already a sacred book.

Its subject is the same as that of the six books composing the *Vishṇu Purāṇa*, which is the Bible of the Vishnuites.[3] The mystic and theologian Ramanuja, the "Lord of Ascetics", who founded the Vishnuite sect in the twelfth century, treats this Purāṇa as an authority on questions of *bhakti*.

[1] *The Purāna Text of the Dynasties of the Kali Age*, Oxford, 1913.

[2] Hastings, *Encyclopædia of Religion and Ethics*, x, p. 455, quoted in **CCLXXXVIII**, iii, p. 632.

[3] Translated into English by H. H. Wilson, London, 1840; also by Manmatha Nath Dutt, Calcutta, 1894.

These two Purāṇas tell much the same story as the *Harivaṃśa*, though in a livelier way. But the object of the two collections is not merely to relate the avatars of the Hindu god. They set forth the doctrine of Vishnu, lord and creator of the absolute universe, not perceived coldly by the intellect but adored amorously.

Other Purāṇas are partly Vishnuite and partly Sivaite. In some of them the supreme god is now Siva and now Vishnu—for example in the *Kūrma Purāṇa*, which relates the avatar of Vishnu as a tortoise, or in the *Garuḍa Purāṇa*, in which the eagle Garuda on which Vishnu rides expounds Vishnuite theology and the mystical cult of Siva is also described.

The Purāṇas are encyclopædias of all the knowledge of the Indian Middle Ages. Their principal features, their qualities and defects of style, their abundance of detail and their love of exaggeration, and even the rhythms of their verse passages, appear again in the Buddhist works of the Mahāyāna, devotion to Vishnu being replaced by adoration of Buddha. Their Sanskrit is not very good. It is, as Senart calls it, "Mixed Sanskrit," mingled with the Prakrits or popular dialects. The prolixity, repetitions, and lack of plan are also characteristic of Pali writings.

IV

PALI AND PRAKRIT LITERATURE

The art of the *Rāmāyaṇa* is not an isolated fact. The grammarian Patañjali, in his *Mahābhāshya*, quotes very fine verses from poets whom he does not name. Pingala, probably his contemporary in the second century B.C., wrote an important work on prosody entitled *Chhandaḥ Sūtra*. He is no longer concerned with Vedic prosody, the *chhandas*, but with profane poetry, and first and foremost with erotic poetry. His verse is wrought with studied art.

But no work on a larger scale has come down to us, and, indeed, we have no Sanskrit work at all from that period. On the other hand, the Prakrits, which were living tongues, asserted their existence as literary languages.

The ancient variety of Prakrit named Pali, adopted by the Buddhists for writing the greater part of their canon, became the instrument of a whole literature.

In that literature teaching pure and simple alternates with works of imagination which, though naïvely didactic, are sometimes charming. The Pali canon contains everything—sermons, anecdotes, hymns. If we would understand the rise of lyric poetry we cannot neglect the *Thera-gāthās* and *Therī-gāthās*,[1] the hymns of monks and nuns to the glory of Buddha. Tradition already ascribed some of these to Ananda, the favourite disciple of Buddha, and Moggallana (Sanskrit Maudgalyayana), one of the first doctors of the Buddhist church. In that case they would date from some centuries before Christ. But the tradition only proves that the names of the real authors were not known and that it was desired to give this devout poetry an origin worthy of the public esteem.

It is, however, possible that in all the 107 *Thera-gāthās* there are a good many remnants of an ancient cycle. Many of the hymns consist of unconnected bits which look like fragments which have been given a tinge of severe, monotonous piety and exaggerated renunciation. Only the feeling for nature, which in the Hindu survives the death of the desires, gives a brighter tone to the drab uniformity. The "Nuns' Hymns" are much more interesting. One can distinguish different authors, mostly women, so delicate is the touch and so simple are the stories. Women were only admitted into the Buddhist community with great difficulty. The gifts of their piety were accepted readily; Buddha, according to the story, rested in the house given to him by a converted harlot. It was considered natural for rich, and even poor, women to provide for the needs of the monks. But it was not allowed that they could embrace the monastic life and found convents for themselves officially. Buddha opposed it. When Ananda asked "Why do you withstand this?" he answered, "Women are foolish, Ananda . . . Women are envious, Ananda . . . Women are spiteful, Ananda".

Buddha's adoptive mother entreated him long before

[1] Translated into English by Mrs. Rhys Davids, *Psalms of the Early Buddhists*, i. *Psalms of the Sisters*, London, Pali Text Soc., 1909.

he allowed her to found an order of women. At last Ananda succeeded in overcoming his resistance, but the Buddhist canon did not thank him, and he is heaped with reproaches for his feminist attitude.

The *Therī-gāthās* which have come down to us reveal a knowledge of the art of poetry as set forth in the works on " ornaments " (*alaṃkāra*). They have a developed style such as we do not find in the inscriptions before our era. It may, therefore, be a second, later stratum of *Therī-gāthās* that we know.

The general theme of all these hymns, monks' and nuns' alike, is the joy of renunciation. The women add moving stories of their conversion, the opposition of their kinsfolk, the temptations of love, and so on. Some hymns are in dialogue form, particularly when a tempter comes in, man or demon. Often they are real ballads. One of the most beautiful is that of the young and pious Subha pursued by a lover, like St. Lucy or St. Bridget. She plucks out her eyes that men may not be led aside from the way of salvation, but the Master gives her back her sight.

The *Gāthās* are human documents. In some the monks confess their weaknesses and blame woman, the source of all evil. In others they glory in having had the courage to trample on their duties as husbands and fathers to give themselves wholly to Buddha. A certain self-assertion is noticeable. The women are simpler and more melancholy. Most took to religion after losing their children ; having found consolation, they tell of their serenity under misfortune. Harlots sated with pleasure aspire only to Nirvana. Young girls leave the world, just as in the early centuries of Christian mysticism.[1] There are heart-rending pictures. But one also finds humour and even gaiety of a simple-minded sort. A nun declares that all that she has renounced is the upper and lower millstones and a hump-backed husband, and that for whole days she used to grind the rice and listen to her husband swearing. A monk leaves the convent to marry, but a fortnight later becomes once more convinced of the nothingness of things and returns to his comrades. Some of the hymns are keen satires on bad monks ; one can see that Buddhism is no longer in its first stages. A commentary,

[1] Cf. R. Spence Hardy, *Eastern Monachism.*

doubtless not the first, on these hymns was written in the fifth century.

By the side of these works, which partake of the character of popular literature, the first centuries of our era saw the rise of an artistic and profoundly philosophic literature in Pali—the *Milinda-pañha*, or " Questions of Menander ". It deals with the problem of personality from the Buddhist point of view. It is not only a philosophic treatise, but a work of art. The heroes are a doctor of the Buddhist church named Nagasena and the Indo-Greek king Menander, Milinda in Pali. The latter reigned between 125 and 95 B.C. over a large district extending from the Indus and the Gujarat country to the middle course of the Ganges. He was a Greek. He was believed to be a convert to Buddhism, but this is not certain, although he is represented on coins with a *chakra*, or Wheel of the Law.[1] In his case India—North-Western India, it is true—seems to have abandoned its traditional hostility to foreigners. If we can believe Plutarch, several Indian cities contended for the ashes of Menander, shared them among themselves, and set up a commemorative monument for each portion. The story is too much like that of Buddha to be accepted without caution. However that may be, Menander was the only Greek whom India adopted.

The *Milinda-pañha* is a fine philosophic novel. We have no notion whether it has any foundation in fact. Possibly the author wanted to present the doctrine of negation in artistic form, and the persistent memory in Northern India of an Indian king of Greek race suggested that he should contrast the Greek spirit and the Indian.

Of the seven books of which the work is composed, at most the second and third are authentic, and even they contain late interpolations. The beginning of the first book, describing the capital, is doubtless by the first author, whose name is unknown.

The King is resting after reviewing his army. But the night is fine, and instead of sleeping he would have a bout of argument with some ascetic or pious Brahman. The courtiers take him to a famous hermit who lives near the city. The discussion starts, and the sage is soon reduced to silence, not knowing what to answer to the arguments of the King. Other renowned sages are met, with the same result. Menander exclaims in disappointment, " India is empty ! People here can only prate ! "

[1] Cf. S. Lévi, **XXV** (i), xxiii, p. 43 (1891).

Meanwhile the Buddhist doctor, Nagasena, passing through the country, has stopped near the capital. The King is advised to visit him. Menander goes, and we witness the most remarkable, and indeed the most passionate contest that the world has seen.

" How are you called, venerable one ? " the King asks. " I am called Nagasena, but that is only a name, an assemblage of sounds with no reality in it," answers the sage. And in a dialogue in which the King stands for what one may call the positive spirit and the sage for the speculative, it is proved to us that the " I " does not exist, being only a transitory manifestation of a collection of phenomena.

The most awkward questions are answered in a manner as witty as unexpected. Menander asks whether a man who dies and is born again is the same or somebody else. " Both," answers Nagasena. " You, O King, are you now the same as the little child (and so on) that you once were ? " " No." " Then if you are not the same, you have had no father, no mother (etc.), and you have not lived before this moment at which you are speaking." And by a series of parallels Nagasena proves to the King the continuity of phenomena, the only thing that we are able to admit.

Menander might have said that as soon as there is no personality there is no obligation or responsibility, and would thereby have overthrown the whole of Buddhist ethics.

While Pali was reserved for works of Buddhist inspiration, chiefly propagandist and educational, profane literature developed in Prakrit languages. Sanskrit was not given up, but, having been set up as a sacred language, it was not suited for familiar use. It did not become the idiom of chancelleries and government offices until fairly late. About the beginning of our era Middle Indian came into use in the administration. This is the language used by Asoka to teach his people the Law to which he himself has been converted. His many inscriptions on pillars and rocks are written in local dialects. In any case the Prakrit works followed their Sanskrit models. Tastes were the same, being imposed by the upper classes ; those who wrote on poetics (*alaṃkāra*) addressed themselves to all writers without distinction. Sanskrit, the noble language, Pali, the sacred language of the Buddhists, and the Prakrits, which were regional κοιναί, lived side by side, although they flourished variously according to the place, the time, and the importance of the ideas which were clothed in them.

The inscriptions of Asoka taught his subjects *dharma*, the Buddhist Law, in Middle Indian. The Prakrit inscriptions which one finds scattered about India during the first centuries of our era, especially under the Gupta dynasty from the fourth century on, informed the people of the virtues of their king. Composed by court poets in verse or prose, they were generally distinguished by the exaggeration of their eulogies and the abuse of ornaments of style.

In the first or second century after Christ, Prakrit had the glory of producing a charming work ascribed to Hala Satavahana or Salivahana, the poet king. The Purāṇas call him the seventeenth king of Andhra, in the north-eastern Deccan. He is the author of the *Sattasai* (*Saptaśatī*, " Seven Hundreds of Stanzas "), a collection of love-songs, composed on the pattern of the popular songs which accompany dancing.[1] They are moving, often witty, and always of an artful simplicity. A husband caught erring throws himself at his wife's feet and implores forgiveness. There is a prospect of a dramatic scene. But the little boy takes the opportunity to climb on to his father's back, the parents laugh, and reconciliation follows. Others are sad and sentimental. A young woman starts to count on her fingers and toes the days that her beloved is absent. She counts them all, and still he does not come, and she can only weep.

Some are more frivolous. The husband is away, the house is empty, and the young wife calls in her lover ; she is afraid of thieves with the house empty. Others yet speak of the great disillusionment and weariness of the world ; only the deaf and the blind can be happy, for the deaf hear no wicked talk and the blind see no bad deeds.

The finest lines are those which praise love or sing the beauty of women. There are pretty little pictures, swiftly sketched, of family life. Descriptions of nature have a large place.

The metre of the *Sattasai* is the *āryā* characteristic of popular poetry, a verse of two lines, each of seven and a half feet. Each foot has four morae except the sixth of the second line, which is only a short syllable. A long is equivalent to two shorts, as in Greek verse, but contrary to Vedic usage. This stanza produces the effect of something light and airy. It is perfectly suited to the simplicity of the images and the softness of the Prakrits. Moreover, Hala employs the best

[1] See the extracts translated into German in **CCLXXXVIII**, iii, pp. 98 ff. The best translation, though incomplete (in German), is A. Wilbrandt's in *Neue Freie Presse*, 1899, and *Westermanns Ill. Monatshefte*, 1900 ; cf. **CCLXXXVIII**, iii, p. 97 n.

of the Prakrits, namely Maharashtri, the dialect of the Marathas, which is wonderfully adapted to singing. It became almost a rule in Indian drama that the sung parts should be written in Maharashtri.

The *Sattasai* had a great influence not only on Prakrit authors but on Sanskrit writers, who were rather less frequent in this time when literature in living languages was flourishing. Even late in the eleventh century when the Jain Hemachandra writes a grammar of the Apabhramsa dialect, he composes examples in stanzas modelled on the *Sattasai* to illustrate his rules. In the seventeenth century, again, when the mystic Bihari Lal (1603–1663) sings the loves of Krishna and Radha in Hindi of Mathura, the chief seat of the worship of Vishnu, he is inspired, if not directly by the *Sattasai*, at least by imitations of it.

Prakrit found protectors among the kings, many of whom, as is said of Hala, did not know Sanskrit. Other circumstances helped it. After the empire of Asoka was broken up it developed in the north-west. The Brahmanic tradition could not be strong there. Buddhism, on the other hand, was firmly established, and that religion, speaking to all without distinction of caste, did not make especial use of Sanskrit. Certain Prakrits, too, had reached the dignity of literary languages.

V

SANSKRIT LITERATURE OF BUDDHIST INSPIRATION

Asvaghosha and Aryasura

The beginning of our era, probably the first century, is marked by a great poet, Asvaghosha,[1] who wrote lyrics and dramas in Sanskrit. About his life we know very little. From certain allusions contained in his works, he seems to have come from Ayodhya, the present Province of Oudh. His mother was named Suvarnakshi, "of the Golden Eyes." Born and brought up as a Brahman, he was converted to Buddhism and became a supporter of the school of the Sarvāstivādins

[1] See S. Lévi, "Le *Buddhacarita* d'Açvaghosa," in *Journ. Asiat.*, 1892, and other articles by him in the same journal 1898, etc.

of the Hīnayāna. But his poetic temperament drew him to the enthusiastic love (*bhakti*) of Buddha, and it was as a forerunner of the Mahayanist movement that he wrote his *Buddha-charita*.[1]

The lyrical works which Asvaghosha composed in honour of Buddha have not survived. Hiuen Tsang in the middle of the seventh century and I-tsing in its last years speak of Asvaghosha as " a poet famous in old times ". A biography, quite uncritical, was written by a Tibetan monk. According to this, he was a musician, wandering about the country with a troupe of singers. In that case he would belong to the not very reputable caste of strolling players (*nartaka*), and it is hard to explain his wide and profound erudition. It is true that a Brahman kept the privileges of his caste, whatever trade he took up. In any case, Buddhism paid no attention to the prohibitions of the Brahmans. As a true, convinced Buddhist, Asvaghosha sang of the nothingness of existence. His beautiful voice, doubtless more than his theme, enchanted his hearers, and many, it is said, were converted.

The pious Tibetan's story can only be true of part of Asvaghosha's life, for we know that he spent his old age at the court of Kanishka.[2] That king, of Scythian origin, was a great protector of Buddhism and patron of learned men.

Fragments of the dramas of Asvaghosha were identified quite recently (1911) by H. Lüders in the collection of manuscripts brought from Turfan in Central Asia.

It is to Sylvain Lévi [3] that Europe owes its knowledge of the *Buddha-charita* and of Asvaghosha himself, the greatest poet of India before Kalidasa and a worthy successor of Valmiki in the art of the epic.

As its title shows, the *Buddha-charita* is a poetic history of Buddha. Written in a style of sometimes studied simplicity, with only moderate use of metaphors and other *alaṃkāras*, this epic is a *mahākāvya*, a perfect pattern of classical poetry, but sincere in its expression. Yet the author has invented nothing. Canonical works like the *Mahāvastu* [4] or the *Lalita-*

[1] Translated into English from a Chinese adaptation by S. Beal in *Sacred Books of the East*, xix.

[2] Cf. S. Lévi, in **XV**, 1896.

[3] **XV**, 1892.

[4] Published with an introduction and commentary by E. Senart, Paris, 1882–1897.

vistara[1] gave him his subject ready-made. The poet was able to give it charm and solid construction. The description of the city holding holiday when the young prince goes through with his following inspired Kalidasa with a scene in his *Raghu-vaṃśa.* The scene at night, when Buddha looks sadly at the women of the palace sleeping after their play, but presenting in that moment of unconsciousness all the signs of human misery, was adopted by the continuers of Valmiki and placed in the *Rāmāyaṇa* where the palace is Ravana's and Hanumat is the onlooker.

Asvaghosha combines a sense of reality with that of fiction. The three encounters of the prince, with an old man, a sick man, and a dead man, are presented not only without any exaggeration, which could easily be avoided, but in such a fashion, at once delicate and vivid, that we share the melancholy reflections of the hero. The passages in which the *purohita* tries to turn the young man from his desire to leave the world and speaks to him of the duties of a prince show a profound knowledge of the *nīti-śāstras.* Buddha's struggle with the tempting demon Mara proves that the author was familiar with the heroic poetry of the *Mahābhārata* and the *Rāmāyaṇa.* If to all this one adds his knowledge of the *Kamasūtra,* which is obvious wherever he introduces women, one will conclude that this monk was not only a poet by nature but a highly cultivated man.

The same remarks apply to others of his works, such as the *Saundarānanda* and the *Sūtrālaṃkāra.* It is always the life of Buddha that he relates, in one of its stages.

> Nanda, Buddha's brother, is made a monk against his will. He is much distressed, and his wife, the lovely Sundari, laments. Buddha does not want his followers to be unhappy, but at the same time he knows that to send them back into the world would be to keep them from the road to true happiness. Then he takes Nanda by the hand and leads him to heaven. In the Himalaya they meet a horrible ape, and higher up the divine Apsarases. Nanda sees that these latter surpass his wife in beauty as much as she surpasses the ape. To merit the joys of heaven, Nanda, returning to earth, dedicates himself to penances. But Ananda, the favourite disciple of Buddha, proves to him that heaven is nothing compared with the eternal bliss of salvation. Nanda is converted and becomes an Arhat. But Buddha tells him not to be content with his happiness, but to go and preach salvation to men.

[1] Translated by P. E. Foucaux in *Ann. du Musée Guimet,* vi and xix, Paris, 1884, 1892.

The *Sūtrālaṃkāra* [1] is a series of legends, most of them well-known, in prose and in verse. The original is lost, but there is a Chinese translation, in which the art of the poet still makes itself felt.

Asvaghosha founded a school. The poet Matricheta, who comes not long after him in time, is so like him in his Buddhist hymns that it is hard to distinguish between their work. Taranatha, the Tibetan historian, even says that there was only one poet, who bore both names. It is hard to say what is the truth. The Chinese pilgrim I-tsing, at the beginning of the eighth century, is full of the praises of Matricheta, " a nightingale in a previous life, singing the honour due to Buddha."

Matricheta is only known, as is Asvaghosha in certain respects, by fragments of his works discovered in the present century at Turfan. About Aryasura, of the same school, we have more information. Although he was later, for he seems to have lived in the fourth century, Aryasura was strongly influenced by Asvaghosha. The style of his *Jātakamālā*, which is ornate and studied, but without artificiality, is clearly affected by the *Sūtrālaṃkāra*. Like his model, he did not invent much, and confined himself to embellishing the legends of the previous lives of Sakyamuni. For before Buddha attained complete illumination, he made himself worthy of it by acts of charity and superhuman self-denial. So the " Necklace of Tales of Births " sets forth his acts for the admiration of the faithful and the æsthetic enjoyment of the reader. Certainly there is much to admire and enjoy in the story of Buddha offering his body to a hungry tigress! We also see him, in the form of King Sibi, causing his eyes to be taken out and given to a blind Brahman who asks for them. Unfortunately the lofty tone sometimes gives place to sentimentality, creditable but rather silly, a simple means of edification.

The thirty-four jewels of this " Necklace " are almost all taken from the Pali Jātakas,[2] which were old popular tales

[1] Translated into French from the Chinese version, by E. Huber, Paris, 1908.

[2] Translated into English under the direction of E. B. Cowell, Cambridge, 1895–1907.

adapted to the preaching of the Buddhist doctrine of renunciation. They are found all through the literature of *avadāna*, or " Great Deeds ". Only one is unknown, being merely mentioned in the eleventh century by the prolix and erudite Kshemendra in citing an old stanza.

The story of Buddha and the tigress is the first and the most affecting. In spite of occasional longwindedness and unnecessary argument—for example, when Buddha wishes to save the famished tigress from the crime of eating her own cubs—the intermingled prose and verse make a harmonious whole.

So, in the first centuries of our era, a Buddhist literature triumphed. The favourite type was a medley of prose and verse. This was created under the influence of popular narrative literature. The people had not produced an epic, but it liked to hear strange deeds told in song. These songs, which were never made into a consecutive poem, were collected by reciters or bards, who illustrated them by prose commentaries. These commentaries swelled, and became the real story, while the *gāthās* remained as mere illustration. This type, which is later than the *Mahābhārata* or the canonical poems of Buddhism like the *Dhamma-pada*, is characteristic of the literary activity of the first centuries after Christ.

Since the only hero worthy of being celebrated was Buddha, the only subject worthy of narration was his acts. To these two motives every possible anecdote was attached, just as historical, mythical, and moral subjects had been hung on to the adventures of the Pandavas. These collections of Buddhist *gestes* are called *avadānas*. Usually Buddha himself tells of things which have happened in the past or which will happen as a result of *karman*.

One of the oldest of these collections, probably of the second century, is the *Avadāna-śataka*,[1] a " hundred " of narratives treating of subjects in series. The very interesting fifth book speaks of the world of the souls in torment. A saint goes there to ask them the cause of their sufferings, and Buddha explains it and gives a lesson in morality.

A later work, for it is of the third century with some very

[1] Translated into French by L. Feer, in *Ann. du Musée Guimet*, xviii, Paris, 1891.

ancient parts, is the *Divyāvadāna*, the " Heavenly Avadāna ". It is very unequally written. Sometimes it is in correct and simple Sanskrit, sometimes in the studied style of the *kāvya*, with abundance of ornaments, involved turns of phrase, and long compounds, and sometimes it is already in debased Sanskrit. The prose is frequently interrupted by ancient stanzas (*gāthā*), and it also contains short pieces of modern, cultured poetry.

By the side of this heavenly cycle we must place the contemporary cycle of Asoka, the *Aśokāvadāna*,[1] an elegant and refined work in style, metre, and language. Its hero is the Emperor Asoka and its finest legend is that of his son, Kunala. A stepmother causes his eyes to be put out, but, full of Buddhist indulgence, he feels no hate for her. The narrative is distinguished by truly dramatic expressiveness, and the unknown author gives proof of this quality again when he describes the demon Mara imitating Buddha so well that a pious monk falls on his knees before him and worships him, although he knows that he is only a demon.

Avadānas and *mālās* continued to be written for centuries.

Amid all this mass of works, in which Buddhist piety was dressed as fiction, we must mention one which is not lacking in poetry, the *Saddharma-puṇḍarīka*, the " Lotus of the Good Law ".[2] In it nothing is left of Buddha the man. He has become a god above the gods, an eternal, infinite being. He is everything, the absolute. But this " absolute " is full of compassion for suffering humanity and shows it the way of salvation, which consists chiefly in devotion. It is a Mahayanist work. It abounds in descriptions and comparisons intended to give a notion of the celestial glory of Buddha, of the happiness of his worshippers, and also of the virtue of the book itself. The woman who hears it read will never be reborn as a woman. The man who finds pleasure in it will henceforward breathe the perfume of the lotus and his whole body will have the odour of sandalwood. Exaggeration reaches its height in the figures. Reckoning is no longer done in miserable little thousands as in the popular epic ; myriads of myriads are the order of the day.

The matter and form of the work lack unity. The good

[1] Cf. S. Lévi, in *T'oung Pao*, viii.
[2] Translated by E. Burnouf, Paris, 1852.

Sanskrit prose and the *gāthās* in Mixed Sanskrit indicate that it was written at different dates. It seems that it was at first all in verse, and that the prose was added later. But it must have been completed before the third century, for it was already translated into Chinese about 300.

Let us now turn to the poetry of the court, *kāvya*, which is an artistic production, in matter and in form the opposite of Buddhist poetry. The style of the inscriptions proves that it existed before the time of Christ. It flourished chiefly from the advent of the Guptas onwards.

CHAPTER III

The Age of Kāvya

I

KALIDASA AND OTHER EPIC POETS OF THE TIME. THE THEORY OF POETICS

At the end of the fourth century, if it was not much later,[1] for the dates will always be a weak point in these studies, there lived at the court of a king called Vikramaditya the greatest poet of India, Kalidasa.

He was the son of a Brahman, but, having lost his father early, he was reared by a cowherd. Coarse and quite uneducated, but handsome, he was married to a princess. Legend is not troubled by social inequalities, and in any case it says that the marriage was brought about by the trick of a minister. The young man's ignorance made his wife ashamed. He therefore called on the goddess Kali for help, dedicating himself to her entirely. So he got his name of " Slave of Kali ".

From the less fabulous but very scanty information furnished by the poet's own works, we can gather that he was really a Brahman, a follower of Siva and the Vedānta, and in addition an elegant and cultured man of the world, an aristocrat through and through. He loved the city of Ujjayini and knew the country under the Himalaya. But we have no ground for believing a late stanza which makes him one of the " nine jewels ", the poets and scholars who adorned the court of King Vikrama. For the names of the other eight " jewels " belong to another age, and only a very vague, remote tradition has linked them together. The surname of Vikramaditya, " Sun of Heroism," was bestowed on several kings. However, after the work of Sylvain Lévi, Jacobi and Bühler have proved that one cannot place Kalidasa later than between A.D. 350 and 472. In that case his royal patron would be Chandragupta II, a contemporary

[1] Cf. G. Huth, *Die Zeit des Kâlidâsa*, Berlin, 1890, and B. Liebich, in *Indogermanische Forschungen*, 1912, pp. 198 ff.

of King Matrigupta of Kashmir. The latter was not only a protector of letters but a poet himself.

Kalidasa's inspiration is lyrical, but that did not prevent him from writing dramas and epics. He took his subjects from the Purāṇas or the great epics, and a brief remark in the Veda was enough for him to conceive a work full of charm.

His epic poems are the *Kumāra-sambhava*, the " Birth of Kumara ", and the *Raghu-vaṃśa*, the " Race of Raghu ". Kumara is another name of Skanda, the war-god.

The gods, in their unending war with the Asuras, need a leader. Such a leader can only be begotten by Siva, and Siva is vowed to asceticism. On a mountain-top, seated on the tiger-skin, with his head encircled by snakes and his body clad in the hide of a black antelope—a Brahmanic feature—he remains deep in meditation, from which nothing can tear him. The fair Uma, also called Parvati, the daughter of the Himalaya, goes to Siva to try to win his love. At the bidding of Indra, Kama goes to support her, accompanied by his wife Rati, " Pleasure of Love," and his friend Vasanta, " Spring." Kama bends his bow and lets fly an arrow, but with one glance of his third eye the god reduces him to ashes. For the sake of the lamenting Rati, the gods soften the severity of Siva, and Kama is restored to life.

Uma's devotion and the cruel mortifications which are destroying her delicate body at last move Siva. In the disguise of an aged ascetic he advises her to cease to do penances for the sake of such a terrible being as Siva. She replies with a passionate eulogy of the god, the Lord of the Three Worlds. " He grants all desires," she says, " and is himself without desire ; he dwells in dead places but himself gives life." Seeing her great love, Siva decides to marry her and, proceeding according to the precepts of the Gṛihya Sūtras, he sends venerable friends to ask for her hand. The go-betweens are the Seven Sages (*rishi*) who shine in the sky in the Great Wain (the Great Bear) and the aged Arundhati, the pattern of a faithful wife, who is also a star in that constellation. The King of the Mountains, Himalaya, and his wife receive the messengers in accordance with the rules of etiquette, and presently the wedding is held—a picturesque and vivid picture of Indian life. Kalidasa depicts the emotion of Uma's mother so touchingly that the reader too is affected. The married bliss of Siva and Uma is then described in such lively colours that European taste is sometimes embarrassed by all this frankness. But it never descends to commonness, or even to sensuality pure and simple ; on the contrary, the story is throughout enveloped in a haze of the most exquisite poetry.[1]

[1] Nevertheless, the opinions of Indian philologists were divided. Some thought that it was indecent to describe the amorous antics of the gods, as it would be to describe one's own parents in such a situation (Winternitz, iii, pp. 57 and 58 n.). Such is the opinion of Mammata, a Kashmiri Brahman of the eleventh century, who wrote a *Kāvyaprakāśa*. He holds that the true art of poetry consists in not saying everything but leaving much to be understood. This is the theory of *dhvani* " tone " and by extension

The *Raghu-vaṃśa* [1] is a work of Kalidasa's maturity, presenting the genealogy of Rama.

He was, as we know, a descendant of Raghu. His ancestors are all—except one, Agnivarna—steeped in Brahmanic piety, all are stainless heroes, lovers of knowledge and models of virtue, and all retire into the forest at the end of their life. Much of the poem is taken up with devotion to Nandini, the wonderful Cow. If she is satisfied, she will give the childless King a son. So the King offers his life to save her from the claws of a lion. His devotion is rewarded. The lion is a divine messenger who has come to test the King's courage and to announce to him the birth of a son, Aja. Aja is to make a *svayaṃvara*, or marriage of free will, with Princess Indumati. But he is treacherously attacked and only defeats his enemies by his courage.

Then comes a description of family life, the birth of a son, Dasaratha (afterwards Rama's father), and the peaceful reign of a king devoted to his subjects' good. But one day, when Aja is taking his pleasure in a park with the Queen, a garland of flowers falls from heaven and kills the Queen. The husband's despair is told in some very fine stanzas, which end with a sentence characteristic of that chivalrous but warlike age : the King will not ascend the pyre after his beloved wife, solely in order that people may not say contemptuously of him, " He died for a woman."

Only one king of this model dynasty fails to come up to its standard—Agnivarna. He is the Indian Don Juan, who puts the principles of the *Kāmasūtra* into practice. The poet seems to have introduced him in order to show his own knowledge of that textbook of the art of love and to condemn the application of it. Agnivarna neglects his duty, despises his subjects, and spends his life among women. He dies young, before seeing the birth of his son. Here there seem to be reminiscences of the *Mahābhārata* floating about. The First Queen or chief wife being with child, the ministers consecrate her Regent, and " the water of consecration extinguished the fire of the grief with which the widow had been consumed since the death of her husband."

The *Kumāra-sambhava* and *Raghu-vaṃśa* as we have them are unfinished, but both were continued by other writers and have given rise to twenty and thirty-three commentaries

" allusion ". Anandavardhana, a Kashmiri of the ninth century, who was the true creator of the theory of *dhvani*, is more indulgent. In his remarkable *Dhvanyāloka*, a commentary on Udbhata's book on *rasa*, he points to the eighth book of the *Kumāra-sambhava* as showing how much poetic talent and command of language are needed to escape the difficulties of an improper subject. Yet the rules which he laid down in the *Dhvanyāloka* are very strict. True poetry, he says, is that in which the " unexpressed " plays the chief part. His very pure notion of poetry was somewhat distorted after his time. The word *vakrokti* " oblique " or even " tortuous speech ", was invented to designate what should be the greatest quality of a work of imagination. This was going contrary to the master's intention, and poetry was reduced to tricks of language.

[1] Translated into French by L. Renou, Paris, 1927.

respectively. The best are by Mallinatha (fifteenth century). Both also served as models to authors, who imitated them much, and they became the type of cultivated poetry for theorists of the poetic art, who quoted Kalidasa's lines in their works as examples.[1]

The poet has been credited with works which are not his, including a Prakrit epic named *Rāvaṇa-vadha*, the " Slaying of Ravana ", or *Setu-bandha*, the " Building of the Bridge " which was to take Rama's army to the island of Lanka. Apart from its virtuosity of style and the poetry of certain images, which perhaps remind one of Kalidasa, this poem reveals the degenerate taste of a later age in its superabundance of stylistic ornaments and its interminable compound words, filling whole lines.

Shortly after Kalidasa, two epic poets, Bharavi and Magha, enjoyed a great reputation. Bharavi's poem, *Kirātārjunīya*,[2] describes in eighteen books the war of Arjuna and Siva. The latter, to test the hero's courage, takes on the appearance of a half-savage hillman of the Kirata tribe. The story is of little importance. The value of the work lies in descriptions of nature which are almost equal to Kalidasa's. Bharavi's sunsets recall those which are so much admired in the *Kumāra-sambhava*, when Siva and Parvati, sitting on a rock in a Himalayan forest, watch the sun go down with emotion and enchantment (vii, 45 and 54). Bharavi has original images and unexpected thoughts. Thus, the sun inclines earthwards, drunk with the honey which he has drawn with his hands (*kara* means " ray " and " hand ") from the cups of the lotuses of day. The moon is a silver cup which the night brings for the consecration of the King of Love. The golden pollen of the lotus which quivers in the breeze above a group of flowers is the golden parasol which reflects the face of Lakshmi while it shades it.

What most pleased contemporaries was the tricks of the trade and the acrobatics of form. They enjoyed lines which gave the same words when read in either direction, stanzas in which the second part was composed of the same syllables as the first but making other words and an opposite

[1] Cf. Hari Chand, CCXCVII.
[2] Translated into English by C. Cappeller, *Harvard Oriental Series*, xv.

meaning, lines which contained only certain consonants, and the like.

Magha outdoes even Bharavi in the art of versification, for he uses twenty-three different metres as against Bharavi's nineteen. Unfortunately he also outdoes him in tricks. Lines which have two meanings, according to the way in which the compound words are divided, lines which have an opposite meaning when read backwards, stanzas in which the syllables are repeated so as to form geometrical figures, and, more extravagant still, the use of only two consonants in a line (in *Śiśupāla-vadha*, the story of Vishnu's fight with the demon Sisupala, xix, 3) are the final achievement of this over-ingenious poetry.

Yet Magha was a poet, a poet of love, or rather of the art of love. Women of fulsome beauty and their amorous frolics with the Yadavas are the subjects of his poem. Nature, although he paints it in splendid colours, is only there as a background to the beauty of the female body. The story of Vishnu is quite secondary and the battle-scenes have no truth in them.

We must not leave epic poetry without mentioning a composition, later by eight centuries, which is partly epic poem and partly history and claimed to be a scientific work, the *Rāja-taraṃgiṇī* or " River of Kings " of Kalhana.

The author, the son of a minister at the court of Kashmir, was at an early age initiated into politics. Having had a good education, he was able to see and judge without bias. In his chronicle of the Kings of Kashmir, which he brings down to 1148, he makes it his aim to tell nothing but the truth ; at least, wherever he can ascertain it. He knows that he is a poet, but he regards this gift as necessary if he is to make the past live. In fact, he paints characters with rare acuteness. This does not prevent him from believing in myths and marvels blindly. He relates the legend of the Nagas, the divine serpents which were so intimately linked with the pre-history of Kashmir in the popular mind, without criticism. A king may rule three hundred years or die from the curse of a Brahman. Witchcraft lies at the source of many historical events, and the idea of *karman* is confirmed at every step. Being permeated with a profound sense of morality, he makes his history a *magistra vitae*, but not in the political or social sense; what he wants to show is the triumph of good. He can despise upstarts and hate oppressors. When he speaks of the great famine, he castigates the ministers who had laid in stores beforehand and sold corn to the people at the price of gold; through their fault, he says, the ground was white with bones.

His portraits of sovereigns are expressive. He gives some pictures of women, such as the cruel and depraved Queen Didda, putting her grandson to death in order to reign alone, but a wise ruler for all that; or Suryamati, so haughty and passionate that she was bound to end tragically.

> Ruling in the place of her feeble husband, she caused her son to be recognized as crown prince and gave him wide powers. Presently a conflict broke out between the father and the ambitious youth. The King reproached his wife as the cause of all the trouble, and flung in her face the suspicion, which he had long harboured, that the prince was not his legitimate son. At the insult Suryamati was furious, and heaped contumely on the King, whom she had always despised for his weakness. The King slew himself for shame, and then Suryamati cursed all who had sown discord between her and her husband and flung herself into the flames.

Tragic, too, was the end of King Harsha.

> Endowed with rare talents and famous for his good government and piety, he fell under the influence of evil counsellors, and became cruel and suspicious. Abandoned by all, an outlaw in his own country, he was assassinated by his troops.

Kalhana often reminds one of Tacitus. He is a very trustworthy guide for the history of Kashmir at the end of the eleventh century and the beginning of the twelfth. His lack of simplicity, of mastery of form and of construction, prevents his work from being a true epic. He has poetry in him, but he is not a poet. He is important to history without being a true historian.

II

KALIDASA AND LYRIC (EROTIC) POETRY

A tendency to lyricism marks all the poetry of India. Kalidasa, who is so "un-epic" in the *Kumāra-sambhava* and the *Raghu-vaṃśa*, where the subject lends itself to epic treatment, achieves lyrical perfection in the *Megadhūta*, the " Messenger Cloud ".[1]

The subject of the poem is married love.

> A Yaksha, a divine being in the service of Kubera, god of wealth, is banished by his master. He has to leave his wife and spend a year in the south of India. At the beginning of the rainy season he sees a cloud drifting before the wind towards the north. There stands the snowy mountain of Kailasa, and there, clinging to its side like a loving woman, is the town of Alaka, with Ganga at its feet like her fallen veils. In the house whose portal " is graceful as Indra's bow ",[2] in the garden where a pond " covered with lotuses with golden hearts " spreads coolness, the Yaksha's wife, thin with sorrow, " sets out the petals of flowers on the threshold ", to count the days which have passed and those which still divide her from her husband's return. His love, his home-sickness, his hope of reunion—all this he bids the cloud tell as his message.

It has been doubted whether the *Ṛitu-saṃhāra*, the " Seasons ", another descriptive poem, is really by Kalidasa. But summer, the rains, autumn, winter, the cool season, and spring are painted in so many colours, nature is so finely observed, and the love-making of each time of the year is so delicate and so ardent that it can hardly have been written by anyone but the Slave of Kali.

A small collection of erotic stanzas, the *Śṛingāra-tilaka*, attributed to Kalidasa, recalls the *Sattasai* of Hala, but it has more delicacy of form and wit. Stanzas in varied metres tell again and again, but always in a new way, of the cruelty of the adored maiden. Her eyes are likened to blue lotuses (*nīla*, " blue-black "), her teeth to jessamine, her body to the young sprouts of plants, her heart to stone. This simile became a cliché.

Of clichés there were more and more as time went on, and the art of writing poetry became a matter of stringing them together. The lotus at night is always in love with the moon and opens its cup at the advent of the lover. The *chakora* bird always drinks the nectar of the moon-rays and is another name for the lover, for whom nectar is the sight of the beloved face. The bee (*bhramara*, " the beast with two *r*'s ") is always drunk with the honey of the flowers. The elephant in rut, mountain caves sounding with the roaring

[1] Translated into French by Hippolyte Fauche, Paris, 1865 ; A. Guérinot, Paris, 1902 ; and Marcelle Lalou, Paris, n.d., 1920.

[2] From Mlle Lalou's translation.

of lions, clouds swollen with rain, and a quantity of other images accepted as beautiful recur under the pens of the poets. All nature is classified in metaphors for the use of authors.

The *Ghaṭa-karpara*,[1] the "Broken Pitcher", owes its name to the challenge which the author casts at his rivals. He undertakes to bring water in a broken pitcher to anyone who shall surpass him in the art of versifying. Its only interest is the use of the *yamaka*, the repetition of the same syllable in different combinations with varying meanings. Kalidasa excelled in this device; Ghatakarpara (the author has the same name as his work) abuses it.

Since I have had to mention Hala and erotic poetry again, let me here add that this type, which Kalidasa merely touched (if the *Śringāra-tilaka* is indeed his work), was much practised in India. What Hala was for Prakrit, and Amaru soon after him, Kalidasa was for Sanskrit.

The *Amaru-śataka* ("Hundred Stanzas of Amaru") is rightly admired for its delicacy and elegance. Sometimes, too, the author can embody a profound observation in a short stanza. India, which has little to show in painting comparable to the Persian miniatures, seems to have confined its genius to this type of miniature, in which the colours are words. It is needless to say how many imitations these stanzas inspired. They were quoted in anthologies and explained by commentators centuries afterwards, but nothing is known of their author or his date. For a time it was thought that they could be ascribed to Sankara, the great Vedantine philosopher of the end of the eighth century. The story is that he was a rigid ascetic who took the shape of Amaru, King of Kashmir, to make experiments in love with his hundred wives. The name of Amaru, however, does not appear in the list of the Kings of Kashmir. All that we can say is that the author of the *Śataka* was very much a man of his age, an age of amorous poetry and ready smiles. His heroes are passionate but frivolous. The great sorrow is separation—not the breach caused by psychological complications so dear to the West, but departure on a journey, on business as we should say now. Homesickness brings tears to the eyes of women and men alike. Weary of waiting by

[1] Translated into French by A. Chézy in *Journal Asiatique*, 1823.

the roadside, the desolate lady, as evening falls, goes slowly home, when a sudden thought leaps to her mind, "Perhaps he is coming now!" She turns quickly, but there is nothing on the great road.

There are the same ideas and the same pictures as in the *Sattasai*, and the same pessimism, hidden under laughter, or rather the same resignation in the presence of the fragility of happiness.

III

BHARTRIHARI. GNOMIC AND EROTIC POETS

We now come to one of the most gifted men that India has produced, and one who has the further merit of being historical and datable.

I-tsing wrote in 691 that forty years before there had lived in India a grammarian of great renown, Bhartrihari by name. The features which he describes in the grammarian are what we expect to find in the poet. Bhartrihari is said to have renounced the world seven times and to have seven times returned to it. One of the last times, as he entered the convent, he had his carriage kept near in order that he might escape as soon as the temptation became too strong and the resolve of renunciation too weak. In a line quoted by I-tsing he accuses himself of being the toy of his double inclination.

On the strength of these indications Max Müller[1] concluded that the grammarian and the author of the delightful *Śṛingāra-śataka* are one and the same person. H. Oldenberg doubts it,[2] and so does Winternitz.[3] According to I-tsing, Bhartrihari was a zealous Buddhist. Yet the Bhartrihari of the *Śataka* prostrates himself at the feet of Siva. Possibly the Chinese pilgrim, rather a simple-minded soul, having heard stories of the life of the great poet, thought that they referred to the grammarian. In that case, Bhartrihari's date would still be uncertain. Three series of "Hundreds" are ascribed to Bhartrihari—*Śringāra-śataka* "Love", *Nīti-śataka* "Wisdom", and *Vairāgya-śataka* "Renunciation". The first collection is certainly the work of one man.

[1] *India: what can it teach us?*
[2] *Die Literatur des alten Indien*, Stuttgart and Berlin, 1903.
[3] **CCLXXXVIII**, iii, p. 139.

The other two may have been only a compilation, but tradition is unanimous in making Bhartrihari their sole author.

According to H. Oldenberg, if Amaru is the poet of the moment of passion, Bhartrihari gives us the philosophy of love. It is a very simple philosophy: woman is joy and sorrow, trouble and appeasement. It is she who stops us on the way by her glances. It would take less long to traverse the ocean of suffering which is our life if woman did not complicate our voyage and turn us from our goal. The torch of wisdom burns clear until lovely eyes throw their radiance into it. Yet what is the highest object of our power of sight? To see woman. Of our faculty of hearing? To hear her speak. Of our thought? Her youth and beauty. But the continual thirst of love brings disappointment. Unsatisfied in himself, the poet seeks the fault in woman, the eternal culprit. "In this dirty little girl, fool and liar that she is, what is it that I have adored?" he cries. From loving too much, he ceases to love at all, and takes refuge in asceticism, but not for long. It is very Indian, this oscillation between two poles, frantic desire to live and complete abnegation, and so is the exaltation of love for love's sake and the amorous cult, not of a particular woman, Beatrice or Laura, but of woman as such, provided she be young and beautiful. One is inclined to ask, "But what about other interests? Are there none?" The strife of contrary passions and great conflicts did not lend themselves to artistic presentation.

Bhartrihari was the first Indian poet to be known in Europe. The Dutch missionary Abraham Roger, who wrote the first Sanskrit grammar (1651), translated the *Nīti-śataka* and the *Vairāgya-śataka*. These two poems are already gnomic in character. This form was practised in India and was introduced into every other form. The Vedas offer examples of it. The great epics are full of maxims. Aphorisms travelled through India, and things well said (*subhāshita*) were appreciated. For her talent in saying them aptly, Yama grants Sāvitrī her husband's life. There is no work in Indian literature in which general ideas do not occupy an important place. Aphorisms are introduced into the dialogue of plays; the chapters of novels begin and end with them; columns of aphorisms serve as a framework to the short tales of the

Pañchatantra. India loves the general; the particular serves only to illustrate it. A cultivated man should be able to quote on every occasion one of the general thoughts of which he finds a large selection in the anthologies.[1] Without that, "his tongue would be but a piece of meat hidden in his mouth for fear the crows should take it."

Before Bhartrihari's time, a *Śataka* of Chanakya, the minister of a Maurya king, was known. This Chanakya, who was surnamed Kautilya, from *kuṭila*, "tortuous", is the supposed author of the *Arthaśāstra* (above p. 92). Not content with the prose work in which he had set forth his Machiavellian doctrines, he expressed his acute observation of life in verse. "One must not be particular," he says, "about three things—food, money, and one's own wife. Be exacting about three others—study, penance, and alms." "Empty is the house without children, empty the country without parents, empty the heart of a fool, and poverty is emptiness itself."

Bhartrihari, although perhaps less witty than the supposed Chanakya, far surpasses him in elegance and beauty in his philosophic verse. He was, therefore, often imitated. Silhana of Kashmir, some centuries later, carried the asceticism of the *Vairāgya-śataka* still further in his *Śānti-śataka*, which treats of the nothingness of existence.[2]

From the seventh century we have, besides the *Śataka* of Bhartrihari, an *Ashṭaka* (eight stanzas) of Mayura. The subject is a young woman at a tryst and her return. But this slight theme is enough to allow the author to display profound knowledge of the *Kāmaśāstras* and to give proof of an extraordinary command of language. The story goes that Mayura sang of his own daughter, and she, taking offence, cursed him, whereupon the gods punished him with a skin-disease. Having sinned by poetry, it was by poetry that he was absolved. A hymn to the Sun won his pardon—the *Sūrya-śataka*, which is ingenious in style and often original in similes. Aruna, the "Red", Surya's charioteer, is likened to the

[1] O. Böhtlingk has collected two volumes of *Indische Sprüche*.

[2] As a specimen of this gnomic poetry, see the *Bhāminī-vilāsa* ("The Sport of the Fair One") of Jagannatha (seventeenth century), translated by A. Bergaigne, in *Bibl. des Htes. Études*, i, 1872; Victor Henry, *Trente Stances du Bhâminî-Vilâsa*, translated, with fragments of the unpublished commentary of Manirama, Paris, 1885.

manager of a theatre reciting the prologue, and the series of parallels is continued. It is they which, together with the ornaments of style, account for the popularity of the poem.

The Indian imagination liked to brighten the drab realities of biography by ascribing the most extraordinary histories to authors. When Bilhana of Kashmir won the public favour by his *Chaurīsurata-pañchāśikā*, a whole legend was embroidered on the associations awakened by the word *chaurī*. In Sanskrit *chaura* means " thief ". The title, which means " The Joys of Clandestine Love ", suggested the secret loves of a lady of high degree with a man of lower station but rare intelligence. It was accordingly related that Bilhana was the lover of the King's daughter, was found out, and was condemned to death. Led to the place of execution, he breathed his despair and love in fifty burning stanzas, perhaps too vivid for our taste. Each begins " Only to-day (I held her in my arms, and so on) ". The King, who was fortunately a good judge of literature, was enchanted, and gave the poet a free pardon and his daughter. One need not add that Bilhana himself had no notion that he was the hero of this stirring episode.

He wrote a historical work in verse on the deeds of the princes of the Chalukya dynasty. It contains a kernel of truth, for the inscriptions confirm it, but it is full of myth. Indra blows his conch and flowers fall from the sky at the birth of a king. At the same time the author describes the village in which he was born charmingly, and with a truth which strikes one even now. He had studied all the science of his day, travelled to improve his mind, and taken part in poetic contests with success. Established at last at the court of King Vikramaditya VI (1076–1127), he obtained from that prince the title of *Vidyāpati*, "Master of Science," and the privilege of the blue umbrella. His wife was a lady of rank.

The *Kuṭṭanīmata*, or " Bawd's Lessons ", of the end of the eighth century is pornographic.[1] An old professional teaches a beginner how she should behave in order to seem to be in love with a rich young man. So the work is didactic in its kind. The author, Damodaragupta, was the chief minister of Jayapida, King of Kashmir. At the same court had lived

[1] Bühler, in *Indian Antiquary*, xiv (1885). Quoted in **CCLXXXVIII**, iii, p. 151.

Vamana, who wrote on the theory of literature and was the first to raise the question of the definition of poetry and answered it rather mechanically, starting from style. The harlot of the *Kuṭṭanīmata* is an actress, and this work shows what an important place the theatre had in the life of the Indian upper classes.

There were many works like the *Kuṭṭanīmata.* Licentious in appearance, they have a moral purpose—to warn the reader against dangers and abuses. They throw a new light on the position of certain classes of society, such as courtesans, bogus ascetics, and strolling singers.

A work of this type, but of a severer tone, is the " Dialogue of Suka and Rambha on Love and the Highest Knowledge ".[1] Rambha the harlot speaks in a lively strain, full of imagery, of the pleasures of love, and ends by saying, " Vain has been the life of a man who has not tasted the joys of love." Every verse of Rambha is answered by the man, Suka, in a contrary verse, which he ends with " Vain has been the life of a man who has not sought wisdom and knowledge ". The author and date of this work are not known.

A word on the love sung by these too numerous erotic poets. It is sensual love. It is not conducted without scratchings, bitings, and other proofs of ardent passion. A woman, seeing fresh nail-marks on her lover's chest, knows that he has been unfaithful to her. A lover's lips are so bitten that he cannot pronounce certain sounds, and the poet has to use all his skill to avoid giving his hero words containing labials, *b*, *p*, etc., to speak. Lovely damsels bend under the weight of their bosoms, and can only hold themselves up by means of the counterweight of their hips, and so on. The frolics of the lovers, too, seem over-lascivious; at least they are exhibited with much frankness.

But this poetry does not deal entirely with amorous adventures. The love of husband and wife inspires the poets as often. Tender affection ennobles sensuality and respect gives dignity to what would otherwise be trivial love-making. In addition, there are the elegance of expression, the wit, the delicacy, and the vast culture possessed by the representatives of this aristocratic literature.

[1] Published by J. M. Grandjean (text and translation) in *Annales du Musée Guimet*, x (1887).

IV

EROTIC MYSTICISM

Jayadeva

Eroticism is not far removed from mysticism, which in many poets is simply inverted eroticism. This is all that can be said of such poems as the *Chaṇḍī-kucha-pañchāśikā*, "Fifty Stanzas on the Breasts of Chandi." Chandi is a goddess, otherwise called Uma, Devi, Durga, Parvati, Kali, etc., the wife of Siva and the divine Mother of the World (*Jaganmātṛi*), worshipped as the common origin of Vishnu and Siva. She is the energy (*śakti*) of her husband, and her worshippers, who are numerous at the present day, call themselves Śaktas.[1] The hymns to Devi, which were unknown in the old days of the Vedas and Brāhmaṇas, are the product of early Hinduism. These still deserve the name of literature, which can no longer be applied to the somewhat later Buddhist *stotras* or the *dhāraṇīs*, the invocations and spells of degenerate, popular Buddhism, from which the Tantra sect sprang.[2]

To the great Vedantine philosopher Sankara, of the end of the eighth century, are ascribed certain religious poems entitled *Devyaparādhakshamāpaṇa*, "Prayer to Devi for Pardon of Sins." They are imbued with burning piety and a truly filial love. Each stanza of this poem of penitence and hope ends with the refrain, "For a bad son is born often, but there never was a bad mother."[3] This devotion is the more remarkable because Sankara as a philosopher is an absolute monist and declares in one poem that he never bows to any god.

A celebrated poem, at once religious and erotic, is the *Gīta-govinda*,[4] the "Herdsman (Krishna) in Song", of

[1] For the Śaktas, see Winternitz, "Die Tantras und die Religion der Śāktas," in *Ost-asiatische Zeitschr.*, iv (1916); Sir J. Woodroffe, *Shakti and Shâkta*, London, 1920; Ellen and Arthur Avalon (Sir J. Woodroffe), *Hymn to the Goddess*, London, 1913.

[2] Cf. **CCLXXXVIII**, ii, pp. 266–277; A. Barth, *Religions de l'Inde*, **III**.

[3] **CCLXXXVIII**, iii, p. 123.

[4] Translated into French by G. Courtillier, with a preface by S. Lévi, Paris, 1904.

Jayadeva. Jayadeva lived at the end of the twelfth century and was contemporaneous with four other writers who adorned the court of King Lakshmanasena in Bengal. These "five jewels" are better supported by history than the earlier nine to whom Kalidasa is supposed to have belonged. Yet legend has not failed to obscure the true facts of Jayadeva's life. It is said that he had been a Yogi in his youth and had wandered about India in that capacity until a Brahman made him marry his daughter.

The *Gīta-govinda* is a lyrical drama, which tells how Radha in jealousy left her faithless husband Krishna, but in her solitude did not cease to think of him, how she opened her heart to a woman friend, how Krishna sported with the herd-girls, how in spite of all he still loved Radha and his love for her increased, and how the two were at last reunited. It is doubtless based on some popular rite in honour of Krishna and has a certain dramatic quality, but is not written as a play for acting. It is composed of songs which are obviously meant to be danced; the sounding lines have the rhythm of a ballad and sway like a dance. The stanza introducing each part states in a few words the subject of the coming song. Thus, Radha's companion sings of the dances of Krishna with the herd-girls. Three intermediate lines speak of spring and announce a new song, in which the companion depicts the gaiety of the herd-girls, their delight in the young god, and their calls to love. Again the stanza, probably intended to be spoken, tells in the form of a prologue that Radha, tormented by jealousy, has retired into the shadow, and the two following songs, placed in Radha's mouth, complain of the unfaithfulness of her beloved while they express an ardent desire to be able to forgive him. So it goes on till the reunion of the lovers and a eulogy of Krishna, the one god.

Some have seen mystic allusions in this poem. Radha, they say, is the soul, fallen into confusion, chaos, and suffering as soon as it ceases to be in union with the divine. The return to that union is supreme happiness. There is no doubt that the work has a religious character; it is inspired by *bhakti*, amorous devotion to Krishna. But of symbolism there is no trace. Jayadeva is content to be a poet without aiming at philosophy.

He can pour the fire of passion into a faultless mould. Now short words follow in quick succession, and again there is a slow, measured movement of solemn compounds. Alliteration and rhyme add charm to this musical invention, sweeter than anything known before Jayadeva's time. Here the nobility of Kalidasa's lyricism comes into full flower.

CHAPTER IV

THE DRAMA [1]

I

THE NĀṬYA-ŚĀSTRA

FRENCH Indology is fortunate in possessing a remarkable work on the Indian drama, the *Theâtre indien* of Sylvain Lévi. In the following chapter I shall make much use of the teaching of this master of Indian studies in France.

The Indians themselves place the dramatic art above all others. But they say nothing of its beginnings. They present us with the complete theory of the drama, and playwrights are obliged to follow the strict rules and classifications of this form, which developed early and soon became fixed.

The *Ṛigveda* and *Atharvaveda* already furnish rudimentary specimens of the dramatic art, in the dialogue *ākhyānas* and the hymns, which seem to call for miming. When Pururavas begs Urvasi to come back to him and she refuses implacably, when Yami begs her brother Yama for his love, when Sarama demands Indra's kine of the Panis, we are in the presence of true drama.

One can hardly imagine poems being recited without gestures. Dances were a part of worship no less than hymns. Sacrifice itself, with the prescribed gestures, the correctly intoned prayers, and all its symbolic actions was a religious drama. The officiants and participants were the actors and audience. As the cult of Krishna came to take a place by the side of the Brahmanic and Aryan rites, miming played a more and more important part. Long before our era the loves of Krishna and the herd-girls, the exploits of Arjuna, the adventures of Rama, and other such stories were acted.

[1] H. H. Wilson, *Select Specimens of the Theatre of the Hindus*, London, 1827 ; S. Lévi, *Le Théâtre indien*, Paris, 1890 ; A. B. Keith, *Sanskrit Drama* ; Sten Konow, *Das indische Drama* ; H. Oldenberg, *Die Literatur des alten Indien*, Stuttgart and Berlin, 1903, pp. 236–281 ; A. Barth, in *Revue critique*, 1892, pp. 185 ff. ; **CCLXXXVIII**, iii, pp. 160–265 ; A. Gavronski, " Notes sur les sources de quelques drames indiens," in *Mémoires de la Commission orientale de l'Académie polonaise des sciences*, Cracow, 1921.

They are acted at this day in the temples and elsewhere in Bengal, the Deccan, and the East Indian Islands. And still, following old tradition, in the intervals of the action a clown comes on to the stage, grotesquely garbed and painted, and keeps the audience amused by his fooling.

There are several words to designate the actor. Not to mention the unflattering *jāyājīva*, " man who lives on his wife's earnings," probably an old term of abuse which had lost its meaning in the course of time, his usual names are, among others, *bhārata*, *śailūsha*, and *kuśīlava*. *Bhārata* seems originally to have meant " one of the Bharatas ", a clan of bards or warriors, who already appear in the *Ṛigveda* as a great Aryan tribe. The origin of *śailūsha* is uncertain. Kusilava is the name of the two sons of Rama who came to their father's court in the guise of strolling bards, and the word therefore means more particularly a singer.

The ordinary appellation of a man who performs a part in a play is *nāṭa*, literally " dancer ". A dramatic work is called *nāṭaka*, and the theatrical art, the art of acting, *nāṭya*. All these terms clearly owe, if not their origin, at least their pronunciation, to popular, living languages (Sanskrit, *nart*; Prakrit, *nāṭ*), and all have " dance " for their primary meaning. In the popular dance and the mime of the popular festivity we must seek the origin of the Indian drama.

Of popular drama nothing has come down to us. Its elements were absorbed by the artistic composition, in which they were subjected to the polishing activities of the theorists. At the moment when we are first introduced to the Indian drama it has been classified, described in detail, and set out in watertight compartments.

In the first centuries of our era (the second or third) the *Bhāratīya-nāṭya-śāstra* was written, " Bharata's Treatise on the Theatre." [1] As usual, we know nothing or next to nothing of the author. We hear of an ascetic (*muni*) named Bharata who published a work on music. Is he the same man ? Moreover, *bhārata* means " actor ". Was the Vedic proper name afterwards extended to a whole body of professionals, or was the common noun, in the sense of " the actor ",

[1] P. Regnaud, **CCXIX** (*Bhāratīya*, chaps. vi–vii) ; *Ann. du Musée Guimet*, i, ii (*Bhāratīya*, chaps. xv–xvii) ; J. Grosset, *Contribution à l'étude de la musique hindoue*, Paris, 1898 ; S. Lévi, in *C.-R. de l'Acad. des Inscr. et Belles-lettres*, 1899.

taken for a proper name? The *Nāṭya-śāstra* is an encyclopædia of the arts of the theatre. It gives the impression of being a collection of extracts taken from several different works. It is written partly in verse, the epic *śloka* and the popular *ārya*, and partly in prose, and in style recalls the Purāṇas.

It opens in heaven. At the wish of Indra, Brahma creates the theatre (*nāṭya*) as a fifth Veda. Siva, like Dionysos among the Greeks, teaches the actors the violent *tāṇḍava* dance, which we know from many bronzes of Siva dancing, and Parvati teaches the graceful, feminine *lāsya* dance to the actresses. A play is given, representing the victory of the gods over the Asuras. The latter, who are present, are angry, and by their magic spoil the performers' diction and make them forget their parts. The manager of the theatre, Bharata, is embarrassed, but Brahma persuades the Asuras to be reasonable, telling them that henceforward the theatre will represent the truth alone and life itself. It will show both the good and the bad deeds of gods and of the humblest of mortals alike. Religion, knowledge, and virtue will be reflected there, and men will be encouraged on the good road by noble examples and will be amused by the weaknesses of their neighbours.

But even in these early days in heaven the theatre revealed one of the dangers to which it was always exposed.

On once occasion the Gandharvas and Apsarases ventured to represent the absurdities of a *ṛishi* on the stage, and he, offended, cursed the actors. Thereupon they came down to earth, and have been despised ever since. They trade in the virtue of their wives,[1] they sell their children. But the drama itself remains a noble and imperishable thing.

There were actors who were not only highly talented but well educated and the friends of poets and princes. Yet public opinion looked askance at them. It was the King's duty to maintain troupes of actors, but in case of war actors, singers, and dancers were driven out of the besieged city first, and after them the other useless mouths. The code of Manu is very hard on people who wander about the country like thieves and brigands, much as a number of sham Yogins do even now. They are usually said to have come from the south.

[1] There is evidence for this ill opinion at an early date. Patañjali, in his *Mahābhāshya* (second century B.C.) gives the following sentence as an example of a grammatical rule: "When an actor's wife appears on the stage, ask her, 'To whom do you belong?' She will always answer, 'To you'" (**CCXCIV**, p. 380). Elsewhere we read, "Actresses are like the vowels which go with any consonant."

The *Nāṭya-śāstra* explains the method of building the theatre and consecrating it by solemn rites, the poses and gestures to be used by the actor according to the sentiments which he has to express, the correct make-up, costume, and jewellery for each part, and the dialects to be used by the author.

Sanskrit is the noble language, to be used by the King, his minister, the Brahman, the ascetic, and the learned nun. Other characters understand Sanskrit and may speak it on occasion—for example, high-born ladies, and in an exceptional situation—but generally they use Prakrit, and even then the author must carefully choose his dialect so as to indicate social distinctions.

The art of the theatre is set forth in the smallest details. The *Nāṭya-śāstra* is an actor's handbook. The theatre was based on the communion of stage and audience. The audience, which was a select one, had to be worthy of the play, which was always very lyrical, noble, and harmonious, and the actor had to be worthy of his audience, which consisted of the court and of learned Brahmans and great lords invited to the entertainment. For the spectacle was reserved for a closed circle ; this is the great difference between the Indian theatre, which was aristocratic, and the Greek, which was open to all. India built no great amphitheatres in which the multitude, sitting on the stone tiers, acclaimed poets. Platforms of carved wood were erected under a silk awning, and servants, chariots, and elephants made a living wall all round. Everything could be assembled and dispersed in a few days at the caprice of the monarch. More often the performance took place in a court of the palace, or, still better, in a large hall, where at ordinary times the zenana took its lessons in singing and dancing. The people had its own shows, which were simpler and coarser. These still exist. It is in the popular performances given near temples on the occasion of the spring and other feasts that the abduction of Sita, the death of Ravana, and, most of all, the story of Krishna are given in mime, dance, and song to-day. The old aristocratic theatre no longer exists save at Java in the marionette theatre, at Bali in the exquisite art of the dancing-girls, and in Cambodia in the royal ballet, now incapable of revival and dying of old age.

A very important chapter of the *Bhāratīya-nāṭya-śāstra*

is that in which the author gives the theory of *rasa* (" sap, juice, taste ").

> A work should be " juicy ", full of savour. The sentiments (*bhāva*) which the actor's playing represents should create in the audience certain states of soul which outlast the transitory impression and penetrate it deeply with sensibility. Bharata distinguishes eight *rasas*—love, mirth, pity, fright (" terror " would be too strong a word for the gentle Indian drama), heroism, fear, disgust, and admiration. These are the categories of sensation which should cause the souls of the spectators to quiver, but inwardly, leaving a memory as certain savoury dishes are followed by a delicious after-taste.

Bharata and his successors classify everything—sentiments and impressions no less than gestures, attitudes, and types. The theory is evidence that the form of art not only was developed but had reached a stage of fixity. Fortunately, true poetry is always there to triumph over obstacles.

There are ten kinds of higher theatrical representation (*rūpaka*), in which the poetry is the chief thing.

> The noblest is the *nāṭaka*. Its subject must be taken from mythology, history, or imagination, the hero is a king, god, or other such person, its language and sentiments are lofty, and heroism and love are indispensable. The number of acts is between five and ten. Commoners appear but little on the stage—five persons at most. The hero of the *prakaraṇa* may be a Brahman, a minister, or a wealthy merchant. Harlots, rakes, and inferior persons are introduced. In other respects, it is the *nāṭaka* popularized. Briefly, it is an adventure-story in dramatic form. The *bhāna* is a performance by a single actor, who by changes of voice and action represents the conduct of several persons in a comic situation.

In addition there are farces (*prahasana*), fairy-plays (*ḍima*), and various kinds of show, heroic or comic, gay or sad. The categories are purely conventional, and, as if there had not been enough of them, Bharata added eight more, in which dancing, singing, and love were essentials. One even finds a sort of opera and every kind of interlude. Women play an important part.

The performance was given by day, from the morning on. It commenced with a *nāndī*, the remnant of an old religious ceremony accompanied by music and dancing, reduced in the more highly developed drama to a brief invocation. Then comes the prologue (*prastāvanā*), in which the manager (*sūtradhāra*) holds a conversation with one of his assistants or the principal actress, who is usually his wife. The object of the prologue is to announce to the audience the title and author of the play about to be performed. And, as in the French classical drama, the last words of a scene announce the character who is about to appear in the next. The manager has an opportunity to display the extent of his knowledge.

"Musical instruments, technical treatises, the various dialects, the art of government, the business of the harlot, works on poetics, ways of standing and moving, elocution, dramatic business, the industrial arts, prosody, the planets, the lunar zodiac, the local speech, the earth and its countries and mountains and inhabitants, ancient history, royal pedigrees—all these the *sūtradhāra* has to know. . . . He has a good memory, wit, dignity, nobility. He is strong, honourable, in good health, amiable, patient, self-controlled, affable in speech, truthful, courteous, and without greed."[1]

Equally high are the physical and moral qualities required in the actor.

He must have "freshness, good looks, a broad and pleasant face, long eyes, red lips, good teeth, a round neck . . . well-made arms, a slender waist, wide loins, and big thighs, besides charm, grace, dignity, nobility, and pride."

The audience must be up to the standard of the actors.

"The true spectator is happy when the hero is happy, sad when he is sad," etc. In addition to this sensibility, he must have education and a sense of beauty, be able to appreciate the orchestra, understand dancing and acting, and "show his satisfaction by generous gifts".

The religious, or at least pious (originally magical) character of the theatre appears in all the preparations.

The gestures of the *sūtradhāra* as he measures the hall, of the subordinates as they try the costumes, and of the actor as he grinds the ingredients of the make-up are accompanied by propitiatory formulas. The wings hum with murmured prayers.

Only a difference of level separates the stage from the audience. The curtain is at the back, and serves to hide the space behind the scenes where the performers dress (*nepathya*). A whole modern theory, that of the Greek origin of the Indian theatre, owes its existence to the name of this curtain. For it is usually called *yavanikā*, and Yavana was the name for the "Ionians", the Greeks who remained in possession of land in the Punjab and Bactriana under the successors of

[1] Op. cit., p. 380.

Alexander. Some scholars, and first and foremost Windisch,[1] after comparing the facts, have held that India took its theatre from the Greeks. Sylvain Lévi at one time combated this view keenly,[2] plausible though it seems. There is no doubt that the company of actors which followed Alexander and the performances which it gave on great official occasions must have stimulated the Indians. But it is very difficult to determine the limits of an influence. The word *yavanikā*, which, by the way, is not the only name for the curtain, may simply indicate the name of the material, if it was made beyond the Indus, or even the way in which it was used. The other words connected with the arts of the theatre are of Prakrit origin, proving that the drama existed in a living language of the people.

This does not prove that the Indians, with their passion for singing and dancing, did not widen their æsthetic horizon by a knowledge of the theatre of the Greeks. But we should have to know what the Greek theatre as they knew it was like. Plays intended for the amusement of the troops and their leaders in war-time would not be the same as the dramatic performance of peace-time. It is probable that the repertory of the theatre of Alexander and the Greek Kings of Bactriana consisted of fairy-plays, triumphal allegories, and other such shows, mounted in a spectacular fashion to impress their new subjects. On the other hand, Greek mimes,[3] who were strolling players, travelled far into Asia and could easily come into contact with their Indian brethren. The comic types of the two theatres are the same. What is more, they are almost the same from the Indus to the Thames, and the similarity of the Indian theatre and that of Shakespeare has already been noted.[4] The likeness extends even to the colour of the curtain, which was black when the play was sad, and red when it was gay (in England) or violent (in India). A white curtain announced a drama of love.

Women's parts were at first taken by men. They still often are in popular shows. But the classical drama mentions actresses both in the prologue and in the body of the play,

[1] *Der griechische Einfluss im indischen Drama*, Berlin, 1882.
[2] In his *Théâtre indien*.
[3] H. Reich, *Der Mimus*, Berlin, 1903 ; J. Horovitz, *Spuren griechischer Mimen im Orient*, Berlin, 1905.
[4] L. v. Schroeder, *Indiens Litteratur und Cultur*, Leipzig, 1887.

and certain parts are, without any doubt, written to give the actress a chance of displaying her grace and her singing.

Contrary to the Greek usage, the Indian drama does not observe the three unities. According to the treatises on poetics, the action may cover a year. But in *Śakuntalā* several years pass in the interval between the last two acts; the child not yet born in the fifth act is playing with a lion-cub in the seventh. Not much more attention is paid to unity of place. The first four acts happen at the hermitage, the two following at the King's court, and the seventh in heaven. There was no scenery to hamper these changes of locality; words and action took its place.

Unity of action was given to a certain extent by a predominant *rasa*. In *Śakuntalā* the *rasa* is at once erotic and heroic, the love of Dushyanta and Sakuntala with its vicissitudes being the main theme, of which heroism and nobility are the ornament. As a general rule, the Indian play has only one plot and few psychological complications. It avoids bringing violent actions on to the stage, such as a fight or a death, which might arouse painful emotions or make the audience feel uncomfortable. So there is no despair in the theatre, no tragedy. We have not only one life; what does not happen in one will happen in another; injustices will be repaired and efforts rewarded. One must only know how to wait. But the stage presents an abridgement of a life or lives. The good result, the happy ending, must be soon perceived by the audience which has followed the ups and downs of fortune. And, just as the music of Bach, even if it has been played in the minor key, returns to the major in the last chord, so the Indian drama, when all complications are ended, closes in calm and harmony.

The setting was of the simplest kind. There were always garlands and decorations, and there might be properties, such as chariots, weapons, a throne, but there was no scenery. Its place was taken by a description delivered by the hero, as that of action was in the French classical theatre. Moreover, the audience was presumed to have a lively imagination and a quick intelligence. The actions of the players were of the greatest importance; it was they that had to say everything and produce the desired impression. So the treatises on acting describe the conventional gestures in minute detail. For the theatre was old. It had long lost the spontaneity of the popular spectacle. Elegant and refined as it was, it was also conventional. Manifestations of feeling are classified, feelings are catalogued, and so are costumes and colours, make-up and situations.

When a young girl picks a flower (an imaginary one), "her left hand is flat, arranged in an *arāla*,[1] her fingers apart with a slight curve, the forefinger in an arc and the thumb completely curved," and so on. The position of the right hand is described in the same detail. Nothing is left to the actor's invention. The heroine simulates fear—her lips must tremble and her fingers must have such-and-such a position and no other. She is lovesick—she must stand thus. The hero mounts on a chariot (imaginary)—this is how he must raise his legs in succession, thrust his feet forward, etc.

The royal ballet of Cambodia may give us some notions of this strictly regulated mimicry.[2]

There are five moral situations in drama (enterprise, effort, hope, certainty, success) and sixteen kinds of hero, who may, according to the category of the play, be of upper, middle, or lower class, so that there are forty-eight varieties of him altogether.

The hero (*nayaka*, "leader" of the drama) is endowed with high native qualities, among which impassibility, honour, and elegance hold the first place. The heroine (*nayikā*) may be innocent, brazen, or something between, and these three species are further subdivided according to the situation.

The situation is likewise of three kinds.

The heroine belongs to the hero, being his wife; or she belongs to others as a young girl belonging to her parents or guardian; or she belongs to everybody as a courtesan. A married woman should not be the subject of dramatic sentiment, but there are exceptions to this rule. Nevertheless, the desire for another man's wife never appears as the subject of an Indian work of literature.

The heroine may stand in eight situations with reference to the hero.

"She is tormented when she finds on her lover the marks[3] of another love, and she reddens with jealousy"[4]; she is betrayed, she repents of her cruelty, etc., etc.

She has twenty native graces. Other theorists require twenty-eight, pride being one.

[1] Curved in a hook.

[2] M. G. Groslier, "Le Théâtre et la danse au Cambodge," in *Journal Asiatique*, ccxiv (January–March, 1920), p. 125.

[3] The marks of nails, bites, etc., as in erotic poetry.

[4] **CCXCIV**, p. 76.

The signs of modest and semi-modest love are classified according to the situation. Counting them all, we get 384 classes of heroine, almost as many as for the heroes. The playwright had only to make his choice, but once he had chosen he had to stick to his category. In practice, however, characteristics were mingled, and, fortunately for us, genius overcame scholasticism.

Other classifications deal with dramatic means, principal and auxiliary, men's parts, and women's parts. The treatises even give the correct manner of addressing a person and the colours of the costumes to be worn. The stage represents types. There is a type of King, of First Queen, of loving maiden, etc. Everything is laid down beforehand, moral and physical qualities and attitudes. It is a theatre of living marionettes. Talent reveals itself in infusing blood into these puppets, and genius in extracting a drama from the conflict of types and circumstances.

II

THE FORERUNNERS OF THE CLASSICAL THEATRE

A. *The Religious and Epic Drama. Asvaghosha and Bhasa.*

The earliest known dramas belong to Buddhist Sanskrit literature. Among the fragments discovered at Turfan part of the last act of a play about the conversion of Sariputra and Maudgalyayana, two of Buddha's first disciples, has been identified. The last sheet of the fragment bears the title, *Sāriputra-prakaraṇa*, and the author's name, Asvaghosha.

For a pious Buddhist to write plays when the canonical *sūtras* condemned dancing and music, the love of the stage must have been stronger than the fear of prohibitions. Three hundred years before Christ, Asoka caused severe censure of theatrical amusements to be engraved on rocks. But they won the day. " A respectable man could not dispense with the study of the arts of the stage, and the biographers of Buddha found themselves compelled to ascribe this pernicious lore to him." The dancing girl Kuvalaya attains to sainthood, having taken part, in a previous life, in the performance of a *nāṭaka* in the Master's honour.

The recent discoveries in Central Asia, which have been

studied by Lüders, prove that the technique of the drama had been completely worked out a hundred years before our era. It had reached a point at which it could influence the creation of the theatre in adjoining countries—Burma, Tibet, Sogdiana, China—where it came in with Buddhism.

In 1910 an Indian scholar, looking for manuscripts in the south of Travancore, discovered ten complete dramas, part of an eleventh, and yet two more complete ones.[1] They were written by the Brahman Bhasa, whose name had hitherto been known only from vague allusions. Neither his time nor his country is certain. He was a Vishnuite, and knew the legend of Krishna and his avatars. If that legend, which is of non-Aryan origin, took shape in India in the first centuries of our era, Bhasa would belong to that period at the earliest, and must have lived about a hundred years before Kalidasa and some hundred and fifty after Asvaghosha. In technique he is nearer the latter. He is a poet, and, what is more, a dramatist. He takes his subject from the *Mahābhārata*, from the legends of Krishna and Rama, and perhaps also from the tales of Gunadhya, unless both authors drew from the same sources. Although his invention is poor, his plot rather simple, and his form still too like that of the epic, he can create striking situations.

His drama, *Pañcharātra* ("Five Nights", or "Five Days"), deals with an episode in the war of the Pandavas to recover their kingdom. It is not lacking in dramatic moments; it is pure *Mahābhārata*, but made more varied and interesting. In the *Dūtavākya*, the "Message", in which Krishna is the messenger of the Pandavas, a picture is brought and described. It required great histrionic talent to give life to this.

The *Pratimā-nāṭaka* (the "Play of the Image") contains a striking scene of Dasaratha's despair at having driven away his son Rama. The old king wanders over the stage, mad with grief, and dies, calling on the ancestors whom he thinks he sees coming at his call. The act, which ends with the lamentations of the onlookers and presents a death-scene, is contrary to the rules of Indian drama. So, too, in the first act of the *Abhisheka-nāṭaka*, the "Play of the

[1] *Thirteen Trivandrum Plays attributed to Bhasa*, translated by A. C. Woolner, 2 vols., Oxford, 1930–1.

Coronation ", Vali, King of the Monkeys, dies tragically on the stage. But a talent which could move men's hearts was forgiven. Another peculiarity strikes one in the former play. The image which gives it its name is the statue of the King, placed in the temple after his death. To it the widowed queens bring an offering of flowers. There is nothing in the information which we possess which authorizes us to believe that India ever had the custom, so common in Imperial Rome and Greek lands, of exhibiting the effigies of princes and paying them divine honours. Bhasa presents us with some very curious problems.

His masterpiece is *Svapna-Vāsavadattā,* " Vasavadatta in a Dream."

Reasons of State demand that King Udayana should marry Padmavati, the sister of the King of Magadha. But he loves his wife Vasavadatta too much to take another wife. The wily minister, Yaugandharayana, engineers a conflagration and causes it to be reported that he has perished in it with the Queen. Then, in the disguise of an ascetic, accompanied by Vasavadatta, he goes to the court of Maghada and entrusts his " young sister ", as he calls her, to the Princess. We know nothing of what Vasavadatta thinks. We can only suppose, as is confirmed later, that this is a sacrifice which she makes for the good of the King and the State.

Udayana asks for the hand of Padmavati. Vasavadatta, still in the guise of the young sister of the ascetic and chamber-woman of the Princess, has to weave garlands for her husband's wedding and, although she knows that it is only a political marriage, she suffers sorely.

The two women have become intimate friends, and are never separated. One day they overhear the King talking with his confidant (the *vidushaka*, an ignorant, absurd, cowardly Brahman, but the faithful friend of the hero). The King is affected by Padmavati's grace, but he still loves Vasavadatta deeply, and as he speaks of the wife whom he supposes dead he weeps. This detail would not suit the European stage, which is more reserved and harder about outward manifestations of suffering. The Brahman brings him water with which to wash his eyes, and when Padmavati comes forward the King tells her that some flower-pollen has fallen in them.

One day, when asleep in the baths, he dreams of Vasavadatta. She comes in person at that very moment, expecting to find Padmavati. He hears her name, and she fits herself into his dream, but vanishes as soon as he wakes. This is a touching scene. The elegance of the sentiments bears witness to a life which is not only cultivated but highly refined, although rather idle. In the end, through a portrait of Vasavadatta sent to Udayana by her parents, she is recognized. She becomes First Queen once more, and Padmavati is the second. The minister confesses his plot ; policy is satisfied and so is the heart.

This is the drama of fine sentiments. The two young women are noble and unselfish. The King is at once a faithful husband and an elegant lover, divided between his gay, sensual love for Padmavati and his deep affection for Vasavadatta.

Bhasa composed another play on the same subject, *Yaugandharayana Keeps his Promise*. The prevailing sentiment is the fidelity of a minister who succeeds by the sacrifice of himself in bringing about a useful alliance.

B. *The Middle-class and Political Drama. Sudraka and Visakhadatta*

An unfinished play of Bhasa, *Chārudatta*, was rewritten by King Sudraka. I say " rewritten " because the first four acts are repeated with few changes. We know nothing of the later author. He is mentioned only by an eighth-century theorist named Vamana. His period cannot be determined. Sylvain Lévi [1] refuses to place him before Kalidasa, who " does not mention him in the prologue of *Mālavikā* among the famous playwrights ". All that we know of him is taken from the prologue of his drama. " He knew the *Ṛigveda*, the *Sāmaveda*, arithmetic, the art of the courtesan, and the management of the elephant." By the grace of Siva he was cured of an ailment of the eyes. When his son was established on the throne and the horse-sacrifice was made, he went on to the funeral pyre at the age of a hundred years and ten days. " The prologue, which ascribes the play to King Sudraka, hardly deserves confidence, for it describes the death of the poet who wrote it "—unless these lines were added afterwards by other editors.

Sudraka is not highly regarded by the theorists, and is quoted little and only late. Possibly this is because he was of the Śūdra caste, or it may be because his adaptation of Bhasa's play, under the title of *Mṛichchhakaṭikā*,[2] the " Little

[1] Op. cit., pp. 196 ff.

[2] Translated into French for the first time by Hippolyte Fauche (in *Une Tetrade, ou Drame, hymne, roman, et poème*, i), Paris, 1861 ; by Paul Regnaud, Paris, 1877 (*Bibl. orientale elzévirienne*, vi–ix. Translated into English by H. H. Wilson in *Select Specimens* ; by A. W. Ryder in *Harvard Oriental Series*, ix, 1905.

Clay Cart ", does not conform to the rules of dramatic poetry. For this latter reason it is the more appreciated in Europe. Two French adaptations have unfortunately not been successful on the stage.[1]

The merchant Charudatta, a Brahman by caste, is noble and cultured, but has impoverished himself by his generosity. He loves the courtesan Vasantasena. She is persecuted by Samsthanaka, the brother of the royal concubine, a coarse, insolent upstart, who is powerful through the favour of the King. Vasantasena takes refuge temporarily in the house of Charudatta, where she insists on leaving her jewel-case for safety. The poor Brahman Sarvilaka steals the jewel-case in order that he may sell its contents and buy the freedom of Madanika, a young slave-girl of Vasantasena. He is dissuaded from his project by the girl herself, and returns the case to Vasantasena (who has been present at their conversation unseen) as if he had been instructed to take it back to her. In return, Vasantasena gives Madanika to him without payment. The consequence is that the former slave acquires a higher social rank than her mistress, for Vasantasena, for all her wealth and culture, belongs to the low caste of harlots——a hereditary profession—and is not free. Only a king can liberate her, as happens at the end of the play, when the herdsman Aryaka, a friend of Sarvilaka, is suddenly placed on the throne by a revolution.

But before that Vasantasena is knocked down by Samsthanaka, in his rage at her scorning his overtures. He thinks her dead and, burying her under dry leaves, accuses Charudatta of her murder before the courts. However, the crime has been witnessed by a Buddhist monk, to whom Vasantasena has done a service. He had once been a masseur and a gamester, and, having been driven out of the gaming-den by the proprietor, had taken refuge with the courtesan, saying that he was an old servant of Charudatta. Vasantasena had paid off his creditors and he, sick of the world, had taken to a religious life. He now revives Vasantasena, takes her to his convent, and tends her, and presently the two of them appear in court to overthrow the false accusation. They arrive just as the executioner is raising his sword over Charudatta.

The death-sentence is based on the fact that certain jewels of Vasantasena were found in the hands of the clown, Charudatta's friend. She had put them in a toy cart of clay belonging to Charudatta's little boy, in order that he might buy the gold cart which he wanted. Hence the name of the play.

In the tenth act all ends happily. Samsthanaka flies in shame ; the ex-masseur monk becomes a superior of convents ; Charudatta is made governor of a province by the new king ; Vasantasena, now a free woman, becomes his second wife. For he has a first one ; we must not forget that. She has even shown her devotion to her husband by sending Vasantasena her last necklace, to make up for the lost jewel-case. Now she shows her delight as she accepts the lovely courtesan as a sister.

[1] By Méry and Gérard de Nerval, Paris, 1850 ; by V. Barrucand, Paris, 1895.

The *Little Clay Cart* is packed full of situations and types. It is the life of every day. We are even shown a traffic-block. An unintentional exchange of palankeens, the flight of an outlaw, the brawls of a gambling-house, children at play, a concert (described with enthusiasm by Charudatta on his return from it), a storm, a lovers' meeting, ruses and intrigues and the opulent life of high society, the insolence of favourites and the quick wit of burglars, all are full to overflowing of liveliness and swift action. This drama, breaking all the rules and partaking of two forms of art, is really a novel set forth on the stage.

Bhasa, who is still governed by the spirit and tone of the epic (except in the *Svapna-Vāsavadattā*), chiefly uses Sanskrit. Sudraka, bringing in people of the middle and even lower class, makes them speak the Prakrits. Seven varieties of them occur in the play. This would be evidence against its supposed antiquity, especially since the Sanskrit is somewhat debased. But this defect might suggest that the author, who is obviously steeped in Buddhist ideas, was not a Brahman, and therefore did not know the sacred language thoroughly. Certain simplicities of technique, such as the suppression of intervals of time between the actions of the characters and the change of place with almost every scene, may indicate a period before Kalidasa. The descriptions, which are too long for the stage, although they take up slightly less room in Bhasa, still point to epic methods transported into the drama.

There is something of politics, as a *deus ex machina*, in the *Little Clay Cart*; there is more in the *Pratijñāyaugandharāyaṇa* of Bhasa; there is nothing else in the *Mudrā-Rākshasa* [1] (the "Seal of Rakshasa") of Visakhadatta or Visakhadeva.

As with most Indian writers, we know nothing of the author. There is not even agreement about his probable date. Serious scholars place him in the eighth or ninth century, and others, no less serious, make him almost contemporaneous with Kalidasa. His drama, his only work, was probably written about A.D. 410. It is a curious play, without a love-interest and without a heroine. But of politics there is plenty.

[1] Translated into French by Victor Henry, Paris, 1888 (*Coll. orientale*, ii). Also in H. H. Wilson, op. cit.

The praise of politics is sung in the prologue, and about politics the plots are wound and unwound. There is no love, but there is passion—loyalty to the King and his glory. The play, which in its workmanship is not unlike the *Little Clay Cart*, has an unattractive subject for us, but the author's skill makes it thrilling.

The minister Chanakya dethrones the Nanda king, who has insulted him, and sets up in his place a Sūdra named Chandragupta. In his determination to destroy the last member of the Nanda house and to obtain for Chandragupta the support of the former minister Rakshasa, he resorts to every means. Rakshasa flies, and works for his masters abroad. Chanakya surrounds him with spies and corrupts all his friends, except Chandanadasa, who is faithful to the death. Chandanadasa is accused of having sheltered Rakshasa's family and is led to execution, whereupon Rakshasa, to save him, gives himself up to Chanakya. This last bids him choose between acting as minister to Chandragupta and seeing his friend put to death. Rakshasa avows himself defeated. His King is dead, his plots have failed, his allies have betrayed him. He accepts the generous offer of his adversary and enters Chandragupta's service. Having secured for the throne the assistance of an able and devoted minister, and having restored peace in the land, Chanakya retires from the world, presumably to write his *Arthaśāstra*.

"The author of the *Mudrā-Rākshasa*," Sylvain Lévi writes, "deserves to be compared to Corneille. Both, in bringing politics on to the stage, have had the happily-inspired courage to choose the sentiment of admiration as the mainspring of drama."[1] For it is with the sentiment of admiration that the play ends. Rakshasa cannot help admiring his conqueror. Chanakya admires Rakshasa's talents and dignity of character, while he circumvents his plans of resistance and brings him over to the side which he has been combating. The play is intensely interesting but, unlike the drama of Corneille, it lacks grandeur, and it also lacks pity. The cause of the downfall of a dynasty and of civil war is a mere personal insult. Although Chanakya, the author of all these disasters, acts for the good of the king whom he has set on the throne, our moral sense is not satisfied. The tragic death of the last of the Nandas is merely a murder in disguise. All this abyss of intrigue and spying, of cold, calculated cruelty, inspires us with aversion for the hero. The two ministers are equally skilled in policy and equally devoted to their masters. One might say that they are equally

[1] Op. cit., p. 228.

treacherous, but Rakshasa, being attached to those who are destined to be defeated and perish, being defeated himself, and, lastly, being capable of strong friendship, attracts us more. Chanakya is admirably drawn as a powerful, menacing intelligence. The beginning of the play shows him devising his schemes in a series of short, rapid scenes; the end shows him satisfied in his hate and in his loyalty.

III

KALIDASA. THE CLASSICAL THEATRE

Here again we must return to Kalidasa, who covers the field of the Indian drama as he does those of epic and lyrical poetry.

The poet's first work was the *Mālavikāgnimitra.*[1] This drama is so unlike the others that H. H. Wilson, who translated it, expressed doubts as to its origin. His scepticism was unfounded. Kalidasa amuses himself by describing a petty intrigue of the zenana, not devoid of humour. That it is a first work we gather from the prologue, in which the manager apologizes to the audience for neglecting the famous authors and introducing an unknown man.

For the theme of many plays of this type we may again turn to Sylvain Lévi.[2]

"A princess, who is to marry a king, falls victim to some accident which seems to make the marriage impossible. Without being recognized, she enters into the service of the Queen whom she should have supplanted. The King sees her, is struck by her beauty and distinction, and falls in love. He overhears the confidences of the girl, who has not given her heart elsewhere. The lovers make an assignation, but the blundering of the clown enables the Queen to break in on their first meeting. She is furious, and the King tries to pacify her, but she again catches him straying. A chance circumstance changes the Queen's temper. She is softened, and herself offers the King her rival's hand, and usually this new marriage brings the King, in fulfilment of a prophecy, universal sovereignty. That is the scheme of the *Mālavikā*, *Ratnāvalī*, *Priyadarśikā*, *Karpūra-mañjarī*, *Karṇa-sundarī*, and other plays. The only variation is in the incidents which bring the lovers face to face, lead the Queen to the meeting, suddenly pacify her fury, and so on.

[1] Translated into French by Ph.-Ed. Foucaux, Paris, 1877 (*Bibl. orientale elzévirienne*, xiv); by Victor Henry, Paris, 1889; into English by Tawney, 2nd ed., Calcutta, 1891.

[2] Op. cit., pp. 167–8.

The main object is to depict the states of mind of the two lovers in pleasing verse and to introduce a few descriptions or landscapes."

In the play with which we are dealing, the King has seen Malavika's portrait, and wants to see the original, but the Queen in jealousy hides her. However, a dancing competition brings her on to the stage, and the King's heart is enraptured. The two First Queens react each in her own way. Dharini, who is noble and proud, finds some forgetfulness in long conversations with the nun Kausiki, "whose powerful intelligence adapts itself to all circumstances," while Iravati, who is violent and masterful, spies on the lovers, insults the King, and has Malavika imprisoned. When things are at their worst, a body of prisoners from Malavika's country recognize their princess, who was believed dead. At the same time it is reported that Dharini's son has gained a great victory. She marks her joy by presenting the King with Malavika as his third wife, and Iravati has to agree.

In the first act there is a quarrel between the two ballet-masters, who are jealous of the King's favour. This comic incident is soon raised to a higher level by a speech on dancing, the divinest of all arts. At the end the nun Kausiki delivers a very reasonable stanza on women who, themselves true and chaste, bring their husband a new bride, therein being like rivers, which do not prevent other streams from flowing into the sea. King Agnimitra, amorous, sensual, refined, delicate, and full of consideration for the women whom he deserts, will appear again under other names, as he has already been seen in the affectionate hero of the *Svapna-vāsavadattā*.

Of the arts, according to the Indian theorists, the best is the drama; of dramas, *Śakuntalā*; of *Śakuntalā*, the fourth act; and of that act, the verses in which Kanva bids farewell to his adopted daughter. And indeed in the *Abhijñāna-Śakuntalā*, the "Recognition of Sakuntala", Kalidasa's genius attains its highest point.

The subject is taken from the *Mahābhārata* and perhaps also from the Purāṇas.

King Dushyanta, hunting in the forest, comes to the hermitage of Kanva. The hermit is not there, and a girl comes forward to pay the duties of hospitality to the King. It is Sakuntala, the daughter of the Apsaras [1] Menaka and the sage Visvamitra. Abandoned by her mother, for the Apsarases do not rear their children, she has been taken in by Kanva and brought up by the hermits. She herself relates to the King her origin—how the ascetic had been seduced by the Apsaras, whom the gods had sent on purpose to destroy the fruit of the holy man's penances. The King falls in love at first sight, and learns with joy that the maid is not of the Brahman caste, which would have prevented their union. King though he be, he has not the right to take a wife of a higher caste. Nor can the simple-minded, honest Sakuntala conceal her love. She writes verses, or rather scratches them with her nail on a lotus-leaf. The King offers her marriage in the

[1] One of the Nymphs of the Celestial Waters, the Dancing-girls of Heaven.

Gandharva fashion—that is, a marriage contracted without the knowledge of the parents, but none the less legal. Sakuntala accepts. Presently the King, being recalled to his capital, leaves the hermitage, promising to send for Sakuntala in great pomp, and gives her his ring.

Then troubles begin. Sakuntala, deep in memories of her happiness, does not hear the summons of the severe and irascible ascetic Durvasas who, passing by the hermitage, asks for hospitality. He curses her: " May he for whom you forget respect for holy men forget you! " At the entreaty of Sakuntala's friends, the maidens Anasuya, " Unjealous," and Priyamvada, " Speaking-pleasant-things," he mitigates his curse; when the loved one sees the ring he will remember. But Sakuntala, lost in her dream, knows nothing at all of what has happened, and her companions are careful not to distress her.

Kanva returns. The voices of heaven have told him of Sakuntala's wedding and of the glorious destiny which awaits the son whom she will bear. It is time to hand her over to her bride-groom, who is strangely late in sending for her. She sets off, accompanied by good Gautami, her adoptive mother, and two ascetics. In this fourth act, Sakuntala's farewell to the forest is capable of moving even one who dislikes the Indian drama. The fanciful is mingled with the real. The trees bend in friendship over her who has tended them, and the voices of genies utter blessings. She sheds tears as she leaves the jasmine bush which she has reared, and her gazelle runs after her a long way, to lead her back to the hermitage. Kanva speaks of the solemn duties which await her, and of his paternal love which makes him at once happy and unhappy, and her friends advise her in whispers to show her ring to the King if he does not know her immediately. At that Sakuntala shivers with foreboding. Turning round once again, she asks Kanva when she will see the hermitage again. " When, having served your husband for long years and reared up a son worthy of his name, you see him give the reins of government to that heroic son, then, with your husband, you will come back to the repose of our retreat."

A cloud lies on the King's memory. When he sees Sakuntala, he dare not lift his eyes to her, for she is with child, and therefore married. He remembers nothing. She would show him the ring, but it has fallen into the river. The King sees in this only feminine guile. Sakuntala is hurt and angry. The ascetics tell her nevertheless to remain in her husband's house, and they withdraw. In despair she cries out, " Earth, open under my feet! " She calls on her mother, the Apsaras, to help her, and as she is being led away a cloudy shape seizes her and vanishes with her into the tank.

In the seventh act, a fisherman is arrested for the theft of a ring, which he declares that he has found in a fish. The King recognizes his own ring, and his memory returns. Regrets, melancholy. Time passes. The gods give the King an opportunity to fight and defeat the demons. On the car of Indra, by the side of the divine charioteer Matali, he comes to receive his reward from holy Maricha and his wife Aditi, the august ancestors of the world. In the abode of the gods he sees a young boy playing with a lion-cub. Two attendants warn the child against the lioness, but he is not afraid.

He is Bharata, the King's son. Sakuntala is there, as an ascetic, sad but peaceful. The lovers are reunited. Maricha prophesies that Bharata will have the empire of the world, and allows the whole family to return to earth, to Dushyanta's kingdom.

The *Abhijñāna-Śakuntalā* is not a drama in the Greek and European sense. H. Oldenberg criticizes it very severely.[1] Nothing in it is explained by the natural course of things. The curse is pronounced by a " sage " who cannot control himself, and therefore lacks the first qualification of the sage. The King, though guilty in fact, is fundamentally innocent. Sakuntala's misfortune is immense and unjustified, for what we might regard as light conduct in a woman was nothing of the kind in India, where the Gandharva marriage was lawful. It is by mere accident that Sakuntala does not hear the sage calling and afterwards loses the ring. Only the faults of a past life can explain what is inexplicable in our trials. This is a convenient theory, and Kalidasa may have used it as an excuse for introducing into his work an element defying all psychology. But if he had not introduced it his hero would have been really guilty, and that is not allowed by Indian dramatic theory.

The play was translated into English by Jones in 1789, and from English into French in 1803, and it aroused the enthusiasm of Goethe, who in 1791 composed his famous elegiacs :—

Will ich die Blumen des frühen, die Früchte des späteren Jahres,
will ich, was reizt und entzückt, will ich, was sättigt und nahrt,
will ich den Himmel, die Erde mit Einem Namen begreifen,
nenn ich, Sakontala, dich, und so ist alles gesagt.[2]

The play has several times been translated into French,[3] and it has been performed on the French stage. Sarcey, who was not likely to find poetry of this type congenial, said, more wittily than justly, " *C'est l'enfance du théâtre et le*

[1] *Die Literatur des alten Indien*, Berlin, 1903, p. 261.

[2] Flowers and fruit, all that delights and all that sustains, all heaven and all earth, are expressed in the name Sakuntala.

[3] Translated into French from Sir W. Jones' version by Citizen A. Bruguière, Paris, 1803 ; from the Sanskrit by P. E. Foucaux, Paris, 1867 and 1874 ; by Abel Bergaigne and Paul Lehugueur, Paris, 1884 ; into English by Monier-Williams, 6th ed., London, 1894.

théâtre de l'enfance." It is true enough that for the manufacturer of well-constructed middle-class comedies the curse which sets the play in motion is merely ridiculous, and the theme of the ring (or other means of recognition) intolerably hackneyed. This theme recurs in Indian literature *ad nauseam*, as it does in all literature.[1] Yet one could hardly find a more poetical work. The verses are simply enchanting. No translation will ever convey their beauty.

A fairy-tale of the love of a goddess and a mortal, a type called *troṭaka*, is the subject of *Vikramorvaśī*,[2] "Urvasi won by Heroism," the third and last play of Kalidasa. It already shows signs of commencing decline. There are as many versions of it as of *Śakuntalā*, and they are so many and so different from one another that it is difficult at this day to know what the original was. It has been translated into European languages, and an opera has been made of it at Munich. The audiences have felt the lack of dramatic plot. Certain verses of the *Ṛigveda* (x, 95), the dialogue of Pururavas and Urvasi (cf. above, p. 238), have furnished Kalidasa with matter for five acts. But here the nymph is not cruel, but affectionate and tender.

> Having been carried off by the demons, she is liberated by Pururavas and brought back on his chariot. They fall in love. Urvasi returns to Indra's heaven, but at the first opportunity she appears in the King's park and there leaves a love-letter for the King (like the verses which Sakuntala wrote on a lotus-leaf). Needless to say, it falls into the hands of the Queen and she is angry.
>
> A play is performed in heaven, in which Urvasi acts the part of Lakshmi. At the question, "Who is the lord of thy heart?" instead of answering "Purushottama" (i.e. Vishnu), she says "Pururavas", so lost is she in her love. Then Bharata curses her, but Indra pities her and modifies the curse: she may remain united to Pururavas until he sees his son, born of her. But in a moment of jealousy Urvasi, wandering wildly, enters the sacred wood forbidden to women, and at once Bharata's curse acts and the nymph is changed into a creeper. The King is in despair, and seeks her in vain. He addresses a complaint, beautiful but rather long, to beasts, insects, and birds, mountain, river, and forest, until at last, under the influence of a magical stone, he clasps a creeper and finds Urvasi in his arms. It is by chance, too, that he finds his son, whom Urvasi has caused to be kept secretly in a hermitage. She then returns to heaven, and so is lost once more. But the victory of Pururavas over the demons induces Indra in gratitude to allow him to take back his wife, this time without conditions.

[1] A. Gavronski, *Notes sur les sources de quelques drames indiens*, Cracow, 1921, p. 39.

[2] Translated into French by P. E. Foucaux, Paris, 1861 (also in *Bibliot. orient. elzév.*, xxvi); into English by Wilson, op. cit.

Between the fourth and fifth acts several years pass, as between the fifth and seventh acts of *Śakuntalā*. Here again heroic conduct on the part of the child reveals his race. But in this case Pururavas " learns of his fatherhood only to find at the same time that they must part ".

The verses of Pururavas, who is rather a pallid hero, are too lyrical. But this very defect attracted the successors of Kalidasa, and the play was much imitated. It won the public favour. No one has equalled Kalidasa in the art of calling up the most delicate shades of feeling, and no one has painted nature as he has done. There have been more colourful writers, such as Harsha in the *Ratnāvalī*, and others whose dramatic talent stirs us more deeply, but none has had his grace, his elegance, or, above all, his noble rhythm.

IV

THE SUCCESSORS OF KALIDASA

For some time yet, with Harsha and Bhavabhuti, the drama was kept at the high level to which Kalidasa had brought it. After them came inferior writers who exaggerated its qualities but multiplied its defects.

It was as a crowned monarch, enjoying a well-earned rest after thirty-seven years of hard conquest, that Harsha wrote his dramas. He reigned from 606 to 647 at Kanauj, which political revolutions had made the ruling power of India. His friend the poet Bana has left a biography, conventionally exaggerated, of this amazing king, and his guest and admirer, Hiuen Tsang, tells us what he was able to see between 630 and 644, thanks to the favour given him by the sovereign. Inscriptions and coins tell the rest. It might be maliciously suggested that, amid all this information, we are not told whether Harsha really wrote his plays himself. This doubt is no longer possible ; Siladitya Harsha, " Harsha, Sun of Virtues," has plundered his predecessors in too royal a fashion for it to be possible to suspect a hand invested with less authority.

By race Harsha was eclectic. His grandfather was a worshipper of Siva, his father of Surya, the Sun, perhaps under influences from beyond the Indus, and his brother and sister were Buddhists. Hiuen Tsang's residence at the court led the King to incline towards Buddhism, and he even composed hymns in honour of Buddha.

He is likewise eclectic in his work. He draws on the *Mālavikāgnimitra*, and makes out of it two pretty heroic comedies (*nāṭika*), the *Ratnāvalī* [1] and *Priyadarśikā*,[2] and out of three different subjects inspired by his own imagination he composes a mosaic entitled *Nāgānanda*,[3] of which the introduction is dedicated to Buddha and the end to the goddess Gauri.

The subject of the *Ratnāvalī*, the "Pearl Necklace", is as follows:

> The Princess of Ceylon is to marry the King of Vatsa. Her ship is wrecked. She is picked up by unknown folk and becomes an attendant of Vasavadatta, the Queen. The King notices her, and she thinks that she sees in him the god of love himself. They love. The Queen rages, and then herself offers the King the hand of the Princess, who is moreover her cousin, when she is recognized by her necklace.

Harsha embroiders this stale old theme with delicate arabesques. The spring feast is for the reader a feast of sound and colour. The imagination revels in the pictures which are presented in profusion by the verses of the author, who is more artist than poet, but a decorative artist and a musician.

Sagarika, as the Princess calls herself in her disguise, paints the King's portrait for herself and discloses her feelings to a friend. One should note how cultivated these dramatic heroines are. Sakuntala composes verse, Sagarika paints, all dance and make speeches, and they understand Sanskrit and speak it in solemn moments. The heroes, too, resort to painting to remind themselves of the features of their lady-loves. These repeated characteristics help the play along, and so do familiar situations. In the *Ratnāvalī*, a monkey escaping from its cage causes the disorder which leads to the discovery of the heroine's secret love. The same device

[1] Most of it is translated into French, in fragments, in Sylvain Lévi; into English by Wilson.

[2] Translated into French by G. Strehly, Paris, 1888 (*Bibl. elzévirienne*, lviii).

[3] Translated into French from the Sanskrit and Prakrit by A. Bergaigne, Paris, 1879 (*Bibl. orient. elzév.*, xxvii); into English by Palmer Boyd, London, 1872.

is used twice by Kalidasa, in one case an elephant being the cause of the trouble and in the other a monkey. These two are the favourite animals of the drama and the tale. Often a parrot is brought in, which repeats the conversation of the heroine and her girl friend to the King.

Knowing that he is loved, the King declares the ardour of his passion to the Princess, but the Queen comes in, sees the portrait, guesses what is happening, and goes out, cold and injured. The King implores her forgiveness. "Queen, my treason is but too plain. Yet hear me. As I lie prostrate at your feet, my humiliated brow reddens with the lacquer with which they are painted, but if it can also take the redness of anger from your face, lovely as the moon, then, O Queen, have pity on me!" [1]

The story of *Priyadarśikā* is very similar, and in the third act there is a play within the play. As in *Hamlet*, it serves to tell the truth. It tells it only too well, and gives rise to complications. According to a custom, which no doubt gave the audience pleasure but is not in the least necessary to the action, it is announced towards the end that the generals have won a victory in the King's name. The hero is thereby covered with new glory, and can give himself up to his love.

The *Nāgānanda*, the "Joy of the Serpents", has no value as a drama. Yet some passages have merit. The typical man of pleasure (*viṭa*) and the humbler folk are well drawn, especially in contrast with the delicate scene between the newly married pair, Prince Jimulavahana and Princess Malayavati. The Prince chooses the inopportune moment when the enemy are attacking his country to reveal that he is a *bodhisattva.* In this the author follows the *avadāna*, which had spread as far as Mongolia. In virtue of the character of its hero, this play had great success in Buddhist circles as a religious drama, and I-tsing, twenty years after Hiuen-Tsang, speaks of performances of it with songs, music, and dancing.

The cult of Gauri, the terrible wife of Siva, as described in the first and last acts, is of interest to the student of religions. Gauri appears with her arms entwined in snakes. But, though she is the cruel, implacable goddess of the Tantric orgies, she can have pity for those who call upon her, and she restores the *bodhisattva* Jimutavahana to life.

The Indians themselves place the dramatist Bhavabhuti

[1] From S. Lévi's translation, **CCXCIV**, p. 87.

immediately beside Kalidasa. " Kalidasa suggests feeling, Bhavabhuti expresses it," with disturbing intensity. He lived at the court of Yasovarman, King of Kanauj, who reigned at the end of the seventh century and in the first half of the eighth. Although devoid of any inventive power, Bhavabhuti was one of the most learned men of his time, and had an unequalled mastery of language. No one excelled him in handling Sanskrit and in restoring all their power of expression to old words already obsolete.

Three dramas of Bhavabhuti are known. Two, the *Mahāvīra-charita* and the *Uttara-Rāma-charita*,[1] are taken from the *Rāmāyaṇa*, while the third, the *Mālatī-Mādhava*,[2] is a bourgeois drama, one might say a comedy, with a subject taken from a collection of tales and the accessory details from observation.

The plays dealing with Rama are merely series of pictures, without much unity or life. They seem to be intended to be read, not acted. There is more action in the *Uttara-Rāma-charita*. From the *Uttara-kāṇḍa*, a late addition to the *Rāmāyaṇa*, the poet takes the idea of telling the story of the second part of Rama's life in his partly dramatic but mainly lyrical manner.

Rama and Sita look at the picture-gallery in which the painter has depicted the life and deeds of Rama in exile. Their memories revive, and Sita says that she would see once more the forest in which she has lived with her husband, in exile but happy. This passage will produce a highly dramatic effect later. The two, united at last after long suffering, love each other the more tenderly. Sita is with child. A messenger from the holy man Vasishtha advises Rama to obey every wish of the Queen in her present condition, but " above all to respect his duties to the people ". It is like the first rumbling of the approaching storm, and Bhavabhuti is a master in the preparation of effects. Rama, under the dominion of his memories, asks Ganga, the deified Ganges, to protect his wife always, and he begs the magical weapons, which the gods had given him, to transfer themselves to his son born of Sita as soon as he shall be old enough to handle them. Desiring to know the feelings of his people, he maintains spies, as is a king's duty. Now one of these informs him that the people are murmuring against Sita on the ground that she has lived too long in the palace of Ravana to be worthy to be their Queen. Rama broken-heartedly

[1] Translated into French, with an introduction on the life and works of Bhavabhuti, by Félix Nève, Brussels and Paris, 1880 ; into English by Wilson, op. cit.

[2] Translated into French by G. Strehly, with a preface by A. Bergaigne, Paris, 1885 (*Bibl. elzévirienne*, xlii) ; into English by Wilson.

submits to his duty. He will send Sita away. She will be taken to the forest, but she will not come back.

In the third act we learn that Ganga has saved Sita when she wished to die after giving birth to twin children, that the twins have been given into the care of Valmiki (cf. above, p. 256), and that she herself is coming unseen to visit the places which she once loved. Rama arrives also. In their emotion both faint, each into the arms of an attendant. Sita, still invisible, approaches Rama, and their mere contact brings back their knowledge of their lost happiness. This scene is a model of the Indian *rasa*. Pathos is mingled with pity, and the tenderness of lost love, the vain attempt to seize the dear shadow, the melancholy diffused in a world half unreal, half human, all in a language in which every word seems to tremble with emotion, are sheer magic.

The three next acts introduce us to the sons of Rama, who are not yet full-grown but are already heroes. The magical weapons have, of course, come into their possession, but Rama does not yet recognize his children. In the seventh act, when Rama witnesses the play which Valmiki has written about his life,[1] the final recognition takes place. The goddesses take part in the performance, which is accompanied by a series of faints on the part of Rama, so great is his emotion. At last Arundhati, the divine wife of the wise Vasishtha, takes Sita by the hand and brings her, restored to life, to Rama, while Valmiki presents the two princes to the people, who acclaim them and their mother.

The comedy, if it is not a tragedy, of *Malati and Madhava* is the story, in ten acts, of love triumphant over many obstacles. Some, hailing Bhavabhuti as an Indian Shakespeare,[2] have found in it a likeness to *Romeo and Juliet*.

Malati loves Madhava, and their parents consent to the union. But Nandana, the King's favourite, wants Malati for his wife, and her father, not daring to resist, promises her to him. Thanks to the intervention of the Buddhist nun, Kamandaki, all turns out well and the lovers are united.

Kamandaki, who is the big mind of the play, is a consummate diplomatist, knowing life as if she had had a long experience of it ; one may, indeed, call her a go-between, and one understands why Bhavabhuti, an orthodox Brahman, made her a Buddhist. But there is nothing dishonourable in her conduct, and if the author was to bring in a clever woman independent enough to be able to act of her own authority, he had little choice. Nuns were the only women who did not belong to their parents, or their husband, or everybody.

Old tricks—the scene with the picture and a verse of

[1] A play within a play is called *garbhānka*, " embryonic act."
[2] Cf. **CCLXXXVIII**, iii, p. 235 n.

declaration, the non-recognition of a lover, an escaped tiger (instead of the monkey or elephant)—fill up time, complicate the direct action, and serve to explain the most unexpected events. What is new is the fifth act, in which Madhava, in despair at the approach of his loved one's marriage to another, calls on the demons for help.

> He goes by night to the burning-place, and in the midst of a veritable witches' and demons' Sabbath, calls up evil spirits (*bhūta*) to offer them new flesh, his own. Cries are heard from the neighbouring temple of Durga. He rushes in and sees Tantric rites in progress ; before the statue of the dreadful goddess a priest lifts his knife to sacrifice Malati, who has been drawn to the temple by magical means. Madhava kills the priest, rescues his love, and with her flies from the vengeance of the priestess. But we are still shown the wild dance which Durga, with her head and arms wrapped in snakes, performs in honour of her husband Siva.

Bhavabhuti loves contrasts of light and shade, violent emotions, terror. His contemporaries called him *Śrīkaṇṭha*, "Divine Throat," which is also a surname of Siva. Siva burnt his throat by swallowing the poison which was about to destroy the world. For this he was called "*Nīlakaṇṭha*, "Black Throat," or, in reverence, *Śrīkaṇṭha*, "Glorious Throat" or "Divine Throat". Did Bhavabhuti get this name from his love of the horrible and of painful impressions, like Siva, who haunts cemeteries and wears a collar of skulls ? Perhaps ; but for other reasons, too—his inexhaustible vocabulary, the sonorous effect of his complicated metres, and his powers of expression.

One cannot imagine an ordinary audience listening to Bhavabhuti's plays and at once understanding his long, and too long, compound words. His works demand an audience of connoisseurs. It was to be found in the limited circle of highly cultivated men who surrounded the Maecenas princes of ancient India.

V

THE DRAMA AFTER BHAVABHUTI

Bhavabhuti ends the great age of dramatic literature. After him we come to an age of lesser men. Skill in versification takes the place of the poetry which is lacking, and erudition is displayed where there should be inspiration. Even the old masters were not strong in invention. Out of respect for texts and traditions, or out of contempt of the real life surrounding them, they preferred to draw on the immense fund of legends which India offered. Their successors continued to work on the same materials, the *Mahābhārata*, the *Rāmāyaṇa*, the Krishna cycle, and, exceptionally, the legend of Siva. Real life was left to humbler writers, and it was among them that dramatic talent found a refuge.

The anthologies often quote fragments of the *Veṇī-saṃhāra*, the "Binding of the Braid of Hair". Draupadi (see above, p. 251) swears that she will not bind her hair until the insult done to her is avenged. It is the same idea as in the *Mudrā-Rākshasa* (p. 306), in which Chanakya swears to leave his lock unbound until he has won Rakshasa for Chandragupta.

Polished Sanskrit stanzas were still turned out, but the living tongues were used to represent life.

At the beginning of the tenth century Rajasekhara of Kanauj wrote, among several plays very popular at the time, a drama in Prakrit. He was not another Hala, who wrote in Prakrit because he did not know Sanskrit. Rajasekhara knew the sacred language thoroughly, and it was to prove his mastery of the Prakrits that he wrote his *Karpūra-mañjarī* in a living language. The interest of the play lies in its very lively pictures of popular merrymakings. In his description of the Feast of the Swing, on which a girl mounts in honour of the goddess Gauri, he uses alliteration, repetitions, internal rhymes, etc., in such a way as almost to give the impression of gentle swaying. He is a master of the harmonious and sounding line. But there is no action ; he only makes allusions to it, and amuses himself by startling us with his twists of speech (*vakrokti*), which are practically riddles.

Anandavardhana, a theorist of the ninth century, quotes the *Mahā-nāṭaka*, the "Great Drama", in which Kalidasa's practice of introducing stanzas into the dialogue is carried to extreme lengths. The *Mahā-nāṭaka* is nothing but a series of stanzas and comes half-way between drama and epic. Ascribed to the celebrated monkey Hanumat, Rama's friend, it returns to the epic narrative of the *Rāmāyaṇa*. But it seems to be intended for a shadow-theatre. In that case the stanzas would be recited by a single speaker, as in the popular spectacles. There was a legend about its authorship. It was said that Valmiki feared that his *Rāmāyaṇa* would be outshone by Hanumat's drama, and that Hanumat, who had carved his work on a rock, advised Valmiki to cast the rock into the sea. Centuries went by, then the broken fragments were found and taken to King Bhoja (eleventh century), himself an author. It is unnecessary to say that the *Mahā-nāṭaka* was probably written in Bhoja's reign and perhaps at his suggestion.

At the solemn assemblies of the Bhaktas, who worshipped Vishnu, it was the custom to perform the mystery-play of the *Gopāla-kilichandrikā*, the " Moonlight of the Herdsmen's Games ". Its theme is the oneness of Krishna and Radha. She is the energy (*śakti*) of her husband, but really they are one. This is the subject of the *Gīta-govinda* (see p. 290). One actor recited the poem in the wings and his words were enacted in mime on the stage.

Another religious drama, which is known all over India and has been the subject of much commentary, is the *Pārvatī-pariṇaya*, the " Marriage of Parvati ". The hero is Siva, who very rarely appears in drama. Five acts without any action tell how Kama was burned by one glance from the third eye of Siva, and how at last Parvati got her husband. This slavish imitation of Kalidasa's *Kumāra-sambhava* (see p. 277) was for long attributed to Bana, the court poet of Harshadeva. It is of much later date, probably of the fifteenth century, and was written by the " Second Bana ".

The tradition of the allegorical drama goes back, if not to Asvaghosha, at least to the Buddhist dramas in general, in which personified abstractions were brought on the stage. The most celebrated is the *Prabodha-chandrodaya*, the " Rising of the Moon of (true) Knowledge ", probably written in the first years of the twelfth century for a royal patron of letters. The author, at once an orthodox Vedantine and a Vishnuite, effectively combats heresies with his undeniable gifts as a playwright and poet.

The *Bhartṛihari-nirveda*, or " Disillusionment of Bhartrihari ", a fifteenth-century work, is not allegorical but philosophical. It might be called " The Strange Ending of a Mad Love ". In it we find Sivaite asceticism and Buddhist renunciation mingled.

King Bhartrihari loves his wife tenderly. She declares that she could not live without him. To test her, he causes it to be reported that he has been eaten by a tiger while hunting. His wife falls dead at the news. In despair, the King wishes to mount on to the pyre to be burned with his wife's body. A Yogi arrives and by his anecdotes persuades the King that nothing is of value save renunciation. In consequence the King loses all interest in his wife, even when she is restored to life by the ascetic. The poor Queen brings her child, but the love of the father is as dead as that of the husband.

VI

FARCE

The masses needed the theatre as much as the select few and if nothing or almost nothing has come down to us of the works intended for the people, it is because they were not considered worthy of preservation. Yet the court did not disdain the rather shallow gaiety and humour of the farce. It found it in the *bhāṇa*, a monologue, and in the *prahasana*, or farcical comedy.

Works of this type chiefly developed the characters of the *viṭa* and the *vidūshaka*. They became principal instead of incidental parts. The *viṭa*, who appears quite rarely in the *nāṭaka*, is the usual hero of the *bhāṇa*, in which he mimes and relates his exploits or his conversations with other people. He has literary culture and a complete knowledge of the courtesan. The *bhāṇa* and the *prahasana* " take for their heroes debauchees, libertines, and vagrants, and for their subjects the vilest actions and the most scandalous intrigues. The world which they paint is doubtless only a conventional caricature, but the exaggerations of oddity and vice are on the whole less far removed from real life than are the pictures of ideal virtues . . . They constantly verged on true comedy without ever touching it ".[1]

A *bhāṇa* of the fifteenth century, *Śṛingāra-bhūshaṇa*, the " Ornament of the God of Love ", by Vamana Bhatta Bana, the author of the *Pārvatī-pariṇaya*, is summarized by Winternitz as follows.[2]

The man of pleasure (*viṭa*, whom Sylvain Lévi calls the *bel esprit*), after a night of gaiety, having saluted the sun in choice verse, strolls in the harlots' quarter. He meets whores, bawds,

[1] **CCXCIV**, pp. 155–6.
[2] **CCLXXXVIII**, iii, p. 260.

> parasites, clowns, and so on, chats with them more or less wittily, and takes the words out of their mouths. For instance : " But who is that, the girl in the belvedere of that palace ? With her eyes she follows her lover, whom her old mother has just driven out of the house. Why, it is Vasantika, Madhavi's daughter ! " (Approaching) " Little Vasantika, what are you doing there, on that high terrace ? You say that you are admiring the spring-time verdure of the grove from aloft ? " He laughs and quotes a verse which proves that he has not believed her for a moment. The street seethes with life. Dancing-girls go to the theatre. The *viṭa* goes in, admires the grace of the artistes, and does not fail to make declarations of love. An old harlot runs to the law-court to complain against a young man who has married her daughter for six months but has not paid her the money he owes. We also see a cock-fight, a fight between rams, and an athletic contest.

The Hindus, incapable of creation in sober, straight lines, excelled in the observation of detail. It is for the reader or spectator to reconstruct the general plan of the work in his imagination.

CHAPTER V

Narrative Literature

I

FOLK-TALE AND FABLE

As the *Gīta-govinda,* a work on the border-line of lyric poetry and drama, led us to speak of the drama, so the Indian drama, which is essentially lyric and narrative, leads us on to the form for which the Indian spirit has shown the greatest aptitude, narrative literature. We have seen the heroes of the *Mahābhārata* diverting themselves in their distress by listening to fables and stories. In discussing Buddhist literature I have mentioned the *avadānas* and the " Garland of Jātakas ". Let us remember that at an early date India possessed the largest collection of stories in existence, the Jātakas.

The Jātakas were written in prose, often interspersed with stanzas (*gāthā*). The Pali of this verse is older than that of the prose, which seems to serve as an explanation. Sometimes, however, there is no connection between the verse and the story. Only the verse stanzas were admitted into the Buddhist canon. The prose is merely a commentary added later, after the constitution of the canon.

The collection, containing over five hundred tales, was translated from Pali into Cingalese at an uncertain date, no doubt shortly after Buddhism had spread to Ceylon. The *gāthās* were not translated, and we still have them in the old original Pali. In the fifth century, or somewhat later, the stories were translated back from Cingalese into Pali, and this is the Jātaka which we know to-day.[1]

[1] Translated under the direction of E. B. Cowell, Cambridge, 1895–1905, and into German by Julius Dutoit, Leipzig, 1920. For French translations, see Léon Feer's articles on the Jātakas in *Journ. Asiatique*, 1875, 1895, 1897. The fundamental edition is V. Fausböll, *The Jâtaka together with its Commentary, being Tales of the Anterior Births of Gotama Buddha*, i–vii (index by Dines Andersen), London, 1877–1897.

They are popular literature—if not created, at least adopted by the people. But some of the stories bear the mark of conscious literary workmanship. They have descended into the popular domain, like the Mediæval romance, which was originally intended for the upper classes. Thus the Jātakas are hybrid works in their evolution and hybrid also in their foundation, for they consist of two chief elements, tales and fables.

The origin of fables has long been discussed. Some scholars said that they had their birth in Greece; others, perhaps with more effective arguments, attributed them to India. Reciprocal influences and exchanges occurred. India seems to have given more than it took. Theodor Benfey, whose translation of the *Pañchatantra* [1] was the foundation of comparative literature, maintained that the tale and the anecdote were purely Indian, whereas the fable came from Greece. He also recognized the part played by the Buddhists in propagating this literature. To-day discussion would be idle, for no one any longer seeks to find the birth-place of all tales and fables in one country.[2] Only there are peoples with greater inventive faculty, while others are more expert in literature. The lively imagination of the Indian, fostered by an inactive life and a climate which encouraged rest and meditation, the hordes of pilgrims, ascetics, and beggars who attracted custom by telling marvellous or amusing stories, and lastly the belief, fundamental in India while fairly common elsewhere, that the beasts are not a different world from ourselves, all prepared a soil in which both tales and fables sprang up in abundance. The *Pañchatantra*, the "Five Threads" or "Books" on politics and the art of government, has not come down to us in its original form. It is composed of remnants of a *Tantrākhyāyika*, or "Collection of Little Tales", and various other elements, traces of which are preserved in the Kashmiri, Nepalese, and Southern Indian versions. The *Pañchatantra* which Europe knows in editions [3] and translations is a late work, reconstructed on the lost ancient original and probably a good deal different

[1] Leipzig, 1859.

[2] E. Cosquin, *Études folkloriques. Recherches sur les migrations des contes populaires et leur point de départ*, Paris, 1922.

[3] Ed. by F. Kielhorn and G. Bühler, Bombay, *Sanskrit Series*, i, iii, v.

from it. The researches of Johannes Hertel[1] and the attempt of F. Edgerton to construct the original text justify one in concluding that it was a hand-book of politics (*nīti-śāstra*) for the teaching of young princes.

The *Tantrākhyāyika* seems to belong to the age of the Guptas[2] and to have come originally from Kashmir, which is supposed, according to R. O. Franke,[3] to be the birthplace of Sanskrit itself. The unknown author of the collection had not only the language but the style of the *kāvya*, but, being a man of taste, he did not consider it suited to the little stories which he told quite simply, but not without wit and delicate irony. He used old and in part popular materials, but by polishing and transforming them he gave them the air of a personal creation. One cannot say whether the fashion in which the tales are boxed one within another is his invention; we find the same thing in the *Arabian Nights*, a work which betrays Indian influence, if not origin. In the course of conversation, a speaker quotes a proverb in verse in this way: " If you did thus, you would be like the ass in the barley-field." " How so ? " asks the other. " Hear then," says the first, and he tells his story. Very often a character in that story does the same thing, and another story is started. Gradually they get back to the first.

There are stories showing how one should acquire friends, for even the weak are strong when united, and how war is waged, and how one can deceive or be deceived, and how it is a mistake to judge hastily.

A story added later, but full of humour, is that of Vishnu and the weaver.

> A poor weaver saw a princess and fell sick of love. His friend the cartwright made him a Garuda of wood, the Garuda being the mythical eagle on which Vishnu rides. The weaver went up on his wooden eagle, wearing the attributes of Vishnu, and entered the girl's apartments. She fully believed that it was Vishnu, and, yielding to his entreaties, she made a Gandharva marriage with him. To her parents, at first furious and then marvelling, she announced that they had Vishnu for a son-in-law. At night they saw him come down from the sky on his eagle, bearing the disk, the conch, and the other signs of his power, but they dared not speak

[1] *Tantrâkhyâyika*, translated into German with introduction and notes by Hertel, Leipzig and Berlin, 1909; ed. by J. Hertel, Berlin, 1910; the *Pañchatantra* translated into English, Trichinopoli, 1887.

[2] CCLXXXVI, p. 105, London, 1927.

[3] *Pali und Sanskrit*, Berlin, 1902.

to him, for a god does not suffer the approach of mortals. Proud of such a son-in-law, the King provoked his neighbours to war. Presently his capital was besieged, and disaster stared him in the face. The supposed Vishnu calmed the fears of the princess and prepared to fling himself into the fray next morning, for he had no longer anything to lose and it was better to die as a hero. Now the real Vishnu was embarrassed; either men would see the god vanquished or he must aid the impostor. He chose the latter course, and the weaver was victorious.

One cannot quote even the most amusing stories. There is the little hare who outwitted the lion or the elephant. There is the mouse who was turned into a maiden and had to choose a husband; in every one she found some drawback—in the sun, in the cloud, in the wind, and in the mountain—the rat alone seemed perfect, and him she chose. Everything that irony and malice can invent is in them.

The ideal of the *Tantrākhyāyika* and the *Pañchatantra* is the average man, a good householder and a good father. Hospitality and loyalty to his friends are his chief virtues. The duties of a king are very clear—he must fight bravely and give up his life for his subjects. At all times he must protect the innocent and rule the land with the help of wise ministers.

At a very early date the *Pañchatantra* made its way into the literature of the world. A north-western version was translated into Pehlevi [1] in the sixth century by a Persian physican named Burzoë at the order of his master, King Chosroes Anushirvan. From this translation, the text of which is lost, a new translation was made into Syriac about 570 under the title of *Kalīlag and Damnag*, from the names of two jackals, Karataka and Damanaka. An Arabic version, amplified, was made in the eighth century under the title of *Kalīla and Dimna*, and it was this that served as the basis of the European and other translations. In 1816 Silvestre de Sacy translated it into French.[2]

But this work was known to Europe much earlier. In the eleventh century it appeared in Greek and was translated from that into Latin, Italian, German, and other languages. In the twelfth century there was a good version in Hebrew,

[1] A language which may be called Middle Persian, in relation to Old Persian and Avestic on the one side and modern Persian on the other.

[2] English translation of *Kalīla and Dimna*, by Keith-Falconer, Cambridge, 1885.

which was translated into Latin in the thirteenth as *Liber Kalilae et Dimnae, directorium vitae humanae,*[1] for it was generally regarded as the most perfect manual of practical morality and wisdom. Another Hebrew version of the thirteenth century was translated into French in 1644 by David Sahid and Gaulmin as *Livre des lumières, ou la conduite des roys,* and a Turkish translation of the Persian work, dedicated to the Sultan Soliman I (sixteenth century), was translated into French by Galland and Cardonne at the beginning of the eighteenth century. From French it has been translated into Malay.

La Fontaine says in an introduction to the second edition of his *Fables,* in 1678, that he owes several of them to the "Indian sage" Pilpay, but by his time almost all the subjects already bore the stamp of the European mind.

At this day the fables and tales of the ancient *Tantrākhyāyika* have sunk so deep into Western literature that only an expert can identify them in the *fabliaux* or in the *Gesta Romanorum.* A curious instance of the way in which an Indian story may be disguised in an European folk-legend is given by Winternitz,[2] who has shown, beneath the Welsh story of Gelert, the Indian fable of the faithful mongoose killed in error. The Gipsies, who came from India and spread over Europe, may have carried tales to very distant regions. The Mongols, in their advance on Russia and Poland, may have brought some Buddhist stories with them, although their raids in Central Europe were of short duration. Lastly, Arab and Greek merchants, and above all Byzantine popular literature, carried ideas from East to West and from West to East. Persia has always played a very great part in the propagation of ideas; without it we should never have known the *Pañchatantra.*

On the north-western version of the *Pañchatantra* is based the collection entitled *Hitopadeśa,* Useful Teaching,[3] which has the same didactic object. Its author, Narayana, probably a Bengali, was initiated into the Tantric cult. In one of the

[1] The Hebrew and Latin translations were translated into French by J. Derenbourg in 1881.
[2] **CCLXXXVIII**, iii, p. 305.
[3] Translated into French by L. Langlès, Paris, 1790; into English by Pincott, 1880.

first stories we read that young girls had to be offered in sacrifice to the goddess Gauri (cf. *Mālatī-Mādhava*, above, p. 318). Sacrifices of this kind are never mentioned in the ancient texts. Therefore this story, if not the whole *Hitopadeśa*, is of the time when the Tantra sect had spread to Bengal and had already acquired some importance. We have a manuscript of this work dating from the fourteenth century.

II

THE LITERARY STORY

The Bṛihat-kathā,[1] *Kathā-sarit-sāgara, and Suka-saptati*

The great epics were the two chief reservoirs on which writers never wearied of drawing. But there were others of less importance. One was the cycle of King Udayana, narrated by Gunadhya.

When did he live ? We cannot say. A verse in the *Megha-dūta* (see above) says that the old men of the city of Avanti loved to tell the story of King Udayana. The commentators suppose that this remark refers to the *Bṛihat-kathā*, the " Great Romance " of Gunadhya about the King. In that case the author would be much earlier than Kalidasa. If, too, as is probable, Bhasa (see above, p. 302) took the theme of his play *Svapna-Vāsavadatta* from the *Bṛihat-kathā*, the " Great Romance " would be earlier than the third century. A fairly late tradition, only mentioned in the eleventh century, makes this mysterious Gunadhya, of whom the romance-writers Dandin, Subandhu, and Bana speak with such respect, the minister of a King Satavahana. But there was a whole dynasty of Satavahanas ; we know of one of them, Hala, who wrote the *Sattasai*. It is therefore useless to try to place Gunadhya in the Andhra country in order to have more exact information. The geography of his work, if it has any, rather suggests a northern district.

To crown our misfortune, the work itself is lost. We only have minute fragments, a few verses inserted in the Prakrit

[1] Félix Lacôte, *Essai sur Gunâdhya et la Brhatkathâ*, Paris, 1908 ; Leo v. Mankowski, *Der Auszug aus dem Pancatantra* in *Ksemendras Brhatkathâmanjarî*, introd., text, trans., and notes, Leipzig, 1892 ; Y. S. Speyer, *Studies about the Kathâsaritsâgara*.

grammar of Hemachandra. We only know that it was written in the Paisachi language, the language of the demons according to the theorist Dandin ; more probably in some Prakrit dialect not known from other works of literature, perhaps of the Vindhya region, according to A. B. Keith,[1] or of Kashmir, according to Grierson.[2] We have already seen that the period about the beginning of our era was marked by great activity in the Prakrit tongues, and Sylvain Lévi tells us [3] that an inscription (unfortunately of the ninth century) calls Gunadhya the friend of the Prakrit language. In any case, what we know of the *Bṛihat-kathā* shows clearly that it was intended for the cultured few.

Three principal works, not to mention the less important, owe their origin to Gunadhya and are transformations of his Paisachi work into Sanskrit.

Of the Nepalese recension of the *Bṛihat-kathā* there is an abridgement in verse, the *Bṛihat-kathā-śloka-saṃgraha* [4] of Buddhasvamin, who is supposed to have lived in the eighth or ninth century. The fifth book (*sarga*) of the *Śloka-saṃgraha* mentions the Greeks as clever craftsmen and artists, gives scenes of their life, and speaks of flying-machines made by the Ionians. Is this a reflection of the artistic age of Gandhara ? [5] It is a further proof that the original of the *Bṛihat-kathā* belonged to the north-west and to the first centuries after Christ, the place and age in which Hellenic art and culture made their influence keenly felt in India. The scenes of the life of the *hetairai* and the descriptions of their quarter and of the palace of the fair Kalingasena in the tenth book find an echo in the *Little Clay Cart* (see p. 305) and the *Śringāra-bhūshana*.

The Kashmir version of the *Bṛihat-kathā* was used by Kshemendra and Somadeva, both of the eleventh century. The former has left a work in verse which his mannered style and extreme concision make extremely hard to read, *Bṛihat-kathā-mañjarī*, the " Bouquet of the Great Romance ", full of erotic passages. The latter, whose style is simple and

[1] **CCLXXXVI,** 2nd ed., p. 90.
[2] A. Grierson, in *Indian Antiquary,* 1901.
[3] In **XV,** 1885.
[4] Cf. Lévi, in *C. R. de l'Acad. des Inscr. et Belles-Lettres,* 1899.
[5] On the Græco-Indian art of Gandhara, cf. A. Foucher, *L'Art gréco-bouddhique du Gandhâra,* Paris, 1905, and below, part iv.

elegant, has written what is almost a masterpiece, the *Kathā-sarit-sāgara.*[1]

It is indeed an "Ocean of Rivers of Tales", with its three hundred and fifty episodic narratives very loosely connected to the main story which forms their framework. One finds everything in it. Tales of marvels, novelettes, stories of sailors, brigands, and thieves, picaresque novels, love-stories, myths, and legends, a great part of the *Pañchatantra*, and an independent series of "Tales of the Vampire" are jumbled together and between them make a huge novel of manners which gives us a view of the real life of India. But of what period ? Of two or three different periods—that of Gunadhya, the earliest, then the very long period during which his work was swelled by additions, and lastly a time not far from that of the composition of the *Kathā-sarit-sāgara.*

The narrative which forms the framework, or rather fails to do so, for it is lost in the mass of stories piled on to it, begins by having for its hero Udayana, King of the Vatsas in Northern India.

> He marries Vasavadatta, and afterwards Padmavati, as we know from Bhasa's drama. The two marriages are described as an introduction to the story of Maravahanadatta, Udayana's son. He is born with the thirty-two auspicious marks of the *chakravartin* ; this means that if he leaves the world he will become a Buddha, and if he adheres to the secular life he will be an emperor. After a life of adventure, in the course of which he loses his beloved and wins her back, he becomes King of the Vidyadharas, the semi-divine inhabitants of the Himalaya.

His adventures with his betrothed (the fourteenth book of the *Kathā-sarit-sāgara*) recall the abduction of Sita in the *Rāmāyaṇa.* The minister needed to bring things to a happy conclusion is here called Gomukha, and he displays the qualities which Bhasa, borrowing from the *Bṛihat-kathā*, gave to Yaugandharayana. The heroine has her counterpart in the Vasantasena of the *Little Clay Cart*, being a courtesan (in this case only a prospective one) who wishes to emancipate herself from her trade.

The whole story is divided into a hundred and twenty-four "waves" (*taraṃga*), or, like Gunadhya's work, into

[1] English translation by Tawney, 2 vols., Calcutta, 1880, 1884 ; new ed., pr. pr., 1924–8.

eighteen books, fifteen of which are authentic. Of the remaining three, the sixteenth tells of the death of Udayana and his wives, who decide that it is time to go to heaven, and kill themselves. The last two books give some legends. Somadeva is a born story-teller. He shapes the rough stones of popular literature into gems sparkling with gaiety.

Among the people whom he describes are the fool who, being hungry, has eaten seven cakes and wishes that he had started with the seventh ; another who, having been told to guard the front door, puts it on his back and goes off to the theatre with it ; and the three fastidious persons of whom the first cannot eat rice because he perceives the taste of everything which its roots have drawn from the ground, the second complains that his girl smells of the goat's milk on which she was fed as a baby, and the third cannot sleep because there is a hair under his seven mattresses.

Thieves were always severely punished in India. But their cunning is admired. It is the same with the worthless man who has risen to high office ; we laugh at his tricks and jeer at his dupes. Kings and even gods are outwitted by rogues, and their difficulties are a source of fun.

The most amusing anecdotes deal with feminine frailty.

The miraculous elephant of a king has been hurt by a fall. A voice from heaven announces that it will rise again when it is touched by a chaste women. The ladies of the zenana and those of the city, to the number of eighty thousand, pass before the elephant, without producing any effect whatever. At last a poor servant, ugly and dirty, performs the miracle.

Other stories are in honour of the tender, faithful wife. An old couple recall their past lives and see themselves always united—an Indian Philemon and Baucis. But as a rule the woman and the ascetic are objects of satire.

While Gunadhya sometimes follows Buddhism, Somadeva is decidedly a Sivaite and a worshipper of Durga. He describes the bloody orgies performed in her honour. The half-savage Bhils conduct man-hunts in order to supply their goddess with regular victims, and magical rites are performed with blood and entrails. The cult of the " Mothers " and the activities of witches are painted in lively colours. We see women and girls praying in the temple of the phallus (*linga*).[1] Siva floats above all, and the author even makes him receive

[1] There is nothing obscene about this cult. See A. Barth, *Religions de l'Inde* in III, vol. ii, Paris, 1914.

worship from a *bodhisattva,* Jimutavahana. Harsha (see above, p. 313) does the same thing in his *Nāgānanda.* For the life of the middle classes the *Kathā-sarit-sāgara* is an invaluable source of information.

Within this collection is a smaller collection entitled the *Vetāla-pañchaviṃśatikā,* the "Twenty-five Tales of the Vampire", by an unknown author of unknown date. The versification is simple, the foundation is Tantric, and the whole seems to be intended as an exercise in posing riddles.

Every day a Yogi brought to King Vikramasena a fruit, which, according to the custom, the King handed to his treasurer. But one day the tame monkey bit the fruit, and out fell a priceless jewel. Honour obliged the King to return the Yogi an equal service. He therefore agreed to go by night to the burning-ground, and at the bidding of the Yogi—it is a very striking scene—he brought him the body of a hanged man, which he had to seek at a certain place and in a certain manner. According to Brahmanic ideas, to touch a corpse was the worst defilement, and burning-grounds were the scene of demoniacal orgies. The King, true to his promise, took the corpse over his shoulder. Then the vampire which dwelt in the body said, "O King, the road is long. To beguile the way, hear this story"—and so the first story begins. It ends with a point of casuistry which the King must settle under pain of a curse. Hardly has he given his opinion, when the corpse is again hanging on its tree, the King must again detach it and place it on his shoulder amid the fiendish laughter of the *bhūtas,* and again the vampire says, "O King, the road is long," and so on.

Some of these tales are cruel and relentless in their painting of human perfidy, others are amusing and witty.

For example, the daughter of a Brahman was asked in marriage by three suitors. While her father was puzzled which to choose, she stepped on a black snake and fell dead. Witch-doctors came to revive her and, after many incantations, declared that, having been bitten by a black snake, she was indeed dead. Her funeral ceremonies (*saṃskāra*) were performed, and of the three lovers one climbed on to the pyre by her side, another established himself as a Yogi on the place where her ashes were, and the third took to wandering as a mendicant monk (*parivrājaka*). He happened to go into the house of a Brahman, and was horrified to see the mother, angry with her child, which would not leave her in peace to do her cooking, throw it into the fire. He refused to take food in the house, but the Brahman calmed his scruples by taking a book and reading a *mantra,* or spell, whereupon the child rose, rested as if he had slept. At night the young monk stole the book and ran to the burning-ground. He read the spell, and his beloved rose, living, and with her the suitor who had been burned with her. The Yogi was there too, and there they were, all three, again claiming the lady. Who should have her ?

The King answered: "The man who reanimated her is her father, because he gave her life. He who was reborn with her is thereby her brother. Only the man who did nothing at all, the Yogi, can be her husband.

A problem which the King cannot solve is that of the relationship between the children and grandchildren of a mother married by her son and of her daughter married by her father.

But the vampire, who is Siva himself, satisfied with the King's constancy, reveals to him the evil intentions of the Yogi, who wishes to kill the King with the aid of the demons and, by doing magic with his body, to obtain occult power. The King slays the Yogi and gets the magic power for himself, and the "Tales of the Vampire" end.

Many of the stories in this work appear in other literatures, without it being possible to determine their origin or line of descent. Western motives are to be found in it. One such is the story of the Trojan Horse, which occurs three times in Indian literature, in plays or tales, with the local difference that the animal is an elephant.

Needless to say, the *Kathā-sarit-sāgara* was likewise much imitated. The manner in which the stories in it are boxed one in another is simpler, but less natural, than in the *Pañchatantra*, in which they are introduced according to the sense and serve to prove an argument.

The "Seventy Tales of the Parrot", *Śuka-saptati*,[1] is a work of the same type, but not of the same value, as the *Kathā-sarit-sāgara*.

A young merchant, being obliged to go on a business journey, leaves his wife in the keeping of two parrots, which are really two Gandharvas which have been compelled to live in this form among men for a certain time. On the first day the young wife mourns her absent husband; on the second she is bored; and on the third she complains to her friends. On their advice she accepts an assignation, and adorns herself to go to it. The hen parrot reproaches her, and nearly has her neck wrung for it. The cock, on the other hand, approves of the woman's purpose, but warns her that if she is caught she will have to extricate herself like a certain womar, whose story he proceeds to relate. It is an intensely exciting story, and the wife puts off her meeting till the next day in order to hear the end. But the parrot does not tell the end until the following evening, and at once begins another story. The assignation is put off from evening to evening, and after seventy evenings have been spent in hearing stories of the faithlessness of women, which is reprehensible, of that of men, which is pardonable, of harlots, thieves, bogus ascetics, and other kinds of rogue, the husband returns from his journey and all is well.

[1] Richard Schmidt, *Sukasaptatî, textus simplicior*, ed. and trans., Kiel, 1894; *textus ornatior*, ed. and trans., Stuttgart, 1899.

Pornographic and obscene stories are found side by side with others, subtle and ironic, which, it is true, are considerably fewer. On the whole, it is " a very mediocre collection, interesting only for the great extent to which it spread outside India ".[1] For this work, the author of which is unknown, is one of those which has been most widely read and translated. It was through Persian translations, the first of which, the *Tūtīnāma,* is of the fourteenth century, that the " Tales of the Parrot " entered the literature of the world. Europe was particularly taken by one story of an ordeal by fire imposed on a young woman, the theme of *Tristram and Yseult.*

We shall never be able to say how much India gave and how much it took. The story of Sindbad the Sailor seems, on the evidence of the Arab historian Mas'udi (tenth century), to be of Indian origin. It begins just like the *Pañchatantra.* A king entrusts his sons to a wise man, who promises to make them learned at the end of six months. Who knows how many Indian elements there are in the Story of the Seven Sages (Viziers) ? The construction of the *Arabian Nights* is entirely Indian. It is said that the prototype of the containing narrative is to be found in a Jain commentary,[2] and that the chief elements in the collection are Indian subjects.[3]

We should also mention the " Thirty-two Tales of the Throne ", the " Thirty-two Tales of Mendicant Monks ", and the " Ocean of Tales ". They differ greatly in age, and also in value. The period round about the fourteenth century was favourable to the output of such works, which were produced to satiety. India, adapted to Mussulman rule and divided into small states, lived shorn of her ancient glory. The great men of her history were made the subject of tales without a shade of truth. Writers found a cantankerous pleasure in telling the great ones of the earth what they thought about them.

In the *Purusha-parīkshā*, the " Test of Men," a thief condemned to death (theft being very cruelly punished because it was very difficult to detect the author) says that he has the secret of growing gold and making it bear fruit. The King leaps at the chance of

[1] **III**, vol. iii, p. 410.

[2] Jarl Charpentier, *Paccekabuddhageschichten*, Upsala, 1908.

[3] E. Cosquin, " Le Prologue cadre des Mille et Une Nuits," in *Revue biblique*, Paris, 1908.

making himself rich, and calls the thief to him. The latter prepares the ground for sowing, and then says that a sower must come to do his part. A thief, he says, cannot sow gold, for his trade is to steal it ; so a man who has never stolen is needed. Such a man is not to be found, the King himself is not blameless, and the thief is pardoned.

III

THE ROMANCE

Dandin, Subandhu, and Bana.

Except that they are written in prose, the Indian romances have the qualities and defects of the poetry of the *Kāvyas*. There is the same superabundance of descriptions, far-fetched images, unexpected similes, puns, and long compound words which demand sustained attention from the reader and, when the sentence ends, give him the pleasure of having solved a problem. The subject is usually taken from folk-tales, fairy-tales, and other works of imagination. This nucleus of fiction is wrapped in a mass of details taken from life. So, although the plot is improbable, the romance brings before our eyes scenes which are at once picturesque and real. What distinguishes it from the tale is its finished form. The construction is the same as that of the collections of tales—episodic stories contained in a connecting narrative.

The most famous romance-writer of India is Dandin (seventh century), the learned exponent of poetic theory and author of the *Kāvyā-darśa*, the " Mirror of the Art of Poetry ". Maintaining that verse is not a necessary attribute of poetry and that it sometimes clothes the prosiest ideas, he uses prose in his poetic work, the *Daśakumāra-charita*,[1] the " Adventures of Ten Princes ", written in the " style of Vidarbha " (Berar). In Dandin's time different regions had their own poetic style. That of Vidarbha aimed at the ten chief conditions of beauty, which include the use of compounds, but also clarity, rhythm, sweetness of sound, and pleasantly surprising metaphors. The style of Gauda in Bengal was suited to lofty subjects, and set out to render their majesty by complicated turns of phrase and very long compounds. Dandin avoids this style ; that of Vidarbha, embellished with ornaments

[1] Translated into German by J. J. Meyer, Leipzig, 1902.

(*alaṃkāra*), suits the easy narrative of his picaresque romances. The adventure of each of the ten princes is a romance, full of ruses, an Indian *Gil Blas*. As a romance of manners, the *Daśakumāra-charita* is of the highest interest. We witness the daily life of a king, with its duties and its advantages. The latter are comparatively few; boredom and fear seem to be royal prerogatives. A princess plays at ball in honour of the goddess, and the game is a prelude to the choice of a husband. This trace of an old non-Aryan custom is of great importance to folklore. Popular festivities are given in detail. Drama and farce have sometimes taken scenes from Dandin (e.g. the *Little Clay Cart*). Never has the underworld of a city been better painted.

Dandin is an enemy of all hypocrisy. The frankness of his heroes always borders on cynicism, if not on lack of conscience, fundamental non-morality. One of them orders a town to be looted. It is full of old skinflints, he says, who are too fond of their money, and they must be shown that the goods of this world are perishable. Besides, the proceeds of the pillage will enable him to restore the fortunes of a poor man who has been ruined by a courtesan.

Another commends an adultery by which poor parents have been rescued from poverty. What is called crime may have the religious merit of a good deed. Love-scenes are especial favourites with the author. The incident of Prince Pramati falling asleep in the forest and transported to the bed of Princess Navamalika is of great delicacy. On another occasion Dandin creates for himself extreme difficulties of language, as we have already seen, for a lover whom his girl has bitten on the lips cannot pronounce labials, and the author performs the most remarkable *tours de force* to avoid them. As a master of Sanskrit he is incomparable. The sweetness and musical harmony of his style have never been equalled.

While Dandin's painting of reality is intensely interesting, the adventures of his heroes leave us cold. There are too many marvels. The gods take charge of the heroes as soon as real danger threatens them, and fate (*karman*) has predetermined everything. We know that all will end well, and are merely amused where we should like to be moved.

The work is divided into chapters entitled " Sighs " or

" Breaths " (*uchchhvāsa*). It was left unfinished, or else it has been mutilated, more probably the former. Instead of ten romances we have seven, and the beginning is by another hand.[1] In this respect Dandin's work has been as unfortunate as the *Kumāra-sambhava*, the *Raghu-vaṃśa*, and other works.

Subandhu, the author of a much admired romance, *Vāsavadattā*, gives us talking birds, enchanted horses, and such like, and plunges us into the Gauda style, with its interminable compounds, puns piled on puns, and too clever similes. His work is untranslatable and barely readable. One must be very well up in the philosophic and religious controversies of the seventh and eighth centuries, in the various *Śāstras*, and in *alaṃkāra*, to have an idea of the pleasure which a learned and cultivated Hindu derives from this laborious reading.

The subject of the book is as follows :—

> A prince sees an unknown princess in a dream and falls in love with her. She does likewise. The conversation of two parrots which the prince overhears one night tells him of her love. With the aid of the kindly birds the lovers are able to meet, and on the night before the princess is to marry the ruler of the Vidyadharas at the King's command they flee on a magical horse. After various adventures, Vasavadatta is turned into stone, but the touch of the prince restores her to life, as in the *Vikramorvaśī*.

The interest lies in the descriptions—those of the beauty of the princess, which are too frank for our taste or too complicated (she is *raktapāda* like a grammar-book, her feet being painted with red lacquer as the sections of the grammar are marked with red lines) ; and those of nature, such as that in which the lion of the dawn has clawed the elephant of night so that the rising sun is blood-coloured.

There are yet two other works of the seventh century which are still famous, the *Harsha-charita* and *Kādambarī*.

Harsha has already been mentioned in connection with his plays. His court poet, Bana, wrote a romantic biography of his sovereign, the *Harsha-charita*, which is a panegyric in prose with occasional passages in verse. Religious ceremonies take up a considerable place, and Bana, a pious Brahman, does not lack opportunity to describe them in detail. Yet another quality makes him useful ; he likes to

[1] A. Gawronski, *Sprachliche Untersuchungen über die Mrcchakatikâ und das Daçakumâracarita*, Leipzig, 1907.

talk about himself, and so we can reconstruct the life of a man of letters of the time.

The extravagant praise of the King, of his outward man and his talents, hardly interests us, except that it is written in a choice and careful style. Bana, who is more of a poet than Subandhu, writes in a less complicated style, although strings of adjectives and participles make him monotonous to read. When he describes the death of King Prabhakaravardhana, Harsha's father, he achieves a dramatic note. One of the physicians, a youth of eighteen, fanatically attached to his sovereign, kills himself on a pyre. The Queens, including Harsha's mother, resolve not to survive, and bid touching farewells to all around them, even to the flowers in the garden.[1]

Another romance of Bana is *Kādambarī*, which was left unfinished by the author but was continued by his son Bhashna Bana. Its subject is taken from the *Kathā-sarit-sāgara*, and it too consists of a series of stories one within another. A young Chandala girl[2] brings a parrot to King Sudraka. The bird, which has lost its mother and has been piously brought up by a devoted father, as Bana was himself, tells its own story and then repeats the story which it has been told by the sage Jabali, whose eye sees past existences through the present. The story is very involved. Two pairs of lovers aspire to reunion and reach it only after long and cruel waiting. But death itself is the moment of rebirth, and the tears of grief are tears of joy—in another life.

The text is very hard to read, even for one who knows Sanskrit thoroughly. But Indian critics have admired this work, with all its difficulties. They have above all esteemed its power of suggestion (*dhvani*), which causes the reader to live in a dream-world. For us there are too many assonances, as in Subandhu, and the abundance of mythological allusions sometimes makes it hard to follow the story, which is already complicated enough.

Bana was severely criticized fifty years ago by A. Weber.[3]

[1] An abridgement of the subject is given by F. Lacôte in *Mélanges S. Lévi*, Paris, 1905; English translation by Cowell and Thomas, London, 1897.

[2] The Chandalas are a mixed and despised caste, born of the marriage of a Śūdra man and a Brahman woman. *Kādambarī* is translated by Ridding, London, 1896.

[3] In *Indische Streifen*, i.

Weber likens his prose to a rank jungle in which one has to cut down the undergrowth before one can penetrate it, and difficult and unknown words lie in wait for the reader as wild beasts watch for the traveller. But one should recognize Bana's gift of description, his art of using contrast (e.g. the peace of the hermitage and the bustle of the King's court), and above all his love of colour. Long after one has read him, when one has triumphed over sentences a page and a half in length, one's eyes are still dazzled.

BOOK TWO

THE ART OF INDIA

Introduction

I SHALL here attempt to show in succession the evolution of the chief æsthetic tendencies to which the art of India has been subject. With this purpose, I shall sometimes simplify greatly, at the risk of being incomplete and slightly distorting the facts. A sketch, as we know, in a few lines, which are usually untrue because they are isolated and exaggerated, often renders a movement more correctly than a drawing which copies the model faithfully in all its details. After following the various lines of development which we encounter from the third century B.C. to about the eighth century of our era and sketching some of their later extensions, all that will remain for me to do will be to put together, to tie as in a bouquet, these various tendencies which curve, cross, and mingle, that we may have a general view of the whole of Indian art and determine its position among other arts. So we shall have quite a different view of that art from that given by an examination of its various periods in order of time, which I have attempted elsewhere.

The art of India has a very great evocative power, chiefly, perhaps, with those who do not know much about it, and very different conceptions are the result.

People usually think of dark temples overloaded with decoration, or shadowy caves in which horrible angular gods stand scowling above pyres on which widows are burned, or ride on cars over the bodies of their worshippers. If we clear away the theatrical aspect and reduce the picture to true proportions, we cannot say that it is entirely wrong, but it represents only one part of late Hindu art or certain forms of the Tantric art of Tibet.

In Great Britain the fame of the Taj Mahal has established a picture of an India of white marble palaces inlaid with coloured flowers, with bulbous domes and minarets reflected in still tanks of water-lilies. That India exists, but it is a comparatively late Mahommedan India, whose art, already in decay, is chiefly connected with Persia.

The discovery of Græco-Buddhist art made a great impression on those who believed in the absolute supremacy of the Greek genius and held that the excellence of an art lies in the accuracy with which it copies the real. To them Græco-Buddhist art seemed the norm to which everything should be referred, while the other tendencies of Indian art could only be decadence.

There is something to be said for all these various points of view, but they only touch the edge of Indian art. They seize upon only one aspect of it, a decadent or unoriginal aspect, which is, moreover, presented in a distorted manner. So they miss what is essential in that art, its central part —the age of complete maturity, which idealizes forms (Gupta art, that of Ajanta and Ellora, from the fifth to the ninth century); the age of youth, of love of direct, lively naturalism which preceded it (the art of Bharhut, Sanchi, and Mathura, from the third century B.C. to the second of our era); and that very personal art of Southern India which formed a bridge between the two periods (the art of Amaravati, from the second century to the fourth).

There are certain conceptions which are found in almost all religious arts. They seem so obvious that one hesitates to mention them. Let us, however, run over them briefly.

A religious art, as we know, does not try to create original and individual works; nor does it as a rule try to imitate nature and to be anatomically correct. Each artist receives a tradition, and he tries above all things to respect it, while setting his own stamp on it, almost in spite of himself, and so contributing to development. He wants to represent the beauty and power of the gods. In India that power is indicated by the many arms of the god, which also serve to multiply the number of his attributes.

In the reliefs, the chief persons are sometimes made larger than the others, in order that the story may be clearly understood, and also that they may provide centres to attract the eye and so produce a pleasant composition and prevent monotony. The same person may appear several times in various episodes, for the object is to tell a story, often a complicated one, while preserving unity of composition and decoration and keeping the episodes connected. The perspective is vertical, things at the back being placed high.

In decoration India does not usually aim at the impression of harmony and calm given by motives set in front of a detached background, without overlapping each other. It has, on the contrary, a love of the impression of life, vibration, and movement given by motives piled one on another and intertwined, what is commonly called *horror vacui*.

Spreading as it did over a huge sub-continent, in the course of over twenty centuries, Indian art has many different aspects. Yet to the eye which tries to see it as a whole it presents undeniable continuity and even a certain unity. One can realize this if one contrasts it with the arts which surround it, and follows, through their development, certain motives, such as the slanting hips (see below, p. 380). What is constant and personal in Indian art emerges when it is compared with Khmer art, for instance. Indian art is sensual, living, and essentially graceful, and it sets great store by decoration both in sculpture and in architecture. In its most different aspects one finds the sinuous line of the human body, exaggeration of the signs of feminine beauty, the slanting hips, and the crowding and overlapping of figures in the reliefs. In Khmer art, on the other hand, the Indian tilted hips soon disappear and bodies tend to the straight, vertical line, to hieratic poses and frontality. A man coming into contact with these two arts for the first time is seldom equally attracted by both. If he is drawn by the life, the voluptuousness, the casualness and fancy and luxuriance of the art of India, Khmer sculpture will at first seem cold and stiff; if he is susceptible to the hieratic dignity and restrained grandeur of Khmer art, he will be embarrassed by the opulence and over-fluid intertwining lines presented by Indian figures and decoration.

PRE-INDIAN ART

Harappa and Mohenjo-Daro

The art of Harappa and Mohenjo-Daro is much closer to that of Sumer and Susiana, that is, of Mesopotamia and Persia, with which, however, it must not be confused, than to the Indian art which succeeds it. In religion the relations seem to have been the same. It is not, therefore, as Indian art, but as a branch of the great civilization which seems to have had its centre in Persia and Mesopotamia that this art should be studied. Nothing of what will be essential to later Indian culture seems to exist yet. I shall therefore speak very briefly of the art of Mohenjo-Daro. It is a prologue to the art of India, but a prologue quite distinct from the main theme, although we are beginning to suspect that certain traditions may perhaps have survived.

Seals of the Mohenjo-Daro style were found a long time ago, but it was only lately that excavations in the Indus valley brought to light two large cities, regularly built of brick, with thick walls, the construction of which reminds one of Mesopotamia, and many admirably engineered water-channels. Various objects have been discovered—a curious little bust (Pl. I, A), a statuette of a dancing-girl, painted pottery, jewels, and, above all, quantities of seals. These seals have an undeniable family likeness to those of Susiana and Mesopotamia, but their style is peculiar and the signs which they bear, not yet deciphered, are quite unlike those of cuneiform writing and look less developed. Whereas cylinders are frequent in Mesopotamia, none is found in the civilization of Harappa and Mohenjo-Daro. Most of the seals are adorned with the same bull (Pl. I, B), showing only one horn, in front of an uncertain object, which is always the same. This subject recalls the religions of Sumer. Some seals are decorated with essentially Indian animals, such as the elephant and zebu (Pl. I, C). These very well-executed designs already herald the animal art of India, and the style of the modelling makes it difficult to place them very early.

The date of the ancient civilizations of the Indus is not yet established. Marshall, who is responsible for the excavations and for the principal work dealing with these questions, is inclined to give them the earliest possible date, the third or even the end of the fourth millennium B.C. It is true that single seals, inscribed with characters of the Indus script, have been found in the lower strata of the Sumerian excavations, but it is not absolutely certain that these seals, which were chiefly found in cleared-away rubbish, really belonged to the stratum to which they are ascribed; moreover, the civilization which used the script which we find on the Indus may have developed in the course of long ages and in different places. While some indications tend to make us date the Mohenjo-Daro culture further and further back, others point in the opposite direction. On some seals the modelling of the Indian animals seems fairly late. One bears a stylized tree which recalls certain Indian conceptions; another, a human figure seated in the Indian fashion. In the few sculptures in the round discovered in the Indus valley, certain details, such as the flattened skull and the hair-dressing, appear to show connexion with the ancient sculpture of India. Vases, with fairly complicated decoration, remind one of the pottery of the second millennium. There are other such evidences.

So, although the Indus culture is almost certainly pre-Aryan, it may perhaps not be as ancient as was at first supposed. A thorough examination of a certain painted ware all over its area of dispersion, from the valley of the Indus to Baluchistan (Nal, etc.), and of the different prehistoric finds in India and other parts of Asia will doubtless shed light on this problem.

CHAPTER I

Architecture and Decoration

ARCHITECTURE

FOR the Vedic cult neither permanent buildings nor representations of the gods are necessary. Did an architecture in durable materials, stone or brick, exist from the earliest days of Indian civilization properly so called? It is hardly likely, for no trace of any such architecture has survived, and the caves cut in the rock reveal imitation of wood in almost all their details (Pl. II, B). Save, therefore, for a few copies of foreign architecture, we may take it that all the ancient architecture of India, apart from the caves, was wooden. We know what it was like from about the second century B.C. onwards from the imitations of it in the rock-hewn caves, from the monuments represented in reliefs and paintings, and from the balustrades of the *stūpas* (Pl. II, A), which we shall discuss presently.

As soon as architecture makes its appearance in India, two distinct currents are seen. Some motives are derived from the local wooden construction, others are imported from the formerly Achæmenian and now Hellenized world. The development of these motives is clear enough. To describe it, I shall make use of the work of Jouveau-Dubreuil, adding several observations of my own.

Is the wood construction purely local? It is hard to say. Combaz points out curious likenesses to the wooden architecture of Lycia, but the forms which he mentions seem to result from the very use of wood, and they may well have been invented simultaneously in different regions. Indeed, the long form with the "Gothic" vault (Fig. 20) is found in the huts of the Todas of India to-day.

The most important motive in this wooden architecture, the essential feature of all façades, is the horse-shoe-shaped projection forming a kind of canopy over a door or window (Pl. II, B). It is often, perhaps always, the end of a vault of the same shape, supported by beams, the square ends of which are seen on the front of the building on the inner side of the horse-shoe (Pl. II, B). In time this opening gradually changes; the ends tend to turn in and to become ornate (Pl. III, A). In addition, smaller openings appear beside the main one. On the façades of the caves, from the very beginning (Pl. II, B), one finds false windows of every size under horse-shoe arches. As art develops, these arches become more and more numerous and smaller and smaller. It is an architectural motive which gradually becomes a decorative motive. The false windows, which stood under the horse-shoes in the oldest examples, disappear first of all. Then the arches, supported only by balustrades and stepped cornices, tend to appear in continuous rows. Later, the balustrades and stepped cornices disappear in their turn, and their place is taken by curved cornices along which the arches, now minute, are set in lines, as at Ajanta (Pl. III, A); they are called *kuḍu*. Then a head appears in these tiny niches, but it does not persist long (sixth to ninth centuries). Later still, fairly large false arches are used to decorate the towers (*śikhara*) of Northern art. In the Dravidian art of the south they continue to be made small and to be used on cornices under the name of *kuḍu*. These *kuḍus* gradually close up completely and are ornamented; then they open out again, so as to give a new effect, which is what we see at the present day. They are also found in the first period of Khmer art (the pre-Angkor art of Cambodia, seventh century), the art of Champa, and the first period of Javanese art.

The horse-shoe arches, as we have seen, are not the only feature of the ancient façades of caves. There were also (Pl. II, B) trapezium-shaped openings, doors or windows (the jambs and columns of the wood construction usually sloping slightly inward), wooden balustrades like those which we shall see round the *stūpas*, and stepped cornices, generally widening upwards. These cornices, which are likewise imitated from wood, are also found on the top of *stūpas*, *dāgabas* (see p. 361 and Pl. III, B), and capitals (Figs. 3, 4). Balustrades and stepped cornices disappear from façades, as I have said, in the sixth century, and instead we have the curved cornice adorned with *kuḍus*. About the same time,

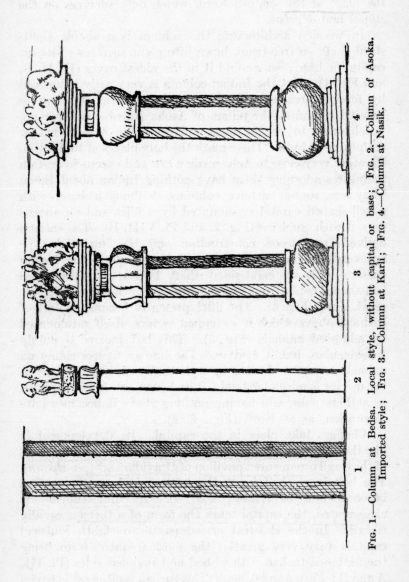

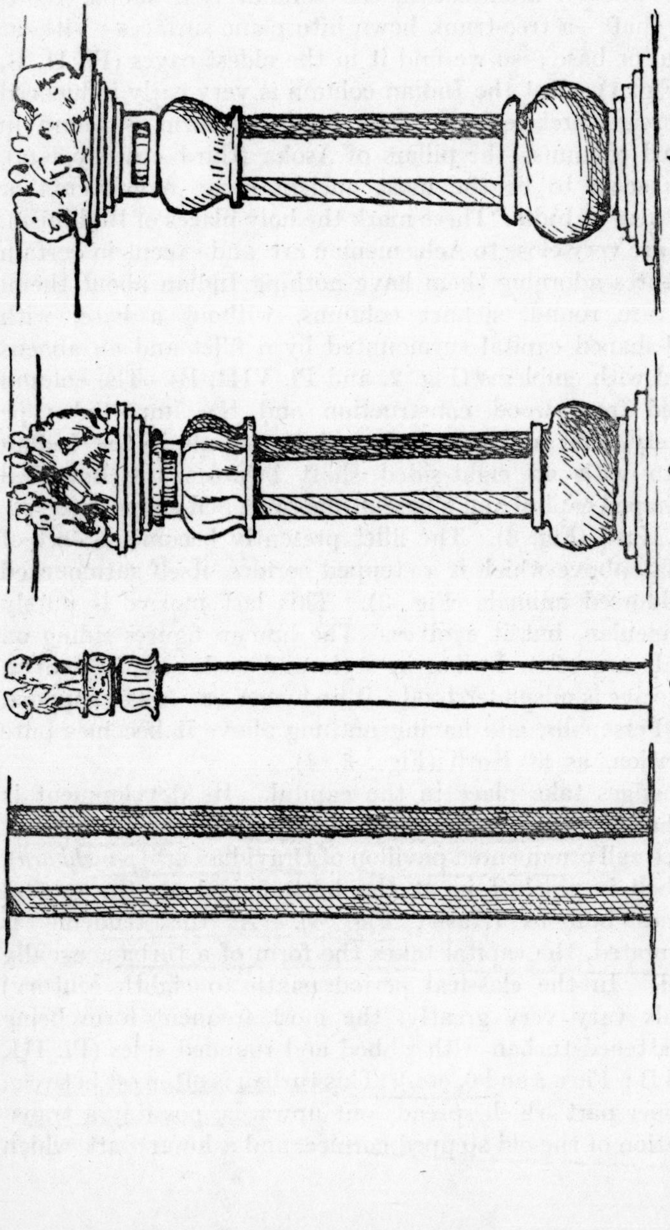

FIG. 1.—Column at Bedsa. Local style, without capital or base; FIG. 2.—Column of Asoka. Imported style; FIG. 3.—Column at Karli; FIG. 4.—Column at Nasik.

above the capitals of pillars an elongated slab, with its ends curved on the underside so that they form brackets, takes the place of the stepped form, which only survives on the *stūpas* and *dāgabas*.

In wooden architecture the column is a simple eight-sided shaft—a tree-trunk hewn into plane surfaces—without capital or base; so we find it in the oldest caves (Pl. II, B, and Fig. 1). But the Indian column is very early influenced by foreign architecture. The imported form is found in isolated columns—the pillars of Asoka (third century B.C.), which seem to be the most ancient stone monuments or sculptures in India. These mark the holy places of Buddhism. They are very close to Achæmenian art, and except in certain sculptures adorning them have nothing Indian about them. They are round, slender columns, without a base, with a bell-shaped capital surmounted by a fillet and an abacus carved with emblems (Fig. 2, and Pl. VIII, B). The column derived from wood construction and the imported type are very soon amalgamated, and the result is the Indian column with an eight-sided shaft between the imported bell-shaped capital and a base of the same bell-shape inverted, as at Karli (Fig. 3). The fillet presently becomes a sort of cushion, above which is a stepped cornice, itself surmounted by addorsed animals (Fig. 3). This last motive is purely Achæmenian, but it evolves. The human figures riding on animals are often Indian in style and costume. Moreover, the motive is misunderstood; it no longer serves as a support, as at Persepolis, and having nothing above it becomes pure decoration, as at Karli (Figs. 3, 4).

Changes take place in the capital. Its development is like that of the *stūpa*, the *dāgaba* (see p. 362), and the summit of the small ornamented pavilion of Dravidian art (*paṇchhara*). The bell is pinched in at the bottom and so the capital becomes bulbous (Nasik, Fig. 4). As this tendency is exaggerated, the capital takes the form of a turban, usually ribbed. In the classical period (sixth to eighth century) capitals vary very greatly, the most frequent form being the flattened turban with ribbed and rounded sides (Pl. III, A and B; Figs. 5 and 6, etc.). This turban is often set between an upper part which spreads out upwards, possibly a transformation of the old stepped cornice, and a lower part which

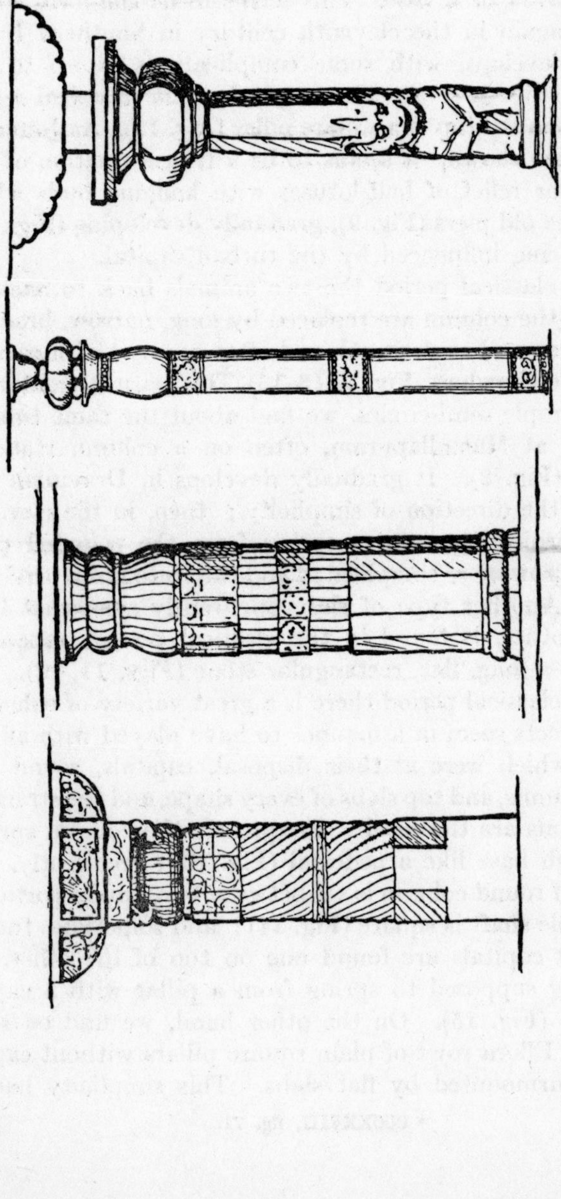

5 6 7 8

FIGS. 5–6.—Columns at Ajanta; FIG. 7.—Light wooden column, from a painting at Ajanta; FIG. 8.—Column at Mamallapuram.

spreads downwards and forms the top of a column (Fig. 6.). Sometimes this last element seems to emerge from a thick square pillar (Fig. 13). In wooden architecture the capital has exactly the same shape, as we see in the frescoes (Fig. 7), but the turban is small and the part below looks like the cup of a flower or a vase. This seems to be the form which one finds again in the eleventh century in Southern India, where it develops, with some complications, down to our own time (Fig. 16). Another capital of the classical age is the basket on the top of a square pillar (Fig. 12). As Jouveau-Dubreuil has shown,[1] it seems to be a transformation of the semi-circular relief of half-lotuses with hanging buds which adorned the old piers (Fig. 9), gradually developing (Figs. 10, 11), and being influenced by the turban capital.

In the classical period the two animals back to back on the top of the column are replaced by long, narrow, bracket-like slabs, curved underneath and often covered with carving (Ajanta and elsewhere, Figs. 5, 13–15). This feature, unadorned save for simple semi-circles, we find about the same time in the south, at Mamallapuram, often on a column standing on a lion (Fig. 8). It gradually develops in Dravidian art, at first in the direction of simplicity ; then, in the eleventh century, projecting corners spring from the rounded part, and these grow more complicated and turn into floral pendants (Fig. 16). Another type of slab, apparently somewhat later than the other, is found in the classical period, especially at Ellora—a long, flat, rectangular stone (Figs, 11, 12).

In the classical period there is a great variety of columns. The architects seem in a manner to have played with all the elements which were at their disposal, capitals, round and square columns, and top slabs of every shape, and the strangest combinations are the result. Frequently the column springs from a high base like a pedestal (Fig. 13) ; frequently, too, a section of round column is set between two square portions ; or the whole shaft is square (Fig. 14) ; and sometimes turban and basket capitals are found one on top of the other, the shaft being supposed to spring from a pillar with a capital of its own (Fig. 15). On the other hand, we find on some façades at Ellora rows of plain square pillars without capital or base, surmounted by flat slabs. This simplicity has its

[1] **CCCXXVIII**, fig. 71.

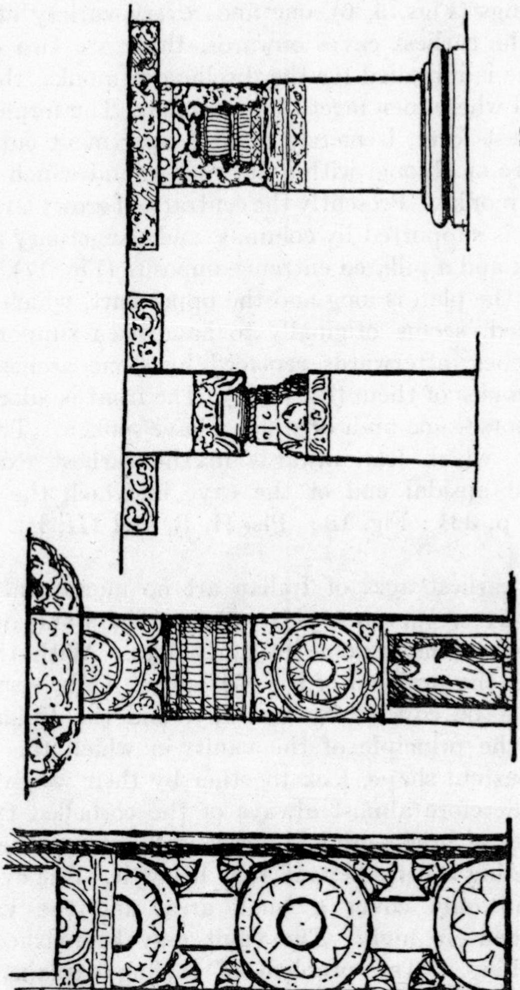

9 10 11 12

Fig. 9.—Pilaster at Nasik; Fig. 10.—Pilaster of a façade at Ajanta; Figs. 11–12.—Pillars at Ellora.

character, but it may perhaps only mean that the cave was not completed. Between these plain shafts and combinations of pedestal and column presenting the most complicated form (Fig. 15) and ornament, such as bands and straight or spiral flutings (Figs. 5, 6), one finds every variety of fancy.

From the earliest caves onwards, there are two distinct plans. One is intended for the dwelling of monks, the other for the hall where men meet to do worship. The former type, in its earliest form, is merely a small apartment cut in the rock, square or oblong, with a flat roof, round which are the cells of the monks. Presently the central hall grows larger, the upper part is supported by columns, and a sanctuary appears at the back and a pillared entrance opposite (Fig. 17). In the other type the plan is long and the upper part, which is high and rounded, seems originally to have been supported by wooden arches, afterwards replaced by stone arches which are exact copies of them (Pl. II, B). The front is adorned by the great horse-shoe arch of which I have spoken. Two rows of columns, which lean inwards in the earliest examples, lead to the apsidal end of the cave in which the *dāgaba* stands (see p. 361 ; Fig. 18 ; Pls. II, B, and III, B).

Of the earliest ages of Indian art no monument, other than the caves, survives. Architecture in stone or brick must, therefore, have come in fairly late. With the new architecture the problem of the roof arose. Only very small spaces could be covered horizontally, and the Indians did not know the principle of the vault, in which the stones, cut in trapezium shape, lock together by their weight. The roof was therefore almost always of the corbelled type, in which stones or bricks are laid horizontally one on the other, each projecting a little beyond that below it. But even this method will only cover a small area, and the vault is disproportionately high. The vault may be masked by a wooden ceiling. The problem of roofing explains many peculiarities of Indian architecture, which shows great virtuosity in handling rather primitive technical methods.

In the buildings made of lasting material we find again the two forms which we have seen in the caves, based on wood construction—the square or oblong building, a *cella* when the walls are low and far apart and a tower when they

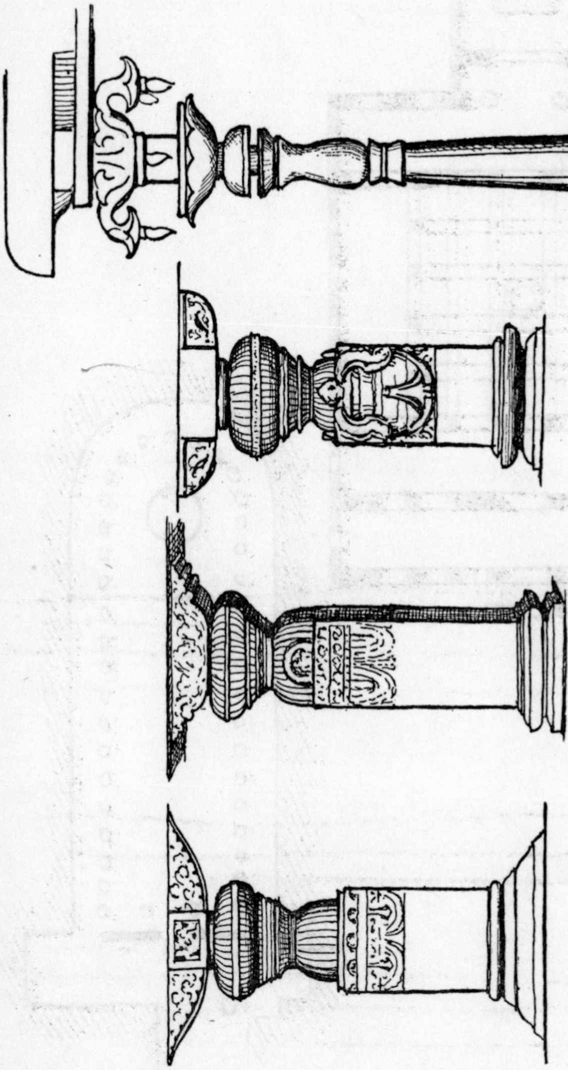

13 14 15 16

FIGS. 13–14.—Pillars at Badami; FIG. 15.—Pillar at Ellora; FIG. 16.—Late Dravidian column.

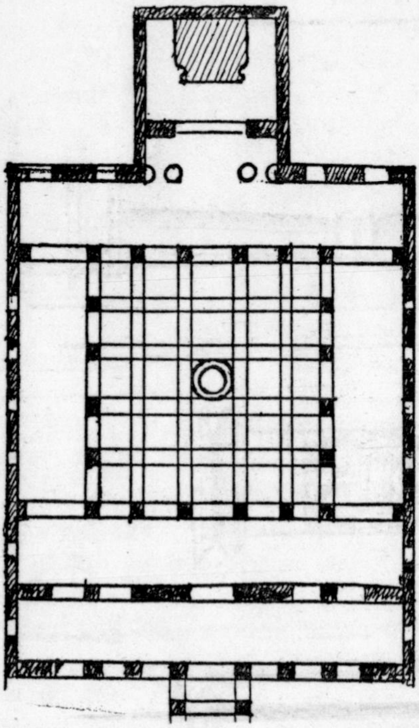

17

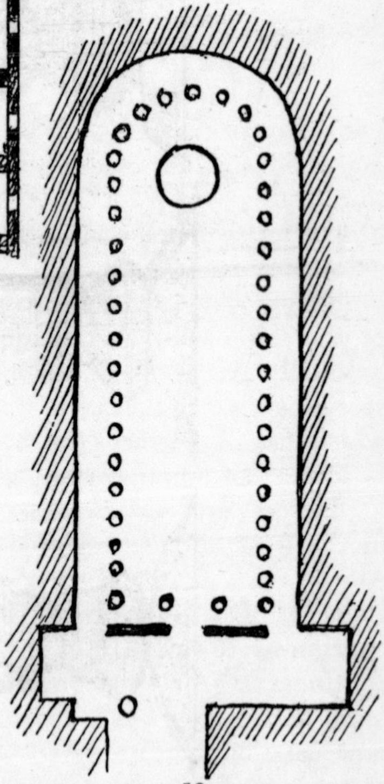

18

FIG. 17.—Square plan. Cave 1 at Ajanta; FIG. 18.—Long plan. Karli.

are high and close together, and the long building, which afterwards grows still longer and becomes a gallery. The simplest type of *cella* is found, with a row of columns on one side, in the small temple at Sanchi (fifth century, Fig. 19),[1] and, without a colonnade, in the smallest *ratha* at Mamallapuram (seventh century), which has a large roof with four curved sides (Pl. IV, A). The long building, with its curved roof terminating at each end in a horse-shoe arch, exists in its most primitive form at Chezarla and Ter (Fig. 20).[2]

Soon buildings become more complicated. Both types grow larger, and sometimes have a porch in front. At the same time they grow taller, and the *cella* or tower seems to rise out of the base, which is widened (Pl. IV, B).[3] The roof of the *cella* is developed and made in many stories, adorned with models of square or long buildings in the round, as at Mamallapuram (Pl. IV, A) and Pattakadal.[4] The *cellae* seem to be the product of stone construction, and the towers, with their curved lines, of the use of brick. For brick is easier to work, so making it possible to heighten the building, and the use of flat bricks produces more and more corbellings and stories, which tend to make the lines curved. The tower at first consists of a *cella* surmounted by a curvilinear portion, as at Sirpur (Fig. 23),[5] and is adorned with relief models of buildings, which we also find on the pre-Angkor monuments of the same period in Cambodia. The curvilinear form is gradually accentuated and the decoration marking the many stories is then composed of *āmalakas*, a sort of ribbed turbans which usually crown the towers. Later, this decoration is formed of small turrets (Fig. 24).

Towers and *cellae* are combined in certain buildings in the west at the end of the classical period (Pattakadal, Aihole, etc.). Later, the very high *cella* becomes the essential element of the architecture of Southern India and the curvilinear tower that of the north. In the south, the *cella* continues to grow in height while the stories of its roof become more numerous ; so it eventually becomes the *vimāna*, the sanctuary of the Dravidian temple, the best-known example of which is at Tanjore (tenth and eleventh centuries, Fig. 21).

1 **CCCVII**, fig. 151.
2 Ibid., fig. 147.
3 Ibid., figs. 148, 153, 188.
4 Ibid., figs. 187–8, 197, 201–2, etc.
5 Ibid., fig. 186.

In time the *vimāna* is as it were flattened, and becomes the *gopura*, or gate-house, characteristic of Dravidian monuments from the thirteenth century to the present day (Fig. 22). The curvilinear tower (*śikhara*) is the principal element of the northern temple from the eighth century to modern times

19

20

Fig. 19.—Temple, Sanchi; Fig. 20.—Temple, Chezarla.

(Fig. 24). Some Jain temples have domed halls. In Mysore there is a peculiar style: the chief part of the temple, which is set on a base, is almost pyramidical, with re-entrant angles in the plan which give it a star shape. This form seems to be intermediate between the northern tower and the southern *vimāna*.

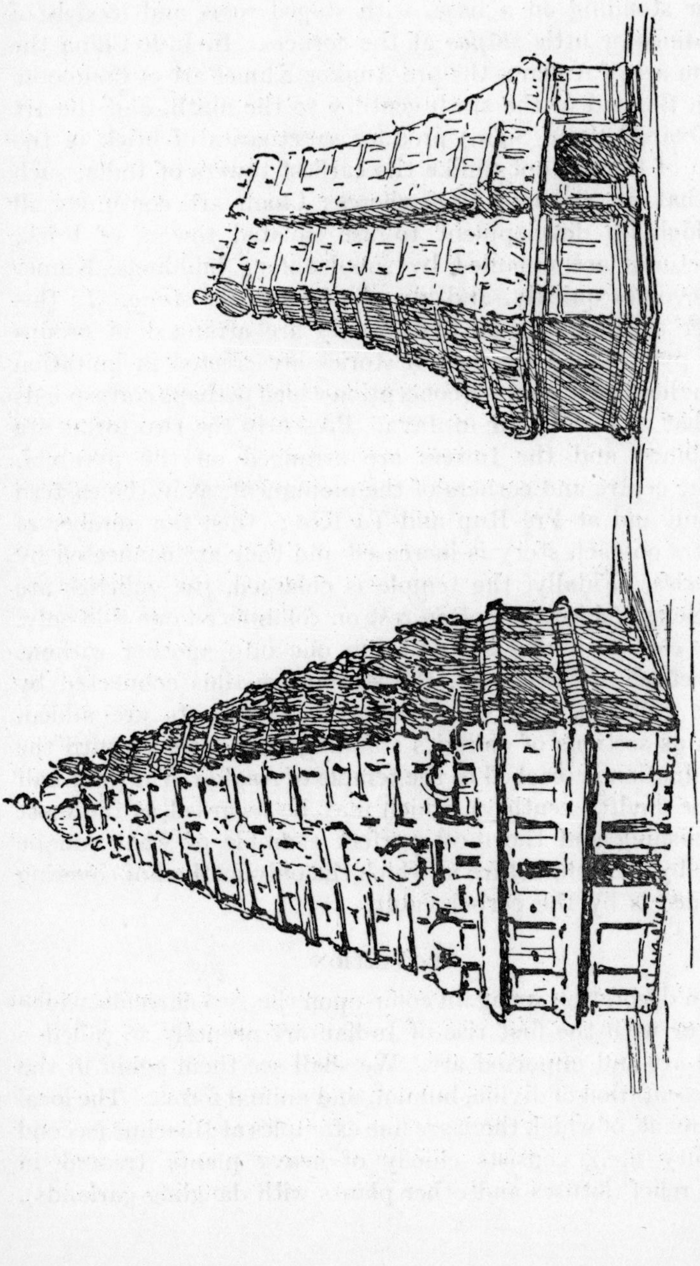

21 FIG. 21.—Vimāna, Tanjore; 22 FIG. 22.—Gopura, Madura.

From the architecture of India in classical times those of Indonesia and Indo-China are derived. In Java, in its first period (eighth to tenth century), the buildings are chiefly *cellae* standing on a base, with staged roofs and models of buildings or little *stūpas* at the corners. In Indo-China the Cham art of Annam, the pre-Angkor Khmer art of Cambodia from the end of the sixth century to the ninth, and the art of Dvaravati (in Siam) produce sanctuaries of brick in the form of towers, not unlike the earliest towers of India, such as that at Sirpur. But whereas Cham art continues all through its development to use isolated towers of brick, sometimes accompanied by small oblong buildings, Khmer art evolves quickly, and abandons brick for stone. In this latter architecture, at first towers are arranged in groups and pyramidical temples in stories are erected in imitation of the holy mountain—a conception which perhaps corresponds to that of Borobudur in Java. Presently the two forms are combined and the towers are arranged on the pyramid, at the centre and corners of the monument, as in the eastern Mebun and at Pré Rup and Ta Kèo; then the number of towers on each story is increased and they are connected by galleries. Finally, the temple is enlarged, the galleries are developed (since they often rest on columns on one side only, they can be multiplied and run one into another without any effect of heaviness), the stories are thus connected by cross galleries, and small isolated monuments are added, such as sections of galleries standing on a terrace, until the culmination is reached in the temple of Angkor Wat (first half of the twelfth century), which may be regarded as the most astonishing and the most perfect example of what can be done by an architecture in which the only method of covering a space is by the corbel vault.

DECORATION

In decoration we again come upon the two currents which appear with the first rise of Indian art properly so called—local art and imported art. We shall see them again in the representation of divine, human, and animal forms. The local ornament, of which there are fine examples at Bharhut (second century B.C.), consists chiefly of heavy plants treated in high relief (lotuses and other plants with dangling garlands),

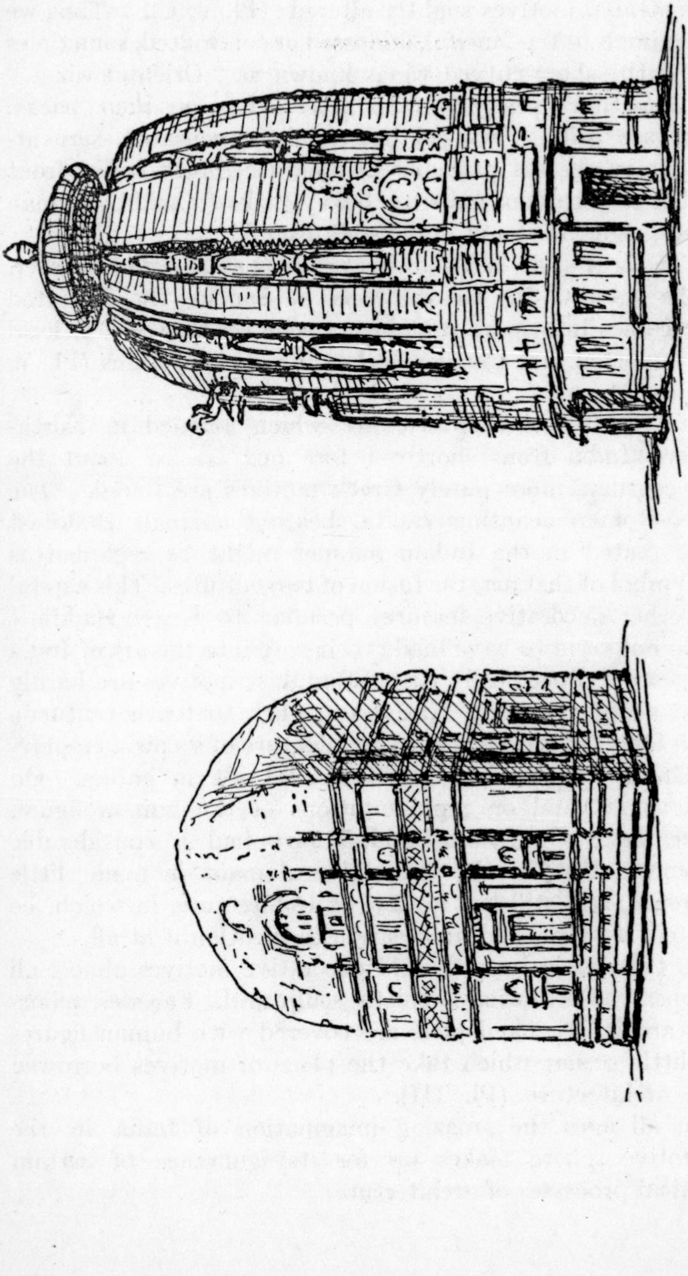

23 24

FIG. 23.—Śikhara, Sirpur; FIG. 24.—Śikhara, Bhuvanesvar.

often accompanied by aquatic creatures, etc. (Pl. V, B). The other type of decoration makes use of a great number of motives from the Hellenized East, which are usually old Achæmenian motives slightly altered (Pl. V, C). Thus we find animals, often fanciful, addorsed or confronted, sometimes having the short curved wings known as " Oriental wings " and sometimes prancing with little riders on their backs. There are griffins, winged horses, lions, centaurs, serpent-tailed men, horses prancing in opposite directions in front of a car seen end on, Atlantes, heavy garlands held by human figures, palmettes, etc. (Combaz's list).

The local style of ornament prevails at Bharhut. Later, on the gates of the Great Stupa at Sanchi, the imported style comes into more prominence and the two styles, local and imported, are found side by side on the jambs (Pl. V, B and C).

In the Græco-Buddhist art which reigned in North-western India from shortly before our era to about the fifth century, more purely Greek motives are found. The Græco-Roman acanthus capital bearing a small Buddhist figure seated in the Indian manner might be regarded as the symbol of that art, the fusion of two cultures. This capital and other decorative features peculiar to Græco-Buddhist art do not seem to have made their way into the art of India in general. Specifically Græco-Buddhist motives are hardly found again except in Kashmir (eighth to tenth century), which for a short time had an architecture of its own, employing Greek columns and trefoil arches set in gables. On religious art and on representations of the human figure, as we shall see, Græco-Buddhist art had a considerable influence. But in the decorative domain it made little difference, and still less in that of architecture, in which, be it noted, we have had no occasion to mention it at all.

In the classical age the old decorative motives almost all disappear. Decoration is chiefly sculptural. Façades, pillar-tops, architraves, and piers are covered with human figures and little scenes which take the place of motives borrowed from architecture (Pl. III).

In all ages the amazing imagination of India in the decorative sphere makes up for its ignorance of certain technical processes of architecture.

THE STŪPA

The *stūpa* (Pl. II, A) is connected both with architecture and with sacred art, and for that reason we shall study it by itself. It is a fundamentally Indian structure, appearing with Indian art itself and spreading with Buddhism. It consists of a hemispherical mound of masonry set on a base and crowned by a cubical " tee " and an umbrella. In small *stūpas* the " tee " is surmounted by a stepped cornice.

The origins and the purpose of the *stūpa* have been very clearly indicated by Foucher. It was originally a funerary monument and tumulus, to hold the ashes of Buddha, which were, it is said, divided into eight parts and laid in eight *stūpas*. In later times Asoka found seven of these *stūpas*; the eighth was lost in the jungle, and it was said that the Nagas who guarded the relics which it contained refused to deliver them up to the king. Asoka collected the ashes, divided them, and built a large number of these gigantic reliquaries for them. So the function of the *stūpa* was extended; it served to protect the ashes of the saints and also, where ashes were lacking, other relics of the Blessed One. Finally, having become the chief form of sacred monument, it was used as a memorial, to mark the scene of a miracle or other great event. So, in districts where the Buddhist faith was lively but Buddha himself had never been in his last existence, *stūpas* were erected where one or another Jātaka, an event in his previous lives, had occurred.

Stūpas were of all sizes. The large ones (Pl. II, A) were often surrounded by balustrades with entrance-gates, doubtless intended to keep out malign influences and to bound the holy ground on which the *pradakshiṇā* was performed, the rite of going round a being or a symbol, keeping it on one's right hand, to honour it. Sometimes smaller *stūpas* containing the ashes of monks were grouped round the main edifice. Inside temples and at the inner end of the oblong buildings which served as a place of prayer there were small *stūpas* called *dāgabas* (see above, p. 352; Pls. II, B, and III, B). As time went on the *stūpa* grew higher and changed its shape. In the earliest examples the dome is as it were flattened and the terrace is low (Pl. II, A). By the first century of our era, both terrace and dome are considerably higher. Passing through an evolution similar to that of the capital, the dome assumes a bell shape, the lower part being drawn in, and the base, especially in certain *dāgabas*, becomes higher than ever (Ajanta, Pl. III, B).

The *stūpa* vanishes from India with Buddhism, but it continues in use down to modern times in the countries where the Buddhism of the Small Vehicle prevails—Ceylon, Burma, Siam, Cambodia, Laos. There it becomes yet taller and more pointed, and is like the head-dresses of the dancing-girls, having the form of a bell, wide at the bottom and ending in a spike above.

The earliest *stūpas* and *dāgabas* are not ornamented with sculpture, but the balustrades surrounding them are covered with medallions and friezes (Bharhut, etc.). Elsewhere, as in the Great Stupa of Sanchi, the balustrades are only a plain imitation of wooden railings, and the reliefs are grouped about the entrances (Pl. II, A). Later the *stūpa* itself is adorned with scenes and decoration, in rows one above the other, running round the base and possibly in a collar round the dome, as at Amaravati. On the very high bases, covered with carving, of the classical *dāgabas* at Ajanta, Ellora, and elsewhere, a large Buddha often stands out prominently, generally seated in the European fashion (Pl. III, B).

CHAPTER II

Religious Art

THE earliest religious art of India known to us is Buddhist. Here again both local traditions and imported influences are at work, but in this domain it is the local traditions which develop chiefly at the beginning, and outside influence only appears with Græco-Buddhist art, shortly before our era. That influence prevails at first in the north-west, on the fringe of India as it were, and then gradually makes its way all over the country.

We find the earliest Buddhist religious works, which belong to the local tradition, carved in durable materials in the second century B.C. The most noticeable thing about them is the absence of any representation of Buddha himself. Whether the cause was the difficulty of portraying such a miraculous being, or religious scruple, or ancient tradition, his place is marked by an empty seat, by his footprints, by a riderless horse, and his presence is indicated by an umbrella. How can this conception have arisen ? The answer is indicated by Foucher's researches. It seems that very soon after the death of the Blessed One it became habitual to make pilgrimages to the sites of the four chief events of his life, the Four Great Miracles—the Birth and Departure from Kapilavastu, the Illumination at Buddh Gaya, the First Sermon in the gazelle park at Benares, and the Death at Kusinagara. It was, and still is, the custom for pilgrims to take small cakes of earth away with them as mementoes and relics. These cakes doubtless bore the four emblems, the vase of lotuses of the Immaculate Birth, the tree of the Illumination, the Wheel of the Law, symbolizing the First Sermon, and the *stūpa* (tomb and reliquary) of the final Nirvana, the Parinirvāṇa, the earthly death of Buddha (Pl. VI, B, D, E, G). Presently worshippers were depicted round these symbols (Pl. VI, D–G). Then it came to be held that the worshippers were not adoring only the symbols, but Buddha himself at the moment when the miracle was being performed, and so the real scene was represented. Since Buddha could not be shown, an empty seat, the mark of his feet, or an umbrella was sometimes inserted to indicate his presence (Pl. VI, D, F, A). In this way the Illumination and the First Sermon were represented, and from the Four Great Miracles the method was soon extended to other scenes in the last existence of the Blessed One. An empty seat with a tree (Pl. VI, D) or an empty seat with a wheel and often with gazelles (Pl. VI, F) indicates Buddha at the moment of the Illumination or of the First Sermon. One finds a still more curious scene—a birth without a child. Maya, the mother of Buddha, is shown (Pl. VI, C) standing or sitting on the lotus while two elephants, carved above her—that is, behind her in vertical perspective—ritually asperse the unseen child, in accordance with the legend. This scene was probably misunderstood, and since the absence of the child and the perspective give the impression that it is Maya that the elephants are aspersing, the Brahman goddess Lakshmi, Vishnu's wife, was afterwards represented in this way. The Departure of Buddha (Pl. VI, A), leaving his family for the wilderness, was represented by a riderless horse under an umbrella, with deities supporting its hooves, as the legend tells. When Buddha, arriving in the wilderness, is bidden farewell by his groom and his horse, we see the groom and horse prostrating themselves before the mark of his feet (Pl. VI, A).

So a whole religious art became established, some of the symbols of which are perhaps old symbols of the Near East, taken over and transformed by India and Buddhism.[1] It is hardly probable that it had any influence in Buddhist countries outside India. It is, however, curious that one often finds in Byzantine art the theme of the Etimasia (ἑτοιμασία), in which angels adore the empty throne on which the Saviour will come to sit for the Last Judgment.

But, while the Blessed One cannot be represented in his last existence, there is not the same scruple against showing him in his previous lives. This fact, combined with the Indian artist's love of depicting animals, explains why early art is so full of Jātakas, miraculous stories of how Buddha, often in the form of an animal, did deeds of charity and benevolence to all creatures (Pl. IX, A).

[1] CCCL.

Græco-Buddhist sacred art is very different. It depicts Buddha himself, and so introduces entirely new treatments. As we shall see later, Græco-Buddhist art, combining Greek methods and Indian religious subjects, seems to have developed from the middle of the first century B.C. onwards in Gandhara and Kapisa, in the north-west of India and south-east of the present Afghanistan. The earliest figure of Buddha—the fact is almost certain, although it is still contested—is a Græco-Buddhist work. It wears the monastic dress treated as classical drapery (Pl. VII, A), and has the signs of perfection of the universal lord and great religious reformer and various other marks of beauty, such as the long ears and the small circle in relief (*ūrṇā*) between the eyebrows. Such a miraculous being could not be represented with his head shaven as the sacred books required, and he was given wavy hair tied on the top into a bun. Later on, apparently under the influence of the art of Mathura, the ritual bun and curls were adopted almost everywhere and took the place of the waved hair, the general form of which was, however, maintained, although not properly understood. Since some of the books declared that Buddha's skull was highly developed, this bun then became a protuberance of the skull, the *ushṇīsha*, an attribute which persisted in all the various renderings of Buddha and was sometimes, but only later and chiefly in Indo-China, surmounted by a flame.

Buddha is not always shown, as is sometimes supposed, sitting cross-legged on the ground (Pl. X, B). This " Indian attitude ", as it is called, is only a position of repose, suited to meditation, intermediate between the upright attitude, which brings fatigue, and the recumbent, which is conducive to sleep. Buddha is frequently represented standing, or, especially in the Ajanta period, sitting in the " European " fashion on a seat with his knees wide apart (Pl. III, B). This last attitude, apparently the royal position of the Asiatic king, seems to have been adopted by the Scythians and by them to have been introduced into Buddhist religious art. It is found again at Dvaravati in Siam and in Java.

The position of Buddha's hands (*mudrā*) has a symbolic meaning. Meditation is indicated when they rest in the lap (Pl. X, B), argument when the right hand is raised with the first and middle fingers joined, and charity when it hangs palm outwards (Pl. III, A). The hand held forward, open, with fingers raised and palm outwards, wards off all fear. Preaching is symbolized by the hands brought together and "turning the Wheel of the Law", and illumination by the right hand, palm inwards, touching the ground, for when the Blessed One became Buddha he took the earth to witness.

Græco-Buddhist art represents the *bodhisattva* as covered with jewels and wearing a moustache, like a Scythian ruler. Another type of *bodhisattva* which should be mentioned here is found in the art of Mathura, a specifically Indian art which developed in the north of India, parallel to Græco-Buddhist art. These *bodhisattvas*, which are dated by an inscription of the reign of Kanishka, are substitutes for Buddha himself, who was not yet represented after his Illumination. It has been suggested that this type is the first representation of the Blessed One, and so earlier than the Greek rendering and fundamentally Indian (Pl. VII, B). For the general aspect of these *bodhisattvas* is that of the typically Indian figures of the art of Mathura—round face, rounded figure, and Indian treatment of clothes. The skull is smooth with a coiled bun, a peculiarity. On the other hand, the arrangement of the drapery is very like what one finds on some Græco-Buddhist *bodhisattvas*; the halo, which is frequent, seems to be a foreign importation, in spite of its peculiar ornament; and the use of the name of *bodhisattva* shows a persistent dislike of representing Buddha after the Illumination. The school of Mathura does not therefore seem to have been the first to venture to defy the old prohibition. Probably these figures are, not a model, but a first repercussion, indirect, it is true, of Græco-Buddhist art on the native art of India. In any case, after fifty years they give place, even in the art of Mathura, to figures copied from Græco-Buddhist types.

Almost the whole expansion of the arts of India can be traced by that of the plastic representations of Buddha. Two different types appear fairly soon. A Buddha with the right shoulder uncovered is found, carved in the round, in Southern India in the first centuries of our era, at Amaravati, and the material in which he is clad is still heavy, with broad, regular folds (Pl. VII, C). We find him again later, in Ceylon; here the material is finer and the folds, which have been preserved, are more numerous. The best example of these Buddhas is perhaps that at Dong-duong in Champa (Annam), which seems to be a Cingalese importation (Pl. VII, D). The Buddha with the bare shoulder also seems to have existed at the beginning of one of the most ancient arts of Indo-China, that of Dvaravati in Siam.

The figure of Buddha with both shoulders covered was still more popular, and seems to have gradually influenced the previous type, and sometimes to have taken its place. This is the Buddha which we usually find in Græco-Buddhist art. We see it penetrating into the art of Northern India in the second Mathura period, about the fiftieth year of Kanishka, and reaching Southern India in the age of Amaravati (second to fourth century), where it generally appears in the reliefs. This Buddha becomes hieratic and stylized in the north, while keeping its harmony. It is an upright figure, with the clothing held up by the lowered forearms and falling in regular lines on each side of the body so as to frame it. The folds are now rendered by curved lines in very slight relief, indicating a fine, transparent material clinging to the body (Gupta period, Pl. VII, E); this drapery is also found in late Græco-Buddhist art, and as far away as China, at T'ien Lung Shan. Presently the folds disappear altogether, and Buddha at first sight looks as if he were naked, for his robes are a transparent muslin, and might be wet, so closely do they follow the modelling of the figure. From the fifth and sixth centuries onwards, Buddha is always represented thus in India, whether he is standing, sitting in European fashion, or sitting cross-legged (Ajanta, Bengal, etc.; Pl. III, A and B), until Buddhism disappears from the country.

In the earliest period of Javanese art (eighth to tenth century) Buddha is clad in this same almost invisible material, but one of his shoulders is bare; often he is inclined to plumpness, with rounded lines (Chandi Mendut, Borobudur, etc.), recalling the Buddhist sculpture of the most ancient caves at Ellora. Another type of Buddhist sculpture in Java is more vigorous (at Chandi Sari, etc) and seems to be related to the art of Bengal. In the early art which develops in Siam, probably from the sixth century (the art of Dvaravati), Buddha is represented seated in the European way or, more often, standing, in his Gupta form, clad in transparent material which frames his body, and his face has a special character which may be racial. It is a Buddha related to that of Dvaravati, but with the Indian hips, that we find, though not often, in the pre-Angkor art of Cambodia from the end of the sixth century to the ninth. In the next period of Khmer art the representation of Buddha seems to have been abandoned, and it is, I think, not till about the beginning of the twelfth century (Phimai, etc.) that he reappears, often dressed in jewellery and almost Khmer in form, then shorn of his ornaments and showing some slight influence of Dvaravati, and finally transformed by the art of the Bayon, which gives transfiguration to the countenance, into the type with the closed eyes and the mystic smile. This expression of the Buddhas, afterwards extended to the *bodhisattvas*, seems to be in part explained by a particularly strong influence from outside, which is very marked in Buddhas derived from the prototype which Commaille discovered on the Bayon. In Siam, under Thai influence, a new aspect of Buddha appears, in which the brow-ridges are marked by two convex lines and the mouth is narrow with upturned corners. There are many different schools of this art, in which the standing Buddha continues, down to our own time, to be framed in his clothing, which is less and less well understood by the artists who copy the type until it is sometimes no more than a flat sheet of metal (Pl. VII, F).

To the north the figure of Buddha serves to mark the route by which art spread to China by way of the oases of Central Asia, following the ancient silk road which turned the plateaux of Tibet. In addition to this land route there was the sea route to China by the islands and Indo-China. In China, as early as the Wei period, we find a completely transformed, hieratic type of Buddha. The thick concentric folds, arranged almost in steps, of these sculptures are also found in Champa (Annam) and even in one example in Indonesia, but one cannot say whether this type of drapery came direct from India or through China. Later, the light, separate folds, carved in relief, indicating thin material, which are characteristic of late Græco-Buddhist art and Gupta art are found in exactly the same form in China, at T'ien Lung Shan. This second wave of influence seems to have brought figures of the Ajanta style to Yun Kang, where they are sometimes found, to T'ien Lung Shan, where they are frequent, and even to Horyuji in Japan, where the paintings show striking likenesses of style and detail to those of Ajanta. The concentric folds and the little stiff folds, which have become mechanical, persist in Central Asia, Tibet, and Japan. In Central Asia we find the influence of India or of China predominating, according to the geographical position; in the latter case the face of Buddha is rounder and the folds of the drapery are harder. Later, in Tibet, Buddhist figures present the same Chinese character striving and mingling with the fragile, less lethargic, but equally rigid Indian type introduced from Bengal through Nepal.

When it became possible to represent Buddha, the rendering of the scenes in which he appears was naturally affected greatly. Their composition was almost entirely changed by Græco-Buddhist art. In the scene of the birth, Maya stands, with tilted hips, with one hand above her head, holding a branch of a tree in the Lumbini garden (Pl. X, A)—the attitude of certain figures at Bharhut and Sanchi (Pl. XVI, A)—while the child, who is now represented, springs miraculously from her side towards the gods who stand ready to take him. In the Departure the horse bears his rider. The thrones of the Illumination and the First Sermon are no longer empty. Græco-Buddhist art even shows the death of Buddha, as, lying on his right side, he enters Parinirvāṇa. In addition to the old scenes, thus transformed, new scenes are shown. The Blessed One is often accompanied by a curious person, Vajrapani, the Thunder-bearer. Since there is no longer any difficulty about representing scenes in the last life of Buddha, and Græco-Buddhist art has not the same love of naturalism and animal figures as that of Bharhut and Sanchi, Jātakas are less frequent.

The art of Amaravati, in southern India (second to fourth century of our era), presents a very singular phenomenon—two manners of representing the divine side by side. The works in which Buddha is not represented happen, in general, to be earlier than those in which he appears, but at one time the two methods coexist. The old scruples and habits seem to have struggled to hold their ground. On the same relief one finds, side by side, one scene in which Buddha is shown and another in which his seat is empty; after several scenes in which he is represented, there is one on the same slab in which his presence is merely suggested; or two separate reliefs show exactly the same group of figures, belonging to the same scene, crowding in the one round the Blessed One and in the other round his vacant throne. The old dislike of representing the earthly death of Buddha persists; in spite of Græco-Buddhist influence, even in scenes where Buddha is shown, his death is symbolized by the *stūpa*.

Yet the strong character of the school of Amaravati stamps this branch of its art, and many details peculiar to it are added to what it derived from the two older traditions.

Buddhist religious art was developed at Ajanta, where, as Foucher has shown, scenes are arranged according to the place of their original occurrence, and not in order of time. But, apart from the great *bodhisattvas*, the spirit of the art of Ajanta, even in religious scenes, is not that of Buddhist beliefs but that of the Sanskrit literature and theatre of the day.

When Buddhism was about to disappear from India, it was in the north-east, about Bengal, that its sacred art lasted longest and developed. In figures set against stelæ and curious ornamented Buddhas we can follow the transformation of the subjects and the multiplication of deities under the influence of the Great Vehicle and Tantrism. It is this north-eastern art which, through Nepal, reaches Tibet.

Other sects had their religious art, beside the Buddhists. The Jains were chiefly content to turn out *tīrthakaras* of one same conventional type, and it would make this treatise too long if I were to discuss them. There is a third and very different art, that of the Brahmans.

Vedic sacrifice, as we have seen, does not require images of the gods. The efficacity of its ceremonies lies in the correct recitation of the texts and the ritual performance of the sacrifice in a place which is consecrated afresh each time. It needs no architecture or divine figure.

The earliest statues of a Brahmanic tendency which we know seem to be of minor deities, Yakshas and Yakshiṇīs, the oldest examples of which seem to date from the second century B.C. The great gods of Hinduism do not appear until much later. We do not know whether there were earlier images which have not survived, or the worship of them was later than is generally supposed, or there was a religious objection to representing the gods, as among the Buddhists.

The *linga* (phallus), treated naturalistically both in India and in Indo-China, appears with the art of Mathura, and the figure accompanying it is related in style to the *bodhisattvas* of the same art and the images of Siva on the reverse of Scythian coins. Only with the coming of Gupta art (probably fourth to fifth century) do we find the great Hindu deities represented frequently—Vishnu and his avatars, Siva, and the rest. These figures have the gentleness and harmony of contemporary Buddhist art. Indian sculpture and painting, as we shall see, had developed, and at every stage of that development gods of different religions were portrayed in such a similar manner that they have been confused when not distinguished by very definite attributes. Thus the Brahmanic figures have the Buddhist softness which affects the whole early period of Indian art, and not until the second period of the classical age, about the seventh and eighth centuries, does the special character of the Hindu religions seem to assert itself in art, with the disappearance of Buddhism. Art has all its old harmony, but a new grandeur takes the place of the Ajanta gracefulness. Tall, hieratic figures stand isolated against detached backgrounds. Thus the avatars of Vishnu are represented, and Siva in his different forms, dancing the *tāṇḍava* (Pl. XV), emerging from the *linga*, and so on.

Towards the end of the classical period and in the succeeding periods, the tendency towards grandeur and violence becomes a love of movement and frenzy, and sometimes even sadism and delight in the horrible. This happens especially in the Dravidian art of Southern India and in Tibet, where Buddhism is influenced by Hindu Tantrism.

This development can be followed in one particular scene—that in which Vishnu, enraged at the impious man who declares that the god cannot be everywhere, comes in the form of a lion out of the pillar which the blasphemer was striking and rends him. At Ellora, about the seventh century, in the Cave of the Avatars, Vishnu, in whom force and balance are united, attacks the blasphemer, whose recoil is striking in the elasticity of its movement. In later versions we see Vishnu seizing his victim and rending him so that his bowels gush out.

There is another and opposite tendency, chiefly in the north, which produces the most indecent erotic scenes and figures of a refined charm which sometimes falls into preciosity. So religious art runs in two directions, to occasionally insipid gracefulness and to frenzied violence, after the harmony of the classical age.

CHAPTER III

SCULPTURE AND PAINTING

IN sculpture and painting the two styles which I have already mentioned several times, local and imported, appear again, and, what is remarkable, the two same developments take place.

I have said that, from the very beginning of Indian art properly so called, architecture and decoration contained, in addition to the local style, imported features, which were at first copied slavishly and then assimilated and blended with native traditions, and that Græco-Buddhist art, which came later, did not have a very great influence. In religious art, on the other hand, the local style alone appears and is maintained in the first period, and it is Græco-Buddhist art, which had practically no influence in architecture and decoration, which then brings in a whole new style, which at first grows up on the fringe of Indian art and is then absorbed by it.

This dual movement is also found in sculpture and painting. As in architecture and decoration, an imported style exists from the very beginning of Indian art. At first it is rare, and has no connexion with the local style (e.g., the animals on the Asoka pillars), but later the two are mingled, as in the gates at Sanchi, the whole remaining fundamentally Indian. Then, as in religious works, Græco-Buddhism artificially applies the Hellenistic style to Indian subjects, after which it develops parallel to the art of India, independently, until it gradually becomes Indianized, for example in the treatment of drapery. Indian art, on its side, without losing any of its original character, absorbs Græco-Buddhist art, is nourished by it, and transforms it until it vanishes, merged in the art of India.

The earliest period of truly Indian art (Pataliputra, Bhaja, Bharhut, Buddh Gaya, Sanchi, Karli, the school of Mathura, etc., from the third century B.C. to the third century of our era) shows a very marked naturalism. It is not a copying of the real in its smallest details, picturesque but destructive of all grandeur, harmony, and life, and indicative of decline, but the naturalism of certain young arts, which simplifies forms, is equally far from hieratic stiffness and from perfect harmony and balance, and keeps in close touch with every-day life. There is neither elongation of figures nor very studied or well-ordered composition, but a keen sense of life, a love of story-telling, direct contact with reality, a movement which is never violent, and straightforward, simple love of all creatures (Pls. IX, A, and VI). There is, not so much sexual provocation, as a diffused, easy sensuality that one seems to find in the very much emphasized and not idealized female figures characteristic of this first period (Fig. XVI, A).

This naturalism is the local element, and is fundamentally Indian. It appears in works which seem to be the most ancient—small terra-cotta heads found at Pataliputra (Pl. VIII, A), a few statues in the round, reliefs at Bhaja, the earlier medallions from Bharhut (Pl. IX, A), and the animals in relief on the Asoka pillars (Pl. XIII, B). The imported art, which is infrequent and is quite unlike the local style, is seen in the animals in the round on the tops of the same Asoka pillars. These are conventional animals, the most remarkable of which are the hieratic, stylized lions, which are cold, academic figures from the Hellenized East (Pl. VIII, B). After this first encounter, the local tendency prevails. The most ancient reliefs tell stories with a simplicity not lacking in charm (Pl. IX, A). The planes are not superimposed; the actors in one same scene vary greatly in size without æsthetic necessity and are often seen from different angles. It is the spontaneous expression of direct observation, trying to say its say without being overmuch troubled by logic. The figures are numerous and the field sometimes, overcrowded, as if the artist had too much to say.

Not long afterwards, in the Buddh Gaya medallions, the older sculptures at Sanchi, and above all the friezes and some medallions at Bharhut, a technical progress appears which soon arrives at real perfection. The sculptors may have mastered their technique very quickly, but that very speed seems to indicate rather an influence from outside, an influence still latent, which appears at this time to have affected methods rather than motives. One is struck, not by the few new motives introduced, but by the sureness of the three-quarter attitudes and the sudden ease with which the sculptor expresses a direct and vigorous naturalism.

The perfection acquired is still more noticeable on the gates of the Great Stupa of Sanchi (probably the first century B.C.), which are perhaps the culminating point of the first period of Indian art (Pls. II, A, V, VI,). Here the imported element is much clearer, but it has been assimilated. Many foreign motives—the fanciful animals mentioned above and decorative features (Pl. V, C)—are mingled in an easy fashion with more particularly Indian elements (Pl. V, B). The wonderful genius for portraying animals already noticeable at Bharhut is maintained, and so is the power of telling a story, but the composition of the scenes is more skilful and better balanced.

The appearance of the figures is thoroughly Indian. The torso is always bare, the drapery is of the Indian kind, folded in front, and a flat collar is worn. The men wear a turban puffed out at one side (later, in the art of Mathura and Amaravati, it is puffed out over the forehead), while the women have their arms and legs covered with bangles (Pl. XVI, A).

The naturalism of early Indian art continues and is exaggerated at Karli and in the art of Mathura, from the first to the third century of our era. The female figures become still more fulsome, and their wide hips and their transparent clothing, which makes some them of look naked, increase the impression of unashamed sensuality (Pl. XVI, B). The pink sandstone figures of the Mathura style have round heads and in many cases a curious fixed smile which recalls the sculpture of Ægina (Pl. VII, B). In its second period this art is affected by various influences.

In all the arts which we have been examining the general impression is quite definitely Indian. On the other hand, Græco-Buddhist art seems, at least at first sight, more Greek than Indian. As we have seen, it flourished probably from the second half of the first century B.C. to the fifth century of our era, in the north-west of India and the south-east of the present Afghanistan, at the same time as the native arts of Mathura in the north and Amaravati in the south. It carried on Hellenistic traditions of which little is known, which may perhaps have been kept alive in the small kingdoms which arose in succession between Asia Minor and India after Alexander's conquest.

At first sight Græco-Buddhist art seems simply to apply Hellenistic ideas of beauty and Hellenistic methods to Buddhist subjects (Pls. VII, A, and X). It differs from the early art of India (Sanchi, Mathura, etc.) in style, e.g. in the treatment of faces, as much as in costume. In contrast to the drapery of Sanchi, treated in the Indian fashion, with the material falling down the front, the torso always bare, and the special ornaments such as collars, anklets, and (in the case of men) turbans, Græco-Buddhist drapery is of the Hellenistic type, sometimes covering the whole body, while the head-dressing and ornaments are different. So Græco-Buddhist art, to one who does not believe in the absolute excellence of Greek art, seems at first to be decadent and devoid of originality, expert in an ancient technique from which the life has fled and reproducing cold, stiff, academic clichés to which the Buddhist religion is incapable of giving a soul. Yet to an observer without preconceptions it may bear comparison with the true art of India, for all the latter's intense vitality and its air of being in constant communion with what it represents.

But the problem is far from being so simple. Besides the large statues, often squat and clumsy (Pl. VII, A), and the schist reliefs, which are usually in the cold style which I have described, there is, at least in the second Græco-Buddhist period, a class of small works in stucco which has been brought to light by the recent excavations at Hadda in the extreme south-east of Afghanistan and Taxila in North-western India (Pl. VIII, C and D). This style is full of imagination. The heads are cast, while the bodies are sculptured on the spot. Some of the drapery is related to late Greek art but recalls the beauty of the drapery of the fifth century B.C. Some of the heads are like Hellenistic models (several remind one of Socrates), but have a new intensity. Others suggest the French art of the thirteenth century (Pl. VIII, C). No connexion is possible, but in the Middle Ages and in the Græco-Buddhist world alike the same Greek style seems to have received new life from a religion in its full vigour. The researches which Hackin and Mlle Hébert are at present conducting are revealing the Hellenistic prototypes from which the figures at Hadda and Taxila are derived. The heads which suggest a Gaul, a Socrates, a Christ, were not invented by Græco-Buddhist art, they were not created by direct observation; they are Hellenistic models transformed, but a new strength and youth have been breathed into them. If the invasions had not killed it, Græco-Buddhist art would doubtless have become, as Grousset holds, a special art, close to that of India but independent of it, and equally different from the Hellenistic art which had given it birth.

The evolution of Græco-Buddhist art is difficult to follow. It is not the normal evolution of an art which has its infancy, prime, and old age. It is an importation, already decadent when it makes its first appearance, and it seems to be gradually rejuvenated under the influence of India. Perhaps it follows certain variations in Græco-Roman art at a distance. We can classify works only by certain details, such as the increasing thinness and softness of the drapery which we have seen in the evolution of the Buddha.

In its turn, Græco-Buddhist art exercises a twofold influence, which we have already seen in religious works and will find again when we study the Indian treatment of the hips. Its influence spread on the one side through Central Asia to China and Japan and on the other in India itself and by the sea to the islands and Indo-China.

The art of Mathura seems to have been the first to come under Græco-Buddhist influence. We seemed to see this double wave of influence in the time of Kanishka, beginning as indirect influence at the commencement of his reign, in *bodhisattvas* which are very Indian in style and drapery (see above, p. 366) and appearing fifty years later in the imitation, often clumsy, of Græco-Buddhist models. About this latter time, the sculptures of the Naga kings, of which there is one in the Musée Guimet, seem to combine Greek harmony with the old naturalism. The figures are slenderer and there is a new vigour. The art of Mathura seems also to have received a Scythian influence, which is visible in the standing statues of kings wearing heavy garments spreading at the bottom and boots pointing outwards, and also in similar figures seated on a throne with the knees wide apart, a royal pose which was afterwards assumed by the Buddhas sitting "in the European fashion".

Not until later, in Northern India, does the Græco-Buddhist influence appear, at once dominant and completely assimilated, in Gupta art, which perhaps reacts in its turn on late Græco-Buddhist art. The figures, especially the Buddhas (Pl. VII, E), seem to be the direct result of a Græco-Buddhist development. The halo has become very large and is covered with decoration. The treatment of the eyes, brow-ridges, and lips is that of Græco-Buddhist art transformed, and will survive all through the classical art of India. The drapery, which is thin, with folds rendered in relief, seems to be related to Græco-Buddhist drapery, in spite of differences which are chiefly due to the difference in the material represented. But though in all their details these figures are related to Græco-Buddhist art, their style is totally different. They have become wholly Indian. We can trace the origin of each detail, but the whole has a new and living harmony. Harmony, proportion, and balance seem to be the predominant characteristics of these works, and they do not exclude elasticity, life, or the delicate, vigorous treatment of the face.

While Græco-Buddhist art was developing on the borders of India and the art of Mathura, followed by that of the Guptas, in the north, there was an art in the south known as the art of Amaravati (roughly from the second to the fourth century; Pls. IX, B, and XVI, C). Various styles seem to arise in succession in this art, yet it keeps a strong general unity.

By its position in the artistic development of India, the art of Amaravati is transitional, but it has none of the factitious air usually produced by the artificial combination of various tendencies. Elements which at first seem contradictory are intimately blended in it so as to form one of the most beautiful and most characteristic arts that India has brought forth. The old naturalism is there, but it has become more delicate (Pl. IX, B). A new sense of movement, in which all the figures are caught up, is very marked. This is perhaps a local tendency, for we shall find it again in the south after the harmony of the classical period. Later it seems as if the Greek harmony absorbed by this art embraced and gave balance to the almost acrobatic suppleness of the female figures, and medallions and other sculptures show amazing composition, in which the figures are as numerous and the tendency to movement is as great as ever. In addition, the charm and grace of the coming age, that of Ajanta, begin to make themselves felt in the elongation and fluidity of forms, in which the signs of feminine beauty are very much accentuated and even provocative (Pl. XVI, C).

It is difficult in the present state of our knowledge to follow the evolution of the school of Amaravati. According to Jouveau-Dubreuil, the most characteristic marks of this art (movement combined with naturalism, faces with very marked features, and absence of representations of Buddha) represent a first style, while the more harmonious, better composed, quieter sculptures are later. Separate mention should be made, without it being possible to place them exactly, of certain less perfect sculptures, perhaps relatively late, in very low relief.

The art of Ajanta (west of India, chiefly, about the sixth century) is represented (Pls. XI–XIV) by the paintings in Caves 1, 2, 16, and 17 at Ajanta and perhaps the frescoes at Bagh and Sigiriya, to which the most ancient paintings of Afghanistan are related, and also by almost contemporary sculptures (those at Ajanta, chiefly in Caves 19 and 26, and at Deogarh, Aihole, and elsewhere). The art of Ajanta is a creative art, which seems to unite the traditions of the north and the south. The harmony, serenity, and balance of the Gupta style of the north, which seem to mark the commencement of the classical period, are combined with the suppleness, grace, and flexibility of the art of Amaravati, but the marks of female beauty are less emphasized and an easy relaxation is introduced into the figures. The old naturalism, which remained in close contact with reality, and the rushing movement have gradually disappeared. A refined, idealized, fairy-tale atmosphere reigns in their place. But I shall examine the general characteristics of these paintings later. Here I shall merely try to define the various styles which can be determined by careful study of the frescoes of this period.

The art of Ellora and Elephanta (Pl. XV), which is found again in other caves in the west and elsewhere in India, is a development of that of Ajanta, and indeed its earliest works may be contemporary with it. On the whole it presents Hinduist tendencies as against the Buddhist tendencies of the art which preceded it. As we have seen in religious sculpture, it retains the harmony of Ajanta but transforms its grace into power. Large figures are set up against a detached background, and the small size of the minor figures accentuates the stature of the principal ones. The superhuman enters the domain of art. Many examples show this combination of harmony and grandeur, which does not exclude suppleness (see above, p. 371); the most remarkable are perhaps the sculptures of Ellora (the Cave of the Avatars and that of Ravana ka Khai, Pl. XV), which present an admirable union of tension and relaxation, and sometimes that mysterious smile of the Ajanta *bodhisattvas* which seems to express serenity and love for all creatures. One should also mention the *trimūrti* and certain figures in the caves of Elephanta, etc., and the contemporary art of Mamallapuram (seventh century)—relief sculpture in the rock and the reliefs of the *rathas* with tall, slender, cold figures of quite a special type.

Here we come to the end of the period with which this volume deals. In order to trace, in very summary fashion, the later developments of the tendencies and main streams of influence which I have mentioned, it will be most effective to study them in special instances. The treatment of Buddha and other divine persons has enabled us to obtain a first view of these lines of development. I shall review them again in an examination of the treatment of the hips, and shall sum them up in the chapter on the evolution of Indian art.

THE EVOLUTION OF THE TRIBHANGA

The danger of a survey such as I have attempted is that it may lay too much weight on the very real diversity of the different periods of Indian art and fail to show the unity which nevertheless connects them. So I shall here, as a parallel to my previous study of the history of the figures of Buddha, try to follow one of the most characteristic attitudes of Indian sculpture—the triple bend, or *tribhanga*.

This attitude, which is a kind of " Praxitelean bend ", seems to combine suppleness with balance, the suppleness being sometimes provocative, sometimes merely sensual, and sometimes relaxed and weary, to symbolize the voluptuous, swaying aspect of Indian art, and we find it all through the history of that art from its birth to our own time (Pl. XVI).

In the very earliest Indian sculpture, at Bharhut, the *tribhanga* is frequent. We find it bound up with the naturalism described above, with an impression of health and direct contact with life, with the fulsome, accentuated forms of the female body which seems to unfold and offer itself in all simplicity, without provocation or coquetry. It remains in evidence at Sanchi (Pl. XVI, A) and at Karli, and corresponds to the whole of the first period of Buddhist religious art. It is particularly marked, with a very definite tendency to sex-appeal, in certain statues of the Mathura type (Pl. XVI, B).

The attitude of the female figure with tilted hips, seizing a branch with one arm held above the head, is found at Bharhut and Sanchi, where it plays an important part in the decoration of the sides of the entrances (Pl. XVI, A). Græco-Buddhist art afterwards takes it up to represent Maya, the mother of Buddha, at the moment of his birth (Pl. X, A). In this way the treatment of the hips so as to form a triple bend enters Græco-Buddhist art and examples of it appear in the Greek style. But it is far more frequently employed in the art of Northern and Southern India. In the second Mathura period Greek influence appears to give harmony, slenderness, and a new springiness to the figures of the Naga kings treated in this way.

At Amaravati the *tribhanga* is constant, and is very highly marked. It does not seem to be merely a relaxing, but a movement of provocation. The crossed position of the legs and the slant of the hips emphasize the slightness of the contact of the body with the ground, while the long lines of the legs, spreading at the top, exaggerate the fullness of the hips (Pl. XVI, C). Thus the *tribhanga* gives the

Amaravati tendency to movement together with the old naturalism, and in addition a more markedly provocative effect and a new harmony and lightness and slenderness in the human figure.

In the art of Ajanta, Gupta harmony, combined with Amaravati grace, gives a less accentuated triple bend in figures which are idealized and less opulent, in which a new sense of relaxation, of lassitude and abandonment, is accompanied by the balance of a figure sinking back on itself (Pls. XIII, XIV). Later, in discussing the connexions between painting and literature in the Ajanta period, I shall attempt to show all that is expressed by this triple bend in one of the finest periods of Indian art.

In the art of Ellora and Elephanta, the evolution which I have already described gives the *tribhanga* less grace and more strength, while preserving its balance (Pl. XV).

Later, in the south, figures, at first a little cold, soon reveal a love of movement and violence and at the same time become hard and stiff. The dancing Siva shows these tendencies, while keeping the old balance. Other figures are overloaded with decoration, prancing animals and the like. In this evolution, the triple movement is exaggerated and strained, and sometimes the hips are merely tilted while the torso remains straight, so that the figure soon becomes rigid (Pl. XVI, D). In the north, on the other hand, the suppleness is what prevails, especially in the erotic scenes in the temples, and the triple bend is very marked, although soft and graceful. These figures (Bhuvanesvar, Konarak, Khajuraho) have profound charm (Pl. XVI, E), but they have lost their grandeur and tend to be feeble. Presently they become rigid and petrified. The slender, graceful *tribhanga* hardens, like the jewellery, which no longer hangs according to the laws of gravity, but forms lines of decoration. This is the *tribhanga* which, through Nepal, entered Tibet, where it has survived to the present day.

Like the figure of Buddha, the triple bend will show us the lines along which the art of India spread. Northwards, we find the Gupta *tribhanga* and that of Ajanta at Dandan Uiliq in Central Asia,[1] at T ien Lung Shan in China, and at Horyuji in Japan. Later we find it, transformed, in figures

[1] CCCVII, fig. 283.

of Indian tendency at Tun Huang on the borders of China. Still later, in a slender, hardened form, it enters Nepal and Tibet. In all these districts of Central Asia and Tibet where we find belated Græco-Buddhist influences mingled with those of Persia, China, and India, the *tribhanga* marks the Indian contribution, accompanies the Indian style, and so is carried with certain waves of influence to China and Japan.

On the sea route the *tribhanga* likewise points to Indian influence. It also shows—and this is very important—by its disappearance, the reaction of local influences. These local arts, as they move further away from their Indian prototypes, gradually reject the sloping-hipped figures in favour of upright, hieratic statues. This development is found in all the arts of Indo-China and the islands, varying in speed and strength according to the creative power of each. The earliest styles also produce upright figures, but, as in India, they generally surround them with figures with slanting hips. Afterwards these latter, which are contrary to local tendencies, are rare or disappear altogether.

In Java the difference between the two great periods is very marked. In the first (the art of Central Java, eighth to tenth century) the triple movement is constantly represented and the connexion with India is emphasized by the likeness of the slanting-hipped figure of Chandi Pawon in Java and the Ganga at Besnagar in India.[1] In the second (Eastern Java, thirteenth to fifteenth centuries) straight, hieratic figures are very frequent and the *tribhanga* is exceptional.

In the art of Dvaravaṭi in Siam the use of the *tribhanga* in Buddhist figures derived from Gupta art is represented by the Buddhas of Préi Krabas, which were found in Cambodia but belong to the art of Siam. It is not long before these figures tend to frontality. The *tribhanga* is, however, sometimes preserved (in a clumsy, exaggerated form, as if it no longer answered to the fundamental needs of the art which employs it), even in sculptures of Brahmanic style which seem to be copied from straight, hieratic pre-Angkor statues of Cambodia.

In Khmer art properly so called the evolution is still

[1] Ibid., fig. 177.

more rapid. Only the small statues, chiefly female, which seem to be the oldest in pre-Angkor art, definitely show the hip-effect, and it is already a stiff pose, the movement of which does not spread throughout the body. In the large pre-Angkor statues surrounded by an arch (seventh century) the *tribhanga* is barely perceptible, and the Khmer statues become upright and hieratic, observing the law of frontality, and remain so all through Khmer art, in which the triple bend is almost unknown. Here we have a striking example of Indian influences being quickly rejected by a local art with a strong character of its own.

CHAPTER IV

The Evolution of Indian Art

If we bring together the various lines of development which we have been following separately, Indian art presents itself to us as follows.

Before Indian art properly so called and Indian civilization (the belief in transmigration, the escape from *saṃsāra*, Buddhism, etc.) came into being, there grew up in the pre-Aryan period in the valley of the Indus an art (that of Mohenjo-Daro and Harappa) which seems to be connected with the great group of Susiana and Sumer (Pl. I). It was represented by large towns, many seals, sculpture, pottery, jewels, etc.

True Indian art appears about the third century B.C. Its sudden advent may have been due to a change-over from wood to permanent materials, but it does not seem to have had a very long past. There was a local art, and there were importations from outside. The local art is represented, in architecture, by the imitation of wood construction (octagonal columns without capital or base, horse-shoe arches over windows, stepped cornices, railings, etc., Pl. II); in sculpture, by a lively naturalism which simplifies forms and keeps in close contact with reality (Pls. VI; VIII, A; IX, A); in religious art, by Buddhist works in which the symbols (Pl. VI) and the representations of Jātakas (Pl. IX, A) are constant and Buddha is never represented (Pl. VI); and in decoration by heavy water-plants in high relief, open flowers, and hanging garlands (Pl. V, B). Imported art brings to architecture the bell capital (Pl. VIII, B) and the addorsed animals; to sculpture, a finished technique and fanciful animals, sometimes treated in a cold, academic manner; and to decoration, various motives—lions, griffins, garlands, palmettes, etc. (Pl. V, C). These two currents first run separate, and then combine, the general aspect remaining fundamentally Indian (Pl. VI). On the entrances of the Great Stupa of Sanchi and on pillars the two kinds of decoration are found together (Pl. V, B and C), and on another pillar of the same monument, representing the heavens one above the other, both kinds of architecture alternate—palaces with octagonal columns having no capital or base and surmounted by a cornice with horseshoe niches, and palaces whose columns have Persepolitan bell-capitals with addorsed animals on top (Pl. V, A).

In architecture the union of the two currents seems to be effected in the cave at Karli (perhaps the first century of our era, Fig. 3). The local current with its naturalism maintains itself in the sculpture of the school of Mathura.

Parallel to the art of Mathura, Græco-Buddhist art develops in the north-west (perhaps from the first century B.C. to the fifth of our era). It is more Hellenistic than Indian (Pls. VII, A; VIII, C and D; X), and at first it illustrates Buddhist themes by stock types of Hellenistic Asia (Pl. VII, A; X) and is quite unlike the fundamentally Indian art of Sanchi, Karli, and Mathura, which is direct and full of life. But it seems to become gradually imbued with a new youth and to tend to form an independent art (Pl. VIII, C and D). In religious art the foreign element appears in the creation of a type of Buddha (Pl. VII, A), which brings with it the creation of a new religious art, in which Buddha himself is shown and even his death is represented.

Græco-Buddhist influences seem to have hardly touched architecture or decoration, except in the short-lived style of Kashmir. But on sculpture and painting, religious and profane, they appear to have had a considerable effect. Græco-Buddhist art spread over part of what is now Afghanistan, whence it afterwards reached Central Asia. In India, Græco-Buddhist sculpture and religious art first affected that of Mathura, and afterwards that of Amaravati, as a diffused influence. Later, in the Gupta art of the north (Pl. VII, E), its influence continued to be more direct, being a sort of new leaven which the art of India absorbed without losing anything of its own character.

Parallel to Græco-Buddhist art and that of Mathura, although perhaps on the whole a little later than the latter, there developed in the south the art of Amaravati (second to fourth century, Pls. IX, B, and XVI, C). In this art the various old tendencies are mingled, the different ways of representing the divine exist side by side, the idealization of the figures of Ajanta begins to make itself felt, and an astonishing sense of movement grows up. But these very different tendencies form a single whole, which is alive, original, and thoroughly Indian.

Meanwhile architecture and decoration develop. The *stūpas* and *dāgabas* rise higher, their domes gradually become bell-shaped, and their surfaces are covered with sculpture (Pl. III, B). The narrow part of the capital is drawn in tighter (Fig. 4) and the decorative motives change.

What is known as " classical " art is at first represented, as a sort of prelude, by the Gupta Buddhist figures (Pl. VII, E), which owe their component elements to Græco-Buddhist art, but present a general aspect which is Indian, in which balance, harmony, suppleness, and serenity predominate (perhaps fifth century).

At this time Indian art receives hardly any influence from outside. It tends to concentrate on its own resources, and to expand and influence other countries. In a first period of the classical style, which I have called the art of Ajanta, painting and sculpture (Pls. XI–XIV) show Gupta harmony combined with the sinuous grace of Amaravati. Naturalism has disappeared, a new relaxed effect has come in, and scenes based on real life have given place to an idealized fairy-tale world. The Buddhas now wear only a thin, transparent garment without folds (Pl. III, A).

After the art of Ajanta a second classical period, which I have called the art of Ellora (probably eighth to tenth century ; Pl. XV) presents a new aspect. The accent becomes Brahmanic more than Buddhist ; the harmony and suppleness remain, but strength takes the place of gracefulness ; the superhuman appears ; the principal figures are larger, and are shown against a detached background. There is a similar sculpture, in which, however, the figures are slenderer and colder, in the south, at Mamallapuram.

Architecture and decoration have developed. We find great ornamented horse-shoe arches, *kuḍu* cornices, turban capitals, elongated slabs at the tops of columns, and pillars in which the various elements are combined in every variety of fanciful manner (Figs. 5–8, 10–15), while reliefs representing scenes often take the place of the old decorative motives.

Buildings made of permanent materials appear—square or oblong *cellæ* of stone (Figs. 19, 20) and towers of brick, which become higher and more elaborate (Fig. 23).

In the south, the *cella* grows yet higher, as a *vimāna* (Fig. 21) and then assumes a flatter shape, as a *gopura* (Fig. 22), and architecture becomes more and more rigid and overladen with ornament. In the north, the tower, with smaller buildings round it, becomes taller, with an incurved line (Fig, 24), and then stiffens. In sculpture, sacred and profane, the coldness of Mamallapuram is maintained in the south until it surrenders to violence, frenzy, tension, and exaggerated lines, which become stiff and angular (Pl. XVI, D). Meanwhile, in the north (Pl. XVI, E), grandeur is succeeded by a rather insipid grace (erotic scenes, etc.), and this grace in its turn becomes set and rigid in Bengal, and subsequently in Nepal and Tibet. The Moslem invasions bring into being and develop an Indo-Persian art which we shall not discuss here. Horror and violence, which have made their way into literature and various religions, find artistic expression in certain aspects of the Dravidian style of the south, in the Tantric tendencies of Sivaism in the north, and in the Buddhism of Tibet, under the influence of Tantrism.

Great streams of influence flow to China, by the sea in the south and by the silk route in the north. It seems that on the sea route the arts are derived from Indian influence but shake it off fairly soon—the art of Dvaravati in Siam, which chiefly continues Gupta Buddhist traditions, the Khmer art of Cambodia, which soon develops a character of its own, the art of Champa in Annam, and Javanese art, which seems to be related to the style of the ancient caves of Ellora and that of Bengal. These arts affect each other, and there are cross-currents of influence. There is the same evolution everywhere, though it varies in speed and extent. The local arts acquire their own character and become independent. They move away from Indian art, they become hieratic, they lose something of their perfection and of their grace and beauty in giving up the hip-effect, the symbol of India, but they gain a new life and strength by coming more into touch with local traditions. In the art of Champa, the styles of Dong Duong and the late styles seem to be opposed to the style of Mi-son. Among the Khmers, although the development is continuous, Angkor art is different from pre-Angkor art, and at the time of the Bayon (end of the twelfth century) art, now less perfect, turns to the observation of local life. The art of Central Java (eighth to tenth centuries) is followed by that of Eastern Java (thirteenth to fifteenth centuries), with its peculiar decoration and its profile figures, which are akin to the Wayangs, the figures of the puppet-theatre. At Dvaravati the evolution is similar, although less apparent; the invasion of the Thais, affecting the countries all round Siam, creates, from the thirteenth and fourteenth centuries onwards, a different art, a continuation of the previous traditions in an altered form, which becomes rigid and is repeated with little variation in Burma, Siam, Cambodia, and Laos.

In the meantime, by the north, along the silk route, the influence of Græco-Buddhist art in its new form may have reached the China of the Wei period. The influence of late Græco-Buddhist and Gupta art, followed by that of Ajanta, spread into Afghanistan and a little later, beyond all doubt, into China, where it appears at Yun Kang and Lung Men and was predominant at T'ien Lung Shan. Ajanta also influenced Central Asia and Tibet and reached Horyuji in Japan. At this time, in Central Asia, influences from India, Persia, and China, met and mingled with Græco-Buddhist survivals; art tended to acquire an independent appearance, but does not seem to have survived beyond the tenth century. In Tibet, on the other hand, it is in late works, chiefly paintings and bronzes, that we see ancient Indian and Chinese influences, with perhaps a certain Persian ingredient. India, which affects the figures rather than the backgrounds, asserts itself in successive waves—the art of Ajanta, the art of Bengal, Rajput miniature-painting—and the oldest traditions of all, those of Ajanta, remain marvellously true to themselves, almost to our own day, as it were petrified in that astonishing country.

CHAPTER V

INDIAN ÆSTHETICS. THE FRESCOES OF AJANTA AND THE SANSKRIT DRAMA

I SHALL conclude this study of the art of India by an attempt to determine certain peculiarities of its spirit by examining its relations with contemporary literature at the high-watermark of Indian civilization.

Thus I shall try to point out what connexions there are between the frescoes of Ajanta and Sanskrit poetry and drama. That poetry and that drama are especially connected with painting, and it is at the beginning of the so-called "classical" period that the connexion seems to be most marked. Fortunately a series of paintings of that very period survives in Caves 1, 2, 16, and 17 at Ajanta. Some of my observations, it is true, will extend beyond the domain of Ajanta and will not apply to the classical Sanskrit drama alone. But it is chiefly in the Ajanta frescoes, both in the composition of scenes and in the treatment of isolated figures, that we shall find the union of a classical kind of balance and harmonious serenity with suppleness and an astonishing fluidity of line, a union of contraries which are at once highly accentuated and intimately blended, which is perhaps the distinctive mark of the Indian genius (Pls. XI–XIV).

The same union and opposition are found in music. While a rigid system and strict rules lay down the modes, indicate the notes to be stressed or omitted, and prescribe the ornaments required for each environment, freedom and elasticity are restored by later rules. Certain notes must be omitted in a rising passage but may be taken lightly in a falling one; there are several ways of approaching one or another note; in some cases one can choose between several fancies or ornaments. So the fluidity of musical line is restored.

A similar phenomenon is presented by the language of literature, Sanskrit. It is a highly elaborate system of construction, and roots are of great importance, prefixes and suffixes being attached to them by very strict rules. There could hardly be a more rational, stricter, more rigidly constructed language. At first the whole seems to be organized so as to give the mind the greatest possible satisfaction in intellectual balance. But the construction comes to be as it were wrapped in rules which are intended to soften its rigidity. Words change their form according to what precedes or follows them ; two successive vowels are combined so as to become long or to alter completely ; words are amalgamated in this way. The sentence becomes continuous, being marked by the musical rhythm of longs and shorts ; hardnesses and jars have vanished. Here again, the line has become fluid and supple ; the skeleton remains, but the resonance of the flexible sentence covers it like living flesh.

It is the same with the paintings at Ajanta. The scenes, which are admirably composed, are not separated from each other by the uncompromising straight lines which one often finds in Italian frescoes, such as those in the Arena chapel at Padua. There is no break between one scene and the next. One runs into another, and the first impression of the visitor is one of confusion. The wall seems to be covered from end to end by a single scene containing too many figures. Like the long musical passage, made flexible by the various possibilities sometimes allowed to the musician, and like the long Sanskrit sentence, made continuous by the combination of words according to the rules of euphony, the long surface of wall forms a single uninterrupted whole. But the observant eye soon sees that the scenes are concentrated upon themselves and are separated, not by their edges, for they have none, but by their centres (Pls. XI–XII). The chief persons are grouped together, and minor figures form a frame to them. The effect of the tilted hips makes it possible to end each scene without an abrupt barrier (Pl. XI, top right). Thus the woman holding a yak's-tail fly-flapper (Pl. XII, top left), by her triple movement and the position of her face, turned towards the chief figures in the scene, leads the eye to the centre of the composition. Elsewhere (same scene, right) the end of the scene is marked by a pair of figures between columns, which balances the groups. A figure with its back to the spectator (Pl. XII, bottom left) separates two compositions placed one above the other and directs attention to the chief figures of the whole of which it is part. Figures belonging to adjoining scenes often stand quite close together, but face in different directions. There is no mechanical repetition, but a spirit of fancy which does not preclude good composition and amazing balance of the figures. One passes easily in a continuous movement from one scene to another, the elements of which are grouped round a new centre. So, in painting as in music and in language, we find carefully composed balance of each part and smooth fluidity of the whole.

In the theatre likewise groupings are carefully studied and the passage from one scene to the next is very easy. No drama is more plastic than the Sanskrit drama of the Ajanta period. It is given up almost entirely to the portrayal of love, and by studying it we shall be able, not to understand the stories told on the walls of the caves, but to feel the spirit which they breathe, not at all the spirit of the preceding art, but one of idealized life, refined and amorous, which we also find in the theatre. The Sanskrit play is divided into a good many acts, and the greater part of each act is usually one long plastic scene, a pleasing, motionless group of characters, like a *tableau vivant*—the first meeting, the love-scene, the distress of the deserted maiden when caught painting the portrait of her beloved (*Ratnāvalī,* Act II), the hero or heroine sick with love and tended by the confidant or serving-woman (*Śakuntalā*). The hero with the fool, his confidant, on the one side and the heroine with her woman on the other often balance each other. Sometimes one of these groups spies on the other unseen (*Vāsavadattā,* Act IV; *Śakuntalā,* Act III). The author seems to have wanted to keep a harmonious composition of figures motionless before the spectators for a long time. In the best-known of all Sanskrit dramas, *Śakuntalā,* there are seven chief scenes, plastic scenes, corresponding to the seven acts—the meeting of the King and Sakuntala; the King's conversation with his confidant; the love-sickness of Sakuntala, discovered by the King, who is in hiding, and its cure; Sakuntala's departure and farewells; her meeting with the King, who does not recognize her; his regret as her portrait brings her back to his memory; and the final meeting of the lovers when the curse has been dispelled.

In the Sanskrit drama the plot and scenes of movement are usually relegated to a prologue, where they are merely related, and to pass from one place to another or from the prologue to the plastic group a few steps on the part of the actor are all that is necessary.

So we see that the stage presents both strong emphasis on the composition of groups, which remain motionless for a long time (what I have called plastic scenes), and extreme fluidity in passing from one scene to another. We note the likeness to the composition of the frescoes, and naturally think that the theatre must have influenced painting or vice versa.

This plastic sense in the drama appears also in the descriptive verses. Stanzas of verse occur at intervals in the text and they often describe the beauty of the hero and heroine, their attitudes, or sports (*Śakuntalā*, Acts I, III, etc.). Sometimes characters are thus portrayed before they appear on the stage. We at once feel that what these stanzas call up is the pliant, refined poses of the frescoes. The characters of the drama are at once conventional and typical figures, remote from realism and having the charm of the fairy-tale or the Italian Comedy—hero, heroine, and their respective confidants. The hero's confidant is also the fool, greedy, cowardly, and bursting with curiosity like a ripe pomegranite. The same atmosphere and similar types are found in the paintings. There is no realism, there is no play of the features expressing joy or sorrow, but there are idealized types, beautiful (the hero and heroine) or grotesque (the palace dwarfs etc.), and a technique which makes use of line and pose rather than of facial expression.

Certain paintings at Ajanta might be those described on the stage, where the stock figures whom I have just mentioned speak of the fresco hall of the palace. Thus, the fool cries to the hero, "King, let your eyes behold! On the ornate wall of the inner crystal chamber, the King is painted playing at dice with the Queen. There is Nagavali, who carries the betel-box; there is Prabhañjanika, waving the fly-flapper; there is the dwarf Nagarakanthaka, and here is Taparakarna the monkey" (*Viddhaśāla-bhāñjika*).

Elsewhere the bearer of the fly-flapper is described as carrying it over her shoulder, and in another play the fool speaks of a young woman hidden behind the pillars. We have descriptions of pleasure-pavilions, where the smoke of aloe perfumes goes up, and strings of pearls hang from pillars (*Priyadarśikā*, Act III), and doves flutter down, and grand couches are set out. Elsewhere scenes of dancing are described. In the frescoes of Ajanta we see those pavilions with the festoons of pearls, the King and Queen on grand couches (Pl. XII), the dancing (Pl. XII, bottom right), the young woman hiding behind the pillars (Pl. XII, right), the woman with the fly-flapper on her shoulder (Pl. XII, left), and the bearer of the betel-box (Pl. XI, bottom right ?). On the stage and on the frescoed walls there is always the same world, the love-story in an unreal fairy-land.

The importance of painting and its connection with poetry and the drama are also proved by the constant mention of it by poets and playwrights. We have seen the descriptions of halls adorned with frescoes. At the beginning of the *Little Clay Cart* the clown, as he picks for food right and left, likens himself to a painter among his paint-pots. The portrait of the hero or heroine is often introduced on the stage. At a wedding the bride or bridegroom, if too far away to take part in the ceremony, may be represented by a portrait (*Vāsavadattā*, Act VI). It is sometimes at the sight of a portrait that the hero or heroine falls in love. The King, who has allowed Sakuntala to go away in consequence of a curse, mourns before her picture, which he is finishing and which the fool describes (*Śakuntalā*, Act VI). These pictures are not portraits as we understand the word. They seem never to show the individual imperfections and other marks by which one person can be distinguished from the general type to which he or she belongs. It is rather by the very perfection of their beauty that the hero recognizes the heroine and she him.

Sanskrit poetry incessantly returns to describing woman, and that description can be applied to the female figures at Ajanta. The lady of the poems has gone to the gazelles for her timid, moving eyes, which reach in curved lines to her ears, eyes with large pupils glancing sidelong and shaded by great lids with the graceful curve of the bow. The blue of her eyes makes that of the lotus look pale. Beside her lips, red as the bimba-fruit, coral seems white. Her hair, on her head and elsewhere, is blue-black like a cloud or a swarm of bees. Her complexion surpasses gold, her face and her body, rubbed with saffron, have the brightness of the moon. Her neck is curved like a conch. She sinks under the weight of her breasts, which are like inverted pots of gold and beautiful as the boss of an elephant's forehead, and project so far that they hide her navel. Her waïst is lithe as a leopard's and so slender that it can be held in the hand of a child, and her hips, like chariot-wheels, are so wide that two arms cannot enfold them. There are three creases in her stomach and her legs have the swell of a quiver. So Bhartrihari, Dandin, and others. This ideal of loveliness corresponds, in rather exaggerated and perhaps late form, to that of the Ajanta paintings (Pl. XIII). These female figures, in literature and in frescoes alike, are often adorned with garlands of flowers and gems. They wear rings (*nupura*) on their ankles, their belts have fringes and little bells which lie against their hips, the charm of their bosoms is enhanced by strings of pearls, and their arms and wrists are adorned with bangles, their ears with earrings, and their hair with a diadem (*Priyadarśikā*, Act III). So as they walk they are surrounded by jinglings, which, so the poets say, are answered by the tinkle of the festoons of pearls hanging from the golden pillars.

The union of pliancy and balance which we have found to be characteristic of the music of India and its language, its drama and its plastic composition, we find here again, in these feminine figures and their movements, in which elasticity, suppleness, and lassitude are combined with harmony. From the creepers swaying in the breeze, the Sanskrit poets say of woman, she has taken the litheness of her body and the grace of her gestures ; her nonchalant, well-balanced gait, rendered slow by the size of her hips, is that of the flamingos ; her moving eyes are those of gazelles ; her arms are pliant branches ; her neck, like the pigeon's, bends to one side ; her hands come together in a cup for greeting ; her voice is that of the *kokila* (*Raghuvaṃśa*, viii, 58, etc.). The lassitude of the hot season adds to her grace, but " the heat does not produce in young women such an enchanting languor" (*Śakuntalā*, Act III); the beads of sweat which follow the delight of the senses are a garland to her and her half-closed eyes shine; "weariness gives her an air yet more charming." Full of love, she speaks slowly, very slowly.

It is this lassitude which makes the body so readily assume the triple bend, the *tribhanga*, which Indian art has given to its most beautiful figures all through its history (see above, p. 380). In the *tribhanga*, pliancy and balance are united. The female figures at Ajanta, by their suppleness and their nonchalant grace, seem to indicate self-surrender, voluptuous delight, and languor; by their balance, which often looks like a backward movement, they appear to express a modesty which makes them as it were recoil upon themselves. This union of contraries, which seems to me to be characteristic of the greatest works of art, and which here consists of passion and self-surrender on the one hand and modesty on the other (Pl. XIII), struck me at my first sight of the feminine figures of Ajanta. For a moment I feared that my imagination was leading me astray, but literature afterwards confirmed my impression. "My body," says Sakuntala, "goes forward, and my mind, which is not at one with it, turns back." The King, speaking of Sakuntala, says more definitely, "Love, its impulse checked by restraint, is neither shown by her nor concealed." Of another woman, a poet says, "In her weakening body, love and shame balance each other at the two ends of her soul" (Tiruvalluva), and yet another is "full of modesty and at the same time shaken by desire". Flights and sudden returns, coquetry and tenderness are constantly expressed in poetry and drama as in painting. The heroine's gaze is at once modest and passionate, her voice is now soft, now ardent, in her are joy and fear, she is now carried away by daring, now held back by modesty, now urged on by desire, now driven away by fear. In the *Nāgānanda*, if it is correctly translated, these contrasts are emphasized by the stage-directions: the heroine looks at the hero "with a mixture of desire and modesty", or "with a mixture of joy and modesty", or as she leaves the stage "she casts a glance at once modest and passionate".

This union in single characters of balance and suppleness,

which often leads to the attitude of the *tribhanga*, does not only express fleshly love, even in its refined form. We find it in flying and prostrate figures, and again in the great *bodhisattvas* of Cave 1 at Ajanta (Pl. XIV). At the end of this cave, their attitude serves to frame the sanctuary without closing it abruptly, just as that of the women carrying fly-flappers divides scenes without making a break. The hips tilt down away from the sanctuary while the head is turned towards it, thus leading the eye to it. These *bodhisattvas* are very like the female figures, for in the Ajanta period the sexes are not highly differentiated—another form of the union of contraries. In almost all the great ages of artistic balance—the fifth century in Greece, the thirteenth century in France, the Italian Renaissance, the classical period in India, the Khmer art of the Bayon—masculine strength and balance are found combined with feminine grace and suppleness in figures of indefinite sex, without these deep-rooted æsthetic tendencies being necessarily connected with any moral perversity. In the *bodhisattvas* of Ajanta the breadth and balance of volumes and the very broad treatment of light and dark is combined with the bending effect of the *tribhanga*, and the serene expression of the faces seems to be mingled with one of melancholy and profound tenderness. What is united modesty and fire in the amorous woman seems to become in the *bodhisattvas* complete detachment from the outer world and concentration inwards in the equilibrium and serenity of meditation, intimately mingled with infinite compassion, tenderness, and love for all suffering creatures.

Later, in literature as in art, we shall find the same tendencies with a love of size and also, presently, of frenzy and horror. Kalidasa was all grace and proportion; Bhavabhuti, who comes next, will already show in his plays frequent swoons and a taste for violent dramatic effect; later still, scenes of burning-grounds and frightful combats will be usual. In art the same tendencies are found, as we have seen, in the relief of Vishnu rending the blasphemer (p. 372). We find them in the Underworld at Angkor Wat (Cambodia, twelfth century), with its frenzied movements and varied torments, very unlike the mild Underworld of Borobudur (Java, eighth century). We find them, too, in Dravidian art, in the representations of Kali, in Tibetan Tantrism (furious wrestlings with Sakti, bloody emblems, skulls), etc. Perhaps these tendencies, both in art and in literature, are to be compared to the morbid taste which developed at the end of the Middle Ages in Europe, to which we owe the Dances of Death and the tomb-figures of bodies eaten by worms.

CONCLUSION

AT the beginning of this book I warned the reader against over-simplified conceptions of India and all that it means. I have said, more than once, that India is in every respect a chaos. The summary nature of this work has compelled us to present the facts, problems, and many factors which make up Indian civilization as being much simpler than they really are. Let us remember, as we come to an end, that what gives form to all this diversity, all this development, is Brahmanic classicism.

The imposition of that form on the "Hindu" material was never so effective as to create either uniformity or tyranny. The dominion of the priestly caste no more stifled other castes and all the variety of other sects than Sanskrit literature impeded other means of expression, and the unity of the plastic style was only an ideal, like the validity of the written law. Life breaks out from rules, and does not cease to proliferate in capricious growths, just as it perpetuates ancient types, long obsolete, among later types, more highly developed. So the "Young India" of our day comes to regard as "broad-mindedness"—in the sense of liberalism—what is really indefinite fecundity of natural genius.

The decoration, sculptural and architectural, of the monuments illustrates processes of composition similar to those manifested in the systems of religion or of abstract thought. Sculptures and paintings everywhere present jumbled masses, imagination run riot, but within symmetrical arrangements. Theories are full of fantastic conceptions, but these are classified under headings governed by analogy. Often richness is accepted as beauty and abundance as truth. If we Europeans prefer those Indian works in which the line seems simpler, let us bear in mind that in judging so we are acting as heirs to Greek æsthetics or logic, and are therein departing from the principles of *alaṃkāra,* sovereign in this land.

India puts things together and co-ordinates them without assimilating them. That is why its civilization preserves barbaric elements more than it transforms them, and mingles them with others far more refined. It loves art passionately, without ever opposing it to nature, doubtless because nature in that country is like art in its creative exuberance. Religious belief and philosophic reflection partake of the nature of art, because they claim, not to treat of a real, independent of thought, but to establish modes of existence by means of the autonomous activity of the mind. Nowhere has the "spiritual life" been as intense as in this civilization, which has hardly ever believed in an immaterial soul. We must not be too much surprised to find that India equally systematically sought pleasure and fought against pleasure, in the manner, one might say, of Bhartrihari. The fanatic of renunciation masters the vital forces only in order to possess them better, that he may acquire, through the resources which they give him if he concentrates them, miraculous powers.

Dives and Lazarus rub shoulders, zeal for fullness and passion for emptiness stand face to face for ever. Let us make our choice without blaming India for the lack of measure in its spirit—which, indeed, as I have pointed out, proceeds according to canons of right conduct. In Greece, ontology has its limits—the nature of essences—and logic has its limits, those drawn by definition. But India dedicates itself to the unlimited because it always operates, even when it seeks to know. When it succeeds in avoiding anarchy, it is because it has found, in its very action, principles of order and guarantees of objectivity.

A. Great Stupa of Sanchi.

(*From a photograph by V. Goloubew*)

B. Cave at Bhaja.

(*From a photograph by Major H. S. Wauchope*)

AJANTA

A. Exterior of Cave 19.

B. Interior of Cave 26.

(*From photographs by E. H. Hunt*)

A. The *Rathas,* Mamallapuram.

(*From a photograph by V. Goloubew*)

B. Temple, Aihole

(*From* Coomaraswamy, *History of Indian and Indonesian Art*)

PLATE V

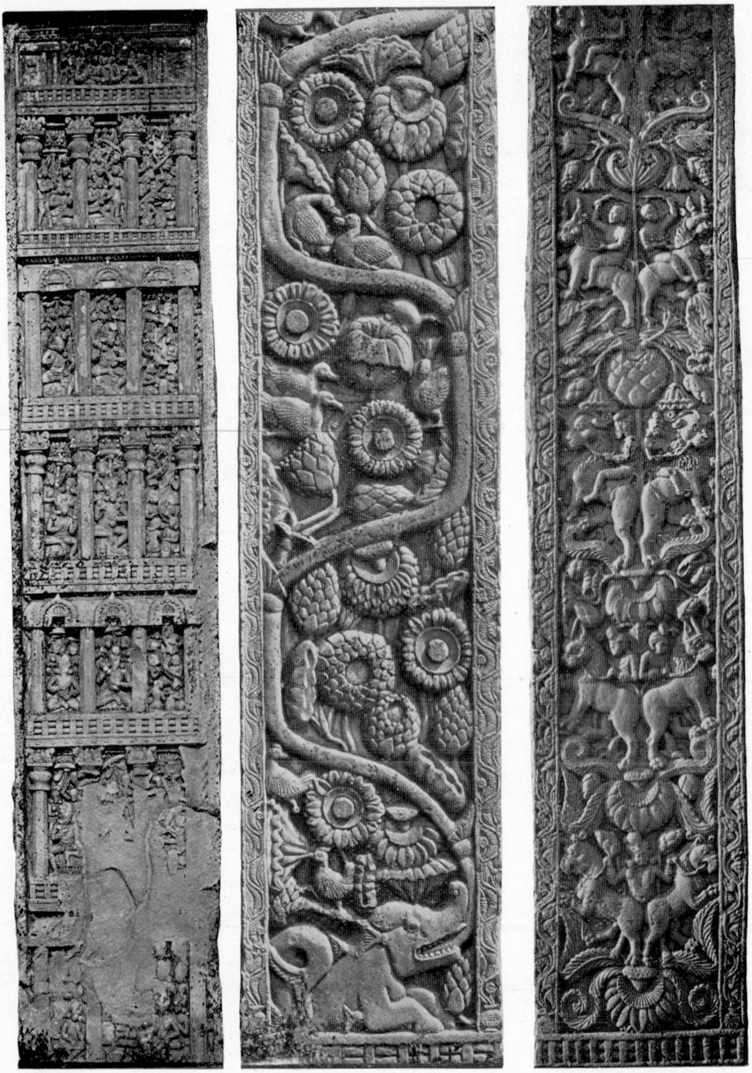

A B C

PILLARS OF THE GREAT STUPA, SANCHI

A. Superimposed heavens. B. Decoration with Indian motives.
C. Decoration with imported motives.

(From photographs by V. Goloubew)

B

A

G

C

D

E

F

GREAT STUPA OF SANCHI. SCENES FROM THE LIFE OF BUDDHA

A. The Departure (lintel). B. Vase of lotuses, symbolizing the Birth. C. The Birth, showing Maya. D. The tree of the Illumination, with empty throne. E. The Wheel of the First Sermon, with worshippers. F. The Wheel of the First Sermon, with empty throne. G. Stupa, symbolizing Parinirvāṇa.

PLATE VII

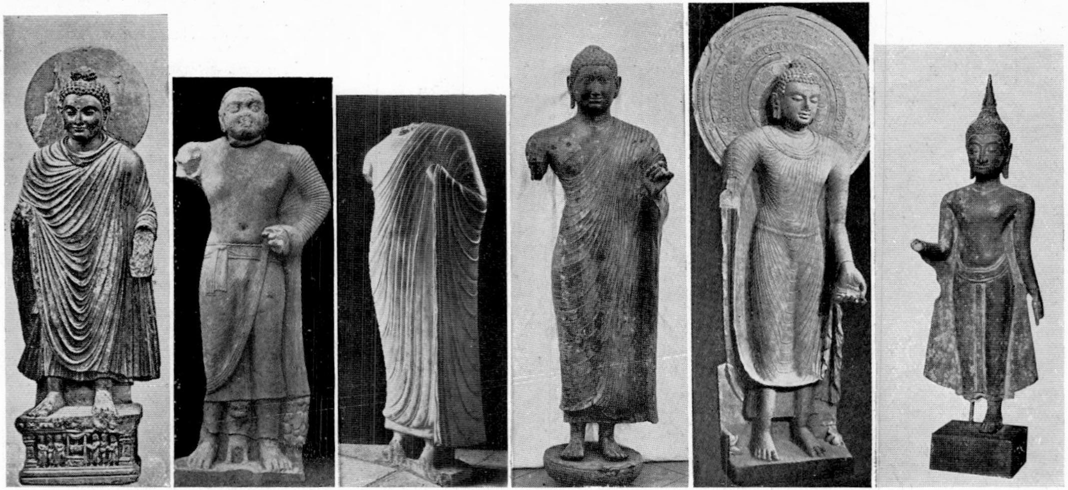

A B C D E F

THE EVOLUTION OF THE FIGURE OF BUDDHA

A. Graeco-Buddhist Buddha (from Foucher, *Art gréco-bouddhique du Gandhâra*). B. Buddha-Bodhisattva from Mathura (from Coomaraswamy, *History of Indian and Indonesian Art*). C. Buddha from Amaravati (*from a photograph by V. Goloubew*). D. Buddha from Dong-duong. E. Buddha of Gupta style (from Coomaraswamy, *op. cit.*). F. Late Siamese Buddha (*in the Musée Guimet*).

Plate VIII

A

B

C

D

A. Head from Pataliputra (from Coomaraswamy, *op. cit.*).
B. Asoka capital (from Bachhofer, *Early Indian Sculpture*).
C. Head from Hadda (excavations of the French Delegation in Afghanistan ; M. Barthoux).
D. Relief from Hadda. The Departure of Buddha.

(*Nos. C. and D. from blocks of the Musée Guimet representing objects preserved there.*)

A. Jataka of the Great Ape, Bharhut.

B. The Gods taking Buddha's Alms-bowl to heaven. Amaravati.

(Both from photographs of the India Office)

PLATE X

A. The Birth of Buddha.

B. The Visit of Indra.

GRAECO-BUDDHIST SCULPTURE

(From Foucher, *Art gréco-bouddhique du Gandhâra*)

AJANTA

Painting in Cave 1, left wall.

(From a photograph by V. Goloubew)

AJANTA
Painting in Cave 1, left wall.
(*From a photograph by V. Goloubew*)

Plate XIII

Female Figures, Cave 1, back wall. Daughters of Mara and a figure beside the large Bodhisattva.

(From photographs by V. Goloubew)

BODHISATTVA, AJANTA, Cave 1, back wall.

(From a photograph by V. Goloubew)

DANCING SIVA, ELLORA, RAVANA KA KHAI

(*From a photograph by* E. H. *Hunt*)

A B C D E

THE EVOLUTION OF THE TRIBHANGA

A. Sanchi. B. Mathura (from Bachhofer, *Early Indian Sculpture*). C. Amaravati. D. Late Dravidian art. E. Northern art. (A and B from *photographs by V. Goloubew*; D and E from *photographs of the Musée Guimet*, representing objects preserved there.)

BIBLIOGRAPHY

GENERAL

MASSON-OURSEL (P.), *Bibliographie sommaire de l'Indianisme*, Isis, No. 8 (vol. iii, 2), Brussels, 1920 I

SCHERMAN (L.), *Orientalische Bibliographie* (begr. v. Aug. Müller), Berlin, 1887, etc. II

INDIAN STUDIES

BARTH (A.), *Œuvres. Quarante ans d'indianisme*, Paris, 1914, 1917, 1918, 1927 III

WINDISCH (E.), *Geschichte der Sanskrit-Philologie und indischen Altertumskunde*, Strasburg, 1917 ; Berlin and Leipzig, 1920 IV

MANUSCRIPTS

AUFRECHT (T.), *Catalogus catalogorum*, 1891, 1896, 1903 . V

CABATON (A.), *Catalogue sommaire des manuscrits sanscrits et pâlis de la Bibliothèque Nationale.* i. *Sanscrits*, 1907 ; ii. *Pâlis*, 1908 ; iii. *Indiens, indochinois et malayo-polynésiens*, 1912 VI

ENCYCLOPÆDIAS

ENCYCLOPÆDIA BRITANNICA VII

BÜHLER (G.) and others, *Grundriss der indo-arischen Philologie und Altertumskunde*, Strasburg, 1896, etc. ; Berlin, 1920, etc. VIII

PERIODICALS

Archæological Survey of India IX

Bulletin de l'École Française d'Extrême-Orient, Hanoï, 1901, etc. X

Giornale della Societa Asiatica Italiana, Florence, 1887, etc. XI

Hindu Thought XII

Indian Antiquary, Bombay, 1872, etc. XIII

Indogermanische Forschungen (Sprach- und Altertumskunde), 1891, etc. XIV

Journal Asiatique, Paris, 1822 XV

Journal of the American Oriental Society, 1843 . . XVI

Journal of the Asiatic Society of Bengal XVII

Journal of the Bombay Branch of the Royal Asiatic Society, 1841 XVIII

Journal of the Pali Text Society, 1882 XIX

Kâvyamâla XX

Journal of the Royal Asiatic Society of Great Britain and Ireland, London, 1834 XXI

Muséon, Louvain, 1881 XXII

Ostasiatische Zeitschrift, 1912 XXIII
Pandit, Benares, 1856 XXIV
Revue de l'Histoire des Religions, Paris XXV
Rivista degli Studi Orientali XXVI
Wiener Zeitschrift für die Kunde des Morgenlandes . XXVII
Zapiski vostotchnago otdieleniia imperatorskago russkago archeologitcheskago obchtchestva, 1886 . . . XXVIII
Zeitschrift der deutschen Morgenländischen Gesellschaft, 1845 XXIX

INTRODUCTION

Physical Geography.

McCrindle, *Ancient India as Described by Ptolemy*, Calcutta, 1927 XXX
Cunningham (A.), *The Ancient Geography of India*, London, 1871 ; Calcutta, 1924 XXXI
Dey (N. L.), *The Geographical Dictionary of Ancient and Mediaeval India*, Calcutta, 1899, 2nd ed., Cal. Orient. Series, 21, 1927 XXXII
Przyluski (J.), *Noms de villes indiennes dans la Géographie de Ptolémée*, Soc. Ling., Paris, 27, fasc. 3, No. 83 . XXXIII
Sion (J.), *Asie des Moussons*, Paris XXXIV

Ethnography and Language.

Baines (A.), *Ethnography*, VIII, 1912 XXXV
Census of India, 1901 and 1911 XXXVI
Grierson (G. A.), *Linguistic Survey of India*, Calcutta, 1903, etc. XXXVII
Meillet (A.) and others, *Les Langues du monde*, Paris, 1924 XXXVIII
Risley (H. H.), *The People of India*, 2nd ed., London, 1915 XXXIX
Ruggeri (G.), *Outlines of a Systematic Anthropology of Asia*, Calcutta, 1921 XL

Predravidians.

Konow (S.), *Munda*, XXXVII XLI
Lévi (S.), *Préaryen et prédravidien*, July, 1923, XV . XLII
Przyluski (J.), *Les Udumbara*, 1926, XV . . . XLIII
—— in XXXVIII XLIV
Rivet (P.), *Le Groupe océanien*, Soc. Ling., Paris, 27, fasc. 3, No. 83 XLV
Schmidt (W.), *Les Peuples môn-khmers*, 1907, X . . XLVI
Skeat and Blagden, *Pagan Races of Malay Peninsula*, 1906 XLVII
Uxbond (F. A.), *Wanderings. The Munda Peoples, a link between Maori and Magyar*, London . . . XLVIII

Dravidians.

Bloch (J.), in XXXVIII XLIX
Brown (G. W.), *The Possibility of a Connection between Mitanni and the Dravidian Languages*, 1930, XVI . L
Caldwell (R.), *A Comparative Grammar of the Dravidian or South-Indian Family of Languages*, 3rd ed., London, 1913 LI

KENNEDY (J.), *The Early Commerce of Babylon with India*, 1898, **XXI** . . . . **LII**
KONOW (S.), *Dravidian*, **XXXVII** . . . . **LIII**

Indo-Europeans, Aryans.

BRUNNHOFER (H.), *Urgeschichte der Arier in Vorder- und Centralasien*, Leipzig, 1893 . . . . . . **LIV**
—— *Arische Urzeit*, Berne, 1910 . . . . **LV**
CARNOY (A.), *Les Indo-Européens*, Brussels and Louvain, 1921 . . . . **LVI**
DUTT (N. K.), *The Aryanisation of India*, Calcutta, 1925 **LVII**
FEIST (S.), *Indogermanen und Germanen*, Halle, 1914 . **LVIII**
GAUTHIOT (R.), *Essai de grammaire sogdienne*, Paris, 1914–23 . . . . **LIX**
GRIERSON (G.), and KONOW (S.), *Indo-Aryan Family*, **XXXVII** . . . . **LX**
KEITH (A. B.), *Early History of the Indo-Iranians*, Poona, 1917 . . . . **LXI**
KONOW (S.), *The Aryan Gods of the Mitani People*, Oslo, 1921 . . . . **LXII**
LA VALLÉE-POUSSIN (L. DE), *Indo-Européens et Indo-Iraniens*, Paris, 1924 . . . . **LXIII**
LÉVI (S.), *Le Tokharien B, langue de Koutcha*, 1913, **XV** . **LXIV**
MEILLET, (A.), *Introduction à l'étude comparée des langues indo-européennes*, 5th ed., Paris, 1922 . . . . **LXV**
—— *Les Dialectes indo-européennes*, 1908 . . . **LXVI**
—— "Le Tokharien," in *Indogermanisches Jahrb.*, 1914 **LXVII**

PART ONE

General History.

COURTILLIER (G.), *Les Anciennes Civilisations de l'Inde*, Paris, 1930 . . . . **LXVIII**
GROUSSET (R.), *Hist. de l'Extrême-Orient*, Paris, 1929 . **LXIX**
LA VALLÉE-POUSSIN (L. DE), *L'Inde aux temps des Mauryas et des Barbares, Grecs, Scythes, Parthes et Yue-tchi*, Paris, 1930 . . . . **LXX**
PARGITER (F. E.), *Ancient Indian Historical Tradition*, Oxford, 1922 . . . . **LXXI**
RAPSON (E. J.), *Ancient India*, Cambridge, 1914. **LXXII**
—— and others, *The Cambridge History of India*. Vol. i. *Ancient India*, Cambridge, 1922 . . . . . **LXXIII**
SMITH (V. A.), *The Early History of India*, 3rd ed., Oxford, 1914 ; 4th ed., 1924 . . . . **LXXIV**
—— *The Oxford History of India*, Oxford, 1919 . . **LXXIV***a*
VAIDYA, *Hist. of Mediaeval Hindu India, from 600 to 1200*, Poona, 1921–6 . . . . **LXXV**

Early Connexions with Western Asia.

BANERJI (A.), *Asura India*, Patna, 1926 . . . **LXXVI**
CHANDA (R.), *Indus Valley in the Vedic Period*, **IX**, 31, 1926 . . . . **LXXVII**
—— *Note on Prehistoric Antiquities from Mohenjo Daro*, Calcutta, 1924 . . . . **LXXVIII**
CHRISTEN (V.), "Beziehungen der altmesopotamischen Kunst zum Osten," in *Wiener Beit. zur K. u. Kulturg. Asiens*, vol. lxiii, 1926 . . . . **LXXIX**

MAITRA (P.), *Prehistoric India*, Calcutta, 1923 . . LXXX
MARSHALL (Sir J.), *Exploration and Research at Harappa and Mohenjo Daro* (**IX**, 1923–4 and 1926) . . LXXXI
—— *Mohenjo-Daro and the Indus Civilization*, London, 1931 LXXXII
WINCKLER (H.), *Vorläufige Nachrichten üb. d. Ausgrabungen in Boghaz-Koi im Sommer* 1907 (*Mitt. d. D. Orientges.*, 35), Dec., 1907 LXXXIII
WUEST (H.), *Über die neuesten Ausgrabungen in N.W. Indien*, 1927, **XXIX** LXXXIV

Connexions with Hellenism.

BANERJEE (G. N.), *Hellenism in Ancient India*, Calcutta, 2nd ed., 1920 LXXXV
CUNNINGHAM (A.), *The Coins of Alexander's Successors in the East*, London, 1873 LXXXVI
FOUCHER (A.), *La Géographie ancienne du Gandhara* **X**, 1901 LXXXVII
—— *Sur la frontière indo-afghane*, Paris, 1901 . . LXXXVIII
GARDNER (P.), *Coins of the Greek and Scythic Kings of Bactria and India, Brit. Mus. Catal.* . . . LXXXIX
GOBLET D'ALVIELLA (E.), *Ce que l'Inde doit à la Grèce*, Paris, 1897 XC
LE COQ (Von), *Auf Hellas Spuren in Ost-Türkistan*, Leipzig, 1926. XCI
LÉVI (J.), *Quid de Græcis veterum Indorum monumenta tradiderint*, Paris, 1890 XCII
RAWLINSON (H. G.), *Bactria*, 1912 XCIII
—— *Intercourse between India and the Western World*, Cambridge, 1916 XCIV
STEIN (Sir A.), "Alexander's Campaign on the Indian N.W. Frontier," in *Geographical Journal*, Nov.–Dec., 1927 XCV
WHITEHEAD (R. B.), *Indo-Greek Coins, Lahore Mus. Catal. I* (Oxford, 1914) XCVI

Connexions with Iran and the Scythians.

PELLIOT (P.), "Influences iraniennes en Asie Centrale et en Extrême. Orient," in *R. d'H. et Lit. rel.*, 1912 . XCVII
SPOONER (D. B.), *The Zoroastrian Period of Indian History*, **XXI**, 1915 XCVIII
BANERJI (R. D.), *The Scythian Period of Ind. Hist.*, **XII**, 1908 XCIX
KONOW (S.), "Indoskythische Beiträge," in *Sitz. d. k. preuss. Ak. d. W.*, 1916 C
LAUFER (B.), *The Language of the Yue-tchi or Indo-Scythians*, 1917 CI
LÉVI (S.), *Notes sur les Indo-Scythes*, 1896–7, **XV** . . CII
THOMAS (F. W.) *Sakastana*, **XXI**, 1906 CIII

Connexions with China.

HERMANN (A.), *Die Verkehrungswege zwischen China, Indien und Rom um 100 n. C.*, Leipzig, 1922 . . CIV
LÉVI (S.), *Notes chinoises sur l'Inde*, **X**, 1905, 253 . . CV

PELLIOT (P.), *Les Anciens Itinéraires chinois dans l'Orient romain*, 1921, **XV** CVI
—— *Deux Itinéraires de Chine en Inde à la fin du VIIIe siècle*, 1904 CVII

Connexions with Turkistan.
GRÜNWEDEL, *Alt Kutscha*, 1920 CVIII
LÉVI (S.), *Étude des documents tokhariens de la mission Pelliot*, 1911, **XV** CIX
LE COQ (Von), *Chotscho*, Berlin, 1913 CX
PELLIOT (P.), *Une Bibliothèque médiévale retrouvée au Kan-Sou*, 1908, **X** CXI
—— *Les Grottes de Touen-houang*, Paris, 1920–4 . . CXII
STEIN (Sir Aurel), *Sand-buried Ruins of Khotan*, London, 1903 CXIII
—— *Ancient Khotan*, Oxford, 1907 CXIV
—— *Ruins of Desert Cathay*, London, 1912 . . . CXV
—— *Serindia*, London, 1921 CXVI
—— " Innermost Asia," in *Geogr. Journal*, 1925 . . CXVII

Southern India.
AIYANGAR (S. A.), *The Beginnings of South Indian History*, Madras, 1918 CXVIII
CODRINGTON (H. W.), *Short History of Ceylon*, 1927 . CXIX
JOUVEAU-DUBREUIL (G.), *Ancient History of the Deccan*, Pondicherry, 1920 CXX

Kingdoms and Empires.
(*a*) Asoka.
BHANDARKAR (D. R.), *Açoka*, Calcutta, 1913 . . . CXXI
HULTZSCH, " Inscriptions of Asoka " in *Corpus Inscriptionum Indicarum*, vol. i, new ed., Oxford, 1925 . CXXII
PRZYLUSKI (J.), (**CCVI**, *infra*) CXXIII
SENART (E.), *Les Inscriptions de Piyadasi*, Paris, 1881–6 CXXIV
SMITH (V. A.), *Asoka*, 3rd ed., Oxford, 1920 . . . CXXV
(*b*) Kanishka.
BOYER (A. M.), *L'Époque de Kaniska*, 1900, **XV** . . CXXVI
KENNEDY (J.), *The Secret of Kaniska*, 1912, **XXI** . . CXXVII
THOMAS (F. W.), *The Date of Kaniska*, ibid., 1913 . . CXXVIII
(*c*) Harsha.
MOOKERJI (R.), *Harsha*, Oxford and London, 1926 . CXXIX

PART TWO

Family Religion.
BANERJEE (G.), *The Hindu Law of Marriage and Strîdhana* Calcutta, 1896 CXXX
CALAND (W.), *Altindischer Ahnencult*, Leyden, 1893 . CXXXI
—— *Altindische Todten- und Bestattungsgebräuche*, Amsterdam, 1896 CXXXII
—— and HENRY (V.), *L'Agnistoma*, Paris, 1907 . . CXXXIII
HILLEBRANDT (A.), *Rituallitteratur. Vedische Opfer und Zauber*, 1897 CXXXIV
JOLLY (J.), *Recht und Sitte*, 1896, **VIII** CXXXV

KANE (P. V.), *History of Dharmaçâstra*, Poona, 1930 CXXXVI
LYALL (A. C.), *Asiatic Studies, Religious and Social*, 2nd ed., London, 1907 CXXXVII
ZIMMER (H.), *Altindisches Leben*, Berlin, 1879 . . CXXXVIII

Castes.

OLDENBERG (H.), *Zur Geschichte des indischen kastenwesens*, **XXIX** vol. li, 267 CXXXIX
SENART (E.), *Les Castes dans l'Inde*, new ed., Paris, 1927 CXL
SHAMA SHASTRI, *Evolution of Caste*, Madras, 1916 . CXLI

Political Doctrines.

KAUTILYA, *Arthaçâstra*, translated into English by Shama Shastri, i–iv, Mysore, 1908 ; v–xv, 1909–1910, **XIII** . CXLII
ALTEKAR (A. S.), *A History of Village Communities in Western India*, Oxford, 1927 CXLIII
BANDYOPADHYAYA (N. C.), *Development of Hindu Polity and Political Theories*, Calcutta, 1927 . . CXLIV
DUMONT (P. E.), *L'Açvamedha*, Paris, 1927 . . . CXLV
FOY (W.), *Die königliche Gewalt nach den Dharmasûtren*, Leipzig, 1895 CXLVI
JACOBI (J.), " Ueber die Echtheit des Kautilîya," in *Sitz. d. k. preuss. Ak. d. Wis.*, 1912 CXLVII
KEITH (A. B.), *The Authenticity of the Kautilîya*, 1916, **XXI** CXLVIII
SARKAR (B. K.), *The Political Institutions and Theories of the Hindus*, Leipzig, 1922 CXLIX

Political Economy.

DAS (S. K.), *The Economic History of Ancient India*, Calcutta, 1925 CL
FICK (R.), *Die soziale Gliederung in Nordöstlichen Indien zu Buddha's Zeit*, Kiel, 1897 CLI
JOSHI (H. C.), *Rech. sur les conceptions écon. et polit. aux Indes anciennes d'après le* Rgvéda, Paris, 1928 . . CLII
MOOKERJI (R.), *A History of Indian Shipping and Maritime Activity*, London, 1912 CLIII
—— *An Introduction to Indian Economics*, Calcutta . CLIV
NARAIN (B.), *Indian Economic Life*, Lahore, 1929 . . CLV
NATH (P.), *A Study in the Economic Condition of Ancient India*, London, Roy. As. Soc., 1929 CLVI
PHILIP (A.), *L'Inde moderne*, Paris, 1930 CLVII
SARKAR (B. K.), *Inland Transport and Communication in Medieval India*, Calcutta, 1925 CLVIII

PART THREE

General Works.

DASGUPTA (S.), *A History of Indian Philosophy*, i, Cambridge, 1922 CLIX
FARQUHAR (J. N.), *An Outline of the Religious Literature of India*, Oxford, 1920 CLX
GROUSSET (R.), *Hist. de la philosophie orientale*, Paris, 1923 CLXI
—— *Les Philosophies indiennes*, Paris, 1931 . . . CLXII
GUENON (R.), *Introd. générale à l'ét. des doctrines hindoues*, Paris, 1921 CLXIII
HEIMANN (B.), *Studien zur Eigenart indischen Denkens*, Tübingen, 1930 CLXIV

MACKENZIE (J.), *Hindu Ethics*, Oxford, 1922 . . . CLXV
MASSON-OURSEL (P.), *Esquisse d'une histoire de la philosophie indienne*, Paris, 1923 CLXVI
—— *La philosophie comparée*, Paris, 1923. (*Comparative Philosophy*, London, 1926) CLXVII
OLTRAMARE (P.), *Hist. des idées théosophiques dans l'Inde.* i. *Brahmanisme.* ii. *Bouddhisme*, Paris, 1906 and 1923 (Musée Guimet) CLXVIII
RADHAKRISHNAN (S.), *Indian Philosophy*, i, 1923 ; ii, 1927; London CLXIX
STRAUSS (O.), *Indische Philosophie*, Munich, 1925 . . CLXX

Vedas.

BERGAIGNE (A.), *La Religion védique*, Paris, 1878–1883 . CLXXI
GELDNER (K.), *Glossar*, 1907–9 CLXXII
GRASSMANN (H.), *Wörterbuch zum Rig-Veda*, 1872 . . CLXXIII
HILLEBRANDT (A.), *Vedische Mythologie*, Breslau, 1891–1902 CLXXIV
KEITH (A. B.), *Indian Mythology*, Boston, 1917 . . CLXXV
MACDONELL (A.), *Vedic Mythology*, 1897, VIII . . CLXXVI
OLDENBERG (H.), *Die Religion des Veda*, Berlin, 1894 . CLXXVII
RENOU (L.), *Les Maîtres de la philosophie védique*, Paris, 1928 CLXXVIII

Brāhmaṇas.

LÉVI (S.), *La Doctrine du sacrifice dans les Brâhmanas*, Paris, 1898 CLXXIX
OLDENBERG (H.), *Die Weltanschauung der Brâhmana-Texte*, Göttingen, 1919 CLXXX

Upanishads.

DEUSSEN (P.), *Allgemeine Geschichte der Philosophie*, Leipzig, 1899 CLXXXI
—— *Sechzig Upanishads des Veda*, 3rd ed., Leipzig, 1921 CLXXXII
GOUGH (A.), *Philosophy of the Upanishads*, London, 1882–4 CLXXXIII
HUME (R. E.), *The Thirteen Principal Upanishads*, trans., Oxford, 1921 (2nd ed., 1931) CLXXXIV
KEITH (A. B.), *The Religion and Philosophy of the Veda and Upanishads*, Cambridge, Mass., 1925 . . CLXXXV
OLDENBERG (H.), *Die Lehre der Upanishaden und die Anfänge des Buddhismus*, Göttingen, 1915 . . CLXXXVI
SENART (E.), *Chândogya Up.*, French trans., Paris, 1930 . CLXXXVII

Jainism.

WINTERNITZ (M.), CCLXXXVIII, II. B., 2. Hälfte, *Die heiligen Texte der Jainas*, Leipzig, 1920 . . CLXXXVIII
GUÉRINOT (A.), *La Religion djaïna*, Paris, 1926 . . CLXXXIX
JACOBI (H.), *Jaina-sûtras* (*Sac. Books of the East*, vols. xxii, xlv), Oxford, 1884–1895 CXC

Buddhism.

WINTERNITZ (M.), CCLXXXVIII, 1. Hälfte, *Die Buddhistische Litt.*, Leipzig, 1913 (Index and suppl. in 2. Hälfte) . CXCI
BURNOUF (E.), *Introd. à l'hist. du Bouddhisme indien*, Paris, 1844, 1876 CXCII

KEITH (A. B.), *Buddhist Philosophy in India and Ceylon*, Oxford, 1923 CXCIII
KERN (H.), *Manual of Indian Buddhism*, 1896, **VIII** . CXCIV
LA VALLÉE-POUSSIN (L. de), *Bouddhisme*, Paris, 1909 . CXCV
—— *La Morale bouddhique*, Paris, 1927 CXCVI
—— *The Way to Nirvâna*, Cambridge, 1917 . . . CXCVII
—— *Nirvâna*, Paris, 1925 CXCVIII
—— *Le Dogme et la philosophie du bouddhisme*, Paris, 1930 CXCIX
LÉVI (S.), *Asanga, le Mahâyâna-sûtrâlamkâra*, ed. and trans., Paris (*Bibl. de l'Éc. des H. Ét.*) CC
—— *Matériaux pour l'étude du système vijñaptimâtra*, ibid., 1932 CCI
OBERMILLER (E.), *Abhisamayâlamkâra-prajñapâramitâ-upadeçaçâstra*, trans. (with T. Scherbatski) (*Bibl. Buddhica*, 23, fasc. 1), Leningrad, 1929 CCII
—— *The Jewelry of Scripture*, by Bu-ston, trans. from the Tibetan, with introd., by T. Scherbatski, Heidelberg, 1931 CCIII
—— *The Sublime Science of the Great Vehicle to Salvation* (*Mahâyânottaratantra*), *Acta Orientalia*, vol. ix, 1931 CCIV
—— *The Doctrine of Prajña-pâramitâ as exposed in the Abhisamayâlamkâra of Maitreya*, ibid., vol. ix, 1932 CCV
PRZYLUSKI (J.), *La Légende de l'empereur Açoka*, Paris, 1923 CCVI
—— *Le Concile de Râjagrha*, Paris, 1926–8 CCVII
—— *Le Bouddhisme*, Paris, 1932 CCVIII
ROSENBERG (O.), *Die Probleme der Buddhistischen Philosophie*, German trans., Heidelberg, 1924 . . CCVIII*a*
SCHERBATSKI (T.), *L'Épistémologie et la logique chez les Bouddhistes tardifs*, French trans. by I. de Manziarly and P. Masson-Oursel, Paris, 1926. CCIX
—— *The Central Conception of Buddhism* (*Dharma*), London, Roy. As. Soc., 1923 CCX
—— *The Conception of Buddhist Nirvâna*, Leningrad, Acad. of Sci., 1927 CCXI
—— *Buddhist Logic*, Leningrad, 1932 CCXII
TUCCI (G.), *Buddhist Logic before Dinnâga*, **XXI**, 1929, 651 CCXIII
—— *Pre-Dinnâga Buddhist Texts on Logic from Chinese Sources*, Baroda, 1929 CCXIV
TUNELD (E.), *Recherches sur la valeur des traditions bouddhiques pâlie et non pâlie*, Lund, 1915 . . CCXV
UI (H.), *Studies in Indian Philosophy* (in Japanese) CCXVI
YAMAKAMI, *Systems of Buddhistic Thought*, Calcutta, 1912 CCXVII

Chinese Evidence on Buddhism.

BAGCHI (P. C.), *Le Canon bouddhique en Chine ; les traducteurs et les traductions*, Paris, 1927 CCXVIII
HIUEN-TSANG, *Si Yu ki*, London, 1906 (cf. Pelliot, **X**, 1905, 423) CCXIX
I-TSING, *Mémoire*, trans. by Chavannes, Paris, 1894 . CCXX
LÉVI (S.), *Les Missions de Wang Hiuan-tse dans l'Inde*, **XV** CCXXI
NANJIO (B.), *Catalogue of the Chinese Translations of the Buddhist Tripitaka*, Oxford, 1883 ; new ed., revised (Takakusu, Watanabe), Tokio, 1926 . . . CCXXII

HOBOGIRIN, *Dictionnaire encyclopédique du Bouddhisme*, from Chinese and Japanese sources, under the direction of S. Lévi and J. Takakusu; ed. J. Demiéville, Tokyo, 1928 CCXXIII

Pali Evidence.

PALI TEXT SOCIETY (many publications), London, 1882 . CCXXIV

Hinduism.

ABEGG (E.), *Der Messiasglaube in Indien und Iran*, Berlin, 1928 CCXXV

AVALON (A.) (Sir JOHN WOODROFFE), *Tantrik Texts*, Calcutta and London, various dates.—*The World as Power*, Madras, 1922–9 CCXXVI

BHANDARKAR (R. G.), *Vaisnavism, Çaivism and Minor Religious Systems*, 1913, **VIII** CCXXVII

GLASENAPP (H. VON), *Der Hinduismus*, Munich, 1922 . CCXXVIII

—— *Madhva's Philosophie des Vishnu-Glaubens*, Bonn, 1923 CCXXIX

JACOBI (H.), *Die Entwicklung der Gottesidee bei den Indern*, Bonn, 1923 CCXXX

KIRFEL (W.), *Das Purâna Pañcalaksana*, 1927 . . CCXXXI

MACNICOL (N.), *Psalms of Mâratha Saints*, Oxford, 1919 CCXXXII

OTTO (R.), *Vishnu-Nârâyana* CCXXXIII

—— *Siddhânta des Râmânuja*, Jena, 1917 . . . CCXXXIV

—— *Dîpikâ des Nivâsa*, Tübingen, 1916 . . . CCXXXV

RADHAKRISHNAN (S.), *L'Hindouisme et la vie*, French trans. by P. Masson-Oursel, Paris, 1930 . . . CCXXXVI

SCHOMERUS (H. W.), *Der Çaiva-Siddhânta*, Leipzig, 1912 CCXXXVII

—— *Sivaitische Heiligenlegenden*, Jena, 1926 . . CCXXXVIII

SCHRADER (O.), *Introd. to the Pâñcarâtra and the Ahirbudhnya Samhitâ*, Adyar, 1916 CCXXXIX

SENART (E.), *La Bhagavadgîtâ*, Paris, 1922 . . . CCXL

Philosophical Systems.

BODAS, *Historical Survey of Indian Logic*, **XVIII**, vol. xix CCXLI

DASGUPTA, *Yoga Philosophy*, Calcutta, 1930 . . . CCXLII

DEUSSEN (P.), *Das System des Vedânta*, 3rd ed., 1920, Leipzig CCXLIII

—— *Die Sûtras des Vedânta*, Leipzig, 1887 . . . CCXLIV

FADDEGON (B.), *The Vaiçesika System*, Amsterdam, 1918 CCXLV

JACOBI (H.), *The Dates of the Philosophical Sûtras*, **XVI**, vol. xxxi CCXLVI

—— *A Contribution towards the Early History of Indian Philosophy*, **XIII**, 1918 CCXLVII

—— "Indische Logik", in *Nachr. d. kgl. Ges. d. Wiss. zu Göttingen*, 1901 CCXLVIII

KEITH (A. B.), *Indian Logic and Atomism*, Oxford, 1921 CCXLIX

—— *Sâmkhya System*, Calcutta and London . . CCL

—— *The Karma-Mîmâmsâ*, Calcutta, 1921 . . . CCLI

GARBE (R.), *Die Sâmkhya Philosophie*, 2nd ed., Leipzig, 1917 CCLII

GHATE (V. S.), *Le Vêdânta, étude sur les Brahmasûtras et leurs cinq commentaires*, Tours, 1918 CCLIII

MASSON-OURSEL (P.), "L'Atomisme indienne," in *Revue philos.*, Paris, 1926, 342 CCLIV
—— "Der atomistische Zeitbegriff," in *Arch. f. Ges. d. Phil.*, Berlin, Bd. xl, H. 1, 1931 . . . . . CCLIV*a*
MULLER (M.), *The Six Systems of Indian Philosophy*,, London and New York, 1899 CCLV
RUBEN (W.), *Die Nyâyasûtras*, Leipzig, 1928 . . CCLVI
SUALI (L.), *Introduzione allo studio della filosofia indiana*, Pavia, 1913 CCLVII
—— "Théorie de la connaissance dans la phil. ind.," in *Isis*, vol. viii, 1920, 219 CCLVIII
TUCCI (G.), *Storia del materialismo indiano*, Ac. dei Lincei, 1923 CCLIX
UI (H.), *The Vaiçesika Philosophy* (*Daçapadârtha-çâstra*), London, Roy. As. Soc., 1917 CCLX
VIDYABHUSANA, *History of Indian Logic*, Calcutta, 1921 . CCLXI
WALLESER (M.), *Der ältere Vedânta*, Heidelberg, 1910 . CCLXII
WOODS (J. H.), *The Yoga System*, Eng. trans. of the *Yoga-sūtras*, Cambridge (Mass.), 1914 CCLXIII

Sciences.

See the *Isis Collection* (Wondelgem-lez-Gand, afterwards Cambridge, Mass.) CCLXIV
BERTHELOT (M.), *Journal des Savants*, 1898, 227 (Chemistry) CCLXV
CORDIER (P.), *Traités médicaux sanskrits antérieurs au XIIIe siècle*, **XXII**, 1930 CCLXVI
CLARK (W. E.), *The Âryabhatîya of Âryabhata, an ancient Indian work on mathematics and astronomy*, Chicago, 1930 CCLXVII
DUTT (U. C.), *Materia Medica of the Hindus* CCLXVIII
HAAS, *Ueber den Ursprung der ind. Medizin* (Susruta), **XXIX**, No. 30, 642 CCLXIX
JOLLY (J.), *Medicine*, **VIII** CCLXX
KAYE (G. R.), "Indian Mathematics," *Isis*, No. 6, fasc. 2, 1919 CCLXXI
—— "Influence grecque sur les math. indoues," in *Scientia*, Jan., 1919 CCLXXII
—— *Ancient Hindu Spherical Astronomy*, **XVII**, No. 15, 1919 CCLXXIII
KIRFEL, *Kosmographie der Inder*, Bonn, 1920 . . . CCLXXIV
KARPINSKI (L. C.), "Hindu Science," in *Amer. Math. Monthly*, vol. xxvi, 298, 1919 CCLXXV
—— "L'unité des contribut. hind. aux sc. math.", in *Scientia*, 1st June, 1928 CCLXXVI
RAY (P. E.), *Hist. of Hindu Chemistry*, Calcutta, 1903 ; *Isis*, vol. ii, No. 6, 1919 CCLXXVII
REY (A.), *La Science orientale avant les Grecs*, Paris, 1930 CCLXXVIII
ROTH, *Caraka*, **XXIX**, No. 26, 441 CCLXXIX
SARKAR (B. K.), *Hindu Achievements in Indian Science* . CCLXXX
—— *The Positive Background of Hindu Sociology*, Allahabad, 1914 CCLXXXI
SEAL, *The Positive Science of the Ancient Hindus*, London, 1925 CCLXXXII

Smith (D. E.), " The Geometry of the Hindus," in *Isis*, vol. i, fasc. 2, 1913 CCLXXXIII
Thibaut (G.), *Astronomie, Astrologie und Mathematik*, VIII, 1899 CCLXXXIV

PART FOUR

Book One

General Works.

Henry (V.), *Les Littératures de l'Inde*, Paris, 1904 . . CCLXXXV
Keith (A. B.), *Classical Sanskrit Literature*, Oxford, 1924 CCLXXXVI
Macdonell (A.), *A History of Sanskrit Literature*, London, 1900 CCLXXXVII
Winternitz (M.), *Geschichte der indischen Litteratur*, 3 vols., Leipzig, 1909–1922 CCLXXXVIII

Epics.

Jacobi (H.), *Der Râmâyana, Geschichte und Inhalt*, Bonn, 1893 CCLXXXIX
Oldenberg (O.), *Das Mahâbhârata*, Göttingen, 1922 . CCXC

Tales.

Cosquin (E.), *Les Contes indiens et l'Occident*, Paris . CCXCI
Lancereau (E.), *Le Pañcatantra ou les cinq ruses*, Paris, 1871 CCXCII
Lacôte (F.), *Essai sur Gunâdhya et la Brhatkathâ*, Paris, 1918 CCXCIII

Drama.

Lévi (S.), *Le Théâtre indien*, Paris, 1890 CCXCIV
Konow (S.), *Das indische Drama*, Berlin and Strasburg, 1920 CCXCV
Keith (A. B.) *The Sanskrit Drama*, London and Oxford, 1924 CCXCVI

Poetic Art.

Harichand, *Kâlidâsa et l'art poétique de l'Inde*, Paris, 1917 CCXCVII
Hillebrandt (A.), *Kâlidâsa*, Breslau, 1921 CCXCVIII
Regnaud (P.), *Rhétorique sanscrite*, Paris, 1884 . . . CCXCIX
Lindenau (M.), *Beiträge zur altindischen Rasalehre*, Diss. Leipzig, 1913 CCC
Schmidt (R.), *Appayadîksita's Kuvalayânandakârikâs, ein indisches Kompendium der Redefiguren*, Berlin, 1907 . CCCI
—— *Beiträge zur indischen Erotik*, Leipzig, 1902 . . CCCII

Book Two [1]

General.

Bachhofer (L.), *Early Indian Sculpture*, Paris, 1929 . CCCIII
Burgess (J.) *The Ancient Monuments, Temples, and Sculptures of India*, 2 vols, 1897 CCCIV

[1] This is only an abridged bibliography. It may be supplemented for recent years by CCCLXXIII and X, and for the years down to 1927 by CCCXII, which is the most complete work on the art of India proper (the parts relating to Further India should be consulted with more caution). The plates in the latter work also serve to illustrate this section ; and those in

CODRINGTON (K. de B.), *L'Inde ancienne* (trans.), Paris (*Ancient India*, London, 1926) CCCV
COHN (W.), *Indische Plastik*, Berlin, 1922 CCCVI
COOMARASWAMY (A. K.), *History of Indian and Indonesian Art*, London, 1927 CCCVII
—— *Les Arts et Métiers de l'Inde et de Ceylan*, Paris 1924 (*The Arts and Crafts of India and Ceylon*, London, 1913) CCCVIII
—— *La Danse de Çiva*, Paris, 1922 (*The Dance of Siva*, New York, 1924) CCCIX
—— *Pou comprendre l'art hindou* (trans.), Paris, 1926 . CCCX
DIEZ (E.), *Die Kunst Indiens*, Potsdam CCCXI
GRÜNWEDEL (A.) and BURGESS (J.), *Buddhist Art in India*, English ed., London, 1901 (*Buddhistische Kunst in Indien*, 2nd ed., Berlin, 1919) CCCXII
HACKIN (J), *Guide-catalogue du Musée Guimet, collections bouddhiques*, Paris, 1923 CCCXIII
—— *Les Sculptures indiennes et tibétaines du Musée Guimet*, Paris, 1931 CCCXIV
HAVELL (E. B.), *Indian Sculpture and Painting*, London, 1908 CCCXV
INDIA SOCIETY (under the auspices of), *The Influences of Indian Art*, London, 1925 CCCXVI
MARSHALL (Sir J. H.), "Monuments of Ancient India," vol. i, chap. xxvi, in *Cambridge History of India*, Cambridge, 1922 CCCXVII
SMITH (V. A.), *A History of Fine Art in India and Ceylon*, Oxford, 1911 CCCXVIII

Architecture.

CHANDA (R. P.), *Beginning of the Sikhara of the Nagara (Indo-Aryan) Temple*, Rûpam, 17, 1924. . . . CCCXIX
COUSENS (H.), *The Architectural Antiquities of Western India*, India Society, London, 1926 CCCXX
—— "The Chalukyan Architecture of the Kanarese Districts," in *Arch. Surv. Ind.*, vol. xlii, Calcutta, 1926 CCCXXI
—— "The Medieval Temples of the Dakhan," ibid., vol. xlviii, Calcutta, 1931 CCCXXII
FERGUSSON (J.), BURGESS (J.), and SPIERS, *A History of Indian and Eastern Architecture*, 2 vols., 2nd ed., London, 1910 CCCXXIII
GANGOLY (O. C.), *Indian Architecture*, Calcutta, n.d. . CCCXXIV

CCCLXVI and **CCCLXX** may be profitably consulted in connection with my last chapter (Indian Æsthetics. The Frescoes of Ajanta, etc.).

I owe a debt of thanks to those who have aided me in my work, M. A. Foucher, Mme de Coral-Rémusat, and M. P. Dumont, and to those who have allowed me to quote certain details from works not yet published, dealing with the differences between the arts of Ellora and Ajanta (Mlle Hallade, Mlle Zentler, Mlle Auboyer), composition in the art of Bharhut (Mlle Hallade), the earliest Brahmanic religious art (M. P. Dumont, Mlle Zentler), pillars with a flat slab supporting the architrave and no capital (Mlle Bruhl), and motives imported from the Hellenized East (M. Combaz). I should like also to say what I owe to M. A. Foucher (the function of the *stūpa*, symbols in early Buddhist art, Græco-Buddhist art) and to M. Jouveau-Dubreuil (evolution of architecture and the school of Amaravati).—PHILIPPE STERN.

Havell (E. B.), *Indian Architecture: Its Psychology, Structure, and History*, London, 1913 . . . CCCXXV
Jouveau-Dubreuil, *Archéologie du sud de l'Inde*, vol i, *Architecture*, in *Annales du Musée Guimet, Bibliothèque d'études*, No. 27, Paris, 1914 . . CCCXXVI
Acharya (P. K.), *Indian Architecture*, Oxford University Press CCCXXVII
—— *A Dictionary of Hindu Architecture*, Oxford University Press CCCXXVIII

Religious Art.

Bhattacharya (B.), *The Indian Buddhist Iconography*, Oxford University Press, 1924 CCCXXIX
Chanda (R. P.), *Four Ancient Yaksa Statues*, University of Calcutta, *Journ. Dep. Letters*, iv, 1921 . . CCCXXX
Cohn (W.), *Buddha in der Kunst des Ostens*, Leipzig, 1925, 2 vols. CCCXXXI
Coomaraswamy (A. K.), *Yaksa*, Smithsonian Institution, 1928 and 1931, 2 vols. CCCXXXII
—— and Duggirala (G. K.), *The Mirror of Gesture*, Cambridge, Mass., 1917 CCCXXXIII
Fergusson (J.), *Tree and Serpent Worship*, 2nd ed., London, 1873 CCCXXXIV
Foucher (A.), *The Beginnings of Buddhist Art*, London, 1918 (a collection of papers which appeared in French in various publications) CCCXXXV
—— *Études sur l'art bouddhique de l'Inde*, Tokio . . CCCXXXVI
—— "Lettre d'Ajantâ," in *Journal Asiatique*, 1921 . CCCXXXVII
—— *L'Iconographie bouddhique de l'Inde*, Paris, 1900–5. CCCXXXVIII
Getty (A.), *The Gods of Northern Buddhism*, Oxford, 1914; 2nd ed., 1928 CCCXXXIX
Jouveau-Dubreuil, *Archéologie du sud de l'Inde*, vol. ii, *Iconographie*, *Annales du Musée Guimet, Bibliothèque d'études*, No. 27, Paris, 1914 . . . CCCXL
Rao (T. A. G.), *Elements of Hindu Iconography*, Madras, 1914–15, 4 vols. CCCXLI
Vogel (J. P.), *Indian Serpent-lore*, London, 1926 . . CCCXLII

Art of Harappa and Mohenjo-Daro.

Hargreaves (H.), "Excavation in Beluchistan," in *Memoirs A.S.I.*, No. 35, Calcutta, 1929. . . . CCCXLIII
Marshall (Sir J. H.), **LXXXII** CCCXLIV

Art of Bharhut and Sanchi.

IX, Annual Report, 1913–14 to 1916–17 CCCXLV
Chanda (R. P.), "Indus Valley in the Vedic Period," in *Mem. A.S.I.*, No. 31, Calcutta, 1928 . . . CCCXLVI
Cunningham (A.), *The Bhilsa Topes, or Buddhist Monuments of Central India*, London, 1854 . . . CCCXLVII
—— *The Stûpa of Bhârhut*, London, 1879 . . . CCCXLVIII
—— *Mahabodhi, or the Great Buddhist Temple at Buddhagaya*, London, 1892 CCCXLIX

FABRI, "Mesopotamian and Early Indian Art Comparison," in *Études d'Orientalisme à la mémoire de Raymonde Linossier*, Paris, 1932 CCCL
MARSHALL (Sir J. H.), *Guide to Sânchî*, Calcutta, 1918 . CCCLI
SPOONER (D. B.), "Terracottas from Pataliputra and Bronzes from Nâlandâ," in *A.S.I.*, *A.R.*, 1917–18 . CCCLII

Græco-Buddhist Art.

BARTHOUX, "Les Fouilles de Hadda" (*Mémoires de la Délégation française en Afghanistan*, vol. iii), Van Oest, 1930 CCCLIII
FOUCHER (A.), *L'Art gréco-bouddhique du Gandhara*, Paris, 1905, 1918, 1922 CCCLIV
HARGREAVES (H.), "Excavations at Takht-i-Bâhî," in *A.S.I.*, *A.R.*, 1910–11 CCCLV
MARSHALL (Sir J. H.), "Guide to Taxila, the Stûpa and Monastery at Jaulian," in *Mem. A.S.I.*, 7, 1921 . CCCLVI
RAM CHANDRA KAK, *Ancient Monuments of Kashmir*, The India Society, London, 1933 CCCLVII
WALDSCHMIDT (G.), *Gandhara-Kutscha-Turfan*, Leipzig, 1925 CCCLVIII

Arts of Mathura and Amaravati.

BURGESS (J.), *The Buddhist Stûpas of Amarâvatî and Jaggayyapeta*, London, 1887 CCCLIX
FOUCHER (A.), "Les Sculptures d'Amarâvatî," in *R.A.A.*, 5th year, No. 1, p. 1 CCCLX
VOGEL (J. P.), "La Sculpture de Mathura," in *Ars Asiatica*, No. XV, Van Oest, 1930 . . . CCCLXI

Art of Ajanta and Ellora.

BURGESS (J.), "Report on the Elûrâ Cave Temples," in *A.S.I.*, *N.I.S.*, vol. v, London, 1883 . . . CCCLXII
—— *Notes on the Buddhist Rock Temples of Ajanta and Bagh* CCCLXIII
FERGUSSON and BURGESS, *Cave Temples of India*, London, 1880 CCCLXIV
GODARD and HACKIN, "Les Antiquités bouddhiques de Bamiyan," in *Mémoires de la Délég. franç. d'Afghan.*, vol. ii CCCLXV
GOLOUBEW (V.), "Ajantâ, les peintures de la première grotte," in *Ars Asiatica*, Paris, x, 1921 CCCLXVI
GRIFFITHS (J.), *The Paintings in the Buddhist Cave Temples of Ajunta*, London, 1896–7 CCCLXVII
HACKIN (J.), "Antiquités bouddhiques de Bamiyan," in *Mémoires de la Délég. franç. en Afghanistan*, vol. iv CCCLXVII*a*
INDIA SOCIETY (under the auspices of), *Ajanta Frescoes*, London, 1915 CCCLXVIII
—— *Bagh Caves*, London . . . . CCCLXVIII*a*
JOUVEAU-DUBREUIL, "Les Antiquités de l'époque Pallava," in *Revue historique de l'Inde française*, 1916–17 CCCLXIX
YAZDANI (G.), *Ajanta*, Oxford University Press, n.d. . CCCLXX

Reviews.

Artibus Asiæ, Dresden CCCLXXI
Indian Art and Letters, India Society, London . . CCCLXXII
Kern Institute, Annual Bibliography of Indian Archæology, Leiden CCCLXXIII
Ostasiatische Zeitschrift, Berlin and Leipzig . . . CCCLXXIV
Revue des Arts Asiatiques, Paris CCCLXXV
Rupam, Calcutta CCCLXXVI

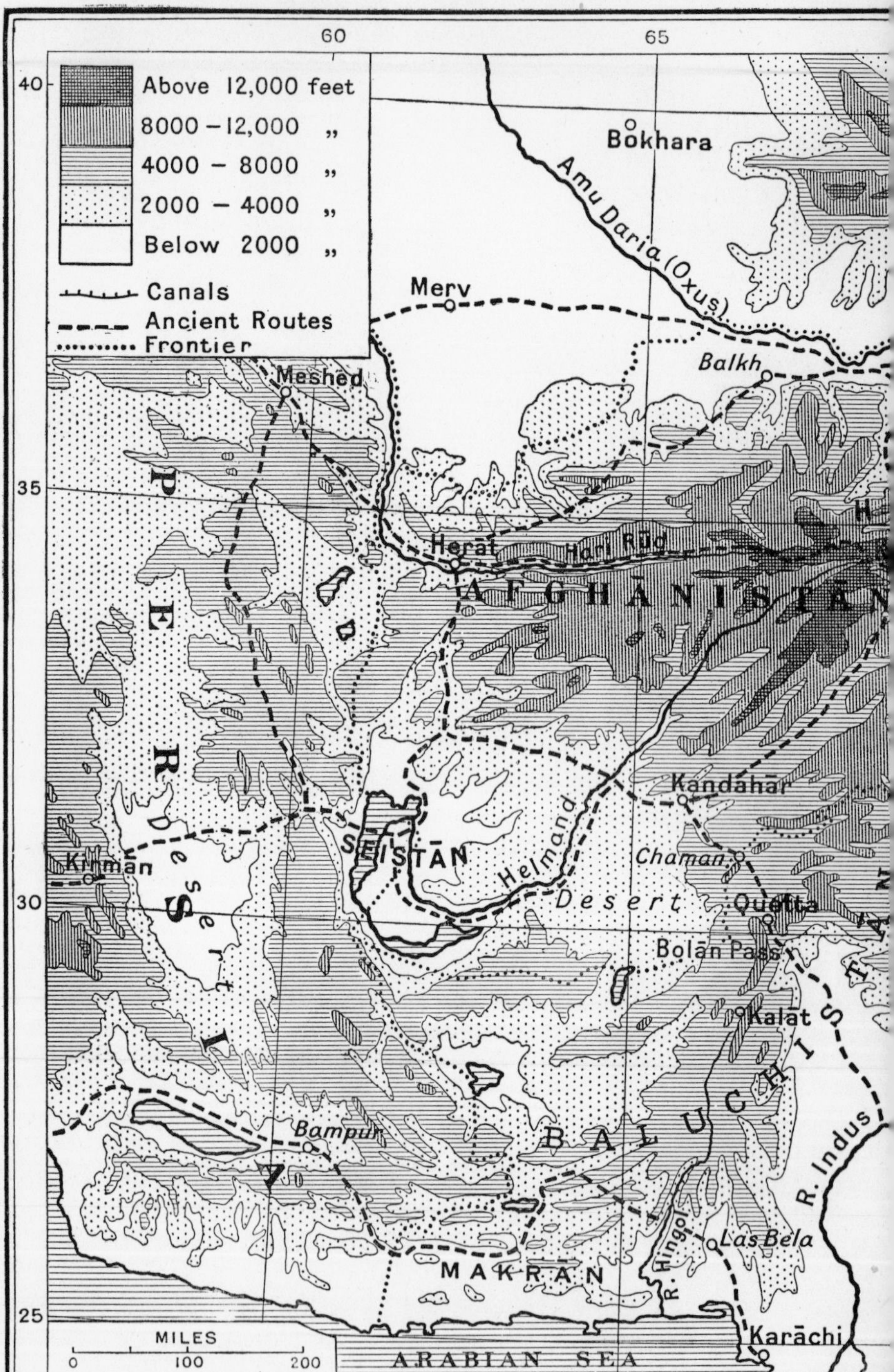

NORT

(From *The Cambridge History of*

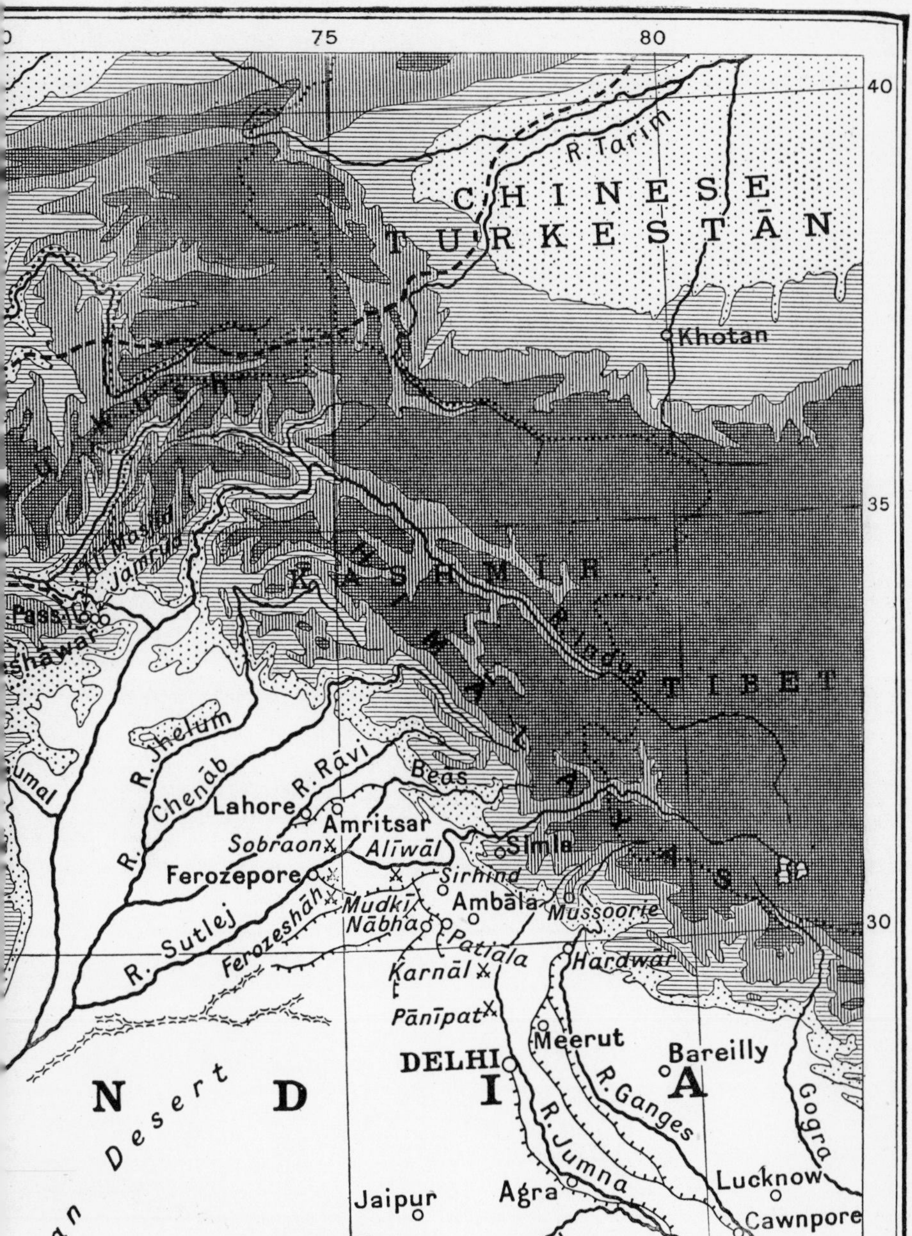

INDIA

l. I, University Press, Cambridge)

[*face page* 416

INDEX

Abhidharma, 161–2, 1, 186–8
Abhisāra, 33
Absolute, see *Ātman, Brahman*
Adam's Peak, 3
Adhṛishṭa, Adraestae, 32.
Ādibuddha, 189–190.
Aditi, 127, 311
Ādityas, 127 ; and see Mitra, Varuṇa
Administration, 103–5
Adraestae, see Adhṛishṭa
Ægean civilization, and Mohenjo-Daro, 19
Æsthetics, *Chitralakshaṇa*. 95, 390–8
Afghānistān, 3, 5, 13, 36 ; art in, 365, 375, 389
Africa, East, trade with, 110
Agalassi, 89
Agathocles, K., 42
Agni, Fire, 126, 238–9
Agnivarṇa, 278
Agra, troops of, 21
Agriculture and stockbreeding, 16, 107–8, 115.
Ahiṃsā, 144, 152.
Ahura, 122
Aihoḷe, 355, 379, pl. iv
Aimaks, 13
Aitareyin school, 63 ; Brāhmaṇa, 62, 236 ; Upanishad 62, 242
Aja, 278
Ajaṇṭā : architecture, 349–351, 354, 362, pl. iii ; art, 362, 365, 367, 369–370, 379–382, 387, 389–397, pls. xi–xiv
Ajātaśatru, Kūṇika, K., 25, 155
Ājīvika sect, 146
Ākāśa, 134
Akriyavādin school, 146
Akshapāda Gautama, 195
Akshobya, Buddha, 190
Alaṃkāra, 267, 399
Al-Bīrūnī, on Purāṇas, 261
Alexander, K. of Epeiros, 40
Alexander III, the Great, K. of Macedon, 7, 30–4, 89 ; influence of his empire, 90
Alexandria in Arachosia, Kandahār, 7, 30
Allahābād, see Prayāga
Almora, 7
Amarasiṃha, 249 ; on *purāṇa*, 260
Amarāvati, 47 ; art, 362, 366–7, 369–370, 375, 378–9, 381–2, 386–7, pls. vii, ix, xvi
Amaru, 283–5
Ambhi, K., 31, 33
Amitābha, Buddha, 163, 180, 189–190
Amitāyus, Buddha, 189
Amoghasiddhi, Buddha, 190
Ānanda, 155, 159, 190, 264–5
Ānandavardhana, on *Kumāra-sambhava*, 277 n.
Ancestors, 66–70, 74, 78
Andaman Is., 2
Andhras, 47–8
Anga, 25–6, 145
Angkor, 358, 389, 397
Animism, 122
Annam, language, 11 ; see also Champā
Anquetil Duperron (A. H.), 223
Antialcidas, K., 42
Antiochos I Soter, K. of Syria, 37 ; II Theos, 40 ; III, the Great, 41–2
Anu, sky-god, 122
Anurādhapura, 40
Anuruddha, 155, 159
Āpam napāt, 67
Āpastamba, Sūtras of, 63–4, 71, 207
Aphorisms, see Gnomic Literature
Apollophanes, Satrap, 34
Apsarases, 238, 294, 309 n.
Arabian Nights, Indian influences in, 325, 334
Arabs, navigation of, 110
Arachosia, 36
Arāḍa Kālāma, 154
Āraṇyakas, 62–3, 156, 217, 240–1 ; and see under *Taittirīya*
Arāvalli Hills, 3
Architecture : Mohenjo-Daro, 19, 343 ; Maurya, 38 ; wooden, 109 ; general, 345–362, 385–8, 399
Ardhamāgadhi language, 148
Arhat, saint, 157, 160, 187, 189
Aria, see Herāt
Arjuna, 172, 254, 259, 279, 292
Arjunaka sect, 172
Ārjunāyanas, 52, 90
Armenia, no Aryan influence, 15
Army, war, 98–100
Arrian : on Assyrian rule of India, 18 n. ; on coins, 114
Arsaces I, K. of the Parthians, 41
Arsaces, K. of Uraśā, see Uraśā

Printed in Great Britain by Stephen Austin & Sons, Ltd., Hertford.

THE HISTORY OF CIVILIZATION

THIS series marks one of the most ambitious adventures in the annals of book publishing. Its aim is to present in accessible form the results of modern research throughout the whole range of the Social Sciences—to summarize in one comprehensive synthesis the most recent findings of historians, anthropologists, archæologists, sociologists, and all conscientious students of civilization.

To achieve success in this stupendous undertaking, the new French series, *L'Evolution de l'Humanité,* in which the leading savants of France are collaborating with the Director of the Bibliothèque de Synthèse Historique, M. Henri Berr, is being incorporated. Distinguished historians, both European and American, are contributing volumes in their several departments.

The field has been carefully mapped out, as regards both subjects and periods; and, though the instalments will be published as they are ready, the necessary chronological sequence will be secured by the fact that the volumes of the French collection will be used as a nucleus. Each work will be entirely independent and complete in itself, but the volumes in a given group will be found to supplement one another when considered in relation to a particular subject or period.

The volumes are uniformly bound in a fine art-cambric cloth, with specially designed gold lettering and emblem, royal octavo in size.

THE TIMES LITERARY SUPPLEMENT devoted a leading article to the first four volumes, in which the series was described as being " composed by all the talents ".

THE MANCHESTER GUARDIAN wrote that " it is a heroic attempt, which will be sympathetically watched, to bring some light into the vast mass of ill-organized knowledge which we owe to modern research and so make it available in the end for the guidance of the world."

NATURE, the leading scientific journal, in a six-column review, provides a striking summary of the aims and objects of the series : " The History of Civilization promises to be perhaps the most important contribution so far undertaken towards the task of organization and systematization of the social studies. A glance at the prospectus makes us anticipate a library of masterpieces, for the best workers of France, Great Britain, and some other countries are contributing from their own speciality and are attempting to bring it into line with the contributions from neighbouring fields and with the results of general sociology. Including all the volumes of the important French collection, *L'Evolution de l'Humanité*, the English library contains additions and improvements which will place it above its continental counterpart. The volumes already issued bear out our best hopes."

*The following plan, comprising just under one hundred titles, though not definitive, will serve to convey a general notion of the nature and scope of the enterprise :**

A. PRE-HISTORY AND ANTIQUITY

I Introduction and Pre-History

*Social Organization	*W. H. R. Rivers*
The Earth Before History	*Edmond Perrier*
Prehistoric Man	*Jacques de Morgan*
*Life and Work in Prehistoric Times	*G. Renard*
*The Dawn of European Civilization	*V. Gordon Childe*
Language: a Linguistic Introduction to History	*J. Vendryes*
A Geographical Introduction to History	*L. Febvre*
Race and History	*E. Pittard*
*The Aryans	*V. Gordon Childe*
From Tribe to Empire	*A. Moret* and *G. Davy*
*Money and Monetary Policy in Early Times	*A. R. Burns*
*The Diffusion of Culture	*G. Elliot Smith*

II The Early Empires

The Nile and Egyptian Civilization	*A. Moret*
The Mesopotamian Civilization	*L. Delaporte*
The Ægean Civilization	*G. Glotz*
*Minoans, Philistines and Greeks	*Andrew Robert Burn*

III Greece

The Formation of the Greek People	*A. Jardé*
*Ancient Greece at Work	*G. Glotz*
Religious Thought of Greece	*L. Gernet and A. Boulanger*
Art in Greece	*W. Deonna* and *A. de Ridder*
Greek Thought and the Scientific Spirit	*L. Robin*
The Greek City and its Institutions	*G Glotz*
Macedonian Imperialism	*P. Jouguet*

IV Rome

Primitive Italy and Roman Imperialism	*Léon Homo*
The Roman Spirit in Religion, Thought, and Art	*A. Grenier*
Roman Political Institutions	*Léon Homo*
Rome the Law-Giver	*J Declareuil*
Economic Life of the Ancient World	*J. Toutain*

* An asterisk denotes that the volume does *not* form part of the French collection *L'Evolution de l'Humanité*.

The Roman World	*Victor Chapot*
*Ancient Rome at Work	*Paul Louis*
The Rise of the Celts	*H. Hubert*
The Greatness and Decline of the Celts	*H. Hubert*

V BEYOND THE ROMAN EMPIRE

Germany and the Roman Empire	*H. Hubert*
Ancient Persia and Iranian Civilization	*Clement Huart*
Chinese Civilization	*M. Granet*
Chinese Thought	*M. Granet*
*Feudal Japan	*G. F. Hudson*
*A Thousand Years of the Tartars	*E. H. Parker*
*Nomads of the European Steppe	*G. F. Hudson*
Ancient India	*P. Masson-Oursel*
*The Heroic Age of India	*N. K. Sidhanta*
*Caste and Race in India	*G. S. Ghurye*
*The Life of Buddha as Legend and History	*E. J. Thomas*
*The History of Buddhist Thought	*E. J. Thomas*

B. CHRISTIANITY AND THE MIDDLE AGES

I THE ORIGINS OF CHRISTIANITY

Israel, from its Beginnings	*Adolphe Lods*
Jesus and the Birth of Christianity	*C. Guignebert*
The Formation of the Church	*C. Guignebert*
The Advance of Christianity	*C. Guignebert*
*History and Literature of Christianity	*P. de Labriolle*

II THE BREAK-UP OF THE EMPIRE

The End of the Ancient World	*Ferdinand Lot*
The Eastern Empire	*C. Diehl*
Charlemagne	*L. Halphen*
The Collapse of the Carlovingian Empire	*Ferdinand Lot*
The Origins of the Slavs	*(Ed.) P. Boyer*
*Popular Life in the East Roman Empire	*Norman Baynes*
*The Northern Invaders	*B. S. Phillpotts*

III RELIGIOUS IMPERIALISM

Islam and Mahomet	*E. Doutté*
The Advance of Islam	*L. Barrau-Dihigo*
Christendom and the Crusades	*P. Alphandéry*
The Organization of the Church	*R. Genestal*

IV THE ART OF THE MIDDLE AGES

The Art of the Middle Ages	*P. Lorquet*
*The Papacy and the Arts	*E. Strong*

V RECONSTITUTION OF MONARCHIC POWER

The Foundation of Modern Monarchies	*C. Petit-Dutaillis*
The Growth of Public Administration	*E. Meynial*
The Organization of Law	*E. Meynial*

VI	SOCIAL AND ECONOMIC EVOLUTION	
	The Development of Rural and Town Life	*G. Bourgin*
	Maritime Trade and the Merchant Gilds	*P. Boissonnade*
	*The Court of Burgundy	*Otto Cartellieri*
	*Life and Work in Medieval Europe	*P. Boissonnade*
	*The Life of Women in Medieval Times	*Eileen Power*
	*Travel and Travellers of the Middle Ages	(*Ed.*) *A. P. Newton*
	*Chivalry and its Historical Significance	(*Ed.*) *Edgar Prestage*
VII	INTELLECTUAL EVOLUTION	
	Education in the Middle Ages	*G. Huisman*
	Philosophy in the Middle Ages	*E. Bréhier*
	Science in the Middle Ages	*Abel Rey* and *P. Boutroux*
VIII	FROM THE MIDDLE AGES TO MODERN TIMES	
	Nations of Western and Central Europe	*P. Lorquet*
	Russians, Byzantines, and Mongols	(*Ed.*) *P. Boyer*
	The Birth of the Book	*G. Renaudet*
	*The Grandeur and Decline of Spain	*C Hughes Hartmann*
	*The Influence of Scandinavia on England	*M. E. Seaton*
	*The Philosophy of Capitalism	*T. E. Gregory*
	*The Prelude to the Machine Age	*Mrs. Bertrand Russell*
	*Life and Work in Modern Europe	*G. Renard* and *G. Weulersse*
	*London Life in the Eighteenth Century	*M. Dorothy George*
	*China and Europe in the Eighteenth Century	*A. Reichwein*

A special group of volumes will be devoted to

(1)	SUBJECT HISTORIES	
	*The History of Medicine	*C. G. Cumston*
	*The History of Witchcraft	*Montague Summers*
	*The Geography of Witchcraft	*Montague Summers*
	*The History of Money	*T. E. Gregory*
	*The History of Taste	*J. Isaac*
	*The History of Oriental Literature	*E. Powys Mathers*
	*The History of Music	*Cecil Gray*
(2)	HISTORICAL ETHNOLOGY	
	*The Ethnology of Africa	*L. H. Dudley Buxton*
	*The Peoples of Asia	*L. H. Dudley Buxton*
	*The Threshold of the Pacific	*C. E. Fox*
	*The South American Indians	*Rafael Karsten*
	*The American Indian Frontier	*J. G. Macleod*
	*The Ethnology of India	*T. C. Hodson*
	*Death Customs	*E. Bendann*

In the Sections devoted to MODERN HISTORY the majority of titles will be announced later.

VOLUMES PUBLISHED

The following volumes have already been issued. They are arranged roughly in the order in which they were published. But their place in the scheme of the whole series may be discovered from the list above:

THE EARTH BEFORE HISTORY: *Man's Origin and the Origin of Life*

By EDMOND PERRIER, *late Hon. Director of the Natural History Museum of France.*

With 4 maps, 15s. net.

"It goes back to the birth of the world and the transformations of land and water, and takes us through the growth of life on the planet, the primitive animal forms, the peopling of the seas, and the forms of life in the primary, secondary, and tertiary periods, to the growth of the human form. Thus, starting from the origin of matter, it leads us in easy stages to *homo sapiens* himself."
Daily News.

"A remarkable volume."—*Yorkshire Post.*

PREHISTORIC MAN: *A General Outline of Prehistory*

By JACQUES DE MORGAN, *late Director of Antiquities in Egypt.*

With 190 illustrations and maps, 12s. 6d. net.

"A notable and eminently readable study in the early history of civilization, and one well worth its place in the great series now being issued by the publishers. It bears on every page the impress of the personality of its author, who strives to give the reader a clear, composite picture of early civilization taking one topic after another."—*Nation.*

"A masterly summary of our present knowledge at a low price. As a full survey the book has no rival, and its value is enhanced by the lavish illustrations."
New Leader.

SOCIAL ORGANIZATION

By W. H. R. RIVERS, LL.D., F.R.S. *Preface by* PROFESSOR G. ELLIOT SMITH.

Third edition, 10s. 6d. net.

"*Social Organization* is the first volume of the series of historical works on the whole range of human activity. May the present book be of good augury for the rest! To maintain so high a standard of originality and thoroughness will be no easy task."—JANE HARRISON, in *Nation.*

The book is a great contribution to the sum of human knowledge in the region of pure sociology."—*Daily News.*

THE THRESHOLD OF THE PACIFIC: *an Account of the Social Organization, Magic, and Religion of the People of San Cristoval in the Solomon Islands*

By C. E. FOX, LITT.D. *Preface by* PROFESSOR G. ELLIOT SMITH.

With 14 plates and 40 text illustrations, 18s. net.

"A masterpiece. One of the very best contributions to ethnology we possess. It has, besides its intrinsic value as a masterly record of savage life, also an indirect one; it is a remarkable testimony to the indispensable need of scientific method for the observer. His account of magical ritual and spells will become a classical source for students. The account of the life-history of the individual is depicted with a clearness and fulness unrivalled in ethnographic literature . . ."—*Times Literary Supplement.*

LANGUAGE: *a Linguistic Introduction to History*

By J. VENDRYES, *Professor in the University of Paris.*

Second impression. 16s. net.

"A book remarkable for its erudition and equally remarkable for originality and independence of thought."—*Sunday Times.*

"As an introduction to philology this volume is a splendid piece of *haute vulgarisation*, for which anyone who at all loves words or who is at all curious about language, must be grateful. It covers nearly all the ground from every useful angle. A wide, level-headed and erudite study."—*Nation.*

A GEOGRAPHICAL INTRODUCTION TO HISTORY

By LUCIEN FEBVRE, *Professor in the University of Strasburg.*

Second impression. With 7 maps, 16s. net.

"A masterpiece of criticism, as witty as it is well-informed, and teeming with nice observations and delicate turns of argument and phrase."

Times Literary Supplement.

"A broad, clear-headed introduction to the fascinating study of human geography. It is much more than a text-book for the student: it is a work that anyone with no knowledge of geography can read with avidity, for it is the greatest of pleasures to watch the clear logical thought of the writer rapidly treating with masterly power these great and important topics."—*Nation.*

THE HISTORY AND LITERATURE OF CHRISTIANITY: *from Tertullian to Boethius*

By PIERRE DE LABRIOLLE, *Professor of Literature at the University of Poitiers.* *Foreword by* CARDINAL GASQUET.

25s. net.

"A masterly volume. A scholar of the finest accomplishment, an enthusiast for his subject, and himself an artist in letters, he has produced a book comprehensive and authoritative, and also a joy to read from the first page to the last."

Universe.

"This interesting and valuable book."—W. L. COURTNEY, in *Daily Telegraph.*

LONDON LIFE IN THE EIGHTEENTH CENTURY

By M. DOROTHY GEORGE.

Second impression. With 8 plates, 21s. net.

" Mrs. George, by her cumulative method, imparts a shuddering impression of the brutalised life led by the masses under the first two Georges. Her work is full of eloquent detail. All who like to get at close quarters with history will feel immensely debtors to her industrious research and faculty of clear statement. And she will have the satisfaction of restoring faith to many minds in the reality of progress."—*Observer*.

" One of the best pieces of research in social and economic history which have appeared for many years."—*Nation*.

A THOUSAND YEARS OF THE TARTARS

By E. H. PARKER, *Professor of Chinese in the Victoria University of Manchester.*

With 5 illustrations and maps, 12s. 6d. net.

" Professor Parker takes us back to a period roughly contemporaneous with that of the foundation of the Roman empire, and shows their history to be, like that of the Northern barbarians and Rome, a constant struggle with China. With an unfamiliar subject the book is not an easy one to read, but the author has done all that was possible to enliven his subject and has certainly succeeded in giving us a most valuable text-book."—*Saturday Review*.

CHINA AND EUROPE: *their Intellectual and Artistic Relations in the Eighteenth Century*

By ADOLPH REICHWEIN.

With 24 plates, 12s. 6d. net.

" Among the volumes of the monumental History of Civilization, this study of the influence of Chinese art and thought on the European art and thought of the eighteenth century will find not the least popular and distinguished place. The chapter headed ' Rococo ' will be of especial interest to connoisseurs. . . The illustrations are numerous and beautiful."—*Sunday Times*.

" A fascinating subject. The references to literature are admirably full and complete."—*Times Literary Supplement*.

THE DAWN OF EUROPEAN CIVILIZATION

By V. GORDON CHILDE, B.Litt.

Second Impression. With 198 illustrations and 4 maps, 16s. net.

" Higher praise of Mr. Childe's book, which forms a volume of the monumental History of Civilization, could scarcely be given than to say that it is in all respects worthy of the volumes which preceded it."—*Sunday Times*.

" He has done a very great service to learning, and given a clear and reliable outline of the earliest civilization of Europe. His book ' fills a gap ' indeed."—*Nation*.

" A very fine piece of work."—*Manchester Guardian*.

MESOPOTAMIA: *the Babylonian and Assyrian Civilization*

By L. DELAPORTE, *Professor in the Catholic Institute of Paris.*

With 60 illustrations and maps, 16s. net.

"This book is for the most part very good. The author has handled his difficult material cleverly. Where he succeeds is in his admirably written description of the social life, of which he makes a fascinating story. Here is presented an entertaining picture of the inhabitants in 2000 B.C. Then from the earlier Babylonians he passes to the Assyrians, dealing with them in a similar excellent way. This is one of the best books of its kind which we have seen for some time."—*Times Literary Supplement.*

THE AEGEAN CIVILIZATION

By G. GLOTZ, *Professor of Greek History in the University of Paris*

With 4 plates, 87 text illustrations, and 3 maps, 16s. net.

"This is a marvellous summary, divided into four books, describing in detail the material, social, religious, artistic and intellectual life of the people. Every one of these sections is full of interesting and new knowledge. A wonderful book, thoroughly scholarly and attractive in presentation."—*Birmingham Post.*

"Reads like a romance . . . presents a very vivid picture of this marvellous civilization."—*Times Literary Supplement.*

THE PEOPLES OF ASIA

By L. H. DUDLEY BUXTON, M.A., F.S.A., *Lecturer in Physical Anthropology in the University of Oxford*

With 8 plates, 12s. 6d. net.

"Although the physical characters of the principal racial strains are described in some detail, the author keeps before his readers the bearing of these data upon the broader problems of racial distribution, as well as the intensely interesting question of the interaction of race, environment, and modification by contact due to migration. The exposition of anthropological method given in an introductory chapter is admirably lucid."—*Manchester Guardian.*

RACE AND HISTORY: *an Ethnological Introduction to History*

By E. PITTARD, *Professor of Anthropology in the University of Geneva.*

Second Impression. With 9 illustrations and maps, 21s. net.

A companion to Febvre's *Geographical Introduction to History,* which estimated the value of "environment" as a factor in history, while the present volume considers the "racial" factor. "No one is better qualified to compose a thoroughly level-headed treatise on the subject of race. For the peoples who occupy a conspicuous place in history, and especially the peoples of Europe, no better guide could be found."—*Times Literary Supplement.*

LIFE AND WORK IN MEDIEVAL EUROPE, *from the Fifth to the Fifteenth Century*

By P. BOISSONNADE, *Professor in the University of Poitiers. Translated with an Introduction by* EILEEN POWER, *D.Litt.*

With 8 plates, 16s. net.

"His work is so interesting that it is to be hoped he will follow Sir James Frazer's admirable example and take each chapter in turn for the purpose of converting its highly concentrated essence of history into a more ample dish for scholars. His subject is attractive and his pages are eminently readable by laymen."—*Times Literary Supplement.*

"There is no book in English which gives so clear and comprehensive a view of the labour question all through the Middle Ages. Readers will find no single volume so useful and so readable as this."—G. G. COULTON, in *Observer.*

LIFE AND WORK IN MODERN EUROPE, *from the Fifteenth to the Eighteenth Century*

By G. RENARD, *Professor at the College of France, and* G. WEULERSSE, *Professor at the Lycée Carnot. Introduction by* EILEEN POWER, *D. Litt., Reader in Economic History in the University of London.*

With 8 plates, 16s. net.

"This can certainly be pronounced a most useful book. There is nothing that covers anything like the same ground; indeed, there is actually no book in English which even pretends to give an outline of European economic history as a whole. It is interestingly written, and is a storehouse of valuable information."—*New Statesman.*

TRAVEL AND TRAVELLERS OF THE MIDDLE AGES

Edited by A. P. NEWTON, *Rhodes Professor of Imperial History in the University of London.*

Second impression. With 8 plates and maps, 12s. 6d. net.

"This work is no mere collection of stray essays, but in some respects the most important contribution to the history of medieval travel since Professor Beazley's *Dawn of Modern Geography* and the new edition of Yule's *Cathay.* . . . We have said enough to indicate that this work is one which should appeal both to the general reader and to the scholar. The illustrations are good."—*Times Literary Supplement.*

CHIVALRY: *Its Historical Significance and Civilizing Influence*

Edited by EDGAR PRESTAGE, *Camões Professor in the University of London.*

With 24 full-page plates, 15s. net.

"This is an excellent book, at once learned and entertaining, a valuable addition to our painfully limited library of medieval studies. The book is worth having, and there is an abundance of beautiful illustrations."—*Daily News.*

"An equally interesting and beautiful volume, a piece of work which appeals alike to the general reader and to the specialist in history."—*Journal of Education.*

ANCIENT GREECE AT WORK: *an Economic History of Greece from the Homeric Period to the Roman Conquest*

By G. GLOTZ, *Professor of Greek History in the University of Paris.*

With 49 illustrations, 16s. net.

"This is a learned but thoroughly interesting description of farming, industry, and business in general in ancient Greece, and should interest the student of economics as well as the classical scholar, since it shows practices developing from their simplest form. Besides giving hard economic facts the author makes interesting remarks on the Greek attitude to slaves, to foreigners, and to labour. This is a very readable and unusual book."—*Spectator.*

"A really fascinating economic history of the Greek people."—*New Leader.*

THE FORMATION OF THE GREEK PEOPLE

By A. JARDÉ, *Professor of History at the Lycée Lakanal.*

With 7 maps, 16s. net.

"One reader at least will tell the world he has enjoyed the book, has profited by it, and is not yet done with it; he means to use it again, and meanwhile ventures to tell others interested that this is a book for them."—*Nation.*

"He has given his readers an analysis of the course of events in the various City states in their external relations *inter se* and with other peoples, of their political, social, and intellectual development, of Hellenic expansion and of Hellenic unity, which is little short of brilliant."—*Nature.*

THE ARYANS: *a Study of Indo-European Origins*

By V. GORDON CHILDE, *B.Litt.*

With 8 plates, 28 text illustrations, and a map, 10s. 6d. net.

"Mr. Childe has followed up his interesting book, *The Dawn of European Civilization*, with another archæological study not less scholarly and sound. By a joint use of philological deduction and archæological induction, he contrives a thoroughly scientific handling of the problem."—*Times Literary Supplement.*

"Here is a book that must be of perennial interest, for it covers the whole field to the time of writing, and is precisely what a work dealing with problems of enormous intricacy should be."—*New Statesman.*

FROM TRIBE TO EMPIRE: *Social Organization among the Primitives and in the Ancient East*

By A. MORET, *Professor in the University of Paris, and* G. DAVY, *of the University of Dijon.*

With 47 illustrations and 7 maps, 16s. net.

"The object of the authors of this valuable addition to the series is to demonstrate how Empires grew from the primitive totemistic clan. Leaving M. Davy's excited, learned, and highly controversial dissertation on primitive society for M. Moret's calm review of the history of the Ancient East is like passing from storm into quiet. M. Moret's story remains the most lucid and satisfactory general survey of the Ancient East that has yet appeared. It is the very romance of history, and he would be dull indeed who did not find recreation and delight in these stirring pages."—*New Statesman.*

THE HISTORY OF MEDICINE, *from the time of the Pharaohs to the end of the Eighteenth Century*

By C. G. CUMSTON, M.D.

With 24 plates, 16s. net.

" Will be an invaluable source of reference to those who wisely remain students all their days. Beginning with the first dynasty of the Pharaohs, the ideas and the personalities of medicine are described in a manner which compels wonder for the amount of literary research, thought, and time which must have been devoted to its construction."—*British Medical Journal.*

"The book should be as interesting to the general public as to the doctors."—*Sunday Times.*

THE HISTORY OF WITCHCRAFT AND DEMONOLOGY

By MONTAGUE SUMMERS, *editor of Congreve, Wycherley, etc.*

With 8 full-page plates, 12s. 6d. net.

" Mr. Summers has just the literary style to do justice to the stewing of witches' broth or the licentious dancing of the Sabbat. This book is one of the most masterly products of psychological-historical literature ; and one feels that the editor of this learned series was perfectly justified in including in it such a storehouse of facts. Mr. Summers has our hearty thanks. His book is enthralling."—*Outlook.*

" No more learned, no more copiously documented work on the subject has seen the light for a long while."—*Birmingham Post.*

THE GEOGRAPHY OF WITCHCRAFT

By MONTAGUE SUMMERS.

With 8 full-page plates, 21s. net.

" The *History* described the general characteristics of European witchcraft in the middle ages ; the present volume gives particulars of actual witches in the various countries of Western Europe. Mr. Summers includes within the scope of his exceedingly painstaking work all the varieties of the black art, from cattle laming to the concoction of love philtres, to demoniac possession and unnatural vice. The book is beautifully produced and contains some excellent illustrations."—*Spectator.*

THE CIVILIZATION OF THE SOUTH AMERICAN INDIANS, *with special reference to Magic and Religion*

By RAFAEL KARSTEN, Ph.D., *Professor at the University of Finland, Helsingfors. Preface by* PROFESSOR E. WESTERMARCK.

25s. net.

" A very solid piece of work. . . Whether Professor Karsten be right or wrong in his contentions, his book can be read with the utmost profit, because he cites the evidence fully and fairly."—*Times Literary Supplement.*

" Dr. Karsten can congratulate himself on having written a work that will form not merely a contribution to the ethnology of South America, but also a valuable addition to the small number of really useful works on the ideas of the less cultured peoples."—*Saturday Review.*

PRIMITIVE ITALY, *and the Beginnings of Roman Imperialism*

By LEON HOMO, *Professor in the University of Lyons.*

With 13 maps and plans, 16s. net.

" This able and scholarly work, which has summoned to its aid all the resources of anthropology, archæology, epigraphy and philology. Here is laid bare the real history of Rome's origins, and especially of her Etruscan origins. A volume characterized alike by scientific caution and a marked power of lucid reconstruction."—*Spectator.*

" He gives us a spirited account of the development of Rome from her obscure origins to her establishment as the dominant power of the Mediterranean world. It would be hard to find a clearer or better proportioned account of the stages by which Rome achieved the miracle . . . ."—*Times Literary Supplement.*

ANCIENT ROME AT WORK: *an Economic History of Rome from the Origins to the Empire*

By PAUL LOUIS.

With 4 illustrations and 6 maps, 16s. net.

" The main stages in Rome's imperial progress are indicated, and the economic causes of her decline are adequately analysed. Agriculture and commerce, industry and finance, roads and communications, slavery and its developments, the rise of the colonate, and the influence of guilds are dealt with in turn, and their bearing on society and the social structure are discussed. . . . The volume presents a vivid, rapidly-moving picture of the economics of the Roman State."—*Times Literary Supplement.*

THE ROMAN SPIRIT *in Religion, Thought, and Art*

By A. GRENIER, *Professor in the University of Strasburg.*

With 16 plates and 16 text illustrations, 16s. net.

" I have not space to set out all the things in the book that have interested me and given me pleasure. The sections on religion and literature are fresh and stimulating. The classical scholar and the general reader can be recommended alike to read every page of this admirable book."—*Nation.*

" A brilliant interpretation of Latin literature and religion."—*New Leader.*

ROME THE LAW-GIVER

By J. DECLAREUIL, *Professor in the University of Toulouse.*

16s. net.

" The level of scholarship is extremely high, and the treatment hardly more technical than the subject-matter demands. The author traces the development of Roman law from its origin to its codification, and on to the later refinements which in their range, subtlety, and realistic logic have given it such unrivalled universality and completeness. While recommending this valuable synopsis as a whole, we may note as specially significant the chapter on the organization of credit."—*Saturday Review.*

THE LIFE OF BUDDHA, *as Legend and History*

By E. J. THOMAS, D.LITT., *Under Librarian in the University Library, Cambridge.*

Second edition. With 4 plates and a map, 12s. 6d. net.

" He has produced an authoritative account of all that is known of the life of the great teacher. We would recommend this important work to all interested in Eastern philosophy."—*Spectator.*

" The treatment of his subject is as thorough as one could wish. His knowledge of the sources, his historical sense, and the soundness of his judgment make him a safe guide in a field in which there are many pitfalls. The book is a worthy addition to a notable series."—*Manchester Guardian.*

ANCIENT PERSIA, *and Iranian Civilization*

By CLEMENT HUART, *Member of the Institute of France.*

With 4 plates, 35 text illustrations, and a map, 12s. 6d. net.

" A very good account of the cultural history of old Iran. A vivid picture of the country and an account of the scripts is followed by a history of the Achæmenids, Arsacids, and Sassanids. The real value of the book consists in the excellent analyses of the cultural data referring to each epoch ; the social organization, the religious cults and beliefs, and the artistic productions. The powerful character sketches of the monarchs and heroes receive new life from the background in which they are set."—*Nature.*

" An admirable epitome of the known facts."—*New Statesman.*

ART IN GREECE

By A. DE RIDDER, *Curator at the Louvre Museum, and* W. DEONNA, *Director of the Geneva Museum of Art and History.*

With 24 plates and 66 text illustrations, 21s. net.

" A fascinating addition to the series. The authors have written attractively not only of Greek art from its beginnings to the Hellenistic period and its final decline, but of everyday Greek life and its relation to art and the artists of the time."—*Daily News.*

" Even on the most familiar ground it is remarkably fresh and penetrating."
New Statesman.

MONEY AND MONETARY POLICY IN EARLY TIMES

By A. R. BURNS, B.Sc. ECON.

With 16 plates, 25s. net.

" He has treated the subject with care and caution and shown clearly what the puzzles are. He deals mainly with Greece and Rome, slightly with Assyria, and gives a paragraph at the end of each chapter to the wholly independent and interesting coinage of China."—*Times Literary Supplement.*

" He is to be congratulated. The book is a striking contrast to the previous superficial treatments of the subject. Documents have been searched and the material obtained, digested, and presented in a most readable form."
Economist.

THE NILE AND EGYPTIAN CIVILIZATION

By A. MORET, *Professor at the College of France.*

With 24 plates, 79 text illustrations and 3 maps, 25s. net.

" This brilliant story of Egyptian society. M. Moret's peculiar contribution to Egyptology is that he has taken the *disjecta membra* of Egyptian history and of them has built anew the living body of that amazing culture. What was it that secured to Egypt a civilization more stable than that of any other of the great kingdoms of antiquity ? M. Moret tells us. It was the Nile, coupled with the establishment of a religious system imposing its sanctions on every social duty. As seen in his sympathetic retrospect, this great religion is curiously attractive. It was the real moral and spiritual force permeating the whole of Egyptian life. Art and science and literature ministered to it, and it sustained for milleniums the most massive, coherent, and amiable civilization the world has known."—*Times Literary Supplement.*

THE HISTORY OF MUSIC

By CECIL GRAY.

Second impression. 12s. 6d. net.

" Here is just the book readers have been looking for, and looking for too long in vain. No music-lover would find it other than arresting from cover to cover. Its distinction of style . . its meticulous accuracy . . its fresh and original standpoint. It is not too much to say that it is one of the most illuminating books of this decade."—SIR RICHARD TERRY, in *Queen.*

" A book which is quite one of the best of its kind."—*Observer.*

THE ROMAN WORLD

By VICTOR CHAPOT, *Professor at the Ecole des Beaux-Arts.*

With 2 plates and 12 maps, 16s. net.

" This survey of the Roman Empire presents in a compendious form an account of the expansion of Rome, the machinery of provincial government, and finally a survey of the Empire and its fortunes province by province. This is the fullest account of the Empire which has appeared in English since the translation of Mommsen's two volumes nearly fifty years ago. It is enriched by the discoveries that have been made in the meantime, and its excellent bibliography brings the sources up to date. The volume has some useful maps."

Times Literary Supplement.

MACEDONIAN IMPERIALISM, *and the Hellenization of the East*

By P. JOUGUET, *Professor in the University of Paris.*

With 7 plates and 5 maps, 21s. net.

" He has told a most fascinating story and told it so well that it forms an excellent sequel to the ordinary histories of Greece. Particularly valuable is his account of the Hellenization of Asia and of Egypt, of the public and private life of the latter, and of the establishment of the Greek and Macedonian military and other colonies. To read his book shows that no one can afford to neglect the study of the Hellenistic period, which was responsible for many fundamental elements of modern civilization."—*Times Literary Supplement.*

THE AMERICAN INDIAN FRONTIER

By WILLIAM CHRISTIE MACLEOD, *Assistant Professor in the University of Pennsylvania.*

With 13 maps, 25s. net.

" It is a tale, alike for its romantic and its historical values, well worth the telling ; and it is not likely to find many tellers so competent and so vivid as Professor Macleod. His book is an important contribution to historical ethnology. The picture of American Indian culture drawn, with a wealth of colour and atmosphere, by this leading authority is in many ways attractive. The erudition is enlivened by innumerable human touches."—*New Statesman.*

GREEK THOUGHT, *and the Origins of the Scientific Spirit*

By L. ROBIN, *Professor in the University of Paris.*

With a map, 21s. net.

" His contribution will probably rank as one of the finest in the series. For immense erudition combined with perfect clarity of expression the book can have few equals."—*Nature.*

" Apart from his account of the three outstanding figures of Greek philosophy [Plato, Aristotle and Pythagoras], a special meed of thanks is due to him for his full treatment of Plotinus and of the Stoics. Professor Robin's work is characterized throughout by an exceptional sense of proportion."—*Times Literary Supplement.*

LIFE AND WORK IN PREHISTORIC TIMES

By G. RENARD, *Professor at the College of France.*

With 9 plates, 12s. 6d. net.

" In a text which is always informing and never dull, it is hard to know where to begin or when to stop [quoting]. Throughout there is a pithiness of diction resulting in memorable epigram. In short, the conjunction of style and matter is so fortunate that it gives the whole volume the individuality that marks a contribution to literature as contrasted with a mere textbook. The student who wishes to use it in the latter capacity will get from it just the right stimulus to send him forward. He will be made to realize the importance of the evolution of the useful and decorative arts. He will be conducted through a veritable museum of curious and telling facts. In short, there is inspiration in everything that Professor Renard has written."—*Times Literary Supplement.*

THE COURT OF BURGUNDY

By OTTO CARTELLIERI.

With 25 plates, 21s. net.

" Professor Cartellieri chose a period steeped in romantic colour. When he began to work he was fascinated by the rich and splendid culture of the brilliant court. But there were bigger matters, as he found the more he explored, and his attention turned to spiritual and social questions. The result is the work of a specialist, who has the gift of attractively presenting pictures of a strange period, its life and manners, its art, literature, and music, its ruler and Court, how the knight and the lady lived, the feasts, jousts, and tourneys."—*Times.*

" His richly-illustrated volume is a learned and engaging guide to the culture of late medieval society at its most brilliant."—*Saturday Review.*

THE HEROIC AGE OF INDIA

By N. K. SIDHANTA, *Professor of English at Lucknow University.*

12s. 6d. net.

"A valuable contribution. The Heroic Age is an epoch in practically all races and cultures. They all show characteristics which the Indian age also displays. The *Mahabharata* is his principal quarry; the heroes of that epic seem near to us. With their drinking and love-making, their chivalry and brutality, they are of the schoolboy age of humanity. It is a delightful world to which Professor Sidhanta transports us. Not only scholars but all who would recapture the illusions of boyhood owe him a debt."

Times Literary Supplement.

THE GREEK CITY, *and its Institutions*

By G. GLOTZ, *Professor of Greek History in the University of Paris.*

16s. net.

"The theme of this admirable book is the autonomous Greek city as it appeared in time from its first dim beginnings in the Homeric age down to its overthrow by Philip of Macedon. It combines great learning with philosophical power, and with a pure and lively style. It, of course, contains the facts, but it contains much more. His remarks on ostracism and the selection of magistrates by lot are good examples of his knowledge and his reasoning power."

Sunday Times.

"He is eminently qualified to write of Greek institutions, and his account of the evolution of man as a 'political animal' in Greece is enriched with the results of discovery since the days of Fustel de Coulanges, whom he rivals in logic and lucidity."—*Times Literary Supplement.*

ROMAN POLITICAL INSTITUTIONS, *from City to State*

By LEON HOMO, *Professor in the University of Lyons.*

16s. net.

"No other English book presents in so convenient a form the story of the stages through which the Roman Constitution arrived at its ultimate form of absolute monarchy and bureaucratic organization. From a description of the rise of the oligarchy, he proceeds to give a lively account of the period of transition in which the ideals of Pompey and Cæsar, Principate and Monarchy, struggle for the victory, and goes on to show how the Principate of Augustus passes by inevitable development into the military monarchy of the later Emperors."

Times Literary Supplement.

THE ECONOMIC LIFE OF THE ANCIENT WORLD

By J. TOUTAIN, *Sometime Member of the French School at Rome.*

With 6 maps, 16s. net.

"He has written a lucid and attractive volume, mainly concerned with Greece and Rome. But he sketches the beginnings of trade in primitive society, the history of Carthage, and the dawn of commerce in prehistoric Italy as well as the development of Etruria. Those who imagine that capital is a modern phenomenon may be commended to the chapter on capitalism in Republican Rome from the Punic Wars onwards."—*Spectator.*

MINOANS, PHILISTINES AND GREEKS : B.C. 1400-900

By A. R. BURN, *sometime Scholar of Christ Church, Oxford.*

With 16 plates, 15s. net.

" A comprehensive study of the Late Bronze and Early Iron Ages in the Eastern Mediterranean for which there is now ample evidence. The author's reconstruction becomes an enthralling, sometimes a thrilling, reanimation, in which a continuous narrative is evolved, and the Hebrew legends of the Judges and of Saul and David and the Greek epic traditions of Minos and Theseus and of the wars of Thebes and Troy are set in historical perspective. A remarkable book."—*Morning Post.*

DEATH CUSTOMS : *an Analytical Study of Burial Rites*

By E. BENDANN, *Ph.D., A.M.*

12s. 6d. net.

" The beliefs and customs associated among primitive peoples with death and the disposal of the body make up a complex manifold, the analysis and explanation of which is a rich field for the ethnologist ; they give us too some insight into savage philosophy. The author makes an intensive investigation in this field, over Melanesia, Australia, North-East Siberia and India. Her criticisms on the Diffusionist school are shrewd and her study is to be commended."

Times Literary Supplement.

CHINESE CIVILIZATION

By M. GRANET, *Professor at L'Ecole des Langues Orientales.*

With 12 plates and 5 maps, 25s. net.

" The imposing story of China's past achievements becomes a clear account of the emergence of an obscure tribe from the unknown lands of central Asia to the proud position of leader of Asiatic civilization. The second part of the book is devoted to a careful analysis of Chinese society, life, customs, cities, feudalism, and the numerous social changes wrought by the change of Court and the growth of moral ideals. The author displays a rare combination of restrained imagination and careful scholarship. The book should be read widely, and will be a necessary part of the equipment of students of Asiatic history for some time to come."—*The Spectator.*

THE END OF THE ANCIENT WORLD, *and the Beginning of the Middle Ages*

By FERDINAND LOT, *Professor in the University of Paris.*

With 3 plates and 3 maps, 21s. net.

" The author strikes a new note in the theory he puts forward that the influx of the barbarian hordes was not the regenerating element which produced the new ideas of the Middle Ages. The author holds that the real regeneration of mankind only appeared when Islam challenged the superstition and idolatry of the Dark Ages, when the reformed Papacy became at last conscious of its mission and when feudalism was able to establish, however imperfectly, something which could give rise to the modern state. The book has an excellent bibliography and index and can be heartily recommended."—*Listener.*

" This masterly book."—*The Spectator.*

ISRAEL, *from its Beginnings to the Middle of the Eighth Century*

By A. LODS, *Professor at the Sorbonne.*

With 12 plates and 41 maps and text illustrations, 25s. net.

This book fills a distinct gap in the long list of modern books on the Old Testament. Its peculiar value lies in the careful and lucid way in which Professor Lods, from his exhaustive knowledge of the results of recent excavation in Palestine, has given us a convincing picture of the early cultural background of the Hebrew people, enabling us to see the religious, social, and political life of Canaan when Abraham and his descendants were settling down in the land. The effect of the culture of the great empires of Egypt and Babylon upon Canaan is drawn in bold outlines, giving us the clue to the unique development of Hebrew religion, at once influenced by and protesting against the religious and social patterns of its environment.

CASTE AND RACE IN INDIA

By G. S. GHURYE, *Reader in Sociology, Bombay University.*

10s. 6d. net.

One of the most remarkable developments in the history of sociology is the institution of caste. To grasp its significance is one of the first requirements for understanding some of the problems of modern India, the history of its social structure, its complex religious development, and its future destiny. This volume has been written by an Indian author who knows the actual facts from within, and who has combined a mastery of the principles of anthropological science with a knowledge of the modern theories of caste.

THE HISTORY OF BUDDHIST THOUGHT

By E. J. THOMAS, D.Litt., *author of "The Life of Buddha".*

With 4 plates, 15s. net.

"Dr Thomas's fine history . . . To approach Buddhism one must learn Buddha's aim. It was astonishingly simple. Buddha believed in re-birth. It clarified the problem of injustice. He was far too practical to care for metaphysics or fruitless debate. But Buddha's followers had no such self-denying wisdom, and the bulk of the commentaries is reckoned to be 700 times that of the Bible. Dr Thomas's erudition in winnowing this haystack is astonishing ; moreover he makes it live."—*The Observer.*

THE RISE OF THE CELTS

By H. HUBERT.

With 47 illustrations and 12 maps, 16s. net.

"The whole problem has never been more completely surveyed than it was by the late M. Henri Hubert. He spent a lifetime on it. . . . Taking as his starting point the Indo-European unity, of which he sees signs in the East, he produced in this, the first attempt to construct a history of all the Celts and a picture of all the Celtic world, a vast encyclopedia, conceived, however, in the spirit of that finely co-ordinated literary unity in which the French mind excels. . . . From the welter of varied data M. Hubert traces the migration of the Celts, and distinguishes more clearly than his predecessors the two great groups, the Brythons of the Continent and Britain, and the Goidels of Ireland and Scotland. . . . He had the double competence of a Celticist and an Assyriologist; and his whole career was inspired by the gift of synthesis."

Sunday Times.

THE GREATNESS AND DECLINE OF THE CELTS

By H. HUBERT.

With 3 maps, 16s. net.

This volume deals with the period of greatest Celtic expansion and the subsequent decline. It describes Celtic settlements in Italy, Galatia, Spain, Gaul and the Danube valley; the adventures of Celtic mercenaries in Egypt and elsewhere on the Mediterranean; the conquest of Celtic countries by the Roman Empire; and later struggles with invaders in Ireland, Scotland, and Wales. A great part of the book is given to a survey of the whole of ancient Celtic life, including such subjects as the survival of primitive customs like potlatch and headhunting, the nature of the clan, the influence of the Druids and the morality of honour.

ANCIENT INDIA, *and Indian Civilization*

By P. MASSON-OURSEL, H. WILLMAN-GRABOWSKA, *and* P. STERN.

With 40 illustrations and 5 maps, about 16s. net.

This work presents native, pre-Moslem India. A description of the country and its races is followed by a summary of its history and an examination of political, social and economic life. In the largest section, dealing with the religions and philosophies, the authors, while emphasizing the different way in which the Indian mind works from the Western, give the essence of the various beliefs and theories with remarkable clarity. The section on literature, with its delightful summaries of the plots of epics, plays, and stories, and that on art, with its interesting remarks on Indian and Western taste, complete a glowing but accurate picture of a past world.

Ready shortly:

JESUS

By C. GUIGNEBERT.